A PALACE IN THE NATION'S CAPITAL

GRIFFITH STADIUM

HOME OF THE WASHINGTON SENATORS

Edited by Gregory H. Wolf

Associate Editors
Len Levin, Bill Nowlin, and Carl Riechers

Society for American Baseball Research, Inc.
Phoenix, AZ

A Palace in the Nation's Capital: Griffith Stadium, Home of the Washington Senators

Edited by Gregory H. Wolf
Associate Editors: Len Levin, Bill Nowlin, and Carl Riechers

Cover Photo:
Cover photo: Griffith Stadium (National Baseball Hall of Fame, Cooperstown, New York)

ISBN 978-1-970159-49-3
(Ebook ISBN 978-1-970159-48-6)

Book design: David Peng

Society for American Baseball Research
Cronkite School at ASU
555 N. Central Ave. #416
Phoenix, AZ 85004
Phone: (602) 496-1460
Web: www.sabr.org
Facebook: Society for American Baseball Research
Twitter: @SABR

TABLE OF CONTENTS

AN INTRODUCTION AND ACKNOWLEDGEMENTS

by Gregory H. Wolf

Griffith Stadium was home of the American League charter member Washington Senators from 1911 through 1960 and the identically named expansion team in 1961. Situated in the middle of LeDroit Park, a former bustling residential neighborhood with tree-lined streets and romantic nineteenth-century architecture and located on what is now the site of the Howard University Hospital, Griffith Stadium was known for its cavernous dimensions, unique outfield notch in center field with a conspicuously large tree behind the wall, cozy quarters, and something no ballpark or stadium in the US had: a presidential box. For more than 50 years, presidents traveled from the White House two miles northeast to Griffith Stadium to throw out the ceremonial first pitch.

About a month before the start of the 1911 season, a fire destroyed Boundary Field, a 20-year-old wooden ballpark where the AL Senators had played since 1904. Club President Thomas C. Noyes commissioned a new steel-and-concrete ballpark to be built on that same site. In less than four weeks, the grandstands were sufficiently built, though not yet covered, that the Senators could take the field on Opening Day, April 12. "Opening of New National Park Is Declared Washington's Greatest Baseball Event," ran a headline in the *Washington Times*.[1] "In the years that baseball has held sway in Washington, there has never been a crowd like the one which packed the Florida Avenue park yesterday," gushed the *Washington Post* about the opener in what the newspaper called American League Park. "Row after row, they sat or stood in a vast human semicircle that embraced the farthermost points of the outfield. Far out by the fences a mighty clan of the faithful stood five deep, inclosing the players in an arena such as gladiators might have longed for in the days of gone by."[2] The highlight of the Senators' 8-5 victory over the Boston Red Sox might have been President William Howard Taft tossing out the first pitch, a tradition he began a year earlier. Boundary Field had been called both National Park and American League Park, hence the newspapers' use of different names. Sportswriters and fans continued to use those appellations, though National Park was more common, until 1922 when majority owner Clark Griffith changed the name to Griffith Stadium.[3] A similar situation existed with the Senators' other familiar nickname, the Nationals. That moniker derived from the first incarnation of the Senators, who played in the National League from 1892 until they were disbanded after the 1899 season.

"Washington: first in war, first in peace, and last in the American League." That quip from the quick wit of Charles Dryden, one of the country's most famous sportswriters and humorists at the turn of the twentieth century, still casts a shadow on the Senators' reputation in the nation's capital well over a century since it first appeared in 1904. And it's not necessarily accurate. It's true that the NL Senators were atrocious and without a winning season in their eight-year existence in the 1890s; and then the AL Senators slogged through a decade of futility, never finishing higher than sixth place; however, Griffith Stadium ushered in a quarter-century of success (1911-1936) with more winning seasons (15) than losing ones (11) for the Senators. The Senators won the World Series in 1924, captured the pennant in 1925, and another in 1933 after winning a franchise-record 99 games, the fourth consecutive season of at least 92 victories in a then 154-game schedule. The club's golden era in Griffith Stadium contrasted sharply with the final quarter-century (1937-1960), when the Senators produced only three winning seasons, and only once, in 1945, contended for the pennant, finishing in second place, 1½ games behind the Detroit Tigers. Nonetheless, by the late 1950s and into 1960, with the team typically mired in the cellar, the nucleus of what would become an annual pennant-contending team after its relocation to the Twin Cities in Minnesota was in place or in the farm system: Harmon Killebrew, Bob Allison, Earl Battey, Zoilo Versalles, Jimmy Hall, Camilo Pascual, and Jim Kaat, all of whom became All-Stars for the Twins. One can only wonder what might have happened had the Senators remained in D.C.

A Palace in the Nation's Capital: Griffith Stadium, Home of the Washington Senators revives memories and the history of Griffith Stadium through detailed summaries of 72 games played there from the inaugural contest in the not-yet completed ballpark on April 12, 1911, to the final baseball game there, the expansion Senators against the original Senators, now called the Twins, on September 21, 1961, as well as insightful feature essays about the ballpark. In our quest to present Griffith Stadium as a locus of baseball history, we've included a broad cross-section of games. You can read about all 10 World Series games the Senators played at Griffith Stadium in the three fall classics, as well as the two All-Star Games the ballpark hosted (1937 and 1956). Some of the games chronicle historic firsts, such as the first Sunday baseball game in Washington history, on May 19, 1918, the first Senators night game, on May 28, 1941, the debut on September 6, 1954, of Cuban-born Carlos Paula, who became the first Black player in Senators' history, more than seven years after Jackie Robinson's debut with the Brooklyn Dodgers, and the only no-hitter, on August 8, 1931, by Bobby Burke, who won just 38 games in his career. Both Walter Johnson and little-known Carl Cashion tossed abbreviated, weather-shortened no-hitters and you can read about them, too. Other essays recount career or season milestones, like the Big Train's 300th victory (in relief), his 400th win, and his 1-0 shutout against the Philadelphia Athletics to record his 36th and final victory of the 1913 season. Johnson's highlights are well represented in our volume; however, you can also read about Stan Coveleski's 20th victory in his final start of the 1925, securing the AL ERA title and helping the club capture its second straight pennant, General Crowder's 15th straight victory to conclude the 1932 season, and also Bob Porterfield's 20th victory in 1953.

With its spacious dimensions, Griffith Stadium suppressed home-run totals for most of its history, but we've included plenty of offense in this volume. Read about Roy Hartzell of the New York Highlanders speeding around the bases to become the first player to hit a pair of home runs, both exciting inside-the-park jobs, in the ballpark's inaugural season. It took another 17 seasons before Red Barnes became the first Senators player to hit two home runs in a game at the ballpark. Joltin' Joe DiMaggio was the first to whack three round-trippers, in 1950, while Jim Lemon (1956) hit the Nats' first trifecta. And don't forget Roy Sievers, whose walk-off blast in the 17th inning against the Tigers on August 3, 1957, made him the club's first hitter with 30 home runs, en route to becoming the first AL player to lead the league in home runs and RBIs for a last-place team. And of course we've included one of the most discussed, indeed mythical home runs of all time, Mickey Mantle's shot in 1953 that cleared the left-center-field wall.

Offense in Griffith Stadium wasn't necessarily about the long ball. Read about the Nats scoring 20-plus runs, erupting for big innings, engaging in high-scoring games, and engineering audacious comebacks. Amazingly, no Senators player ever hit for the cycle in Griffith Stadium, but you can read about the quirky hitting accomplishment by the Yankees' Bob Meusel (1921), the Athletics' Mickey Cochrane (1932), Odell "Bad News" Hale of the Indians (1938), and Vic Wertz of the Tigers in 1947.

Furthermore, the games highlight not only the accomplishments and heroics of Senators Hall of Famers like Walter Johnson, Goose Goslin, Sam Rice, and Heinie Manush, or stars like 1925 AL MVP Roger Peckinpaugh, two-time AL batting champion Mickey Vernon, and seven-time All-Star Camilo Pascual with his knee-buckling curveball; the stories also revive memories of forgotten or overlooked players like Doc Ayers, Jake Early, Sid Hudson, Pedro Ramos, Coot Veal, and many more. Also included are some memorable or historic performances by the Senators' opponents, like Chicago White Sox hurler Jim Scott's no-hitter for nine innings only to lose, 1-0, in the 10th (1914), the St. Louis Browns' Dixie Davis tossing a 19-inning complete-game victory (1921), the Detroit Tigers' Rocky Colavito whacking four home runs in a twin bill (1961), and the Boston Red Sox' Bill Monbouquette fanning 17 batters (1961).

We're especially excited to present some of Griffith Stadium's rich and storied history of Negro League baseball. A feature essay explores the Homestead Grays' tenure at the ballpark, often referred to as their "home away from home" when the tradition-laden club split time in Pittsburgh and the nation's capital. Game stories include the first night game at the park, when klieg lights were installed for a game between the Washington Pilots and the Pittsburgh Crawfords in 1932, as well as five games from Negro League World Series between 1942 and 1945, involving legendary squads, such as the Grays, the Kansas City Monarchs, the Birmingham Black Barons, and the Cleveland Buckeyes. Read about a cast of stars, from Satchel Paige, Josh Gibson, Buck Leonard, and Cool Papa Bell to Jud Wilson, Raymond Brown, Artie Wilson, and Sam Bankhead.

Our feature essays provide context for baseball played at Griffith Stadium. We've included an insightful essay focusing on the history of the ballpark and another on its changing dimensions and configuration. Special thanks go to Clark Griffith, son of former Senators/Twins owner Calvin Griffith, and great-nephew of Clark C. Griffith, for contributing an essay about his most memorable game in the ballpark. Two other chapters shed light on lesser-remembered aspects of the ballpark's history: military drills during World War I and the many sporting (other than baseball) and nonsporting events that took place there. A statistics-oriented piece, "By the Numbers," rounds out this extraordinary volume.

This book is the result of tireless work of many members of the Society for American Baseball Research. SABR members researched and wrote all of the essays in this volume. These uncompensated volunteers are united by their shared interest in baseball history and resolute commitment to preserving its history. Without their unwavering dedication this volume would not have been possible.

I am indebted to the associate editors and extend to them my sincerest appreciation. Bill Nowlin, the second reader; fact-checker Carl Riechers; and copy editor Len Levin each read every word of all the essays and made numerous corrections to language, style, and content. Their attention to detail has been invaluable. It has been a pleasure to once again work on a book project with such professionals, with whom I corresponded practically every day, and typically more than once.

I thank all of the authors for their contributions, meticulous research, cooperation through the revising and editing process, and finally their patience. It was a long journey from the day the book was launched to its completion, and we've finally reached our destination. We did it! Please refer to the list of contributors at the end of the book for more information.

This book would not have been possible without the generous support of the staff and Board of Directors of SABR, SABR Publications Director Cecilia Tan, and designer David Peng.

We express our thanks and gratitude to a number of folks who helped procure photos for this book, including the Topps Baseball Card company for permitting us to use images from one of the golden eras of baseball card collecting. SABR members Linda Hanks and Mike Hanks graciously provided high-resolution scans of those Topps cards. Thanks to Matthew J. Richards, vice president and general manager of sales, and Andy Krause, sport product manager at Getty Images, for their invaluable assistance. Heartfelt gratitude to SABR member Robert E. Wilson, who generously provided his personal photos of Griffith Stadium from his trip there in 1958. Special thanks also to John Horne of the National Baseball Hall of Fame for supplying the cover photo.

We invite you to sit back, relax for a few minutes, and enjoy reading about the great games and the exciting history of Griffith Stadium.

Gregory H. Wolf
April 2021

NOTES

1 "Opening of New National Park Is Declared Washington's Greatest Baseball Event," *Washington Times*, April 13, 1911: 16

2 "Nationals Win, 8 to 5, as 16,000 Cheer Them," *Washington Post*, April 13, 1911: 1.

3 Philip J. Lowry, *Green Cathedrals. The Ultimate Celebration of All Major League and Negro League Ballparks*, 5th edition (Phoenix: Society for American Baseball Research, 2019), 298.

GRIFFITH STADIUM

by John R. Schleppi

When the Washington Senators[1] were founded in 1891, they played their games at Boundary Field in Northwest Washington. Boundary Field was named for its location on the northwest boundary line of the District of Columbia at Boundary Line and Seventh Street. The field is labeled on the 1904 Sanborn Fire Insurance Map as "Athletic Fields," bordered on two sides by a "High Wood Fence."[2] The Senators played there until they were dropped by the National League in 1899 when the league contracted. The new American League brought a franchise to Washington, again the Senators, in 1901. They played at the American League Park in Northeast Washington because the National League retained the lease to Boundary Field. The American League Park, located at Florida Avenue NE and Trinidad Avenue, is noted on the same map as "The American League Ball Park," and the map shows the footprint of the stands.[3] After the 1903 AL-NL Peace Agreement,[4] the Senators returned to the Boundary Field location, renamed National Park, and they took the wooden stands from the American League Park to their new home. The National Park's location was now given as Florida Avenue NW (formerly Boundary Line) and Georgia Avenue (formerly Seventh Street).[5]

Boundary Field began as a simple four-sided field. Over the years its dimensions changed, but the playing surface was always large. As early as 1906, it was evident that Boundary Field needed improvement. The *Washington Post*'s J. Ed Grillo wrote:

> *"[T]here is hardly a minor league city today, unless it [is] of the very lowest class, that cannot boast of a better equipped baseball plant than that on which the Nationals have played for the past years. The local so-called park is antiquated and out of date and far from being in keeping with those in other major league cities and it is commendable that the local owners have finally come to this realization and are at least contemplating improvements. As far as the present site is concerned few cities have one better located or more easily accessible, but the days of rough-built frame stands, lacking even ordinary accommodations and with convenient*

entrances and exits, have long since passed. There are excuses for losing teams, perhaps, but none for such abominable accommodations as the Washington club has furnished its patrons. Men who invested their money in baseball realized years ago that the game had come to stay, and from that time on a most substantial effort to create plants in keeping with the times has been made most everywhere but here in Washington, and it is pleasing to note that there has been an awakening here, even though it is belated."[6]

Finally, in 1910 the club decided to build a new facility.[7] The club's board announced that it was withholding dividends for this investment. The F.J. Osborn Architecture and Engineering firm of Cleveland was selected for the job. Osborn's engineers, with their experience in using steel and concrete in structures, such as bridges, were pioneers in stadium construction and had completed Forbes Field in Pittsburgh in 1909.[8] The plan in Washington was to build stands behind home plate and along first base and third base to seat 15,000 at a cost of $135,000.[9]

On March 17, 1911, a fire destroyed Boundary Field's wooden stands.[10] Spring training had already begun and Opening Day was less than a month away. The Senators' board decided to build the new ballpark on the site and to begin immediately. The *Washington Post* headlines informed the public, "Accommodations for Opening Game Assured – Ban Johnson Here."[11]

Once the remains of the ruined stadium were removed, the new structure rose quickly. The *Washington Evening Star* on April 9 reported, "[D]ay and night the chanting of the negro laborers has been heard in the vicinity. Like Aladdin's Palace the structure rose as if by magic."[12] The playing field was closely aligned with the former one. The left-field line measured 407 feet, right field 328 feet, and center field 421 feet.[13] The center-field line contained a right-angled notch in the fence because homeowners there refused to sell their property to the Senators. The extended left-field foul line proved beneficial when the field was used for football. In addition, home plate was 61 feet from the grandstand, creating a spacious playing area for the catcher.[14] This was a large park compared with other parks of the era.

On Opening Day, April 12, 1911, the stands were completed but uncovered, and ready for a crowd of 16,000 to see the Senators defeat the Boston Red Sox, 8-5.[15] President William Howard Taft threw out the first ball. This tradition had begun two years earlier, on April 14, 1909, in the old ballpark, when Taft was approached by umpire Billy Evans and invited to throw out the first ball to open the season.[16] In previous years, the district commissioner of the District of Columbia had usually done the honors. Eventually a presidential box would be installed in the stadium for the use of future presidents. Calvin Coolidge was the only president to do the honor three times in one season: the Senators' opening game on April 15, 1924, the Olympic Quota Game (a fundraiser for the US Olympic team) on May 19, and the World Series opener on October 4.[17]

Construction continued in earnest whenever the Senators were on the road, and the ballpark was completed for the July 25 game against the Detroit Tigers, which the Senators lost, 5-2. The final structure included a double-decked, covered grandstand around the infield and uncovered single decks along both foul lines. The cost was estimated at $125,000.[18] This was considerably less than the $1 million-plus that had been spent to build Forbes Field,[19] although it should be noted that the Senators' new home was a no-frills structure without the substantial façades of Forbes Field, Comiskey Park, and even Cleveland's League Park, which were all built by The Osborn Company.[20]

The following season, 1912, Clark C. Griffith joined the club as player-manager. He had begun his career with the minor-league Milwaukee Brewers in 1888, and afterward had joined the American Association's St. Louis Browns in 1891. He was released by St. Louis that year and went to the Boston Reds, where he was released again in September.

Batting practice at Griffith Stadium in 1958. The Baltimore Orioles take aim at the left-field bleachers, which angled inward from the left-field foul pole, creating a perfect power alley. (Photo courtesy of Robert E. Wilson)

In 1892 he went to Tacoma, Washington, in the Pacific Northwest League; when the league folded in August, he moved to Missoula in the Montana State League for the remainder of the season.

The start of the 1893 season found Griffith with Oakland in the California League. The league folded in August. In September he moved to the Chicago Colts of the National League. While with Chicago, where he played through the 1900 season, he attended law school at Northwestern University. Following a longing for the outdoors, he also purchased a ranch in Craig, Montana, in 1899.

With Chicago Griffith had six consecutive seasons (1894-1899) of over 20 wins. This is impressive because he had to adjust to the increase in 1893 of the pitching distance from 55 feet to 60 feet 6 inches.[21] His was one of the best pitching records in late-nineteenth-century baseball.

Griffith was a National Leaguer, but he was not happy with the status of players under their current management arrangement with the reserve clause and salary control. He tried to organize players to challenge the status quo; in fact, he wanted to organize a union. He gained only moderate support from the players, who feared for their jobs if they challenged the system. Griffith met with his friend-Ban Johnson, who wanted to form a new league to address some of these issues. Thus began the American League.

Griffith tried to persuade National Leaguers to jump to the new circuit. For his efforts, he was named player-manager of the American League Chicago White Stockings in 1901 and 1902, and led Chicago to the first AL pennant, in 1901. The AL moved the Baltimore franchise to New York as the New York Highlanders in 1903, and Griffith was their player-manager from 1903 to June 1908. A team in New York City was crucial for the success of any league. Finding that the American League management and administration was little different from the National League, he returned to the NL in December 1908 as manager of the

Cincinnati Reds, where he remained through the 1911 season. Ban Johnson drew Griffith back to the American League for the 1912 season as manager of the Senators.

Griffith was always thrifty with money, but in 1912 he purchased a 10 percent interest in the Senators. To raise the funds for the purchase, he "risked everything by mortgaging the Montana ranch he owned with his brother."[22] At the time the club had little going for it talentwise, except for Walter Johnson, but it did have a new ballpark. Even with lesser players, Griffith was still able to take the Senators into the first division several times.

The United States entered World War I in 1917. Griffith, as did many others, believed that military drill for players was patriotic and would prepare them if they were called up for the war effort. On Opening Day, April 25, the players drilled in military formation led by Assistant Secretary of the Navy Franklin D. Roosevelt. In lieu of weapons, the players carried baseball bats.[23] In addition, Griffith raised money to purchase baseball equipment for National Guard camps. He worked out agreements with several sporting-goods companies to supply the equipment.[24]

The next major change to the home of Senators, now known as National Park, came with renovations in 1920s. With improved play on the field and increasing attendance for some visiting teams, such as the New York Yankees and the Cleveland Indians, revenues increased. The stands along the foul lines were given a covered second deck and extended almost the entire length of the foul lines. The second-deck roofs did not connect with the main grandstand because of grading issues. In addition, concrete bleachers were installed behind the left-field fence beyond the stands. These can be seen in a photo of Ty Cobb with the Detroit Tigers sliding into third base in 1924.[25] The distance down the left-field line was 424 feet, the right-field line 326 feet, and center-field (unchanged) 421 feet.[26] This unusual split in the roof line was given a nostalgic nod along the right-field line in Nationals Park, which opened in 2008.

In 1920 Griffith stepped down as manager and devoted himself full-time to administration of the club, with the approval of the Nationals' major investor, William Richardson of Philadelphia. The custom of the era was to name the ballpark after the owner, as in Detroit's Navin Field and Cleveland's Dunn Field. However, although Richardson was the owner, the honor was given to Griffith since he oversaw the operations of the club.

Modifications to the playing area, particularly the relocation of fences, altered the foul lines and center-field distances. In 1926 the left-field line was decreased to 358 feet, the right-field line increased to 328 feet, and center field again remained unchanged. The next alteration came 10 years later, in 1936, when the left-field line was increased to 402 feet, while the right-field line and center-field distance were unaltered. In 1947 the left-field line was increased to 405 feet. The next realignment was in 1950, with the left-field line decreasing to 386 feet. The following year, 1951, the left-field line was increased to 408 feet. In 1955, the right-field line was decreased by 8 feet to 320 feet.[27]

The dimensions proved formidable to hitters. According to baseball-reference.com, "Just two players are known to have hit a fair ball out of Griffith Stadium — Mickey Mantle, who hit the famous '565-foot' blast off Chuck Stobbs in 1953, and Josh Gibson, who reportedly did it twice in the 1940s as a member of the [sometimes] Washington-based Homestead Grays," the Negro League team that called D.C. its second home (along with Pittsburgh's Forbes Field).[28] However, Larry Doby of the Cleveland Indians is credited with a 500-foot home run in 1949. The *Washington Post* declared of the blast, "When Larry Doby pumped that 500-foot home run over the scoreboard, over the Chesterfield sign and onto the rooftop beyond Griffith's Stadium's right field wall the other night, even Clark Griffith could admire the majesty of the swat."[29]

The field's one anomaly remained: the right-angle notch in the center-field fence, created because a homeowner would not sell the property when the park was renovated in 1920. The scoreboard with

Griffith Stadium's deep right-center field with its 30-foot-tall wall in 1958. (Photo courtesy of Robert E. Wilson)

its giant National Bohemian beer bottle was in right-center field.[30] Temporary lights were used for boxing and collegiate football, but not for baseball. Permanent light towers were installed for the 1941 season at a cost of $230,000. Shirley Povich of the Washington Post commented that "the added cash the night games fetched was permitting (Griffith) to go into the market for better ball players."[31] Washington profited from having night games, especially during the war years, which saw a great increase in government personnel in Washington.

Along with the changes in field dimensions, the ballpark's capacity changed as well. In 1921 it was listed as 32,000; in 1936, 30,171; in 1939, 31,500; in 1940, 29,473; in 1941, 29,613; in 1947, 29,000; in 1948, 25,048; in 1952, 35,000; in 1960, 28,669; in 1961, 27,550.32 Note that the capacity averaged almost 30,000 until the 5,000-seat increase in 1952. In eight years, by 1960, the capacity had dropped to below 30,000.[33]

Before the age of loudspeakers or radio and TV broadcasting, the lineups for the game were given to the fans at the stadium by a man with a megaphone. At American League Park in 1901, E. Lawrence Phillips made these announcements along both the left- and right-field lines prior to the game. He did this for 28 years before retiring in 1928 but continued to use his megaphone after he purchased a carnival in 1934.[34] A loudspeaker system was introduced in Griffith Stadium on September 1, 1930. It "seemed to make a hit with the fans, especially the early comers who were treated to a musical program before play started."[35]

Other technological advances affected the game in the 1920s. In 1924, "Thousands of Washington baseball fans, unable to obtain tickets for the World Series games because of the limited capacity of the ball park, are listening in on the games by radio. Play by play descriptions of the games are radiocast directly from the ball park. ..."[36] In this instance, "sport radio's first major star, [Graham] McNamee," broadcast the first of his 12 consecutive World Series.[37] Local radio sales were up 60 percent, but sponsors were concerned that listeners would give up on the poor radio reception and opt for "a first-hand view of the ballgames."[38] The technology continued to improve so that in an article on public-address systems in use in Washington, Fred E.

Kunkel reported that the system "is used at Griffith Ball Park picking up any and all sounds desired, in addition to the speaker's voice announcing the progress of the game. Since most of the games played here by the Nationals are broadcast over the radio, the set has to be perfect in every respect. Pick-up microphones can be focused in any direction the sound is coming from to catch such details as the batter hitting the ball."[39]

With the emergence of a quality team in the 1920s, the Senators won pennants in 1924, 1925, and 1933, crowned with a World Series victory in seven games in 1924 over the New York Giants. These teams were led by players like Muddy Ruel, Joe Judge, player-manager Bucky Harris, Goose Goslin, and Sam Rice. The pitchers included Tom Zachary, George Mogridge, and Walter Johnson, who was nearing the end of his career. Johnson lost Games One and Five of the 1924 Series, but got credit for the win in Game Seven as a reliever.

After the profitable 1924 season, Griffith purchased land for a home in Washington's diplomatic row at 16th and Decatur Streets.[40] The next year saw the Senators repeat as the AL champions. They lost the World Series to the Pittsburgh Pirates in seven games. Johnson pitched three games, winning Games One and Four, but losing Game Seven. Goslin kept his bat hot with eight hits in the Series.

Walter Johnson retired in 1927. When Washington returned to the World Series in 1933, Joe Cronin was the manager against the New York Giants, who took the Series, four games to one. Earl Whitehill won Washington's only game, Game Three, 4-0. Goslin hit one of only two home runs in the series for the Senators along with teammate Fred Schulte.

The Senators hosted two All-Star Games at Griffith Stadium. In 1937, along with President Franklin Roosevelt, 31,391 people watched as the American League won, 8-3. Second baseman Buddy Myer and the Ferrell brothers (catcher Rick and pitcher Wes) represented the Senators. When the All-Star Game returned in 1956, the National League won, 7-3, with Senators outfielder Roy Sievers pinch-hitting in the ninth.

Although the Senators won only three pennants in Washington, they had many outstanding players. The 1902 AL batting champion was Ed Delahanty, who posted a .376 batting average. Leon Goslin won in 1928 with .379; Buddy Myer in 1935 with .349; and two-time winner Mickey Vernon topped the league in 1946 with .353 and in 1953 with .337. Perhaps the greatest hitting feat came from a Senators shortstop in 1941, when Cecil Travis slipped in between Ted Williams and Joe DiMaggio with a .359 average for the season, second to Williams's .406. After spending four years in the military and even enduring frostbite at one point, Travis returned for three seasons and finished his career in 1947 with a lifetime batting average of .314.

Despite the expansive dimensions of their home field, the Senators had two home-run champions, Roy Sievers in 1957 and Harmon Killebrew in 1959, each with 42 round-trippers. They also boasted several basestealing leaders, starting in 1906 with John Anderson, who stole 39 bases. Clyde Milan stole 88 in 1912 and 75 in 1913. Sam Rice led with 63 stolen bases in 1920. Ben Chapman stole 35 in 1937. From 1939 through 1943, George Case took the honors with 51, 35, 33, 44, and 61, respectively.

In the pitching department, 20-game winners include Bob Groom (1912), Stan Coveleski (1925), General Alvin Crowder (1932, '33), Monte Weaver (1932), Earl Whitehill (1933), Emil Dutch Leonard (1939), Roger Wolff (1945), and Bob Porterfield (1953). Walter Johnson topped all Senators hurlers with 12 seasons in which he won 20 or more games. On August 2, 1927, in recognition of his accomplishments and to celebrate Johnson's retirement after 20 years with the team, a granite shaft with a bronze tablet was to be placed in the ballpark. Billy Evans, who umpired Johnson's first game, was to umpire the game.[41] However, this did not occur and the monument to Walter Johnson was formally installed at Griffith Stadium in 1946 and dedicated by President Harry S. Truman.[42] The monument is now installed at Walter Johnson High School in Bethesda, Maryland.

Black baseball also had an extended history at Griffith Stadium. Beginning with the Washington Potomacs (Eastern Colored League) in 1924, several teams used Griffith as their home ballpark. The Washington Pilots (East West League) came in 1932, followed by the Washington Elite Giants (Negro National League) in 1936-37 and the Washington Black Senators (Negro National League) in 1938. None of these teams achieved success either on the field or with attendance.[43] The arrival of the Homestead Grays in 1940 changed this circumstance. During Homestead's tenure through 1948 great players graced Griffith Stadium, including James Cool Papa Bell, Ray Brown, Walter Buck Leonard, and Josh Gibson. The Grays won seven of their 10 Negro National League championships in seasons when they split their home games between Pittsburgh and Washington: 1940, '41, '42, '43, '44, '45, and '48. They won the Negro League World Series in 1943, 1944, and 1948, each time against the Birmingham Black Barons of the Negro American League. In 1946 the Grays hosted the East West All-Star Classic, which attracted a crowd of more than 15,000 and netted $7,500 for the Senators, whom the Grays paid for the use of the stadium.[44]

Washington's black population increased during the war years. To reach this fan base, the Grays used their own public-relations man, who highlighted the team's winning ways. There was easy access to Griffith from nearby Ladroit and Shaw neighborhoods that had large black populations, and the Howard University campus was close by as well. Meanwhile, Clark Griffith, in need of fans to fill the ballpark, lifted the ban on interracial games. With the added attraction of Satchel Paige to hurl several games and the Grays' all-star lineup, both the Grays and Griffith profited. The Senators netted $60,000 from the Grays' 11,600 or so fans per game in 1942, almost double the Senators' average for the season. The next year, 1943, was even better, showing a net profit for the ballpark of $100,000 from the Grays, who drew 225,000 in 26 games. Because of the Grays' drawing power that year, Griffith altered the Senators' schedule so that the Grays could host the 1943 Negro League World Series. "It is easy to see Griffith's reluctance to integrate which would potentially lead to the decimation of the Grays," wrote a Griffith biographer.[45] However, no small consideration may have been that this would result in significant loss of revenue for Griffith.

In addition to major-league and Negro League squads, other baseball teams used Griffith Stadium. In 1931, the Hollywood Movie Stars Girls Baseball Team was in Washington to compete against the Pullman Athletic Club. The *Washington Post* noted, "From all indications, today's game will draw an unprecedented number of fans through the turnstiles to witness a team composed entirely of girls, movie actresses at that, in a baseball game with a rugged group of veteran sandlotters." All redheads were admitted as guests of "Freckles" HooRay of "Our Gang." Griffith donated the use of the stadium for a benefit game for Frank Cinotti.[46] Another charity game, this time to benefit the Metropolitan Police Boys Club, was held on July 12, 1947, and pitted Republican congressmen against Democratic congressmen. Chief Justice Fred Vinson threw out the first ball.[47]

Griffith recognized the value of entertainment for attracting crowds. As an example, he employed two mediocre former Senators, Al Schacht and Nick Altrock, to liven up the game with pantomime routines. In one instance, before a game they mimicked Vincent Richards and Suzanne Lenglen, two well-known tennis players. After the Senators lost to the Athletics, 13-3, the *Washington Post* reported, "(Schacht and Altrock) showed better form than many of the Washington players yesterday."[48] In another show, Schacht was "funmaking around the first base," missed a ball, and was "hit in the back of the head and rendered ... senseless. Spectators did not know whether Schacht was unconscious or whether he was acting. Several buckets of water thrown by Brownie revived the comedian and he resumed his antics to the great amusement of the crowd."[49] The pair were seen at many festivals at

Griffith Stadium and at other ballparks.[50] Besides being a player and comedian, Schacht coached third base for the Senators from 1925 to 1935; he served in World War II and later opened a restaurant in New York City.51 Altrock remained a favorite of Griffith and coached the Senators into the 1950s.[52] Aside from the entertainment value, some of their antics were used as signals for plays, according to Bob Considine in the *Washington Post.*[53]

Other sporting events and entertainments generated additional revenue for the Senators. Football at the high-school, collegiate and professional levels was played at Griffith. The *Washington Post* reported in November of 1929 that "the strong Emerson Institute will host the Baylor Military Academy, prep school champions of Tennessee."[54] On December 7, 1929, Gonzaga played Devitt for the prep-school championship of Washington.[55] Georgetown University used the ballpark as its home field from 1921 through 1950.[56] George Washington University played there during the 1930s and '40s. Schedule conflicts did arise but were worked out between Georgetown and George Washington. The colleges even scheduled night games at Griffith Stadium in 1930. "After-dinner football in wholesale quantities will be offered Washingtonians," reported the *Washington Post.* "... Seven games will be played under huge floodlights. Teams of Georgetown and George Washington University, and the Marine Corps will participate in this first attempt of its kind in the city's sports history."[57] The University of Maryland Terrapins played their home games at Griffith Stadium in 1948 while their own campus stadium was under construction.[58] Howard University, located across the street from Griffith Stadium, used the stadium as the Bisons clashed with "their ancient rival, the Lions of Lincoln, in the thirty-fifth rivalry of their turkey day contest" in 1940.[59]

The Boston Redskins (originally the Braves) of the National Football League moved to Washington for the 1937 season and maintained the Redskins name. They met their opponents at Griffith Stadium for 34 seasons (through 1960). The team was moderately successful; however, in 1940 they lost to the Chicago Bears, 73-0, the worst championship loss in NFL history.[60] The football teams contributed an average of $100,000 annually from rental and concessions alone.[61] Griffith also profited from advertising and concessions for revenue. (Tobacco and beer companies sponsored game broadcasts.) In 1940 Griffith Stadium was spruced up with repainted seats (the paint cost $3,000); 150 truckloads of sod were used to repair the damage caused by the Redskins games.[62]

Boxing was prominent among the other sporting events. On July 25, 1938, Al Reid was an 8-5 favorite over Paul "Tennessee") Lee.[63] It rained, and the featherweight match was held the next night at Turner's Arena. (Reid won a unanimous decision.) Rain often plagued events scheduled at Griffith Stadium.[64] Lewis F. Atchison reported on a "lighting system rigged up to indicate the score of the for the fans' enlightenment."[65] A green light appeared over the corner of the boxer who was leading in the match. A 10-round welterweight match featuring Holman Williams and Izzy Jannazzo was held on September 4, 1940; Jannazzo won the decision before a gathering of 2,500. These bouts were held outdoors, in a ring set up on the infield. The Williams-Jannazzo bout had been postponed a week because of rain.[66] When Henry Armstrong, the welterweight champion, fought Phil Furr on September 23, 1940, a crowd of 15,000 and receipts of between $20,000 and $25,000 were expected.[67] Heavyweight champ Joe Louis defeated challenger Buddy Baer on May 23, 1941.[68] The rough-and-tumble match was ended at the beginning of the seventh round when Baer's manager stopped the fight. The following year, two other heavyweight contenders, Lee Savold and Tony Musto, finally met after rain forced two postponements.[69] On October 3, 1949, Joe Louis, attempting a comeback, returned to Griffith Stadium for an exhibition match against Abe Gestac.[70] It is estimated that more than 150 boxing matches took place at Griffith Stadium.

Wrestling, another physical, combative sport, also was occasionally featured at Griffith

Stadium. Wrestling was a colorful event in 1938, and audience participation was expected. Lewis F. Atchison reported of the Jim Londos-Bobby Bruns match, "[T]is rumored it will be a shooting match. That means only guns, knives and Cyclone Burns shirt will be barred as weapons. It is every man for himself, including the irate customers who inhabit the front row pews."[71] The popular wrestling events continued at Griffith Stadium, bolstered by colorful reporting in the *Washington Post*. For a wrestling card in August 1939, the newspaper commented, "After the culling the ranks of wrestledom – which needless to say are pretty rank – Turner (the promoter) chose the most ferocious of the four wrestling Duseks as the person to break the hindu's celebrated cobra clutch." For this bout between Najo Singh and Ernie Dusek, Turner expected a turnout of 4,000 to 6,000.[72]

During World War II, Griffith Stadium was used to aid the war effort through scrap-metal drives, War Bond sales, and benefit sporting events. The radio personality and singer Kate Smith, a Washington native, appeared for the pregame ceremony before a contest between the Nats and the Norfolk Naval Training Station on May 20, 1943. At home plate she delivered her "notable bond buying speech."[73] Bond buyers received a ticket to the game for each bond purchased in advance. The singer Bing Crosby also was slated to attend the event. During the Korean War, Griffith donated the receipts from the August 10, 1953, game between the Nats and the Red Sox to the Red Cross.[74]

Before the 1960s ballparks were not designed as multipurpose facilities; however, since they were often the largest venue in many cities, they also hosted nonathletic events. Griffith Stadium was a major entertainment center for the capital. It hosted dog races in May 1927. Tiny whippets from across the nation were brought to the city to race for the American Derby title. The weight of the dogs ranged from 10 to 14 pounds.[75] On June 17, 1928, the Masonic Festival highlighted Shrine and Grotto drill teams before a crowd of 8,000.[76] On June 7, 1932, students from the area competed in the Annual Competitive Drill Competition for high school cadet corps.[77] In addition to the drill-team contests, there were also field days. The Colored Elks sponsored one such competition on July 27, 1930, at which events included a fat man race, a tug of war, a sack race, an exhibition drill, a 100-yard race, and baseball; about 2,000 people attended.[78] There was also a "Night of Thrills," an annual circus sponsored by the Masons for the benefit of the Mason and Eastern Star Home. Beginning in 1938, clowns, elephants, and trapeze artists provided annual entertainment.[79]

Griffith Stadium was even used for religious events. On a rainy night in October 1937, 200 people were baptized by immersion by Elder Lightfoot Solomon Michaux. Elder Michaux's church, the Church of God, was across the street from the stadium. For the ceremony, the city Fire Department filled the baptismal tank to a depth of three feet with river water.[80] The Billy Graham National Capital Crusade on June 19-26, 1960, was also held at Griffith Stadium and had an estimated attendance of more than 139,000 over eight days.[81]

Clark Griffith continued to be the administrator for the Senators and Griffith Stadium, but he also worked with his nephew, Calvin Griffith, and Calvin's sister, Thelma Griffith Haynes. Griffith's nephew and niece had been born in Montreal; after their father died, they moved to Washington and adopted the name Griffith.[82] Upon Clark Griffith's death on October 27, 1955, Calvin was elected club president. Clark Griffith left his 52 percent interest in the Senators to Calvin and Thelma, to be shared equally.

The last successful Senators squad was the team that finished in second place in 1945. In 1946, capitalizing on the previous season as well as the postwar return to normalcy, the Nationals drew a record 1,027,216. That was 400,000 more than in 1945 and 200,000 more than in 1947.[83] Calvin Griffith did try to make the experience at the park more enjoyable for the spectators. In 1956, he changed the left-field foul line, which made room for more seating and added a beer garden.[84] However, the ensuing years were marked by declining attendance and the deterioration of the ballpark. Bill DeWitt, president of the St. Louis Browns, declared, "Griffith Stadium is one of the most rundown excuses for a ballpark in the majors."[85] This was harsh criticism from a club spokesman whose own venue, Sportsman's Park, was no palace either.

Calvin Griffith was interested in moving out of Washington because of the deteriorating neighborhood around the ballpark, the racial makeup of the city, and the new competition from the Baltimore Orioles starting in 1954. The American League did not want to lose Washington.

Rumors had circulated as early as the late 1950s about the prospect of a new facility to include the Senators. Finally, after much political maneuvering, the development of a large, dual purpose (baseball-football) stadium began. The proposed location was the end of East Capitol Street near the D.C. Armory.[86] Calvin Griffith had mixed emotions about the prospect of a new stadium in Washington. His reservations were numerous. "Turning to the matter of a stadium in Washington, I feel that the capital of the United States needs one and should have one," Griffith said. "The Washington ballclub would consider playing its games in a new stadium." He was weighing the fact that the club owned the paid-for Griffith Stadium, controlled the concessions, could rent out the facility for added income, and made their own decisions. "We know, on the other hand, that our patrons, who otherwise attend theaters, restaurants, and watch television in the comfort of their home living rooms, have come to expect more and convenient parking, more ample aisle space, roomier seats, more concession stands at our ball park."[87]

Griffith's critics questioned why he listened to offers from other cities. "My answer: I will give that much courtesy to the mayor of any city or his representatives. Besides, the Washington baseball club is a corporation with many stockholders, it is my obligation as their president to listen ... to any proposition that would improve the value of their holdings. We are not seeking offers. ... We do not invite offers. In fact, we discouraged them."[88]

Despite Griffith's frequent expressions of loyalty to Washington, he was interested in moving the club out of the capital. He became enamored with Minneapolis. He gained permission from the American League to move there in 1961. His reasons for moving were not always clear. However, Nick Coleman of the Minneapolis *Star Tribune* reported that Griffith told the Lions Club of Waseca, Minnesota, "I'll tell you why we came to Minnesota. It was when I found out you only had 15,000 blacks here. Black people don't go to ballgames, but they'll fill up a rassling ring and put up such a chant it'll scare you to death. It's unbelievable. We came here because you've got good, hard-working white people."[89] The American League, fearing congressional backlash against baseball's antitrust exemption, awarded an expansion franchise to Washington also, to be known as the Senators. The Los Angeles Angels entered the American League in the same year, making it a 10-team league. The expansion Senators moved into Griffith Stadium in 1961 for one year. The following season they moved to new D.C. Stadium. After 10 years in Washington, owner Robert Short moved the club to Arlington, Texas, in 1972, where they became the Texas Rangers.

In a fitting tribute, the carillon of the Church of God, across the street from the ballpark stadium, rang out with "Auld Lang Syne" on the last day the Senators played there.[90]

EPILOGUE

Howard University purchased the Griffith Stadium site for its University Hospital, and the ballpark was demolished in 1965.[91] The location of home plate is marked inside the hospital entrance. A plaque along Georgia Avenue notes the historic ballpark and notable moments in its history.[92] The spring-training site for the Senators, Tinker Field in Orlando, Florida, became the home for 1,000 seats from Griffith Stadium, which remained there until Tinker Field also was demolished in 2015. [93]

SOURCES

In addition to the sources cited in the Notes, the author also consulted Baseball-Reference.com, Baseball-Almanac.com, and a variety of other sources including:

BOOKS, BOOK CHAPTERS, BOOK SECTIONS

Elston, Gene. *A Stitch in Time: A Baseball Chronology,* 3rd Ed. (Houston: Halcyon Press Inc., 2006).

Lowry, Philip J. *Green Cathedrals: The Ultimate Celebration of Major League and Negro League Ballparks* (New York: Walker & Company, 2006).

Seymour, Harold. *Baseball: The People's Game* (New York: Oxford University Press, 1990).

Snyder, Brad. *Beyond the Shadow of the Senators* (New York: McGraw-Hill, 2003).

Thomas, Henry W. *Walter Johnson: Baseball's Big Train* (Washington: Phenom Press, 1995).

NEWSPAPERS AND MAGAZINES

Atchison, Lewis F. "New Yorker Rallies After Slow Start," *Washington Post,* July 27, 1938: 16.

"Coast Guards Clash With Marines: Teams Appear Well Matched for Service Title Game," *Washington Post,* November 21, 1929.

"Daisy Belles Play Twin Bill Here Tonight," *Washington Post,* May 5, 1951.

"Display Ad 21 - No Title," *Washington Post,* May 24, 1926: 15.

"Girls Teams Play Tonight," *Washington Post,* May 9, 1952.

"G.W.-Ursinus to Attract Notables," *Washington Post,* November 5, 1926.

Johnson, Mrs. Walter Perry, "Loss of Game Was Hard, But 'Luck' at Bat Did It, Says Mrs. Walter Johnson," *Washington Post,* October 5, 1924: 2.

McCannon, Jim. "Famous 'Pebble' Is Forever Lost in Memories of Griffith Stadium," *Washington Post and Times Herald,* March 22, 1964.

"Movie Girls Play Here Tomorrow: Meet Pullman Nine at Stadium in Benefit Day," *Washington Post,* August 8, 1931.

"New Baseball Park: Local Owners Plan Another Home for Nationals," *Washington Post,* January 5, 1910: 8.

"Photo Standalone 1 - No Title," *Washington Post,* April 18, 1927: 13.

Weingardt, Richard G. "Frank Osborn: Nation's Pioneer Stadium Designer," *STRUCTURE magazine,* March 2013: 61-63.

Wyatt, Dick. "Virginia, Maryland Clash in Griffith Stadium Tonight," *Washington Post,*

November 4, 1944.

Young, Frank H. "12,000 Fans Cheer Harris, Johnson, Peck, Others as Youth Is Served in Game," *Washington Post,* August 16, 1932: 9.

ONLINE SOURCES

Bennett, Bryon. "Griffith Stadium and the Site of D.C.'s First National Park," deadballbaseball.com/?p=3073 (deadballbaseball.com/?p=3073), accessed August 20, 2016.

Clem, Andrew. "Clem's Baseball: Our National Pastime and Its 'Green Cathedrals,' Griffith Stadium 1911-1961, andrewclem.com/Baseball/GriffithStadiium.html#Diag (andrewclem.com/Baseball/GriffithStadiium.html#Diag), accessed September 8, 2016.

"Cleveland Architects: Osborn Engineering Company," planning.city.cleveland.oh.us/landmark/arch/pdf/archdetailPrint.php?afil=&archID=189

(http://planning.city.cleveland.oh.us/landmark/arch/pdf/archdetailPrint.php?afil=&archID=189), accessed September 19, 2016.

"Griffith Stadium," ballparksofbaseball.com/ballparks/griffith-stadium/ (ballparksofbaseball.com/ballparks/griffith-stadium/), accessed July 29, 2016.

"Griffith Stadium," projectballpark.org/history/al/griffth.html (Projectballpark.org/history/al/griffith.html), accessed July 29, 2016.

"Griffith Stadium, on Last Legs, Succumbs to Wrecker's Pounding," *Washington Post and Times Herald,* February 12, 1965.

"History," Osborn-eng.com/History (http://Osborn-eng.com/History), accessed July 29, 2016.

"Lease Requirements to Replace Griffith Stadium," ghostsofdc.org/2016/06/29/lease-requirements-replace-griffith-stadium/ (ghostsofdc.org/2016/06/29/lease-requirements-

replace-griffith-stadium/), accessed July 7, 2016.

Richard, Paul. "Lights From Griffith Stadium Towers to Shine Again at City Playgrounds," *Washington Post and Times Herald,* May 14, 1966.

"The Info List - Griffith Stadium," theinfolist.com/php/SummaryGet.php?findGo=

Griffith Stadium (theinfolist.com/php/SummaryGet.php?findGo=Griffith Stadium), accessed October 19, 2016.

"Tradition," dcgrays.com/tradition-2/ (dcgrays.com/tradition-2/), accessed October 13, 2016.

"Where Was Griffith Stadium? - Ghosts of DC," ghostsofdc.org/image/zoom/Griffith-stadium/15346/view (ghostsofdc.org/image/zoom/Griffith-stadium/15346/view), accessed October 12, 2016.

OTHER SOURCES

Washington Nationals 2016 Official Media Guide

ebay (ebay.com)

COLLECTIONS

Baseball Hall of Fame, Griffith Stadium file, courtesy of Cassidy Lent, January 9, 2017.

NOTES

1 The names Senators and Nationals were used interchangeably over the years until the team left Washington in 1965.

2 *Sanborn Fire Insurance Map from Washington, District of Columbia.* Sanborn Map Company, -1916 Vol. 2, 1904 - 1916, 127.

3 *Sanborn Fire Insurance Map from Washington, District of Columbia.* Sanborn Map Company, -1916 Vol. 2, 1904 - 1916, 173.

4 "1903 AL-NL Peace Agreement," roadsidephotos.sabr.org/baseball/1903 AL-NL.htm (roadsidephotos.sabr.org/baseball/1903 AL-NL.htm), accessed October 1, 2016.

5 The multiple names in use for the two sites that the Senators/Nationals called home from 1891 through 1964 cause confusion. The primary location, in Northwest Washington at Florida Avenue NW and Georgia Avenue NW, was known as Boundary Field, National Park, or American League Park II. This is near Howard University and where Griffith Stadium was built. The other site used from 1901-1903 was located at Florida Avenue NE and Trinidad Avenue. It was known as American League Park, and then as American League Park I, to distinguish it from American League Park II.

6 J. Ed Grillo, "Sporting Comment," *Washington Post*, January 6, 1910: 8.

7 "Local Owners Plan Another Home for Nationals," *Washington Post*, January 5, 1910: 8.

8 "Cleveland Architects: Osborn Engineering Company," planning.city.cleveland.oh.us/landmark/arch/pdf/archdetailPrint.php?afil=&archID=189 (planning.city.cleveland.oh.us/landmark/arch/pdf/archdetailPrint.php?afil=&archID=189), accessed September 19, 2016.

9 "Play Ball April 12," *Washington Post*, March 18, 1911: 1.

10 Ibid.

11 "Accommodations for Opening Game Assured – Ban Johnson Here," *Washington Post*, March 20, 1911: 12.

12 "Ready for 'Fans,'" *Washington Sunday Star*, April 9, 1911: 1, 3.

13 "Griffith Stadium," baseball-almanac.com/stadium/st_griff.shtml (baseball-almanac.com/stadium/st_griff.shtml), accessed January 1, 2017.

14 Ibid.

15 "1911 Washington Senators," baseball-almanac.com/teamstats/schedule.php?y=1911&t=WS1 (baseball-almanac.com/teamstats/schedule.php?y=1911&t=WS1), accessed September 15, 2016.

16 Patrick Mondout, "Taft Becomes First President to Throw First Pitch (4/14/1910)," Baseball Chronology: The Game Since 1845," baseballchronology.com/baseball/Years/1910/April/14-Taft (baseballchronology.com/baseball/Years/1910/April/14-Taft), accessed August 17, 2016.

17 "1924 Washington Senators," baseball-almanac.com/teamstats/schedule.php?y=1924&t=WS1 (baseball-almanac.com/teamstats/schedule.php?y=1924&t=WS1), accessed September 13, 2016; "President to Throw First Ball for Olympic Quota," Washington Post, May 17, 1924: 9.

18 "Play Ball April 12," *Washington Post*, March 18, 1911: 1.

19 "Phillies Here First," *Washington Post*, January 25, 1910: 8.

20 "Cleveland Architects: Osborn Engineering Company," planning.city.cleveland.oh.us/landmark/arch/pdf/archdetailPrint.php?afil=&archID=189(planning.city.cleveland.oh.us/landmark/arch/pdf/archdetailPrint.php?afil=&archID=189), accessed September 19, 2016.

21 "National League / Major League Rule Change Timeline: In Chronological Order," baseball-almanac.com/rulechng.shtml (baseball-almanac.com/rulechng.shtml), accessed September 20, 2016.

22 Mike Grahek, "Clark Griffith," sabr.org/bioproj/person/96624988 (sabr.org/bioproj/person/96624988), accessed November 24, 2016.

23 "Franklin D. Roosevelt Opening Baseball Game," gettyimages.com/detail/news-photo/assistant-secretary-of-the-navy-franklin-d-roosevelt-walks-news-photo/514080428#assistant-secretary-of-the-navy-franklin-d-roosevelt-walks the-out-picture-id514080428 (gettyimages.com/detail/news-photo/assistant-secretary-of-the-navy-franklin-d-roosevelt-walks-news-photo/514080428#assistant-secretary-of-the-navy-franklin-d-roosevelt-walks-the-out-picture-id514080428), accessed October 15, 2016.

24 Brian McKenna, *Clark Griffith: Baseball's Statesman* (self-published, 2010), 295.

25 "1924 Detroit Tiger Ty Cobb Safe after Triple Hit Photo Griffith Stadium Baseball," ebay.com/itm/1924-DETROIT-TIGER-TY-COBB-SAFE-AFTER-TRIPLE-HIT-POT-GRIFFITH-STADIUM-BASEBALL-/361584614222 (ebay.com/itm/1924- DETROIT-TIGER-TY-COBB-SAFE-AFTER-TRIPLE-HIT-POT-GRIFFITH-STADIUM-BASEBALL-/361584614222.

26 "Griffith Stadium," baseball-almanac.com/stadium/st_griff.shtml (baseball-almanac.com/stadium/st_griff.shtml), accessed January 1, 2017.

27 Ibid. For diagrams of the field with dimensions and profiles of stands for 1911, 1921, 1954, 1957, and football, see Andrew Clem, "Clem's Baseball: Our National Pastime and Its "Green Cathedrals," Griffith Stadium 1911-1961, andrewclem.com/Baseball/GriffithStadium.html#Diag (andrewclem.com/Baseball/GriffithStadiium.html#Diag), accessed September 8, 2016.

28 baseball-reference.com/bullpen/Griffith_Stadium, (baseball-reference.com/bullpen/Griffith_Stadium), accessed January 5, 2017.

29 Shirley Povich, "This Morning," *Washington Post*, May 27, 1949: B4.

30 McKenna, 274.

31 Shirley Povich, *The Washington Senators* (New York: G.P. Putnam's & Sons, 1954), 219.

32 "Griffith Stadium," baseball-almanac.com/stadium/st_griff.shtml (baseball-almanac.com/stadium/st_griff.shtml), accessed January 1, 2017.

33 Ibid.

34 Bill McCormick, "Phillips Buys a Circus; Now He Can Bark on His Own Hook," *Washington Post*, April 22, 1934: 17.

35 Frank H. Young, "Centerfielder Must Rest Elbow," *Washington Post*, September 2, 1930, 18.

36 "Thousands of Fans Ticketless, Hear of Series Over Radio," *Washington Post*, October 5, 1924: EA10.

37 Graham McNamee," baseballhall.org/discover/awards/ford-c-frick/2016-candidates/mcnamee-graham (baseballhall.org/discover/awards/ford-c-frick//2016-candidates/mcnamee-graham), accessed November 18, 2016.

38 "Thousands of Fans Ticketless, Hear of Series Over Radio."

39 Fred E. Kunkel, "Capitol's Sound Amplifying Systems Serve Many Purposes," *Washington Post*, June 30, 1935: B9.

40 McKenna, 195.

41 "Tablet Given as Johnson Memorial," *Washington Post*, July 23, 1927: 15.

42 deadballbaseball.com/?p=2283 (deadballbaseball.com/?p=228), accessed January 1, 2017.

43 McKenna, 275.

44 McKenna, 276.

45 Ibid.

46 "Hollywood Girls to Play Baseball at Stadium Today," *Washington Post*, September 1, 1931: 15.

47 "Congressmen Play Baseball Today at Griffith Stadium," *Washington Post*, July 12, 1947: 11.

48 "Washington Clowns Aid Mack's Elephants to Stage 3-Ring Baseball Circus," Photo Standalone 1 - No Title, *Washington Post*, April 18, 1927: 13.

49 "Thomas Halts 3-Run Rally in Ninth," *Washington Post*, August 12, 1929: 9.

50 "Masonic Festival Features Delight Crowd at Stadium," *Washington Post*, June 17, 1928: 2.

51 Al Schacht, *My Own Particular Screwball* (Garden City, New York: Doubleday & Company, 1955), 231-235.

52 "The Manager and His Aides," *Washington Nationals Yearbook 1953*: 7.

53 Bob Considine, "Runs-Hits and Errors," *Washington Post*, January 12, 1933: 10.

54 "Color Added to Emerson Contest," *Washington Post*, November 26, 1929: 20.

55 "Gonzaga to Play Devitt at Griffith Stadium," *Washington Post*, November 30, 1929: 16.

56 "History & Tradition: Stadia Of Georgetown, hoyafootball.com/history/stadia.htm (hoyafootball.com/history/stadia.htm), accessed January 8, 2016.

57 "7 Night Football Contests at Griffith Stadium in Fall," *Washington Post*, May 25, 1930: 20.

58 Jack Walsh, "Terps Play Four Grid Games at Griffith Stadium," *Washington Post*, April 4, 1948: C1.

59 "Howard Meets Lincoln at Griffith Stadium," *Washington Post*, November 21, 1940: 31.

60 Al Hailey, "36,000 See Bears Crush Redskins for Title, 73-0," *Washington Post*, December 9, 1940: 1.

61 McKenna, 275.

62 Al Hailey, "Griffith Stadium Gets Annual Face-Lifting," *Washington Post*, March 29, 1940: 23.

63 Lewis F. Atchison, "Reid Rates an 8-5 Favorite Over Lee in Griffith Stadium Battle," *Washington Post*, July 25, 1938: x13.

64 "Reid Rates": 16.

65 "Reid Rates": x13.

66 "Twice-Postponed Welter Battle Goes on in Griffith Stadium," *Washington Post*, September 4, 1940: 24.

67 "15,000 Expected to See Griffith Stadium Bout," *Washington Post*, September 23, 1940: 17.

68 Tony Neri, "Joe Saw Opening, 'Hit Baer as Matter of Routine' in Sixth," *Washington Post*, May 24, 1941: 15.

69 Tony Neri, "Heavyweight Battle Heads Twice-Postponed Card at Griffith Stadium," *Washington Post*, August 16, 1942: SP2.

70 "Bomber Faces Cestac at Griffith Stadium," *Washington Post*, October 3, 1949: 11.

71 Lewis F. Atchison, "Bruns Meets Londos at Griffith Stadium," *Washington Post*, June 16, 1938: 21.

72 "Nanjo Singh Meets Dusek Thursday in Griffith Stadium," *Washington Post*, August 27, 1939: SP3.

73 Shirley Povich, "Kate Smith, 1st Lady of Radio, to Appear at War Bond Game," *Washington Post*, May 20, 1943: 1.

74 "Red Cross Begins Fund Program in Pro Ball Parks," *Spokane Review*, July 28, 1953.

75 "Tiny Whippet Will Race Here," *Washington Post*, May 17, 1927: 14.

76 "Masonic Festival Features Delight Crowd at Stadium," *Washington Post*, June 17, 1928: 2.

77 "High School Cadet Drills End Today," *Washington Post*, June 7, 1932: 18.

78 "Joint Field Day Held by Colored Elks," *Washington Post*, July 27, 1930: M2.

79 *10th Annual Night of Thrills*, May 23, 1947, Souvenir Program, *14th Annual Night of Thrills*, June 8, 1948, Souvenir Program, *15th Annual Night of Thrills*, June 13, 1952, Souvenir Program, *Night of Thrills, June 21st 1940*, Souvenir Program, *Night of Thrills, June 6, 1941*, Souvenir Program.

80 "200 Baptized By Rain, River and Michaux," *Washington Post*, October 4, 1937: 4.

81 "Billy Graham Predicts Christians' Persecution," *Washington Post*, June 27, 1960: B1.

82 "Thelma Griffith Haynes, 82, Baseball Owner," (obituary), *New York Times*, October 17, 1995.

83 "The Senators: Year By Year (1901-1965)," *The Senators 1966 Yearbook*: 55.

84 "Griffith Stadium," thisgreatgame.com/allparks-griffith-stadium.html (thisgreatgame.com/allparks-griffith-stadium.html), accessed October 1, 2016.

85 Chris Elzey and David K. Wiggins, ed. *DC Sports: The Nation's Capital at Play* (Fayetteville, Arkansas: The University of Arkansas Press, 2015), 30.

86 Brett L. Abrams, *Capital Sporting Grounds: A History of Stadium and Ballpark Construction in Washington, D.C.* (Jefferson, North Carolina: McFarland & Company, Inc., Publishers, 2008), 189-195.

87 Calvin R. Griffith, "Griffith Not Happy With Armory Stadium Site," *Washington Post*, January 15, 1958: A18.

88 Ibid.

89 Howard Sinker, "Recalling Calvin Griffith's Bigoted Outburst in Southern Minnesota," Minneapolis Star Tribune, April 2014, startribune.com/recalling-ex-twins-owner-griffith-s-bigoted-outburst/257189521/, accessed on December 8, 2016.

90 Dave Brady, "TV Writes Requiem to Griffith Stadium," *Washington Post*, November 11, 1964, Baseball Hall of Fame, Griffith Stadium file.

91 While in Washington in July 1965, I picked up two bricks from the rubble at Griffith Stadium. They remain proudly in my possession today as bookends.

92 Byron Bennett, "Griffith Stadium and the Site of D.C.'s First National Park," deadballbaseball.com/?=3073 (deadballbaseball.com/?p=3073), accessed August 20, 2016.

93 "Griffith Stadium," thisgreatgame.com/allparks-griffith-stadium.html (thisgreatgame.com/allparks-griffith-stadium.html), accessed October 1, 2016.

GRIFFITH STADIUM OUTFIELD DIMENSIONS

by Ben Klein

Griffith Stadium, a steel-and-concrete ballpark tucked into an urban neighborhood of Washington, D.C., may have lacked the ornamentation of some of its contemporaries, but its irregular and asymmetrical outfield wall conveyed a sense of charm to spectators that was similar to the charm enjoyed by visitors to Brooklyn's Ebbets Field and relished by the Fenway faithful in Boston to this day. This charm, however, may not have been fully appreciated by the players who occupied the Senators' lineup throughout the decades of Griffith Stadium's existence from 1911 to 1961. Those players, often toiling on second-division teams, were acutely aware that the obtuse and right angles of the charming wall enclosed one of the vastest outfields in the major leagues, which compounded the frustrations of a traditionally light-hitting club.

Being located in Washington, Griffith Stadium's outfield dimensions were necessarily at the mercy of the city's layout, which had been developed from the urban plan envisioned by Pierre Charles L'Enfant at the end of the eighteenth century. L'Enfant's plan materialized into a grid, with north-to-south numbered streets intersecting east-to-west lettered streets, and overlaid by avenues sprouting radially from traffic circles arrayed throughout the district. Griffith Stadium was roughly framed by the latitudinal V and U Streets to the north and south, respectively, by the longitudinal Fifth Street to the east, and by the radial, but predominantly north-south-running Georgia Avenue to the west.[1] The plot of Griffith Stadium extended all the way to Fifth Street to the east, but to the south the plot did not extend all the way to U Street, stopping short in order to give way to properties that ran along U Street. Had Griffith Stadium's plot extended all the way to U Street, the left-field and right-field lines — depending on the orientation of the field — could have been close to equivalent, but the accommodation of the properties along U Street had the effect of bringing the right-field wall considerably closer to home plate than the left-field wall, even after the installation of left-field stands.

Although the distance down the right-field line was significantly shorter than down the left-field line, the relatively cozier dimensions of right field

The Senators' Eddie Yost swinging against the Baltimore Orioles in 1958 with a young Brooks Robinson in position at third base. Yost batted only .254 in his 18-year big-league career, but led the AL in walks six times, producing an excellent .394 on-base-percentage. (Photo courtesy of Robert E. Wilson)

were somewhat offset by the imposing 30-foot wall that ran from the right-field foul pole to center field. As the wall approached straightaway center field from right field, it zigged in and zagged out to form the stadium's distinctive "notch," a precise right-angle cutaway in right-center field. The notch separated the playing field's right-center gap from five rowhouses owned by determined homeowners who refused to yield their property to the Senators.[2] The neighborhood side of the notch also hosted an oak tree so massive that its crown peaked above the 30-foot wall. Although the reasons for the rowhouse owners' holdout may be lost to history, any annoyance that they may have felt toward the Senators could have been exacerbated by the oak tree's service as a popular gathering spot for fans before games. According to Maury Povich, son of legendary *Washington Post* sportswriter Shirley Povich, "[i]f you were going to meet somebody to give them a ticket, it was always under the oak tree."[3]

Long before Povich would rendezvous with friends at the oak tree in the notch outside of what would become known as Griffith Stadium, the ballpark opened as National Park on April 12, 1911. At its opening, National Park's dimensions measured a distant 407 feet down the left-field line, an even more distant 421 feet to center field, and 328 feet down the right-field line.[4] The advent of the live-ball era in the early 1920s coincided with the extension of the already rangy left-field line from 407 feet to a remarkable 424 feet in 1921, which denied right-handed hitters the benefits of the livelier ball.[5] Left-handed hitters were slightly aided by the reduction of the right-field line's distance from 328 feet to 326 feet. The liveliest of live-ball lefties, Babe Ruth, was particularly undeterred by the ballpark's spaciousness, collecting two home runs off Eric Erickson and Walter Johnson in two of his first three visits of the 1921 season to Griffith Stadium, in the first week of May. Ruth collected his third home run at Griffith Stadium on May 31 against Tom Zachary. His three home runs at Griffith Stadium that May equaled the output of any individual Senator at Griffith Stadium over the entire 1921 season, with Sam Rice and Joe Judge, both lefties, also managing three round-trippers.

Although the comparative anemia of the Senators' home-run output could largely be attributed to Ruth's singular dominance, Griffith Stadium's spaciousness also played a role in the scarcity of home runs tallied by the Senators at home. The Senators managed to hit 14 home runs at Griffith Stadium in 1921, but slugged exactly twice as many on the road that season. In the seasons that followed, the Senators' home-run statistics saw similar or even more pronounced splits, with 15 at home and 30 on the road in 1922, followed by seven at home and 19 on the road in 1923. Even as they collected their lone World Series title, the Senators' home-run output at Griffith Stadium cratered in 1924, with Bucky Harris's squad eking out only one home run in Washington while collecting 21 on the road. Even that dismal statistic overstates the Senators' power at home in 1924, as the lone home run was an inside-the-park job by Goose Goslin against the Tigers on August 19. Amazingly, the 1924 World Series champions failed to clear the fence of their home ballpark a single time during the regular season. The erection of temporary seats in left field for the World Series briefly made Griffith Stadium more home-run friendly, and five home runs were swatted in D.C. during the Series.

A more permanent move to make the ballpark's confines more hitter-friendly came in 1926, as the left-field line was brought in from 424 feet to a more reasonable 358 feet, even as the right-field line returned to its 1911 distance of 328 feet.6 Despite the moderation to the left-field dimensions, the lopsided home-run splits persisted for the Senators in the decade that followed, with the Senators eclipsing 20 home runs only once between 1926 and 1935 while playing at Griffith Stadium. In 1936 the left-field line was once again moved back, this time to 402 feet, and moved back another three feet in 1947.7 Despite the fact that the left-field line remained more than 400 feet from home during the 1940s, there was one right-handed hitter that Griffith Stadium could not contain. Josh Gibson, the legendary catcher of the Homestead Grays, who split their home games between Washington and Pittsburgh, reportedly hit two fair balls clear out of Griffith Stadium.8

With Griffith Stadium's left-field line consistently measuring over 400 feet, with the 30-foot wall looming in right, and with no Josh Gibson in the majors, it should come as no surprise that Griffith Stadium yielded the fewest home runs among major-league parks for 21 seasons in a row, from 1933 through 1953. One home run that Griffith Stadium did yield in 1953 was certainly notable, however. On April 17, 1953, Mickey Mantle, batting right-handed, hit a ball off Chuck Stobbs that cleared the right-field fence, cleared the right-field stands, and cleared Fifth Street, sending a drive measured by a Yankees official at 565 feet out of Griffith Stadium and into legend.9

In 1954, home runs to left field were made more accessible to the non-Gibsons and non-Mantles, as the line was reduced to 388 feet.10 The following year, relief came to the other side of the outfield, as the right-field line was reduced to 320 feet.11 The left-field line was reduced to 350 feet in 1957, the shortest distance in Griffith Stadium's history.12 Not coincidentally, right-handed slugger Roy Sievers slammed 42 home runs in 1957, including 26 at home, to become the first Senator to claim a home-run crown. Harmon Killebrew would repeat the feat two years later with 42 home runs, including 22 at home. The prodigiousness of Sievers and Killebrew signaled the end of Griffith Stadium's run as the major leagues' leading home-run graveyard, and although the shifting outfield dimensions stripped Griffith Stadium of this distinction, the other defining feature of the outfield – the notch – endured until Griffith Stadium hosted its last game in 1961. The Griffith Stadium notch, however, is not forgotten, as the left-center-field wall of Nationals Park boasts a similar, although less dramatic, notch as an homage to one of Griffith Stadium's most iconic features.[13]

SOURCES

In addition to the sources cited in the Notes, the author also accessed Retrosheet.org, Baseball-Reference.com, SABR.org, and *The Sporting News* archive via Paper of Record.

NOTES

1 Griffith Stadium, ballparksofbaseball.com/ballparks/griffith-stadium/, accessed March 30, 2019.

2 John Schleppi, "Griffith Stadium," SABR, sabr.org/bioproj/park/griffith-stadium, accessed March 31, 2019.

3 Matt Blitz, "Take Me Out to the Ball Game on … Georgia Avenue? Here's the Story of Nats Park's Predecessor," *DCist*, March 28, 2019, dcist.com/story/19/03/28/take-me-out-to-the-ball-game-on-georgia-avenue-heres-the-story-of-nats-parks-predecessor/, accessed April 3, 2019.

4 John Schleppi, "Griffith Stadium," SABR, sabr.org/bioproj/park/griffith-stadium.

5 John Schleppi, "Griffith Stadium," SABR, sabr.org/bioproj/park/griffith-stadium.

6 John Schleppi; "Griffith Stadium," Baseball Almanac, baseball-almanac.com/stadium/st_griff.shtml, accessed March 31, 2019. "Griffith Stadium," Clem's Baseball Blog, andrewclem.com/Baseball/GriffithStadium.html, accessed March 31, 2019.

7 "Griffith Stadium," *Baseball Almanac*.

8 baseball-reference.com/bullpen/Griffith_Stadium; sabr.org/bioproj/park/griffith-stadium; baseball-reference.com/bullpen/Griffith_Stadium.

9 Dan Daniel, "Mantle Makes Home Run History at 21," *The Sporting News*, April 29, 1953: 13.

10 "Griffith Stadium," *Baseball Almanac*.

11 "Griffith Stadium," *Baseball Almanac*.

12 "Griffith Stadium," *Baseball Almanac*.

13 Russell Boniface, "It's a Ballpark," AIArchitect, info.aia.org/aiarchitect/thisweek08/0411/0411n_ballpark2.htm, accessed March 31, 2019.

GRIFFITH STADIUM
THE UTILITARIAN BALLPARK

by Luis Blandon

Many a summer night, the fusion of heat and humidity mingled with the artificial light and odors of the urban night as people filed out of Griffith Stadium. Trolleys picked up passengers. Cars honked horns. The aromas from the baking breads and Hostess Cakes at the Wonder Bread factory (formerly the Dorsch's White Cross Bakery) teased the senses. The spirituals bursting from the choir at Elder Michaux's Church of God soothed fans as they headed home from fights, wrestling matches, and operas.

For 54 years, a ballpark was located between Georgia Avenue and 5th Street NW and between W Street and Florida Avenue NW in Washington's Shaw neighborhood. It looked out of place, surrounded by neighborhoods, houses, and small businesses like the family-owned bakeries lining the streets. The ballpark was minimalist in its appearance. Built quickly, it was considered a charmless relic. It was also situated in the heart of a vibrant Afro-American community served by a series of trolley lines. For decades, a lonely oak tree hovered behind the center-field wall.

Taking a month to build, American League Park opened on April 12, 1911. The stands were completed but uncovered, and ready for a crowd of 16,000 to see the Senators defeat the Boston Red Sox, 8-5.[1] When Clark Griffith assumed control as majority owner of the Washington Senators[2] and American League Park, it became known as Griffith Stadium. It was a family business. Griffith was known for being profane and driven, but also charitable to the community and loyal to his players, his employees, and their families.

For Clark Griffith, the ballpark was a place for baseball and a place to hold events, a community center. The financial benefits to Griffith to host non-baseball and community events were further driven by the Great Depression and poor finances of the baseball team that drove Griffith close to bankruptcy.[3] Structural changes to the ballpark in 1920-1921 were designed to attract nonbaseball events that brought in revenue. From 1911 to 1961, professional, college, and high-school football games were played. Dozens and dozens of boxing and wrestling cards were held. Concerts graced the infield. Political rallies, Masonic festivals, religious rallies, to a myriad other events played out at Griffith Stadium. The ballpark became an integral part of the local black community and a citywide destination spot. Practicing what was described as "mercenary desegregation," Griffith rented his ballpark for boxing matches, community and musical events, and football games.[4] The neighborhood around Griffith was "one of the largest, wealthiest, and best-educated African-American communities" prior to the World War II.[5] Many events brought African-Americans to the stadium.

THE CONGRESSIONAL HORSESHOES TOURNAMENT

The day was cloudy and cool with rain in the air, with the afternoon temperatures hovering in the low 60s.[6] On May 30, 1930, Congress reconvened at Griffith Stadium for the First Congressional Horseshoes Tournament. It was an all-House competition as the senators who agreed to play never showed up and lost by default.[7] In a single-elimination tournament, Rep. Fred G. Johnson (R-Neb.) came away with the winning prize, defeating Rep. Albert H. Vestal (R-Ind.) in a come-from-behind late rally to a 21-20 victory. Johnson was awarded "a set of silver-plated horseshoes in a leather case."[8]

The *Washington Post* described the match as "one-time rural pastime between two one-time country lads."[9] The event was aired live nationally on NBC and locally on WRC with Representative Clarence McLeod (R-Miss.) and Senator Alben W. Barkley (D-Ky.) providing play-by-play. The US Navy Band played between and during the matches.[10] Each finalist, as "guest announcers," provided their own take on the match over the radio.[11]

The tournament was never repeated. Several of the competitors lost their seats, including Johnson, whose athletic proclivities failed to sway his constituents, who voted him out of office the following November.[12]

A WHIPPET DERBY TO DETERMINE THE CHAMPION OF THE EAST

A whippet is a medium-sized breed that encompasses the greyhound, Irish wolfhound, Afghan hound, and others. Whippets were bred to hunt by sight and at high speeds for open-field hunting.[13] The American Whippet Club says "[I]t has long been held that one of the original functions of the Whippet was the 'poor man's race dog' in England."[14] And on a chilly November 19, 1930, about 400 people attended the American Derby races at Griffith Stadium, with 47 whippets competing in seven events. The event was sponsored by the President's Own Garrison, the Army-Navy Union, and the National Capital Kennel Club. Walter Johnson, then managing the Senators, was a judge and entered his own whippet in a race.[15] Johnson's dog was involved in a dispute when it was determined that the dog had jumped into a rival's path.[16]

"30 TONS OF JUNK HEAPED AT THE STADIUM"

During World War II the nation was asked to sacrifice and conserve resources for the war effort. Salvage rallies were held to collect paper, rubber, metals, and other materials that could be recycled and reused for such purposes as "boxes for shipping blood plasma, K rations, medical supplies and ammunition, as well as making bombs, weather parachutes, helmets, life jackets, camouflages, and bomb flares."[17]

Washington was no different. On August 24, 1942, 16,000 people "jammed Griffith Stadium ... to cheer America and whip the Axis with gifts of scrap rubber and metal." It was hoped that Vice President Henry Wallace or Secretary of Interior Harold Ickes would attend. Eleanor Roosevelt was supposed to make brief remarks.[18] Money was not required — admission was a salvage contribution. Screen, radio, theater, and political personalities donated their time. Gene Autry sang his "dreamy tunes." Jimmy Cagney used his acting talents to play the role of a refugee escaping Nazi Germany. The 110-member US Army Air Corps Band played and several orchestras entertained. Patriotic speeches on scrap and salvage echoed through the public-address system. Candidates for the title of Miss Washington made appearances.[19] At the conclusion, the final score was announced: "Spectators, two hours of fun. For America — 60,000 pounds of 'scrap for the Jap.'"[20]

"FOOTBALL IS A GENTLEMEN'S GAME PLAYED BY RUFFIANS, AND RUGBY IS A RUFFIAN'S GAME PLAYED BY GENTLEMEN"[21]

Great Britain in November 1941 was in a deadly struggle against Hitler's Germany. Two British aircraft carriers were docked in Norfolk, Virginia, for needed repairs. A charity event at Griffith to support the British included the two national sports of Britain. Sammy Baugh and several other Redskins were guests of honor along with the paying onlookers, who saw football in a different light "as it's played in Merrie Old England."[22] On Wednesday night, November 12, less than a month before the Japanese attack on Pearl Harbor, soccer and rugby matches were played at Griffith Stadium. The games were sponsored by the American Legion to raise money for the British-American Ambulance Corps, Bundles for Britain, and the local Community Chest. The teams were composed of sailors and Marines from the carriers, HMS Illustrious and HMS Formidable. Before the matches commenced and during the break, the Royal Marine Band of the Formidable,the US Marine Band, and the Washington Gas Light Co. Band provided the sounds of music. "The redcoats are coming tonight," proclaimed the *Washington Post*.[23] Among the dignitaries, Lord and Lady Halifax were among the estimated 20,000 who came or was it 2,000? The local press accounts differ.[24] The outcomes were a minor allegory to the greater cause: Formidable won 2-0 in the soccer game. The rugby match ended in a draw. There was a casualty on the pitch. Stanley Ormond, a Royal Marine and the goalie on the Illustrious soccer team was knocked unconscious in a practice before the game, but played in the game "holding his head and playing through." After the game he collapsed and spent the night at a hospital under observation.[25]

"THERE'LL BE MUSIC IN GRIFF'S BALLYARD"

Opera at a baseball park may seem like an odd marriage, but performances were a common event at Griffith Stadium. Throughout the 1930s, open-air opera performances including Verdi's *Rigoletto* and *La Traviata* were presented annually by the Columbia Opera Company of New York. The August 5 and 6, 1938, renditions were "produced on a stage erected over the pitcher's mound."[26] The August 3, 1932, presentation of *Il Trovatore* attracted 2,000 opera fanatics despite threatening weather.[27] Earlier, on June 19, *Aida* was performed before "an enthusiastic audience of more than 2,500 music lovers."[28]

The National Negro Opera Company (1941-1962) was the first African-American opera company in the United States, directed by Mary Cardwell Dawson. Beginning in 1947, the company held its annual festival at Griffith Stadium. The 1954 program included Muriel Rahm, the star of *Carmen Jones* on Broadway, who sang from *Aida* and *Carmen*. Clark Griffith, as a token of philanthropy, annually gave the troupe free use of the ballpark to help it raise money to build an opera house in Washington and achieve other educational goals.[29] The August 7, 1948, program featured W.C. Handy, acclaimed as Father of the Blues, performing "St. Louis Blues" and other of his compositions.[30] On August 15, 1952, *Faust Comes to Bat at the Park* was presented at the ballpark featuring, in the role of Valentine, baritone Robert McFerrin, the first African-American man to sing at the Metropolitan Opera.[31] (McFerrin was the father of Grammy Award-winning vocalist Robert "Bobby" McFerrin Jr. of "Don't Worry, Be Happy" fame.)[32]

POLITICS, CAMPAIGN RALLY AND FDR

In many ways, to use baseball parlance, Griffith Stadium was a utility player, a journeyman. Griffith's need for income made the park available for many uses. On June 27, 1936, a political rally filled the park with supporters of President Franklin Roosevelt, who at the Democratic National Convention in Philadelphia that day accepted the nomination to run for a second term as president. In Washington, "[S]warming into Griffith Stadium with an enthusiasm undimmed by threatening weather, a crowd of 20,000 men and women celebrated with others."[33] The evening commenced with a torchlit parade that started near the White House and ended at Griffith Stadium The $1 ticket charge included the right to march in the parade.[34] The 100,000 paraders included 3,012 who attended the rally. At the ballpark the crowd heard FDR from 140 miles away at Franklin Field in Philadelphia accept his renomination.[35] The total proceeds of $1 million went to the Democratic National Committee. (Adjusted for inflation, this was equal to $18,205,289.86 in 2019.)[36] As FDR concluded his remarks, the revelers at Griffith Stadium made their way from the stands and "snake danced across the field."[37] Fireworks erupted over the bleachers. Arthur Godfrey, later a TV and radio star, told the crowd, "There are 16 million radio sets tuned in on this park. Let's show them how Washington can yell."[38] The crowd didn't disappoint Godfrey.

THE BATTLE OF THE MUSIC

On July 23, 1942, Adolf Hitler issued Directive Number 45 ordering the Wehrmacht to advance on Stalingrad. A German U-boat laid mines in the Mississippi River delta. On that evening, Griffith Stadium held 20,000 people who paid to watch the "Battle of the Music" between black jazz legend Louis Armstrong and white saxophonist Charlie Barnett and their bands. This event was hugely important to the African-American community living in segregated Washington. It was an organized interracial event and they did not want to miss the "musical fisticuffs."[39] What resulted was a powderkeg that blew into mayhem as Barnett was able to complete his set but Armstrong "was able to blow only one long blast on his trumpet" before the band was forced off the stage for the first time.[40]

The program started 30 minutes behind schedule at 9:00 P.M. as both bands played "The Star Spangled Banner." The bandstands were built on the baseball infield facing those who had seats in the grandstand. MC Willie Bryant flipped a coin to see which act would play first and the honor went to Barnett. He and his band played its four numbers. Then Armstrong came on the bandstand and "the old king of swing blew a couple of notes" and that was it.[41] The crowd seated in the grandstand swarmed onto the field, complaining later that they could not hear the music from the stage built over second base.[42] The music was halted. The Battle of the Music had become an actual battle royal (or "riot" as the press reported).

The overwhelmed police sought to restore order and the decision was made to let the crowd stay on the field. However, those who paid $1.10 for box seats complained that their view was obstructed. Bryant pleaded with the crowd to return to the grandstand, telling them, "This is the first time our race has been able to get Griffith Stadium for an affair of this sort. Let's not make it the last time."[43] Soldiers, sailors and Marines, black and white, linked arms to form a circle to force the crowd back between the baselines and to their seats, albeit for only a short time. Armstrong reappeared with his band and "hit a few hot licks on his trumpet."[44] The crowd again surged toward the band and the concert ended. Efforts were made to push the crowd back, but the servicemen and police were met by a fusillade: "In one spontaneous burst of indignation, the thousands packed in the stands above the field let go with pop bottles, flasks, and anything else they had."[45]

By 11:00 P.M., it was over. The police restored order. The bands packed their equipment and fled the scene. No refunds were issued; according to the promoters the bands made every effort to play. Thirteen people were arrested on charges of drunkenness and disorderly conduct; all were black.[46]

PERFORMANCE ART: WRESTLING AT GRIFFITH

A crowd-pleasing attraction, wrestling matches, filled many dates on the Griffith Stadium calendar from the time Griffith assumed Senators ownership to the ballpark's closing in 1961, providing a steady source of income to the Griffith family. It was performance art and attracted a loyal following.

The National Wrestling Alliance held monthly outdoor cards throughout the 1950s. Two marquee wrestlers were Haystack Calhoun and Killer Kowalski. Calhoun, who weighed an estimated 600 pounds, emerged as a fan favorite during the golden era of pro wrestling starting in the late 1950s. His trademark outfit was blue overalls, a white T-shirt, and a horseshoe around his neck. Walter "Killer" Kowalski starred as a villain who reputation was solidified when he ripped off part of his opponent's ear in 1954. At 6-feet-7 and 275 pounds, the imposing Kowalski delighted in applying his claw hold, a thumb squeeze to an opponent's solar plexus. Calhoun and Kowalski wrestled several times in Washington, with Kowalski defeating Calhoun in one of the last Griffith Stadium matches, on September 19, 1960, before 11,565 fans.[47]

Riots exploded during the September 2, 1937, matches in which "shoes, liniment bottles and other miscellaneous missiles were hurled with reckless abandon" after the last match disappointed the audience.[48] Two 1960 cards attracted 35,000 fans.[49] The next-to-last card, held on August 7, 1961, featured the Argentine wrestler Antonino Rocco in a tag-team match. A highlight was a five-woman "battle royal."[50] The last wrestling card at Griffith Stadium, on September 25, 1961, drew a crowd of 12,000.[51]

JOE LOUIS VERSUS BUDDY BAER

More than 150 boxing cards took place at Griffith Stadium. Boxing was a popular sport in DC and rental fees filled Griffith's coffers. The cards included several title matches. Heavyweight champion Joe Louis made personal appearances and fought at Griffith three times.

The high point of Griffith Stadium boxing was the May 23, 1941, heavyweight championship fight between Louis and Buddy Baer. The 25,000 who brought tickets included Vice President Henry Wallace.[52] The fight was aired nationally on the radio. Louis was the heavy favorite. A defiant Baer told reporters before the fight that he would not become part of Louis's Bum of the Month Club, saying, "I'm saving my wrath for Louis. I'm going to knock that guy flat."[53] Perhaps he wanted revenge for his brother Max, whom Louis had knocked out in the fourth round in 1935. In the event, Buddy became the 17th member of the Bum of the Month Club, although in unusual circumstances. Baer came out aggressively, knocking Louis out of the ring in the first round. Louis climbed back in before the count reached 10. Louis then flattened Baer at the end of the sixth round. Between the rounds, Ancil Hoffman, Baer's manager, urged the referee to give Baer additional time to recover from what he argued was a punch after the bell rang. Hoffman would not leave the ring and the referee disqualified Baer, awarding the match to Louis.[54] Louis's purse was a handsome $105,000. Seventy percent of the paid crowd was black.[55] The importance of Joe Louis for black America was stated by Maya Angelou in her memoir: "If Joe lost, we were back in slavery and beyond help."[56]

"BROTHER GRIFFITH" AND THE NIGHT OF THRILLS

The Night of Thrills was a fundraiser held annually from 1938 until 1963 to benefit the Masonic and Eastern Star Home in Washington. While it may seem odd for a ballpark to host such an event, Clark Griffith was also Brother Clark

Griffith of Harmony Lodge No. 17, donating the use of the ballpark to the Masters Association. This act of charity by Griffith was a major factor in the success of the Night of Thrills,[57] and showed a side of Griffith he did not publicize.

The initial Night of Thrills, on June 15, 1938, attracted 25,000. Reported the *Washington Post*: "[A] long-legged dwarf, 34 inches tall, danced beneath the floodlights at Griffith Stadium, his face smeared grease paint. High above the outfield trapeze performers swung and spun."[58] There was a baseball game, presentation of the queen of the pageant, a circus, and a fireworks show. During the event's 25-year run at Griffith, the average yearly net was $22,400. The worst year was 1938, at $11,300 ($204,500 adjusted for inflation), and the peak was $40,400 ($381,000 adjusted for inflation) in 1953.[59] It became a signature event on the Griffith Stadium schedule.

NATIONAL CAPITAL CRUSADE

"Evangelist Billy Graham will take over second base in Griffith Stadium today and he'll be out there for a week,"[60] announced the *Post* on June 19, 1960. Graham's National Capital Crusade was "going to bat against the devil" before crowds of thousands. Graham stood on a podium behind second base facing the multitudes sitting behind home plate. Straddling the baselines were two choir stands. Admission was free. The opening and closing nights were aired nationally. The theme of Graham's message was that the United States was in decline and needed "a moral and spiritual bath."[61]

During the June 21 event, Graham introduced Vice President and Mrs. Richard Nixon (on their 20th wedding anniversary) and their daughter, along with the vice president of Liberia. The topic of Graham's sermon was marriage and family life, giving several tips to wives such as to "[B]e attractive. Keep the house clean; don't gossip."[62] During each rally, people were asked to come forward as "inquirers" to home plate to "complete their commitment as Christians."[63] Through June 23, more than 2,700 came forward.[64] The choir numbered 1,160.

Attendance exceeded the pace of the 1960 Senators. On its last day the Crusade drew 24,000, for a total of 139,000, averaging 17,375.[65] The Senators' 1960 attendance, in their last year before moving to Minnesota, was last in the league with 743,404 for a home-game average of 9,654.[66] Every night ushers went through the crowd with cardboard boxes. About $85,000 was needed for operating expenses, including rent for the facility.[67]

"HAPPY-AM-I" – ELDER LIGHTFOOT SOLOMON MICHAUX

Elder Lightfoot Solomon Michaux was a pioneer in radio and television evangelism and an influential figure in Washington from the late 1920s until his death on October 20, 1968. The controversial African-American minister was an urban housing real-estate developer, a successful businessman, and a newspaper publisher, as well as a charismatic preacher with his Church of God on Georgia Avenue, opposite the entrance to Griffith Stadium. Known as the "Happy Am I Preacher," he had a national following by the 1930s from his radio show, *The Radio Church of God*, and his efforts to serve the poor. His annual religious revivals, "Ball Park Meetings" at Griffith, became legendary.

The revivals began in 1936 and ended when Griffith Stadium closed in 1961. (Michaux moved the event to Washington's Uline Arena.) Crowds ranged from 10,000 to 25,000. Admission was usually "free" and many were seated in the grandstand, but a donation was collected. Michaux's showmanship was evident when he exhorted "several former invalids whom he apparently cured to make a spirited dash around the bases in a 'home run dash for Jesus.'"[68] *Ebony* magazine called Michaux's meetings "the biggest mass baptism in the nation."[69] Before 1938 Michaux rented a boat each summer to baptize people in the Potomac. After that the baptisms occurred in a pool built over second base, in which the preacher, dressed in a black robe, boots, and a black skullcap, baptized his followers.[70] Another time, Michaux staged a Second Coming tableau using the left-field tower as a prop and the center-field bleachers as part of the Resurrection motif.[71]

As neighbors, Michaux and Clark Griffith developed a friendship. Michaux made Griffith an honorary deacon and gifted him a Bible "to seal the covenant."[72] Griffith allowed Michaux to use his ballpark annually at no charge. Michaux's rallies frequently attracted as many people as the Senators had at the gate.[73] On September 21, 1941, "Elder Lightfoot Michaux met Hitler in Griffith Stadium ... and proved to the satisfaction of more than 25,000 persons that the dictator has no chance of victory."[74] Michaux sermonized that victory belonged to the defeated of Europe and to Christianity. The 156-member "Happy-Am-I" choir sang religious songs "with a bit of boogie-woogie thrown in."[75] Oratory flamboyance and showmanship were characteristic of the annual revivals. The 1938 sermon was "How the Strange Woman Took Your Husband."[76] Then candidates were baptized with water that came from the River Jordan.[77] River Jordan water was used again in the 1950 revival.[78]

In 1934 Michaux filmed a movie called *Happy Am I — We've Got the Devil on the Run* that included a scene shot at Griffith Stadium on September 24 showing the devil and his Imp being driven out, tossed into the Potomac and exiled from Washington.[79]

THE GRIDIRON AT GRIFFITH STADIUM

HIGH SCHOOL

High-school football was the type of local event Griffith wanted at his ballpark. The "colored" high-school city championship was a sought-after ticket. The top Catholic schools scheduled games at the park. The city championship between the public and Catholic league champions was played in late November. Catholic youth leagues played at Griffith as preliminaries to the Catholic league championship game.[80]

Gonzaga College High School, a Jesuit institution, played many football games at Griffith. Most notably was the November 7, 1943, benefit game against Father Flanagan's Boys Town, the Nebraska orphanage for boys. Gonzaga was a local football powerhouse and the benefit was to raise funds for Boys Town. Both teams practiced in secrecy. Gonzaga's motto for the game was "We concede Boys Town the edge in publicity, but we'll try for touchdowns."[81] Eleanor Roosevelt and other dignitaries were among the crowd of 12,000. The Catholic University Cadet Corps and Band were among the halftime performers. Boys Town held off a late Gonzaga drive and won, 12-6.[82] It was a lucrative payday for Boys Town with Clark Griffith presenting a check for $13,094.42 ($191,011.47 in 2019 dollars) after taxes to Senator Elmer Thomas of Oklahoma, chairman of Boys Town. Gonzaga received $1,000 for its athletic fund ($14,587.22 in 2019 dollars).[83] Two years later, Gonzaga won a rematch at the University of Maryland's Byrd Stadium, 9-0 before 8,000.[84] The significance of the games was the all-white Gonzaga Purple Eagles against Boys Town, which had several black players. The game reportedly was the first high-school contest in Washington in which blacks competed against white players.

COLLEGE

Before the end of World War II, college football was a marquee event at Griffith Stadium. From the 1920s until 1961, Maryland, Georgetown, George Washington, Howard, and Catholic University at times called the ballpark home. The Naval Academy team played several games in the 1920s and 1930s as the home team and later as the visiting team.

Georgetown was a tenant from the 1920s through 1950 and enjoyed its greatest success with Griffith as its home. A game against Carnegie Tech on November 18, 1932, ended with a Carnegie win; then "fists, elbows and feet flew thick ... as police, spectators and several burly players battled over possession of the pigskin used in the ... grid clash."[85] Three Georgetown students were arrested for disorderly conduct. A police officer was "kicked and pummeled." Students challenged the police to a brawl. The game ball was considered the property of the winner by the tradition of the time. The Georgetown coach presented a ball to the winning Carnegie team with apologies.[86]

Despite winning the 1936 Orange Bowl over Mississippi, Catholic University stopped playing at Griffith Stadium commencing that fall. It was difficult for the team to get attractive dates to play there with Georgetown and George Washington getting priority. The Flying Cardinals feared slim crowds and hemorrhaged financially.[87]

Maryland played most of its 1948 schedule on the road, including three home games at Griffith Stadium. Because of the limited seating at Byrd Stadium and the 15 percent rental for Griffith Stadium, the Terps chose to be road warriors.[88] A highlight for 1948 was the resumption of the local Maryland-George Washington rivalry after 38 years, with the Terps romping, 38-0, before a crowd of 16,034.[89]

George Washington University played its home games at Griffith Stadium from the 1920s through 1960, then moved to D.C. Stadium. In 1932, the team played a big-time schedule, and drew over 100,000 to home games that featured Alabama, Iowa, North Dakota State, and Oklahoma. From going 0-8 in 1929, they were 6-2-1 in 1932.[90] When George Washington hosted Alabama, Shirley Povich wrote, "Win, lose or tie in the Alabama game tomorrow, George Washington University will have the satisfaction of 'arriving' in the big league circle."[91] Alabama was two years removed from a national championship season. Among the 19,500 who filled the stands, Alabama bought a large contingent of students and their marching band, and won 28-6.

Washington was considered the birthplace of black college football. For a brief period in the 1920s, the Thanksgiving games between Howard and Lincoln University marked an important day for the black community. The games were played in Philadelphia, at Howard's home field, and in 1920, 1922, and 1924 at Griffith Stadium. The games were a source of racial pride and civic unity and a time for activities, parties and the naming of the black All-American team. The games were well attended but with the Depression, the game diminished in appeal after 1929, though the two schools would compete until Lincoln dropped football in 1960.[92] Competition for the financially lucrative Thanksgiving date was fierce. The local white college teams normally were given priority. In 1940 Clark Griffith gave the date to the Howard-Lincoln game. He thought it was right thing to do.[93]

Established in 1942, the Capital Classic was considered the Negro National Collegiate Football Championship and featured teams from the East Coast. The September 30, 1961, game was the last Classic played at Griffith and was the first interracial game in its tenure, featuring the University of Southern Connecticut and Maryland State University.[94]

The President's Cup was an effort by Griffith to bring an annual high-profile college football game to D.C. He had failed to attract the Army-Navy battle and an annual Notre Dame game. He organized an armed services game, proclaiming it the top game over Army-Navy. On December 1, 1923, the first game was played between the Quantico Marines and the Third Army Corps. A crowd of 45,000 was expected.[95] This effort led Griffith to create the President's Cup. Griffith had plans to increase the seating capacity of the park to 75,000 so Washington could be permanent host.[96] The President's Cup commenced in 1924 and lasted for only a few years. It could not compete with the traditional Army-Navy game. Each game featured armed forces teams and the net proceeds went to charity. The 1930 game was played "for benefit of the capital's unemployed."[97]

PRO FOOTBALL

The Washington Redskins were profitable at the gate during their time at Griffith in 1937-1960. Owned by racist dry-cleaner mogul George Preston Marshall, the team was a winner on the field from 1937 through 1945, but in its 13 final seasons at Griffith, it had only two winning seasons (1953 and 1955). The Redskins paid a lofty sum for renting Griffith and felt no need to be part of the community.[98]

When the Japanese began their attack on Pearl Harbor on December 7, 1941, it was 1:25 P.M. in Washington and the Redskins were playing at Griffith Stadium. A reported 27,102 were there to watch Sammy Baugh throw three touchdown passes and lead the Redskins to a come-from-behind victory against the Philadelphia Eagles. Though the newsboys and some reporters in the press box were aware, no one in the stands knew that bombs were exploding and Americans were being killed. Announcements were made over the public-address system ordering military officers and government officials to report to their duty stations. No official notice was made to the fans and players. Baugh said, "We didn't know what the hell was going on. I had never heard so many announcements one right after another. We felt something was up but we just kept playing."[99] John F. Kennedy, then a young naval officer candidate, was in attendance.[100] Nineteen years later, on December 18, 1960, the Redskins played their last home game at Griffith against the same Eagles. Redskins coach Mike Nixon was fired immediately after losing the game, 38-28. The star of the game was backup Eagles quarterback Sonny Jurgensen, who threw two touchdown passes "that broke Washington's back."[101] Jurgensen would be traded to Washington in 1964 and emerged as one of the most popular figures in the history of Washington sports and a pro football Hall of Famer.

Throughout their time at Griffith, the Redskins played under the shadow of racism. As Shirley Povich wrote, "The Redskins colors are burgundy, gold and Caucasian."[102] It would not be until 1961 under federal pressure that the Redskins integrated in order to play at the new federally owned D.C. Stadium.

THE LAST GAME

September 21, 1961, saw the last major-league baseball game at Griffith. On the afternoon of November 19, 1961, 8,500 people witnessed the last high-school football game there. St. John's College High School beat Gonzaga College High School, 20-6, to advance to the city championship game against the public Eastern High School on Thanksgiving at the new D.C. Stadium.[103] That game was played before a record 49,690.[104] In contrast, the 1960 city championship played at Griffith Stadium attracted 24,000. Griffith Stadium now was becoming a decaying edifice. Change had come.

Clark Griffith had died in 1955, transferring control of the Senators and the ballpark to his adopted son, Calvin. Calvin showed none of the loyalty to the city that his father demonstrated. Calvin did not want blacks to attend his team's games. The Senators needed a new facility and he preferred one that catered to whites. He made it known that a new ballpark in Potomac Park without paying rent was desired.[105] Soon after he took control, rumors were heard about a franchise move to Minnesota, which occurred in 1961. What would be the future of Griffith Stadium? A New York real-estate developer saw the old ballpark as a future race track.[106]

The Griffith family rented Griffith Stadium to the expansion Senators for the 1961 season. Then the Senators moved to D.C. Stadium and there were no more games after 1961. Griffith Stadium survived in elegant decay until 1965 as the grounds reverted to back to nature and the edifice was vandalized. The Griffith family sold the ballpark to Howard University in 1964. The university razed it on January 26, 1965, to make way for Howard University Hospital. Home plate is located in the lobby of the hospital.

NOTES

1 "1911 Washington Senators," Baseball-Almanac.com, baseball-almanac.com/teamstats/schedule.php?y=1911&t=WS1, accessed January 16, 2019.

2 The names Senators, Nationals, and Nats were used interchangeably by fans and media. For the purposes of this article, Senators will be used.

3 Blair Ruble, *Washington's U Street: A Biography* (Washington: Woodrow Wilson Center Press, 2010), 153.

4 Ibid.

5 Ruble, 159.

6 "The Weather," *Washington Post*, May 30, 1930: 8.

7 History, Art & Archives, US House of Representatives, "The Congressional Horseshoe Tournament," history.house.gov/Historical-Highlights/1901-1950/The-Congressional-Horseshoe-Tournament/, accessed March 11, 2019.

8 Ibid.

9 "Horseshoe Prize Won by Johnson: Representative of Nebraska Defeats Vestal in Annual Tilt," *Washington Post*, May 31, 1930: 18.

10 Ibid.

11 "Representative Johnson of Nebraska Wins Congress' Horseshoe Pitching Championship," *New York Times*, May 31, 1930: 20.

12 Andrew Glass, "Johnson becomes the Champion Horseshoe Pitcher of Congress," Politico, May 30, 2012.

13 Bo Bengston, *The Whippet - An Authoritative Look at the Breed's Past, Present and Future* (Freehold, New Jersey: Kennel Club Classics, 2010).

14 americanwhippetclub.net/whippet-activities/straight-and-oval-racing, accessed January 17, 2019.

15 "Eight Races Listed with Match Event Topping Program," *Washington Post*, November 16, 1930: 20.

16 Bob Considine, "400 Watch Dogs in Close Finishes at Griffith Stadium," *Washington Post*, November 20, 1930: 18.

17 Ellen Knight, "Town Collected Junk to Jolt the Axis During WWII," *Winchester* (Massachusetts) *Daily Times Chronicle*, October 9, 2017. homenewshere.com/daily_times_chronicle/news/winchester/article_7039da4a-acff-11e7-a0b5-2710f1c00991.html. Accessed January 18, 2019.

18 "D.C. Salvage Rally Set for Aug. 24: Federal Leaders, Top Entertainers to Participate In Stadium," *Washington Post*, August 7, 1942: 23.

19 Dick Pollard, "16,000 Rally with Scrap to Beat Axis: 30 Tons of Junk Heaped at Stadium," *Washington Post*, August 25, 1942: 17.

20 Ibid.

21 An old British saying contrasting football (soccer) with rugby.

22 "Redskins Get Bid to Soccer, Rugby Games Wednesday," *Washington Post*, November 10, 1941: 18.

23 "2 Exhibitions Here Tonight to Aid Funds," *Washington Post*, November 12, 1941: 25.

24 Ibid.; "British Rugby Match Here Ends in Tie," *Washington Post*, November 13, 1941: 27.

25 Ibid.

26 "Verdi's Operas Will Play Here," *Washington Post*, July 24, 1938: TT5.

27 "Trovatore Enjoyed by 2,000 at the Stadium," *Washington Post*, August 4, 1932: 14.

28 W.A. Whitney, "'Aida' is Presented Before Audience of 2,500 at the Stadium," *Washington Post*, June 20, 1932: 14.

29 Paul Hume, "There'll Be Music in Griff's Ballyard," *Washington Post and Times Herald*, August 2, 1954: 14.

30 "Negro Music Festival Set Saturday at Stadium," *Washington Post*, August 1, 1948: L3.

31 "'Faust' Comes to Bat Friday at Ball Park," *Washington Post*, July 20, 1952: L5.

32 washingtonpost.com/archive/local/2006/11/29/robert-mcferrin-sr/fc68d37c-9fbc-4938-aebd-cf9e5ac91625/?utm_term=.6450f4cfeebd, accessed January 24, 2019.

33 "20,000 Throng D.C. Ball Park, Hear Roosevelt," *Washington Post*, June 28, 1936: M1.

34 "100,000 Democrats Will Hear Roosevelt Speech in Stadium," *Washington Post*, June 27, 1936: 1.

35 "20,000 Throng D.C. Ball Park.""

36 "100,000 Democrats."

37 "20,000 Throng D.C. Ball Park."

38 Ibid.

39 "Stadium Battle of Music Turns to Battle Royal: Crowd Engulfs Field; Those Left in Stands Swing with Bottles," *Washington Post*, July 24, 1942: 1.

40 "Arrest of 13 Follows Riot of Thousands at Griffith Stadium: Crowds Surge Onto Field, Pop Bottles Thrown in Melee at 'Battle of Music,'" *Washington Evening Star*, July 24, 1942: A-3.

41 "Stadium Battle of Music."

42 "Arrest of 13 Follows Riot."

43 "Stadium Battle of Music."

44 Ibid.

45 "Arrest of 13 Follows Riot."

46 Ibid.

47 prowrestlinghistory.com/supercards/usa/misc/washington.html#092561, accessed March 10, 2019.

48 "Riot at Stadium; Ray Steele Victor," *Washington Post*, September 3, 1937: 19.

49 "Tag Match to Mark Final Wrestling Card," *Washington Post,* September 18, 1960: C6. prowrestling.fandom.com/wiki/September_19,_1960_NWA_Capitol_Wrestling_results accessed January 28, 2019.

50 https://prowrestling.fandom.com/wiki/August_7,_1961_NWA_Capitol_Wrestling_results. Accessed January 28, 2019.

51 prowrestlinghistory.com/supercards/usa/misc/washington.html#092561. Accessed March 10, 2019.

52 Al Hailey, "Champion Rules 8 to 1 Favorite," *Washington Post,* May 23, 1941: 21.

53 Al Hailey, "Baer Promises He'll K.O. Louis," *Washington Post*, May 19, 1941: 19.

54 "Blow-by-Blow Story of Bout, from a Staff Correspondent," *New York Times*, May 24, 1941: 19.

55 Brad Snyder, *Beyond the Shadows of the Senators* (Chicago: Contemporary Books, 2003), 99.

56 Maya Angelou, *I Know Why the Caged Bird Sings* (New York: Ballantine Books, 2015, 135).

57 dcgrandlodge.org/thevoice/a-look-back-at-the-night-of-thrills accessed January 31, 2019.

58 "Dwarf Dances as Performers Fly Through Air on Trapeze," *Washington Post,* June 16, 1938: 13.

59 dcgrandlodge.org/thevoice/a-look-back-at-the-night-of-thrills, accessed January 31, 2019.

60 "Graham at 2d Base for Stadium Rally," *Washington Post*, June 19, 1960: B4.

61 Ibid.

62 "Nixons, Wed 20 Years, Attend Graham Rally," *Washington Evening Star,* June 23, 1960: B-6.

63 Ibid.

64 "Graham Finds Youth Insecure," *Washington Post*, June 24, 1960: B6.

65 "Billy Graham Predicts Christians' Persecution," *Washington Post*, June 27, 1960: B1.

66 baseball-reference.com/teams/WSH/1960-schedule-scores.shtml, accessed March 10, 2019.

67 Barnard K. Leiter, "Billy Graham Returns: 16,000 at the Stadium for Crusade Opening," *Washington Evening Star*. June 20, 1960: B-1.

68 Frank Rasky, "Harlem's Religious Zealots," *Tomorrow*, November 1949, in W.E.B. Du Bois Papers (MS 312). Special Collections and University Archives, University of Massachusetts Amherst Libraries. credo.library.umass.edu/view/full/mums312-b157-i232: 12.

69 Ibid.

70 Constance McLaughlin Green, *The Secret City: A History of Race Relations in the Nation's Capital* (Princeton, New Jersey: Princeton University Press, 1967), 239.

71 Kenneth Dole, "Elder Lightfoot Solomon Michaux, Negro Religious Leader, Dies at 84," *Washington Post*, October 21, 1968: A17.

72 Green.

73 Snyder, 11-12.

74 Charles Mercer, "25,000 at Stadium Join In; Fireworks Startle Some in City," *Washington Post*, September 22, 1941: 13.

75 Ibid.

76 "Elder Michaux Will Opera Series Here Tomorrow," *Washington Post*, September 3, 1938: X15.

77 Green.

78 "20,000 Witness Baptisms in River Jordan Water," *Washington Afro-American,* September 18, 1950: 1-2.

79 "Elder Michaux Is Starred in Five-Reel Movie Here," *Washington Daily News,* September 22, 1934: 19; "Thousands See First Filming of 'Happy Am I,'" *Washington Tribune*, September 29, 1934.

80 "CYO Intermediate Title Game Is Scheduled Today," *Washington Post*, November 20, 1948: 11.

81 "Local Eleven Is Primed for Charity Game," *Washington Post*, November 7, 1943: R2.

82 Tom Moore McBride, "Locals Miss Tie Game in Final Period," *Washington Post*, November 8, 1943: 13.

83 "Boys Town Gets Check for $13,094," *Washington Post*, November 12, 1943: 14.

84 Ann Cline, "Flashy Gonzaga Ends Boys Town Winning Streak in an Upset," *Washington Evening Star*, December 1, 1945: A12.

85 "Police Battle Stadium Mob; Jail Besieged," *Washington Post*, November 19, 1933: 1.

86 Ibid.

87 Lewis F. Atchison, "C.U. Will Play Home Tilts at Brookline," *Washington Post,* July 17, 1936: 16.

88 "Terps Play 10 Games in 1948," *Washington Post,* December 16, 1947: 19.

89 Morris Siegel, "Turyn Hurls 3 Scoring Passes: Fourth Stringer Races 88 Yards," *Washington Post*, October 24, 1948: C1.

90 sports-reference.com/cfb/schools/george-washington/1932-schedule.html, accessed February 23, 2019.

91 Shirley L. Povich, "This Morning with Shirley Povich," *Washington Post*, October 7, 1932: 11.

92 Ryan A. Swinson, "Less Than Monumental," in Elzey, Chris and David K. Wiggins, eds. *DC Sports: The Nation's Capital at Play* (Fayetteville: University of Arkansas Press, 2013), 37-39.

93 Swinson, 27.

94 Bob Addie, "Stadium Progresses," *Washington Post,* June 2, 1961: D2.

95 "45,000 Are Expected to See Army and Marines in Clash," *Washington Post*, December 1, 1923: 1.

96 "Griffith Planning Seat 60,000 at Army-Marine Game," *Washington Post*, July 18, 1923: 5.

97 "25,000 to Attend Charity Grid Game," *Washington Post*, December 6, 1930: 1.

98 Burton Solomon, *The Washington Century: Three Families and the Shaping of the Nation's Capital* (New York: Harper Collins, 2004), 49.

99 S.L. Price, "The Second World War Kicks Off December 7, 1941 Redskins Versus Eagles on Pearl Harbor Day," *Sports Illustrated*, November 29, 1999. si.com/vault/1999/11/29/270652/the-second-world-war-kicks-off-december-7-1941-redskins-versus-eagles-on-pearl-harbor-day. Accessed March 17, 2019.

100 Mark Kriegel, "NFL Games Two Days After JFK's Assassination a Fitting Tribute," NFL.com, November 24, 2013. nfl.com/news/story/0ap2000000285908/article/nfl-games-two-days-after-jfks-assassination-a-fitting-tribute. Accessed March 14, 2019.

101 Jack Walsh, "Nixon Fired After Redskins End Poorest Season With 38-28 Loss," *Washington Post*, December 19, 1960: A16.

102 Snyder, 198; Ruble, 157.

103 Byron Roberts, "St. John's Beats Gonzaga, Plays in City Title Game," *Washington Post and Times Herald*, November 20, 1961: A22.

104 Byron Roberts, "City Title Game Sold Out: 51,696 Will Watch Eastern, St. John's," *Washington Post*, November 21, 1962: A19.

105 "Griffith Urges Stadium Built in Potomac Park," *Washington Post and Times Herald*, July 19, 1956: 18.

106 Walter Haight, "Horses and People," *Washington Post and Times Herald*, October 17, 1956: C5.

MILITARY DRILLS AT GRIFFITH STADIUM DURING WORLD WAR I

by Gordon Gattie

Baseball had established itself as America's national pastime for over a half-century, and professional baseball existed for over 40 years, when World War I consumed world geopolitics during the mid-1910s. After years of shifting power and alliance-building in international politics, Austrian Archduke Franz Ferdinand and his wife were assassinated on June 28, 1914, in Sarajevo, Bosnia.[1] Their assassination trigged a sequence of events resulting in World War I, starting on July 28, 1914. The Great War ravaged Europe for nearly three years before the United States joined the Allied Powers when Congress declared war on Germany on April 6, 1917. President Woodrow Wilson asserted that the most consequential shift in American foreign policy was desperately needed before an April 2 joint session of Congress, when, in the presence of the Supreme Court, several Cabinet members, and the diplomatic corps, he advocated a change in American foreign policy from an isolationist nation to one making the world "safe for democracy."[2] During the early years of the conflict, the United States had remained neutral while supplying her European allies with critical resources. Although the nation was at first reluctant to become entangled in European politics, Germany's imposition of unrestricted submarine warfare had claimed too many American lives and ships, and a potential developing alliance between Germany and Mexico swayed America's decision to formally join the Allied Powers.[3] Trench warfare dominated continental fighting with no end in sight during the spring of 1917 as America began mobilizing her military forces.

Anticipating the potential involvement of major-league baseball players in the war, Captain Tillinghast L'Hommedieu (T.L.) Huston, co-owner of the New York Yankees, in the winter of 1916-17 developed a plan to increase baseball's military preparedness. His plan required adding military drills at spring-training camps, continuing them during the season by adding drill time in the mornings or afternoons, and opening training camps after the season.[4] Huston, an Army engineer during the Spanish-American War, has generally been credited with the preparedness plan, although the idea may have originated with Washington co-owner and

In a display of patriotism against the backdrop of World War I, Assistant Secretary of the Navy Franklin D. Roosevelt (in suit and hat, third from right) leads the Senators onto the field at Griffith Stadium on Opening Day 1917. (Photo via Getty Images)

manager Clark Griffith in response to a crisis brewing with Mexico.[5] In 1916 Griffith's first-base coach, Nick Altrock, organized a company of Washington rookies who drilled with baseball bats and conducted military stunts. Originally the American League fully supported the military preparedness plan, while the National League was not onboard until months later.

Major-league baseball, facing declining attendance during the 1910s because of the rival Federal League and rising worldwide hostilities, hoped that players wouldn't be drafted for the armed forces if they received military instruction at work. As players reported for spring training before US involvement in the war, AL President Ban Johnson offered a $500 prize to the best-drilled AL team, and another $100 in gold to the drill sergeant who instructed the winning players.[6] In 1917 spring training, Army Corporal John Dean conducted the first military drill for the Washington Nationals in Augusta, Georgia. The initial drill, which included 30 ballplayers, in which Griffith took part, along with team trainer Mike Martin and two newspapermen, consisted of foot movements, saluting, and marching, with simple squad movements planned for the second day.[7] The first game of spring training followed the drill instruction.

Throughout spring training, most teams dutifully performed the drills, though by mid-March players from some teams voted to end drill practice based on time constraints.[8] However, the drill teams were quickly reassembled when war was declared just five days before Opening Day on April 11. The Nationals, under the continued tutelage of Corporal Dean and joined by their manager, conducted more complicated movements; NL clubs were still not drilling as often as their AL counterparts.[9] Teams that did not practice their military drills or otherwise contribute to the patriotic fervor spreading across the country were chastised for not contributing to military preparedness. The Boston Red Sox, for instance, were derided by fans as "American slackers" for not taking part in drills.[10]

When Opening Day arrived on April 20, 1917, in Washington, the Nationals were prepared to showcase their training. Before their opener against the Philadelphia Athletics, players along with soldiers drilled in National Park (later Griffith Stadium)[11] with Vice President Thomas R. Marshall and several members of Congress attending. The soldiers drilled first, followed by the players, carrying bats instead of rifles. The players also formed an honor guard for Assistant Secretary of the Navy Franklin D. Roosevelt.[12]

As war raged overseas, baseball continued with its full 154-game schedule in 1917, though many minor leagues suspended operations. Griffith continued his active support of the military throughout the season, launching a plan to provide baseball equipment to troops overseas.[13] Several ballparks around the country hosted "Griffith Days" to collect donations of equipment.[14] Ballclubs continued their military drills during the season, leading to a final demonstration showdown between the Red Sox and St. Louis Browns at Sportsman's Park in St. Louis; several hundred service members based at nearby Jefferson Barracks were invited to watch the event, and money was collected for Griffith's ball and bat fund.[15] On August 25, after their last regular-season matchup, an Army colonel, judging the drills under military standards, awarded the $500 prize to the Browns, whose ability to change marching from quick time to natural gait without misstep was noteworthy.[16] Washington was subsequently awarded second place as the best-trained AL team and Cleveland was third; the other teams in order of finish were Chicago, Boston, Detroit, New York, and Philadelphia.[17] Also on the 25th, the White Sox, hosting the Senators in Chicago, celebrated their own "Griffith Day" honoring Griffith's work for the troops. White Sox President Charles Comiskey commented, "It was a grand spectacle. I could not stand there and watch those boys marching without choking up."[18]

As the war progressed into its fourth year and more American lives were affected directly and indirectly by world events, the public increasingly asked why major-league baseball and its ballplayers were exempt from the war effort. In one concession before the 1918 season started, major-league owners reduced the schedule from 154 games to 140 games; meanwhile, more minor leagues suspended operations. Ten minor leagues attempted to continue playing in 1918; only the International League survived. The league's resilience was especially noteworthy because before the season four ballclubs in the eight-team league experienced significant changes: The Buffalo ownership changed hands and teams in Richmond, Providence, and Montreal were replaced by teams in Syracuse, Jersey City, and Binghamton.[19]

The AL owners at their annual meeting in December 1917 decided against continuing the military drills in 1918. Although the drills were popular among the fans and beneficial from several perspectives, the owners decided that the difficulty of finding drill sergeants and the uncertainty surrounding team rosters heading into spring training would render drill instruction of little value. The owners did vote to select one day where 25 percent of gate receipts for all games played would be donated to Griffith's bat and ball fund.[20]

One noteworthy change to baseball in Washington was the lifting of the ban on Sunday baseball. Two thousand soldiers in and around the city were to be admitted free and exempted from paying the war tax on tickets. The Nationals successfully argued that other places of public entertainment like moving-picture theaters were open on Sundays, and baseball games would boost morale for both soldiers and civilians.[21] On May 19 the Nationals defeated the Indians 1-0 in 12 innings to provide a dramatic finish for the city's first Sunday game. Clyde Milan hit a sizzling single over third base to score pitcher Doc Ayers with the game's only run. The attendance was more than 17,000, at the time the largest crowd to attend a Nationals game. Attendees included more than 2,000 soldiers, Ban Johnson, members of Congress, diplomats, and "almost as many women as men." One reporter noted, "Many in the crowd were at best lukewarm followers of the national game, but the contest furnished them a place to spend the Sabbath afternoon in a clean, wholesome, and enjoyable manner on an ideal day."[22]

Still, some high-level government officials believed major-league baseball should contribute more resources to the war effort, and in June the military draft director, General Enoch Crowder, issued a "work or fight" order, requiring draft-eligible men working in nonessential jobs to work in essential war-related industries by July 1, 1918, or risk being drafted. On July 19, 1918, Secretary of War Newton D. Baker decided that baseball was a nonessential occupation after an appeal by the Washington Nationals' Eddie Ainsmith regarding his draft status. Baker noted that baseball was accepted as the national sport, supported many businessmen and workers, and offered relaxation and enjoyment; but asserted that "the times are not normal; the demands of the army and of the country are such that we must all make sacrifices, and the nonproductive employment of able-bodied persons, useful in the national defense, either as military men or in the industry and commerce of our country, cannot be justified."[23] More than 90 percent of the major-league players were expected to be affected by the decision. Only four Washington players were unaffected by Secretary Baker's decision: 41-year-old pitching coach-pitcher Nick Altrock, who hadn't pitched more than 40 innings in a season since 1909; 37-year-old shortstop and manager-in-training George McBride; 30-year-old outfielder Clyde Milan; and 35-year-old outfielder Frank Schulte, who was in the final season of his career.

AL President Johnson quickly declared, without consulting the owners, that the season would end two days later, on July 21. Johnson's declaration was rejected by the owners; a second request, to end the season on August 20, was also denied after NL executives insisted on continuing play until Labor Day. The two leagues finally agreed to end the season on September 2, meaning that several teams had to play doubleheaders on the final day. With the War Department's assent, the leagues were allowed to play the World Series as long as 10 percent of its gross earnings were donated to war charities. The 1918 World Series between the Red Sox and Chicago Cubs still holds two noteworthy distinctions: the earliest start date (September 5)[24] and the last Series without a home run.

After the Series, club owners released their players for either the draft or working in an essential industry, with the 1919 season completely unsettled. The war, meanwhile, ended on November 11, when an armistice was signed. Major-league baseball and several minor leagues resumed operations for the 1919 season.

SOURCES

Besides the sources cited in the Notes, the author consulted Baseball-Reference.com, Retrosheet.org, Baseball-Almanac.com, Thedeadballera.com, and the following books:

James, Bill. *The Bill James Guide to Baseball Managers from 1870 to Today* (New York: Scribner, 1997).

Ritter, Lawrence. *Lost Ballparks: A Celebration of Baseball's Legendary Fields* (New York: Penguin Books, 1992).

Thorn, John, and Pete Palmer et al. *Total Baseball: The Official Encyclopedia of Major League Baseball* (New York: Viking Press, 2004).

Voigt, David Q. *America Through Baseball* (Chicago: Nelson Hall, 1976).

Ward, Geoffrey C., and Ken Burns. *Baseball: An Illustrated History* (New York: Alfred A. Knopf, 1994).

NOTES

1 Hew Strachan, *The First World War* (New York: Penguin Books, 2003), 10.

2 A. Scott Berg, *Wilson* (New York: G.P. Putnam's Sons, 2013), 10.

3 Strachan, 227.

4 Jim Leeke, *From the Dugouts to the Trenches: Baseball During the Great War* (Lincoln: University of Nebraska Press, 2017), 6.

5 Stanley T. Milliken, "Griffith Conceived the Idea of Military Training for Ball Players," *Washington Post*, March 5, 1917: 10.

6 "Prize for Drillers," *Washington Times*, March 7, 1917: 10.

7 Denman Thompson, "First Military Drill Given Players of Washington Club," *Washington Evening Star*, March 12, 1917: 12.

8 Joel Zoss and John Bowman, *Diamonds in the Rough: The Untold History of Baseball* (New York: Contemporary Books, 1996), 89.

9 Louis A. Dougher, "Griffmen Will Continue Military Drills - Cobb Faces Punishment from Johnson," *Washington Times*, April 4, 1917: 10.

10 Louis A. Dougher, "Boston Players Are Given Orders to Drill - Carl Mays in Wrong with Teammates," *Washington Times*, April 27, 1917: 12.

11 Griffith Stadium was renamed for owner/president/manager Clark Griffith in 1920. From 1911 through 1919 the facility was named National Park, and was also known as American League Park and League Park.

12 J.V. Fitzgerald, "Friday and Thirteen Prove to Be Allies of Athletics," *Washington Post*, April 21, 1917: 8.

13 Mike Grahek, "*Clark Griffith*," SABR BioProject, sabr.org/bioproj/person/96624988. Accessed July 1, 2019.

14 "Clark Griffith Days Becoming a Fashion," *Washington Post*, August 23, 1917: 8.

15 Clarence F. Lloyd, "Browns Will Show Their Ability in Military Tactics," *St. Louis Star and Times*, August 25, 1917: 9.

16 "Browns Beat Red Sox Drilling, but Lose Game, 3 to 2," *St. Louis Post-Dispatch*, August 26, 1917: 45.

17 Francis C. Richter, "The 1917 Base Ball Season," in Francis C. Richter, ed., *The Reach Official American League Base Ball Guide 1918* (Philadelphia: A.J. Reach Company, 1918), 9.

18 George S. Robbins, "Commy Wants Military Day an Annual Feature in American," *The Sporting News*, August 30, 1917: 1.

19 Marshall D. Wright, *The International League: Year-by-Year Statistics, 1884-1963* (Jefferson, North Carolina: McFarland & Company, Inc., 1998), 205.

20 Richter, 286.

21 "Yanks May Start Sunday Ball Here," *Washington Post*, May 15, 1918: 10.

22 J.V. Fitzgerald, "Milan Hits Nationals to Victory in Twelfth as More Than 17,000 Look On," *Washington Post*, May 20, 1918: 8.

23 J.V. Fitzgerald, "Baseball Players Must Work or Fight, Baker Rules, Dooming National Sport," *Washington Post*, July 20, 1918: 8.

24 "The Star Spangled Banner" was played before Game One, beginning a tradition that continues more than 100 years later, though it did not become the national anthem until 1931.

THE HOMESTEAD GRAYS MAKE GRIFFITH STADIUM HOME

by Alan Cohen

In 1910, so the story goes, "a group of Homestead Negro boys had a ball team known as the Blue Ribbons. Later that name was changed to the Murdock Grays. From that organization came the Homestead Grays in 1912."

— Paul Kurtz, *Pittsburgh Press*, August 6, 1938[1]

Homestead, Pennsylvania, is a steel town of 20,000 inhabitants, seven miles southeast of Pittsburgh. Just when the Homestead Grays team began is a matter of dispute, but when Cumberland Posey, whose father owned the *Pittsburgh Courier*, joined the team in 1912, the troupe of Negro ballplayers made many stops crisscrossing the country. By 1916 Posey was the team's manager.

During the better part of their first two decades, the Grays were a barnstorming team and in 1929 they joined the fledgling American Negro League. They were in the league for three years.

The Grays first played at Griffith Stadium on June 28, 1931. They defeated the Philadelphia Hilldale Giants, 5-2. George Britt outpitched Martin Dihigo, scattering seven hits. The highlight of the game was a homer off the bat of Josh Gibson. Teammate Oscar Charleston doubled in the contest.[2]

In 1932 the Grays were one of a group of teams that formed the East-West League. They played against the league rival Washington Pilots at Griffith Stadium at the end of July. On July 30, the teams played a doubleheader with the Grays winning the opener, 13-8, and the Pilots taking the second game, 4-3.[3] The Grays' 20-hit attack in the opener was punctuated by a three-run homer by Bill Perkins and a solo shot by Ted Strong.[4]

The Grays joined the Negro National League in 1933 for a brief stay, playing most of their home games at Greenlee Field in Pittsburgh. They were suspended from the league on June 24 for alleged tampering in the signing two players (Jimmy Binder and Jim Williams) on the Detroit Stars.[5] The team barnstormed in 1934, appearing at Griffith Stadium on October 7, defeating the New York Black Yankees in the second game of a four-team doubleheader, 5-3. Pitcher Ray Brown struck out 10 in going the route.[6]

The Grays returned to the Negro National League in 1935.

Griffith Stadium was home to the Washington Pilots (1932-34) and welcomed the Washington Elite Giants (1936-1937). The Grays visited the Giants and had a come-from-behind 7-5 win on June 27, 1936, sparked by a Buck Leonard triple.[7]

The following day, the teams played a doubleheader before 3,500 fans. The first game was not played to a conclusion. Lloyd "Pepper" Bassett of the Grays had taken issue with umpire E.C. Turner's call of strike three on him in the eighth inning. Bassett was given the heave-ho, but he refused to leave the field. The umpire ruled the game a forfeit. The second game was a 9-8 Grays win. They staged a two-run eighth inning rally topped off by a game-tying triple by Rap Dixon, who then scored the winning run.[8]

In 1937 the Grays assumed league supremacy, and went on to win eight of the next nine championships. The only year in which they did not win the NNL Championship, 1939, they lost a postseason playoff to Baltimore after leading the league in both halves of the season. They played most of their home games in Pennsylvania and were a fixture at Forbes Field.[9] Changing the fortunes of the Homestead Grays in 1937 was the re-acquisition of catcher Josh Gibson, the pre-eminent slugger in the Negro Leagues. In tandem, he and Buck Leonard were a devastating force.

In 1937 Washington's first home series of the season was against the Grays and on Sunday, May 30, Josh Gibson connected for a homer and two triples as the Grays won, 8-3.[10] On July 11 a smallish crowd of 3,000 saw the Grays and Elite Giants teams split a doubleheader. The Elite Giants won the opener 3-2 in 10 innings on a bases-loaded walk. The Grays won the nightcap 7-2 with a six-run last-inning rally highlighted by a Buck Leonard homer. The Elite Giants relocated to Baltimore in 1938, and for one season the Washington Black Senators played at Griffith Stadium. They finished a very dead last in the league.

> *"Gibson did all that was asked of him in the way of living up to those notices (in the Washington newspapers). The way he handled his pitchers and the manner in which he threw to the bases were incomparable, and his response to the praise given him for his batting was likened to the rare instance when a baby does for company what he does at home."*
>
> — Sam Lacy of the *Baltimore Afro-American* July 22, 1939 after Gibson's first appearance of the 1939 season at Griffith Stadium.[11]

On July 16, 1939, the Grays ventured to Griffith Stadium to face the Philadelphia Stars in a neutral-site doubleheader, and Josh Gibson added to his legend with three home runs and a triple. The homer with the biggest impact decided the opening game. His ninth-inning tie-breaker gave the Grays an 8-7 win.[12] When 4,500 fans showed up at Griffith Stadium on August 27, 1939, to see a three-team doubleheader featuring the Grays, Newark Eagles, and New York Black Yankees, it was an omen that there was interest in Negro baseball returning to Washington. The Grays tied the Black Yankees 2-2. For the next several seasons, the Grays' home schedule included games at both Forbes Field and Griffith Stadium.

The first games of the 1940 season at Griffith Stadium were played on May 12 when the Grays played the New York Cubans. The Grays swept the Cubans, 8-6 and 6-5, after Judge Armond W. Scott threw out the first ball. The Grays, however, did not field a team that was as good as its 1939 squad after Josh Gibson and pitcher Roy Partlow opted for higher wages in Venezuela. Nevertheless, they had sluggers Buck Leonard and Howard Easterling and once again posted the best record in the Negro National League. For one of their games at Griffith Stadium, they had the services of Gibson. On August 18, 1940, he returned to the Grays and homered as they swept a doubleheader from the Philadelphia Stars.[13] The sweep brought the team's record at Griffith Stadium to 9-2 for the season.

Buck Leonard opened the 1941 season with a homer in the first game of a doubleheader with the Elite Giants on May 4. The homer broke a 6-6 tie in a 9-6 Grays win. The Giants won the nightcap, but the 4,755 spectators (including Senators owner Clark Griffith) went home happy. The crowd was the largest of the season in Washington for the Grays.

In 1942 the Grays began to attract large crowds to Washington. Josh Gibson, who had barnstormed with other teams for much of the prior two years, was back and reunited with Buck Leonard to take aim at the fences at Griffith Stadium, Forbes Field, and the other ballparks used by Negro League teams.

Black baseball's biggest drawing card was Satchel Paige, and on May 31, 1942, the largest crowd to date to witness a Negro game at Griffith Stadium saw a contest between the Dizzy Dean All-Stars and the Homestead Grays. Paige, on loan from the Kansas City Monarchs, pitched for the Grays in front of 22,234 fans.

Jack Munhall of the *Washington Post* wrote glowingly of the efforts of Paige. "Swaggering and taunting the batters to connect with his blinding speed, the 34-year-old Kansas City Monarchs' ace permitted five hits but offset them with seven timely strikeouts." In the fifth inning, when the Dean Stars mounted a rally, Paige, "winding and uncoiling his long right arm like a giant spring, fairly blew down two of the Stars' leading hitters (Buzz Boyle and Dick Baker) to end the inning with his sixth and seventh strikeouts."[14]

In the bottom of the fifth inning, it was Gibson's turn to shine. As Munhall reported, "[H]e did nothing to disturb his reputation. He swatted one of (Jim) Duffey's slow balls on a line against the left-field stands and pulled up at second after one of the most gosh awful hard-hit balls you ever saw." Dizzy Dean was chased after hurling only one inning during which he allowed two runs on three hits. The Grays won, 8-1.[15]

Paige and the Monarchs visited Griffith Stadium twice during the 1942 season with the Grays winning two close encounters, 2-1 and 3-2. In the first contest the crowd was 26,113 and in the second meeting, they drew 20,086. The June 18 contest was scoreless through nine innings. (Paige pitched the first five for the Monarchs.) In the 10th inning the two pitchers let their bats make the noise. Kansas City's Hilton Smith, who entered the game in the sixth inning, singled in his team's first run in the top of the inning. The Grays manufactured the tying run in the bottom of the inning and with Jud Wilson on first base, Roy Partlow, who had pitched the entire game for the Grays, stepped in. He tripled over the head of the left fielder to end the contest and was carried off the field by the exuberant fans.[16] In the August 13 contest, Paige pitched the entire 12 innings, scattering seven hits and striking out 12 batters, but the Grays won 3-2 on Dave Whatley's single that scored Vic Harris in the Grays' last at-bat.

Another highlight of the 1942 season was colored Elks' day. The fraternal group, not to be confused with its white namesake, was the largest organization of its kind in black America and used the game as a fundraiser for its activities. Visiting Griffith Stadium for the first time were the Birmingham Black Barons of the Negro American League. The teams split the August 2 doubleheader, with the Barons winning the opener, 11-6, and the Grays winning the second game, 5-2.

At the end of the 1942 season, in the unofficial Negro League World Series, the Grays took on the Monarchs. Griffith Stadium was the site of the first game of the series, on September 8, and the Monarchs defeated the Grays 8-0 behind the pitching of Satchel Paige. The series moved on to Forbes Field, Yankee Stadium, and Kansas City. The Monarchs won at Pittsburgh and New York to take a 3-0 lead in the series, and hoped to clinch at home. The Grays won at Kansas City but were penalized for using four ineligible players. The win was disallowed. Kansas City won the final game of the series at Philadelphia's Shibe Park and was credited with a four-game sweep.

The Grays added veteran James "Cool Papa" Bell in 1943 and blazed their path to a succession of wins at Griffith Stadium. In a May 16, 1943, sweep of Baltimore, Josh Gibson had four doubles (three in a second-game 7-0 win), and his legend continued to grow.[17] Their eighth consecutive win at Griffith Stadium, on May 31, was by far the most impressive. They humiliated the Baltimore Elite Giants, 17-0, with an attack that included two Josh Gibson homers and a double and triple by Buck Leonard. To top things off, pitcher John Wright allowed only one hit, an eighth-inning single by Frank Russell.[18]

On September 2, 1943, a night was held in honor of Josh Gibson at Griffith Stadium. That year the first two games of the Negro League World Series were scheduled at Griffith Stadium, and the fans got more than they paid for. After the Barons won the opener on September 21, the teams played to a 5-5 tie on September 23, as the game was stopped by curfew after 12 innings. They played the next night and the Grays won 4-3 in 11 innings to even up the series. The teams then took the show on the road and the Grays won the series in seven games (eight if you count the tie).

In 1944 the Grays returned to the Negro League World Series, winning in five games. The finale, a 4-2 Grays win, was played at Griffith Stadium on September 24.[19] Two nights after the clincher, the teams played an exhibition, just for the fun of it. Gibson was stationed at third base, Cool Papa Bell patrolled first base, and player-manager Vic Harris went to right field. The Barons won, 4-2.

On June 24, 1945, the Monarchs were in town for the annual midseason clash between the titans of the two Negro Leagues. An estimated 18,000 fans came to see the Monarchs' Satchel Paige and heralded infielder Jackie Robinson. Robinson, in his first at-bat, doubled and scored to give his team a short-lived lead. The game was tied, 2-2, through five innings and Paige, looking for a win, continued to pitch into the sixth inning. The Grays staged a seven-run rally during which Satchel was knocked out of the game. They went on to win the opener, 12-3, and completed the sweep with a 10-6 win in the second game.[20] Robinson's double in the first inning of the opener was his first of seven consecutive hits on the day.

The Grays returned to the Negro League World Series in 1945 and were swept in four games by the Cleveland Buckeyes. The only game of the series played at Griffith Stadium was Game Three on September 18, won by the Buckeyes, 4-0.

Within the next two years, two deaths and one debut would leave the Grays and other Negro teams gasping for breath and recognition.

Cumberland Posey died from lung cancer on March 28, 1946. His accomplishments were by no means limited to the baseball diamond. A star basketball player, he was enshrined in the Naismith Hall of Fame in 2016, 10 years after he was enshrined at Cooperstown. In his 35 years with the Grays, the team had grown from little more than a community semipro team in his hometown of Homestead to the best of Negro League teams.

In 1946 the Grays, run by team co-owner Rufus "Sonny Man" Jackson, not only split their time between Forbes Field and Griffith Stadium, but seemingly made stops at every facility on the path between Pittsburgh and Washington. But their dominance of the Negro National League ended with the Newark Eagles advancing to the Negro World Series.

The 1946 team featured Ted "Double Duty" Radcliffe, sometimes pitcher, sometimes catcher, and always a factor in his team's success. In the first game of a June doubleheader against the Elite Giants, he started behind the plate and went in to pitch when Wilmer "Red" Fields weakened in the ninth inning. There were two on with none out and the score was 9-7. Radcliffe held on for the 9-8 win.[21] On June 30 Josh Gibson, when they weren't walking him, had four hits, including a homer and pair of doubles in a doubleheader sweep of the New York Black Yankees.

Although the Washington fans missed out on the Negro League World Series in 1946, Griffith Stadium played host to an East-West All-Star

Game. The East-West Game had been held annually at Comiskey Park since 1933, and the success of the event led to two games being played in four seasons. Griffith Stadium on August 15 played host to the first East-West game of 1946, and the East, including Grays stars Gibson, Leonard, Sam Bankhead, and Howard Easterling, triumphed 6-3 as 16,268 fans looked on. Gibson and Easterling hit safely during a two-run fourth inning rally that gave the East a lead they would not relinquish.[22]

Josh Gibson died on January 20, 1947.[23] The legendary slugger was only 35 years old. Though his exact home-run totals will never be known, he was a force to be reckoned with in his games at Griffith Stadium.

Luke Easter's prolific home-run bat was added to the Homestead Grays' lineup in 1947, but the team was not able to make it to the top of the league standings, due in large part to Buck Leonard's missing most of the season with a broken hand. In Easter's first at-bat at Griffith Stadium, in an exhibition against the New York Black Yankees on April 27, he hit a two-run homer that traveled an estimated 435 feet.[24] The regular season did not start well for the Grays; they lost a doubleheader to the New York Cubans at Griffith Stadium on May 4. Nevertheless, there were big moments at the ballpark. On May 25 the Grays took a doubleheader from the Black Yankees, winning 12-1 and 11-9. Luke Easter's triple and home runs by Luis Marquez and Bob Thurman were the big blows, and pitcher Genie Smith of the Grays toyed with a no-hitter in the opener.[25] But the team was beginning to perform in a vacuum. Newspaper coverage of the Negro Leagues, even in the predominantly black newspapers, was diminishing after Jackie Robinson's debut with the Dodgers, on April 15, 1947.

Although integration of the major leagues would ultimately bring about the demise of the Homestead Grays, the fans at Griffith Stadium would have, in the twilight of their time in Washington, the opportunity to see players who would make a mark in the big leagues and return to Griffith Stadium as major-league players. One of the best, Minnie Miñoso, was on the Cubans in 1947 and had four hits, including a double on May 4.[26]

On June 8 at Griffith Stadium, the Newark Eagles defeated the Grays, 5-3, and the fans got a glimpse of several other players bound for the majors. The Grays' Luke Easter tripled in the third inning, driving home Luis Marquez to make the score 2-2. Making his last Negro League appearance at Griffith Stadium was the league's leading hitter, Larry Doby. In the seventh inning Doby doubled to bring home a pair of runs, putting his team up 4-2. Easter kept his team in the game. In the eighth inning, he doubled and scored on a fly ball by Bob Thurman, cutting the deficit to 4-3. The Eagles' final tally came across on a fly ball by Monte Irvin.[27] When Doby left for the Cleveland Indians, his batting average stood at .416. He led his league with 18 doubles, 13 homers, and 55 RBIs.[28]

On August 10, 1947, the Monarchs came East to face the Grays at Griffith Stadium. Buck Leonard, fully recovered from his broken hand, was swinging his lethal bat in the first game. Satchel Paige was on the mound for the visitors in the second game. But the turnout was only 5,000. Johnny Wright was on the mound for the Grays in the opener. Unknown by most baseball fans, he had been Jackie Robinson's roommate at Montreal in the early part of the 1946 season before returning to the Negro Leagues. On August 10 he took a shutout into the ninth inning. Buck O'Neil tripled for the Monarchs and came home on a fly ball by Ted Strong, but it was too little, too late as the Grays won, 3-1. They got all the runs they needed on a two-run fourth-inning homer by Leonard. Paige was borderline invincible in the second game. He pitched all nine innings, allowed only four hits and struck out six batters. However, it was not enough to win. The Monarchs staked Paige to a 1-0 lead, but the Grays scored a pair of fifth-inning runs. Igniting their rally was Luke Easter, who tripled off the center-field wall. He came home on a single by Clarence Bruce and Bruce scored the team's second run. Pitcher R.T. Walker made the 2-1 lead stand up.[29]

The Grays were back in contention in 1948, but attendance was dismal and fewer games were played at Griffith Stadium in the early part of the season. They wrapped up their preseason schedule against the Baltimore Elite Giants on April 25, losing 8-6 as their relief pitching was weak, surrendering a 5-2 lead in a five-run sixth inning. Luke Easter had three hits for the Grays, including a first-inning triple and a second-inning homer, both off Baltimore's Bob Romby.[30]

Their home opener was rained out on May 16 and they opened against the New York Cubans on May 20, losing 11-1. The key hit for the Cubans was a three-run homer by Miñoso. In late June and early July, the Grays contended for the league lead. In a key game with the Newark Eagles on July 1, they won 11-2 behind home-run clouts by Luke Easter and Sam Bankhead, but they narrowly missed winning the first-half championship.

In an exhibition game on July 14, the Grays defeated the Indianapolis Clowns, 13-4. In the sixth inning Buck Leonard and Luke Easter homered back to back, and they were hardly finished. Easter also had an inside-the-park homer and Leonard tripled. A crowd of 8,000 showed up to see the game, honor Negro pioneer Mary McLeod Bethune, support the National Organization of Negro Women, and see the antics of the Clowns.[31]

As the 1948 season wore down, the end was in sight for the Negro National League. The integration of major-league baseball had led to decreases in coverage, talent, and attendance. Buck Leonard was still around, and he was honored on September 5. Dr. Claude Carmichael led the fundraising to purchase gifts for the star player.[32] The Grays played the Clowns and won both games, 8-4 and 6-1. Buck Leonard, on his day, singled and scored in the opener and went 3-for-3 with a double and an RBI in the nightcap.[33]

The Homestead Grays went on to have the best record in the league in the second half of the season and defeated the Baltimore Elite Giants in a playoff series for the league pennant. All of the games were played at Baltimore's Bugle Field. The Grays went on to play and win against the Birmingham Black Barons in the Negro League World Series. None of the games were played at Griffith Stadium.

The Negro National League disbanded after the 1948 season. In 1949 the Grays continued to play, and hosted several Sunday doubleheaders at Griffith Stadium. Sam Bankhead replaced Vic Harris as manager, and they joined the Negro American Association. They opened their home season against Charlotte on May 1 and treated the Griffith Stadium fans to a season of winning. In the first half of the season, they lost only three games while winning 27 and finished in first place. The names of the players did not ring with the same resonance of Josh Gibson and Luke Easter, and most of the zip was gone from Buck Leonard's bat, but Wilmer "Red" Fields excelled at bat and on the mound. On July 4 he was sold to the Oakland Oaks of the Pacific Coast League but failed to report, and the deal was voided.[34] On July 10 the Grays defeated the Raleigh Tigers in a doubleheader. Pitcher Roy Partlow, who had played briefly in the Brooklyn Dodgers organization in 1946, was the winner in the 8-5 opener.[35] At the end of the season, they faced Richmond, the second-half winner, winning the best-of-seven playoff series in four games.[36]

In 1950 the Homestead Grays barnstormed much of the season. In July, they joined the Negro American League and played three doubleheaders at Griffith Stadium.[37] When they hosted the Philadelphia Stars on August 6, 4,000 fans came out to see Satchel Paige, who was with the Stars. Paige pitched the first three innings of the opener and was ineffective as his team lost, 7-1. The Grays completed the sweep with a 12-2 win in the second game.[38] Perhaps it was fitting that Paige was there for the last Homestead Grays doubleheader at Griffith Stadium.

On May 22, 1951, it was announced that the Grays were shutting down operations.

SOURCES

In addition to the sources shown in the notes, the author used:

Abrams, Al. "Sidelights on Sports," *Pittsburgh Post-Gazette*, December 26, 1949: 36.

Bush, Frederick C., and Bill Nowlin (eds.). *Bittersweet Goodbye* (Phoenix: Society for American Baseball Research, 2017).

Hogan, Lawrence D. *Shades of Gray* (Washington: National Geographic, 2006).

Lester, Larry, and Dick Clark. *The Negro Leagues Book* (Cleveland: Society for American Baseball Research, 1994).

NOTES

1 Paul Kurtz, "Negro Stars Ready for Celebration," *Pittsburgh Press*, August 6, 1938: 8.

2 "Grays Defeat Hilldale," *Pittsburgh Post-Gazette*, June 29, 1931: 14.

3 "Pilots in Even Break," *Washington Evening Star*, July 31, 1932: 5-4.

4 "Pilots Split Bill with Grays," *Washington Post*, July 31, 1932: 13.

5 William G. Nunn, "Posey Refuses to Return Two Detroit Players," *Pittsburgh Courier*, July 1, 1933: 14.

6 "Pittsburgh Nines Win 2 Games Here," *Washington Post*, October 8, 1934: 15.

7 Elite Giants Beaten, 7-5, by Grays," *Washington Post*, June 28, 1936: X4.

8 "Grays Share Twin Bill; Win, 9-8," *Washington Post*, June 29, 1936: X15.

9 Brad Snyder, "Black Baseball's Return Caught On: Community Flocked to Briggs in '41," *Detroit Free Press*, March 21, 2003: 4E.

10 "Gray Day for Elites," *Washington Evening Star*, May 31, 1937: 16.

11 "Josh Gibson Clouts 3 Homers as Grays Divide," *Washington Post*, July 22, 1939: 22.

12 "Grays' Catcher Hits 3 Homers; Team Takes 2," *Washington Post*, July 17, 1939: 14.

13 "Gibson Clouts Homer, Grays Capture Twin-Bill," *Washington Evening Star*, August 19, 1940: 12.

14 Jack Munhall, "Paige, Grays Beat Stars, 8-1, Before 22,000," *Washington Post*, June 1, 1942: 17.

15 Ibid.

16 Ed Lawson, "28,000 Watch Grays Upset Monarchs, 2-1," *Washington Post*, June 19, 1942: 24.

17 "Grays Annex 2 from Elites, 2-1 and 7-0," *Washington Post*, May 17, 1943: 13.

18 "Josh Gibson's Homers Help Grays Win," *Washington Post*, June 1, 1943: 15.

19 "Grays Earn Baseball Title with Fourth Win Over Barons," *Washington Evening Star*, September 25, 1944: 13.

20 "18,000 Watch Grays Blast Satch Paige," *Washington Post*, June 25, 1945: 9.

21 "Grays Chase McHenry, Nip Elites, 9-8; Then Lose, 7-2," *New York Amsterdam News*, June 29, 1946: 13.

22 Larry Lester, *Black Baseball's National Showcase: The East-West All-Star Game, 1933-1953* (Lincoln: University of Nebraska Press, 2001), 265-274.

23 Wendell Smith, "Grays' Home Run King Dies at 36," *Pittsburgh Courier*, January 25,1947: 1

24 Ric Roberts, "Grays and Yanks Split: Easter Homers in Debut," *Pittsburgh Courier*, May 3, 1947: 14.

25 Roberts, "Grays Grab Four Games from Yanks," *Pittsburgh Courier*, May 31, 1947: 14.

26 Roberts, "Cubans Trip Grays Twice in Washington," *Pittsburgh Courier*, May 10, 1947: 14.

27 Roberts, "Doby's Double Dumps Homestead, 5-3," *Pittsburgh Courier*, June 14, 1947: 15.

28 "Diamond Dope," *Pittsburgh Courier*, July 12, 1947: 15.

29 Roberts, "Grays Top K.C. Twice; Paige Loses to Grays by 2-1 Score," *Pittsburgh Courier*, August 16, 1947: 15.

30 "Harrismen Launch Season Against Elites, Cubans," *Baltimore Afro-American*, May 1, 1948: 29.

31 "Grays Open Second Half in Game with Philly," *Evening Star*, July 15, 1948: C-1.

32 "Clowns, Monarchs, Grays on Buck Leonard Day Card," *Baltimore Afro-American*, August 28, 1948: 2-13.

33 "Grays' Captain Denies Plans to Retire," *Baltimore Afro-American*, September 11, 1948: 2-14.

34 "Fields Deal Off," *San Francisco Examiner*, July 10, 1949: 26.

35 "Homestead Grays Continue Winning," *Pittsburgh Courier*, July 16, 1949: 23.

36 "Grays Whip Giants; Take NAA Laurels," *Richmond Times Dispatch*, September 16, 1949: 33.

37 "Homestead Grays Rejoin Negro American League," *Atlanta Daily World*, July 18, 1950: 5.

38 "Grays Dim Paige's Hope of Big-League Comeback," *Washington Evening Star*, August 7, 1950: 12.

THE SENATORS INAUGURATE NOT-YET-COMPLETELY-BUILT GRIFFITH STADIUM

APRIL 12, 1911
WASHINGTON SENATORS 8, BOSTON RED SOX 5

by Mark S. Sternman

As the 1911 season started, Griffith Stadium represented a work in progress after an off-season fire. Nevertheless, Washingtonians eagerly anticipated their new ballfield. On Opening Day Joe S. Jackson gushed in the Washington Post, "This is the day, and National park the place, on and at which it is expected that all Washington records for baseball attendance and related enthusiasm will be smashed, shattered and tossed into the discard."[1]

Boston arrived in Washington the day before the game "to get in a few licks ... but orders were ... that the team could not practice [at] the [new] park on account of the workmen who were ... clearing away ... debris."[2]

The ballpark received praise from Boston reporter Tim Murnane, a leading knight of the keyboard before his premature passing in 1917. "A new grandstand and bleachers, built in less than three weeks and affording fine accommodations for fully 15,000 spectators, was the work of magic," marveled Murnane.[3]

With "overcast skies and a prediction of rain," the conditions did not live up to the grounds.[4] The "game was slowly played in a chilly east wind. [Making his second Opening Day appearance,] President Taft sat muffled up in a heavy fur overcoat throughout the struggle."[5] Taft had done his Opening Day duties when he "swung his arm and hurled the ball straight and true to 'Dolly' Gray, the Washington pitcher."[6]

Vice President James Sherman joined Taft. "Sherman is a genuine, expert scoring, and peanut-eating regular. Truly, this is an administration which is correct from a base ball standpoint," noted *Sporting Life*.[7]

The politicians missed seeing the ace of the Senators pitch, although before the game "he fooled around in the outfield for quite a while."[8] Demanding a $9,000 salary, Walter Johnson finally signed for $7,000 two days before the opener.[9] As a result, Gray started for the Senators and retired the Red Sox in order in the first inning.

The 21-year-old Smoky Joe Wood, "expected to be the Red Sox star pitcher,"[10] started for Boston. Washington's leadoff hitter, Clyde Milan, reached on an error by Heinie Wagner, one of four committed by the Boston captain in the contest,[11] and stole second. After a strikeout, Kid Elberfeld reached on a fielder's choice retiring Milan and stole second. A foul tip knocked out catcher Red Kleinow[12] in favor of backup backstop Bunny Madden. Wood got another strikeout to escape the eventful but scoreless first.

After a second straight one-two-three inning by Gray, Wood walked John Henry with one out in the second, but got two grounders to strand the Washington first baseman.

Batterymates Madden and Wood, the latter an excellent-hitting pitcher who later became a good-hitting outfielder, hit consecutive singles to begin the Boston third. Wood took second on the throw to put two runners in scoring position with none out. Groundouts cashed in both Bostonians and put the Red Sox up 2-0. Milan singled and stole another bag in the third, but the Senators still could not score.

Boston plated another pair in the fourth. Duffy Lewis hit a ground-rule double into the outfield crowd, and Wagner walked. In his first big-league game, Rip Williams hit to pitcher Gray, who threw wildly to third to load the bases with none out. Clyde Engle reached on a fielder's choice force at the plate, but Madden's single put the Sox up 3-0. Milan threw out Williams trying to score, but Gray uncorked a wild pitch to give Boston a four-run lead.

Henry singled and stole second in the fourth, but remained stranded. Washington had four steals in four innings but no runs. The ease with which the Senators ran the bases boded well for the hosts. "Neither Boston catcher seemed to be in any shape to stop base runners," wrote the *Post*. "In fact, the whole [visiting] team looked far from being ready for a hard season."[13]

After Gray sailed through the top of the fifth, Washington scored in its half with a run on a walk to Gabby Street and singles by Milan and Elberfeld.

Gray set down Boston easily in the top of the sixth. In the bottom of the inning the Senators transformed a 4-1 deficit into a 7-4 lead. With one out, Henry singled. Wagner made another error on a ball hit by George McBride. Street singled in Henry to cut the Red Sox lead to 4-2. Batting for Gray, Wagner fielded Warren Miller's grounder and threw wildly to home as McBride scored to trim the lead to 4-3. Milan's single loaded the bases. Ed Karger came on for Wood, who got little help from his fielders.

Karger "failed to show any real stuff when called upon."[14] Germany Schaefer, the second pinch-hitter used by Washington manager Jimmy McAleer in the inning, singled to tie the game. ("McAleer used excellent judgment ... and won his game by his substitutions in the sixth," the *Washington Post* observed.)[15] Then Elberfeld doubled in two runs and Washington led, 6-4. Bill Cunningham walked to reload the bases, and Karger plunked Doc Gessler[16] to score Washington's seventh run and the sixth in an inning in which nine straight Senators reached.

Pitcher Ewart "Dixie" Walker, the father of outfielders Dixie and Harry the Hat, replaced Gray in the seventh. Each team scored in the eighth. Boston's Harry Hooper walked and Tris Speaker singled him to third. The Gray Eagle tried for second, but Gessler threw him out. Speaker's overaggressive baserunning hurt Boston. Lewis singled in Hooper as the Red Sox edged to within 7-5, but Wagner's misery continued as he hit into a rally-killing double play.

Doubles by Elberfeld and Gessler in the eighth provided insurance for Washington, restoring the three-run margin at 8-5.

In the ninth Walker lived up to his name by walking Williams and pinch-hitter Steve Yerkes. With two outs, Larry Gardner singled to load the bases. With the tying runs on, Hooper sent a fly deep to left, but Schaefer made the catch to end the game.

While a later scorer could would have given Gray the win and Walker the save, the official scorer on this day anointed Walker with the winning laurels (coming off consecutive 19-loss campaigns, Gray could have used the help in 1911, his last season in the majors, which he finished with a 2-13 record). Give an assist to Wagner and the defective

Boston defense. Fans of the Senators may have gotten an exaggerated sense of the team's prowess, as Washington would not score as many as six runs in an inning again until the third frame of a 14-7 win on June 2 against Detroit. On that day, the Senators would make six errors but triumph. On this day, six Red Sox errors gifted Washington with a wild win in the first Griffith Stadium game.

NOTES

1 Joe S. Jackson, "'Play Ball' Today," *Washington Post*, April 12, 1911: 1.

2 "Wood to Be Sent after Senators," *Boston Globe*, April 12, 1911: 1.

3 T.H. Murnane, "Red Sox' 4-to-0 Lead Is Turned into 8-5 Defeat," *Boston Globe*, April 13, 1911: 6. As Retrosheet has no play-by-play data for this game, this account relies on Murnane's reporting to describe what happened.

4 "Baseball's Opening Day," *Boston Evening Transcript*, April 12, 1911: 6.

5 "Taft Starts Senators Off," *New York Times*, April 13, 1911.

6 "Nations Win, 8 to 5, as 16,000 Cheer Them," *Washington Post*, April 13, 1911: 1. Gray kept the ball that Taft threw him and planned to take it to the White House at a later date for an autograph. "Heard and Seen at the Ball Game," *Washington Post*, April 13, 1911: 2.

7 Paul W. Eaton, "From the Capital," *Sporting Life*, April 22, 1911: 3.

8 "Johnson in the Fold," *Washington Post*, April 13, 1911: 8.

9 Shirley Povich, *The Washington Senators* (Kent, Ohio: Kent State University Press, 2010), 58-59.

10 "American League Notes," *Sporting Life*, April 22, 1911: 11.

11 Wagner suffered from a sore arm in this game according to A.H.C. Mitchell, "Boston Briefs," *Sporting Life*, April 22, 1911: 5. Wagner did not play again until May 13.

12 Kleinow did not play again until May 29.

13 "Notes of the Nationals," *Washington Post*, April 13, 1911: 8.

14 "Echoes of the Game," *Boston Globe*, April 13, 1911: 6.

15 Joe S. Jackson, "Nationals Play Better Ball and Deserve Their Victory," *Washington Post*, April 13, 1911: 2.

16 In 1910 Gessler had finished in a three-way tie for the AL lead by getting hit by a pitch 16 times. In 1911 he upped his total to a career-high 20, but finished second behind teammate Elberfeld's 25. Washington finished no better than fourth in any offensive category in 1911 save for its league-leading total of 80 HBPs.

THE SENATORS INAUGURATE COMPLETED BALLPARK

JULY 25, 1911
DETROIT TIGERS 5, WASHINGTON SENATORS 2

by Thomas Kern

In 1911, their 11th year in the American League, the Nationals had yet to have a winning season. The team had been so lackluster in its years in Washington that its ownership solicited fan suggestions and changed its name from the Senators to the Nationals in 1905 in hopes of inspiring a change in fortunes.[1] The team would eventually reach better times, but not yet in 1911.

As if the Nationals didn't have enough to worry about, on March 17, less than a month from Opening Day, National Park burned down. According to the *Washington Evening Star*, "[T]he superintendent of the grounds ... attributes the fire to the carelessness of a plumber who left a blast lamp unwatched for a moment while he left his work to step outside the room. ... The flames ate up the wooden structure with such speed that by the time half the [city's] engines ... were coupled to the hydrants the interior of the park was a great crater of flame."[2] Rebuilding began right away and in a little more than four months, a new park was ready for the Nationals to inaugurate.

After a 20-game road trip ending in St. Louis on Sunday, July 23, the Nationals returned to Washington to open the new park with a three-game midweek series with the Tigers. Walter Johnson would not be available on the 25th, having thrown a complete-game 5-1 victory against St. Louis on Sunday[3] and three innings on Monday at a benefit game played in Cleveland in memory of Addie Joss, who died in April.[4]

Pitching for the Nationals on the 25th would be left-hander Dolly Gray, their Opening Day starter. Washington was 30-58, by now well entrenched in seventh place. The Nationals' opponents, the Detroit Tigers, were 59-28, in first place by four games.

George Mullin pitched for the Tigers. He was 10-5 and had bested Walter Johnson twice earlier in the season.

"Tigers Are Here; Fur Sure to Fly," shouted the *Washington Herald* on the 25th over a story by sportswriter William Peet that began, "Hughie Jennings' Detroit Tigers, leaders of the American League, will oppose the Nationals at the brand new concrete castle on Florida Avenue at 3:30 o'clock this afternoon and a grand surprise awaits the Washington fans. The surprise is in the nature of the ball park, now complete except in a few minor details. ..."[5]

The *Detroit Free Press* noted that "the Tigers were accorded the honor of opening Washington's new ball park and ran true to form to the extent of a whipping their hosts 5 to 2, taking an early start and leading them wire to wire. This new ball park is a sort of Phoenix-like affair, having risen from the ashes of the plant that burned down early in the spring. There was a makeshift arrangement that provided for the earlier games of the season, but today the splendid new concrete stands practically are completed. ..."[6]

As for the game itself, the *Herald's* headline the next day summed it up: "Opening Battle Goes to Tigers: Nationals Unable to Solve Mullin's Shoots when Hits Are Needed – Hughes Does Well after Gray Blows – Score, 5 to 2."[7] Reported Peet, "The Tigers won because George Mullin was able to keep eleven big swats apart, while Dolly Gray gave up the ghost in the second inning, after a quartet of slams and two runs went to the credit of the league leaders. Tom Hughes, who finished the job, was there with bells on. Had he started, the result might have been a different story."[8] Joe S. Jackson of the *Washington Post* could not agree more. "Only the little matter of a misplaced guess stood between the home folk and happiness on the occasion of the return of the Nationals and the dedicating of the revamped ball yard. That guess was on the matter of pitching. Gray ... looked the logical choice against a left handed club like the Tigers. It took less than two innings to prove that he wasn't what we have already said, while the ensuing seven rounds, through which Tom Hughes toiled, serve to show that the long boy might have brought it home had he been first picked."[9]

With the temperature in the low 80s, the game began on a ceremonial note, with Vice President James S. Sherman (but not President Taft) in attendance. In the top of the first, Delos Drake singled but was thrown out on an attempted steal. Donie Bush then walked and took third as Ty Cobb singled. Sam Crawford bunted and Bush scored, beating the tag. Cobb was now on third and Crawford on first. Jim Delahanty hit a fly ball to Clyde Milan and Cobb scored. George Moriarty's grounder to short ended the inning.

In the bottom of the first, Milan promisingly tripled to lead off, but was stranded.

The Tigers scored two more in the top of the second, and in the process drove Gray to the showers. After Charlie O'Leary grounded out, Oscar Stanage singled to right. Mullin doubled off the short right-field wall with Stanage going to third. McAleer removed lefty Gray and brought in Tom Hughes, a right-handed sidewinder. In response to the pitching change, Jennings substituted Davy Jones for Drake, who grounded to first baseman Germany Schaefer. Schaefer threw home and nailed Stanage at the plate. With two outs and men on first and third, the threat was almost contained. However, Bush doubled to bring in Mullin and Jones, making the score 4-0. Cobb then flied out to end the inning.

The score remained unchanged through four innings, although the *Herald* noted, "Mighty good chance to score in the fourth, with three men on bases and only one out."[10] After a walk and two infield hits, the stage was set. J. Ed Grillo of the *Evening Star* reported, "It is doubtful if a faster double play than the one turned by Bush, O'Leary and Delahanty in the fourth inning, with the bases full, has been seen on the local grounds this season. With one out and all the sacks occupied, Wid Conroy hit a sharp grounder to second base. Bush made a great stop, and without steadying himself, threw to O'Leary, who shot the ball to first in time to double up Conroy. The play was worked like a flash, and did much to win the game for the Tigers, for that fourth inning threatened for a time to be disastrous to Mullin."[11]

The Nationals scored a run in the fifth when Eddie Ainsmith tripled past Crawford in right (Peet: "the ball rolling past Sam Crawford, and the fans let out a bunch of roots that jarred the concrete stands"[12]). Hughes hit a grounder to Bush deep in the hole at short and was retired at first; Ainsmith stayed at third. (Some sportswriters thought he could have scored). Milan flied to left to drive in Ainsmith.

In the Tigers sixth, Delahanty singled and took second on one of Walker's two errors. ("Walker is credited with a pair of errors on fumbled balls, but the poor condition of the turf doubtless had a lot to do with Walker's slips, and the fans should not criticize too harshly."[13]) Moriarty's sacrifice moved Delahanty to third. "O'Leary drove up a short fly which Walker gathered in. Delahanty tried to reach home and as the throw as perfect, Ainsmith had his man by two feet, but dropped the ball from the force of the impact."[14] It was one of three errors by Ainsmith in the game, for a total of five Washington miscues. The play made the score 5-1.

"Although the home folks choked a hit out of Mullin in each of the next two rounds, nothing happened, and it was not until the eighth that another tally showed up," the *Herald* reported.[15] In the eighth, Milan singled to left off Mullin, Schaefer struck out, and Kid Elberfeld singled, Milan going to third. Jack Lelivelt grounded to second and, in the words of Joe S. Jackson of the *Washington Post*, "O'Leary grabbed Lelivelt's grounder, and tagged Elberfeld, the latter delaying the play long enough to kill a double [play]. Milan scored while this was going on."[16] Tillie Walker got on board with an infield hit, but George McBride flied out to Cobb to end the inning. That made the score 5-2, Tigers, and that was how the game ended after a playing time of 2 hours before a crowd of 8,000.

The loss put the Nationals at 30-59, but they went 34-31 the rest of the way to salvage something of a lost season. In September the owners hired Clark Griffith as player-manager to replace the departing McAleer. Better times were ahead.

SOURCES

In addition to the sources cited in the Notes, the author relied on Baseball-Reference.com and Retrosheet.org.

NOTES

1. Tom Deveaux, *The Washington Senators: 1901-1971* (Jefferson, North Carolina: McFarland & Company, 2001), 15.
2. "Baseball Park Is Swept by Flames," *Washington Evening Star*, March 17, 1911: 1.
3. Baseball-reference.com: baseball-reference.com/teams/WSH/1911-schedule-scores.shtml.
4. Henry W. Thomas, *Walter Johnson: Baseball's Big Train* (Washington: Farragut Publishing Company, 1995), 83.
5. William Peet, "Tigers Are Here; Fur Sure to Fly," *Washington Herald*, July 25, 1911: 7.
6. E.A. Batchelor, "Tigers Drive Gray to the Bench and Rout Washington," *Detroit Free Press*, July 26, 1911: 8.
7. William Peet, "Opening Battle Goes to Tigers: Nationals Unable to Solve Mullin's Shoots when Hits Are Needed - Hughes Does Well after Gray Blows - Score, 5 to 2," *Washington Herald*, July 26, 1911: 7.
8. Peet, "Opening Battle."
9. Joe S. Jackson, "Tigers Make a Sad Day of New Park Inaugural," *Washington Post*, July 26, 1911: 8.
10. Peet, "Opening Battle."
11. J. Ed. Grillo, "Lively Ball Is No Longer Used in American League," *Washington Evening Star*, July 26, 1911: 10.
12. Peet, "Opening Battle."
13. Peet, "Opening Battle."
14. Peet, "Opening Battle."
15. Peet, "Opening Battle."
16. Jackson.

HARTZELL'S TWO HOMERS IN ONE GAME SET NATIONAL PARK RECORD

AUGUST 12, 1911
NEW YORK HIGHLANDERS 4, WASHINGTON SENATORS 0

by Jimmy Keenan

On August 12, 1911, the Washington Senators played the third of a five-game series against the visiting New York Highlanders at National Park. Washington's home grounds had burned down on March 17, but, amazingly, a new ballpark was built on the site in less than a month. Although it was ready by Opening Day, the final touches were not completed until a few weeks before this game.

The Washington nine had been ensconced in seventh place in the eight-team American League for most of the 1911 season. Recently the Senators had shown some improvement, winning 15 of their last 20 games.

The Highlanders looked like one of the better teams in the loop in the early season but, plagued by inconsistent pitching as well as injuries, they quickly fell out of contention. New York had been fluctuating between the third, fourth, and fifth spots in the junior circuit standings since early April.

After the Highlanders dropped a doubleheader to Washington the previous day, player-manager Hal Chase gave the starting nod to pitcher Ray Fisher (8-7). Nationals manager Jimmy McAleer countered with rookie pitcher Jay Carl Cashion (1-0).

Fisher posted a 24-5 record with 243 strikeouts for the Hartford Senators in the Class B Connecticut State League in 1909. At the behest of Highlanders scout Arthur Irwin, New York purchased Fisher's contract, along with that of infielder Jack Wanner, from the Senators for $5,000. Fisher was allowed to complete his studies at Middlebury College in Vermont before reporting to the Highlanders in 1910.

Fisher had a good fastball along with a variety of curves, yet he was best known for throwing the spitball. Sportswriters who covered his games noted that Fisher didn't throw the spitter on every pitch but went through the motions as if he did. This psychological warfare between pitcher and batter worked to Fisher's advantage throughout his career.

Cashion was playing for the Greenville Spinners in the Class D Carolina Association when he was purchased for $2,500, reported to be the highest price to date for any player from that circuit. Cashion was signed by Nationals scout Mike Kahoe. Cashion had made his big-league debut a week before, on August 4, squaring off against Chicago ace Big Ed Walsh. Cashion allowed just three hits that day in a 3-2 Nationals victory. The youngster's pitching repertoire consisted of a lively fastball, hard-breaking curve and deceptive change of pace, but his control was lacking. Every now and then Cashion would drop down into an almost completely underhanded delivery. Considering his wildness, this submarine pitch created quite a bit of trepidation among opposing hitters.

August 12 started out as a hot and muggy day in Washington. By game time ominous storm clouds had moved directly over the ballpark, limiting the attendance to about 5,000.

Cashion started the contest on a bad note by walking leadoff man Harry Wolter. The next batter, Charlie Hemphill, lashed a single to right, Wolter scampering to the third on the well-executed hit-and-run. Washington right fielder Doc Gessler attempted to throw Wolter out on the play. Gessler's heave from right bounced a few times before being knocked down by third baseman Wid Conroy. Sensing a chance to take an extra base, Hemphill bolted for second. Conroy hurriedly threw toward the middle of the diamond. Off the mark, the sphere rolled into right-center field. By the time the ball was thrown back into the infield, Wolter had crossed the plate and Hemphill was standing on second.

Hemphill stole third as Hal Chase struck out. A wild pitch to Birdie Cree allowed Hemphill to race home with New York's second run. Cree eventually went down on strikes. The next batter, Jack Knight, grounded out to end the inning.

Fisher stymied the Washington batsmen in the bottom of the first, a theme that would play out for the rest of the afternoon. A potential New York rally was thwarted in the next inning thanks to a pair of nice plays by second baseman Bill Cunningham. For the next few frames neither team mustered up much offense.

In the fourth, Highlanders third baseman Roy Hartzell smacked a 3-and-2 pitch from Cashion high over the right-field fence for a home run. Hartzell had broken into the majors with the St. Louis Browns in 1906. After posting a .218 batting average in 1910, he was traded, along with $5,000 to the Highlanders for Jimmy Austin and Frank LaPorte. Hartzell came into the game against the Nationals hitting .300 with 17 stolen bases. This homer was his second of the season.

For the next few stanzas both pitchers were on their mettle. The *Washington Evening Star* observed, "Fisher could not be hit, his speed, control and most deceptive spit ball, which he bluffed with now and then made him almost invincible."[1]

Cashion, behind in the count on nearly every batter, kept Washington in the game by mixing up his pitches just enough to keep the Highlanders batters off balance.

For the remainder of the contest a pitching duel ensued between the two young hurlers.

In the Highlanders sixth, first baseman Chase made a nice defensive play when he snagged a hot grounder off the bat of Clyde Milan then beat him to the bag for the putout.

Bill Cunningham, who recorded the first home run by a Washington player at National Park on June 2, nearly duplicated the feat off Fisher in the seventh. Cunningham's long drive fell just a bit short as Highlanders outfielder Birdie Cree made a nice grab at the left-field fence after a long run.

The Highlanders eighth started with Wolter connecting for a triple. The next batter, Charlie Hemphill, hit a grounder to shortstop George McBride. Wolter, who broke from third on contact, was gunned out at the plate by a perfect throw from McBride.

The Nationals threatened in their half of the eighth. After Gabby Street grounded out, Cashion and Milan reached base via a pair of singles. Germany Schaefer, who already had two hits to his credit, stepped to the plate. With the count full, Fisher spun a slow curveball to the dish. Mistiming the pitch, Schaefer launched a high popup behind the plate that catcher Ed Sweeney was able to haul in near the stands for the second out. At that point

Nationals manager McAleer removed Tillie Walker in favor of pinch-hitter Jack Lelivelt. Walker had been struggling against Fisher, going 0-for-3 with a pair strikeouts. The crowd cheered McAleer's managerial strategy as Lelivelt had tripled in the Nationals' extra-innings victory in the second game of the doubleheader the previous day. On this occasion Lelivelt fell victim to a Fisher breaking ball, grounding out to Chase to end the Nationals' short-lived rally.

With two out in the top of the ninth, Hartzell stroked Cashion's full-count offering into the gap in left-center field, the ball rolling to the fence. Clyde Milan quickly fired the ball toward the relay man, McBride, whose strong throw home landed in the catcher's mitt seconds after Hartzell had crossed the plate, bumping up the score to 4-0. With this second round-tripper, Hartzell became the first player to hit two home runs in one game at the newly built National Park.

In the bottom of the ninth Fisher needed only five pitches to retire the side and seal the win.

He allowed six hits, four of which came with two outs, and walked one batter. He struck out four. No Washington runner advanced past second base. Cashion was touched up for eight hits and walked five in the loss.

Hartzell's long-ball display along with a recent clout by Doc Gessler didn't impress a *Washington Times* sportswriter who wrote under the pseudonym "Senator." "There is something about a home run where the hitter has only to jog around the four sacks that takes much away from the value of his drive as a spectacle," Senator wrote. "Short fences in the National League park at Boston have come close to killing the interest in the sluggers there, and it is to prevent this in Washington that manager McAleer wants a higher fence in right field."[2]

The Nationals went on to post a 17-11 record in August. From there they reverted to their former ways, finishing the 1911 campaign in seventh place. Although he had another year remaining on his contract, McAleer left the Nationals at the close of the season to become president and part-owner of the Boston Red Sox. The underachieving Highlanders ended up one rung above Washington in sixth place. Hal Chase resigned as manager in November.

AUTHOR'S NOTE

There were a few instances of conflicting information in the newspapers regarding specific plays during the game. The author endeavored to discern what actually took place by cross-referencing game information from available articles pertaining to the plays in question.

SOURCES

Baltimore Sun

Baseball-reference.org

Bridgeport (Connecticut) *Evening Farmer*

Cairo (Illinois) *Bulletin*

New York Sun

New York Times

New York Tribune

Sporting Life

The Sporting News

Times Dispatch (Richmond, Virginia)

Washington Evening Times

Washington Herald

Washington Times

NOTES

1 J. Ed Grillo, "Fisher's Pitching Causes the Nationals to Be Shut Out by the Highlanders," *Washington Evening Star*, August 13, 1911: 50.

2 Senator, "Long Clouts by Heavy Sluggers Heighten Fences," *Washington Times*, August 14, 1911: 10.

DOUBLEHEADER DANDY: THE BIG TRAIN WINS AL-RECORD 15TH STRAIGHT; CASHION HURLS SIX-INNING NO-HITTER

AUGUST 20, 1911
WASHINGTON SENATORS 4, CLEVELAND NAPS 2 (FIRST GAME)
WASHINGTON SENATORS 2, CLEVELAND NAPS 0 (6 INNINGS, SECOND GAME)

by Gregory H. Wolf

Washington skipper Clark Griffith had reason to be confident. The former star pitcher, seven-time 20-game winner, and successful player-manager for three different franchises had transformed the Senators from laughing stock to baseball's biggest surprise in his first season in the nation's capital. A charter member of the AL, the Senators had never posted a winning record or finished higher than sixth. Preparing to complete a three-game set with the sixth-place Cleveland Naps (51-61) as part of a three-week homestand, the Senators (69-44) were firmly ensconced in second place, nine games behind the Boston Red Sox. Though the chances of dislodging Boston from their perch seemed slim to none, the Old Fox was not about to give up trying.

Rain the previous day had necessitated a doubleheader on a warm and muggy Tuesday afternoon with temperatures in the mid-80s. Before the twin bill could get underway in the one-year-old steel-and-concrete National Stadium, a controversy erupted when Griffith attempted to jockey for position and pull a fast one. After informing home-plate umpire Tommy Connolly that Lefty Schegg was his starter, Griffith changed his mind when Naps skipper Harry Davis announced that his ace Vean Gregg would start. Griffith quickly recognized that Schegg, a 22-year-old southpaw making his big-league debut, was no match for Gregg, an emerging star coming off 23 wins and an AL-best 1.80 ERA in his rookie campaign. Sensing a disaster, Griffith backtracked and told Connolly that Walter Johnson would start. "Griff forgot the rules," opined D.C. sportswriter J. Ed. Grillo, "and thought that he could announce Schegg as his pitcher and then send Johnson to the slab."[1]

Connelly objected to Griffith's rules violation and ordered Schegg to the mound. In what proved to be his only big-league start, Schegg retired leadoff batter Buddy Ryan and then saw Griffith approach the mound. The Old Fox yanked him and called on the Big Train. The Senators' strong suit was their pitching, which eventually led the AL in team ERA (2.69), more than compensating for an average offensive club. Griffith wanted a matchup of aces, especially with his on a historic roll. The 24-year-old was coming off consecutive seasons with 25 wins and entered the '12 campaign with an 82-78 lifetime slate. Laying claim as the majors' best hurler, Johnson had won his last 14 decisions, tying Jack Chesbro's 1904 AL record, and led all big leaguers with 27 wins (7 losses) and seven shutouts. During the streak, which had begun on July 3, the Big Train had made 17 appearances, 11 of which were starts, logged 113 innings, and limited batters to a paltry .177 average.

After Johnson breezed through the first, Gregg walked leadoff batter Clyde Milan and, like Schegg's, his outing was done. Feeling the pressure to win in the midst of the Naps' steak of 25 losses in their last 37 games, first-year-skipper Davis felt a victory was unlikely against the Big Train, and pulled his star for "supposedly easier game," noted sportswriter Joe S. Jackson.[2] Jogging in to replace Gregg was 24-year-old Bill Steen, a rookie right-hander with a 5-4 slate as a swingman.

Notwithstanding the manipulation of pitchers, the game unfolded as an unlikely pitching duel. Steen held the Senators hitless through four innings. Howie Shanks led off the fifth with a scorcher to Naps shortstop Roger Peckinpaugh, who corralled the ball near the outfield grass, but his off-balance throw, according to the *Washington Post*, eluded first baseman Art Griggs and landed near the stands, enabling Shanks to take second.[3] Shanks advanced to third on Steen's wild pitch and then scored the game's first run on George McBride's single. After Eddie Foster walked in the sixth, Danny Moeller's blast to right field "scratched the paint off the score-board ads," reported the *Washington Times*, for a double.[4] Chick Gandil, acquired in a trade with the Montreal Royals of the International League in late May and in his first full season in the majors, hit a blooper into short center, scoring both runners to make it 3-0.

Staked to a three-run lead and given the way Johnson had pitched since the beginning of July, a Senators victory seemed imminent. The "star slinger was great for six innings," gushed Jackson in the *Post*, and had yielded only three hits, two of which were scratches.[5] Johnson was a different pitcher in the last three innings, when he "seemed to lose everything except a turn of speed," reported Jackson, and the Naps "threatened to annihilate" him, opined sportswriter William Peet of the *Washington Herald*.[6] Shoeless Joe Jackson, who entered the game batting .382 after posting a .408 average the previous campaign, led off the seventh by belting one "far over Milan's head [in center field]," according to the *Post*, and reached third.[7] Nap Lajoie, the former skipper after whom the team was named, followed with a single to put the Naps on the board. Three batters later, Lajoie scored on a single by Fred Carisch, who scampered to second when Milan overran the ball.[8] With the game-tying run in scoring position, Johnson retired Peckinpaugh to end the threat.

The Big Train helped his own cause on the bottom of the seventh. McBride led off with a scratch single to first, moved up a station on Eddie Ainsmith's sacrifice bunt, and then reached third on Steen's wild pitch. Proficient with the bludgeon, Johnson collected one of his 20 RBIs in 1912 by grounding through the box and into center field to give the Nationals, as the club was often called, a 4-2 lead.[9]

Johnson was "forcing himself to the finish line," wrote Grillo in the *Evening Star*.[10] With one out in the eighth, Ryan singled. Joe Birmingham followed with another single, but right fielder Danny Moeller made a remarkable play that the *Post* claimed "probably saved the game."[11] His long and accurate throw to Foster at third nailed Ryan for the second out. Birmingham was subsequently caught trying to swipe second to end the inning. A "combination of bad baserunning and inability to follow up cost the Naps," declared the *Post*.[12]

After Willie Mitchell tossed a one-two-three eighth in relief of Steen, a taxed Johnson took the mound in the ninth facing the heart of the Naps' order. Shoeless Joe led off with a single. Lajoie, who at age 37 was still a threat and batted .368 in '12, went for the win instead of sacrificing and popped up. Griggs's single brought the potential winning run to the plate with only one out. But the ever-cool Johnson retired both Olsen and Carisch on routine flies to Moeller to end the game in 1 hour and 50 minutes.

The Big Train recorded his AL-record-setting 15th consecutive victory and 28th of the season despite yielding 10 hits (his most since a 13-hit complete-game victory over the New York Yankees on May 28 in which he also fanned 10) in 8⅔ innings. He didn't walk a batter and fanned only three. Three days later he tossed a six-hitter to beat the Detroit Tigers, 8-1, for his 16th straight victory. The streak ended on August 26 when Johnson gave up two runs hurling the final 2⅔ innings of relief in a 4-3 loss to the lowly St. Louis Browns. He finished the season with a 33-12 slate and led the majors with a 1.39 ERA and 303 strikeouts.

Less than a month after Johnson's record-setting victory, the Boston Red Sox' Smoky Joe Wood equaled his mark with his 16th straight win. Wood ended the season with a big-league-most 34 victories for the eventual World Series champs.[13] As of 2020, Johnson and Wood still held the AL record for most consecutive victories, and were later joined by the Philadelphia Athletics' Lefty Grove (1931) and the Tigers' Schoolboy Rowe (1934).

The 1912 season was an extraordinary campaign for winning streaks by pitchers. Johnson and Wood fell short of the New York Giants' Rube Marquard, who began the season by winning his first 19 decisions, which as of 2020 was still the major-league record for most consecutive victories in one season. Carl Hubbell of the Giants holds the big-league record for most consecutive victories over multiple seasons, stringing together 24 in 1936-1937.

Davis sent Gregg back to the mound in the second game and had the matchup he wanted against his ace. Carl Cashion, a robust 6-foot-2, 200-pounder, was Griffith's choice. Praised by beat reporter Grillo as the "most promising pitcher on the staff" other than Johnson, the 23-year-old Cashion was in his first full season and had a 5-2 slate (6-7 career) as a swingman.[14] Beat writer Peet asserted that Cashion "would be one of the best in the world [if] he could only control the ball."[15] And for one abbreviated game, he could claim he was.

Gregg, who entered the game with a 14-10 slate en route to winning 20 games, came out "like a house afire," wrote the *Washington Times*.[16] He "had his south side slants working properly," noted Peet.[17] Through five innings, he fanned nine batters, including the side in the fifth; however, he struggled with control in one inning which, along with some shoddy defense, led to his demise.

The bottom of the second commenced innocuously with Gandil whiffing and Ray Morgan being thrown out trying to steal after he had coaxed a walk. Shanks drew another free pass and took a long lead, planning "delayed steal," wrote Peet.[18] Catcher Steve O'Neill rifled a bullet to rookie first baseman Doc Johnston, who had been acquired a week earlier from the New Orleans Pelicans in the Class A Southern Association and was making his first start at first. According to Grillo, Johnston "whirled around and touched the bag," anticipating that Shanks would slide back, but the speedy rookie was well on his way to second.[19] McBride walloped a missile to third, which "nearly knocked the underpinnings off Olson," reported Peet.[20] In an inexplicable move, Ivy Olson took left fielder Buddy Ryan's return throw and attempted to nab McBride at first, but threw the bill wildly past Johnson, enabling Shanks to saunter home for the game's first run while McBride advanced to second. The next batter, John Henry, playing in his first game since July 12 after injuring his left knee, doubled, driving in McBride.[21]

The Senators' two runs were more than enough for Cashion, who "never looked better," gushed the *Times*.[22] Errors by McBride at short gave the Naps one baserunner in each of the first two frames. Catcher Henry atoned for the first by erasing Birmingham on an attempted steal. With two outs in the second Olson hit a screecher to McBride, who according to Peet "got in front of the drive, had both hands on the ball, and fumbled" and had no play at first.[23] In what proved to be the only potentially tricky scoring decision of the game, Peet noted that all three official scorers ruled unanimously that the play was an error and not a hit. Cashion's "speed was terrific, his control good," said the *Times*.[24] The Carolina Curver (Peet's moniker for the North Carolinian[25]), walked only one batter, his mound opponent Gregg, in the third.

Rolling along, Cashion tossed his third straight one-two-three inning in the sixth, but didn't have a chance to finish the game. As reported by the *Cleveland Press*, the teams had agreed prior to the first game to conclude the second contest early so that the Naps could catch a train to Boston, where they had a game against the Red Sox the next afternoon.[26]

Cashion's abbreviated no-no lasted just 65 minutes. He fanned two and faced 20 batters. Over the final six weeks of the season, Cashion proved to be a durable hurler, completing seven of his eight starts; however, he was unable to harness his heaters and curves, walking 7, 8, and 10 batters in three of those distance-going affairs. He concluded the campaign with a 10-6 record and a 3.17 ERA, and completed 13 of 17 starts among his 26 appearances. He walked 103 in 170⅓ innings, which eventually spelled his doom. He made only four more starts for the Senators over the next two seasons, finishing his career with a 12-13 record and one shutout: his no-hitter.

The next truncated no-hitter in the majors was also by a Senators hurler and also took place in Griffith Stadium: Walter Johnson held the St. Louis Browns hitless through seven innings in the rain-shortened first game of a scheduled doubleheader on August 25, 1924. Griffith Stadium witnessed only one regulation no-hitter in its 51-year history (1911-1961) and it came from an unlikely hurler. Swingman Bobby Burke, who made only 88 starts in his 10-year career, defeated the Boston Red Sox, 5-0, on August 8, 1931.

In 1991 Major League Baseball's Committee for Statistical Accuracy changed the definition of a no-hitter, defining it as a regulation complete game of at least nine innings.[27] This definition eliminated 36 shortened no-hitters from the record books, among them Cashion's and Johnson's in Griffith Stadium.

SOURCES

In addition to the sources cited in the Notes, the author accessed Retrosheet.org, Baseball-Reference.com, SABR.org, and *The Sporting News* archive via Paper of Record.

NOTES

1 J. Ed. Grillo, "Griffith's Team Is on Another Winning Streak," (Washington) *Evening Star*, August 21, 1912: 10.

2 Joe S. Jackson, "Johnson Sets New League Record; No-Hit Game Is Pitched by Cashion," *Washington Post*, August 21, 1912: 8.

3 Jackson.

4 Senator, "Johnson and Cashion Make Records at National Park," *Washington Times*, August 21, 1912: 10.

5 Jackson.

6 William Peet, "Johnson Wins Fifteenth; Cashion Allows No Hits," *Washington Herald*, August 21, 1912: 6.

7 Jackson.

8 Jackson.

9 Johnson collected 547 hits and batted .235 in his career. He knocked in a career-best 20 runs twice: in 1912 and 1925.

10 Grillo.

11 Grillo.

12 Jackson.

13 Both pitchers were remarkable during their record-braking streaks, though Johnson might have been slightly better. He made 19 appearances (12 starts, 7 relief outings), logged 130 $^{2}/_{3}$ innings, yielding 87 hits (.186 batting average), fanned 109, and walked 20. Smoky Joe also made 19 appearances, including 16 starts, logged 145 $^{2}/_{3}$ innings, held opponents to a .219 batting average (114 hits), fanned 122, and walked 30.

14 Grillo

15 Peet.

16 *Washington Times.*

17 Peet

18 Peet.

19 Grillo.

20 Peet.

21 Peet.

22 *Washington Times.*

23 Peet.

24 *Washington Times.*

25 *Washington Times.*

26 "Johnson Makes New Record; Naps Tie Old Losing Mark," *Cleveland Press*, August 21, 1912: 10.

27 "Close, but No Cigar," Nonohitters.com (nonohitters.com/near-no-hitters/).

THE BIG TRAIN SPINS SHUTOUT FOR 30TH WIN OF SEASON

SEPTEMBER 5, 1913
WASHINGTON SENATORS 1, NEW YORK YANKEES 0
(SECOND GAME OF DOUBLEHEADER)

by Gregory H. Wolf

"To encounter Walter Johnson even one time during a series is considered misfortune for any ball club," lamented the *New York Times*, "but to inflict him on an opposing ball club twice in the same afternoon verges on downright cruelty."[1] The Big Train, the Washington Senators' hard-throwing right-hander, proved to be the hero of the team's doubleheader sweep of the New York Yankees, extinguishing a fire in the ninth inning of the first game and then tossing a shutout for his 30th victory of the season in the second contest.

The Senators owner-manager Clark Griffith needed a more than miracle for his third-place club (70-56) to have a chance to catch the Philadelphia Athletics, whom Washington trailed by 13 games with a month to play in the season. The Nationals, as sportswriters often called them, had been plodding along since July 31 and had lost 16 of their last 31 games, including the first game of a five-game set against the last-place Yankees (44-80) to kick off a 20-game homestand.

If the Senators had any chance for the AL flag, they'd need Walter Johnson to lead them. The 25-year-old side-armer laid claim the previous season as the best twirler in the sport, winning 33 games (one behind Smoky Joe Wood of the Boston Red Sox) and leading the majors with a 1.39 ERA and 303 strikeouts, the second time in three seasons that he surpassed the 300 mark. In 1913 the "Big Scythe," as the *Washington Times* called him, was on a rampage.[2] He began the day with a 29-7 slate, which pushed his career record to 144-97, and he had something to prove. In his last start, four days earlier at Shibe Park in the City of Brotherly Love, he uncharacteristically struggled, yielding a season-high six runs in a complete-game, walk-off loss in the 10th, his second consecutive defeat after 14 straight winning decisions.

On an unseasonably warm Friday afternoon, with temperatures in the mid- to upper 80s, an estimated 4,500 spectators had gathered for an afternoon of the national pastime at National Park, the Senators' two-year-old steel-and concrete playing field. (It was renamed Griffith Stadium in 1920.) Scheduled to start the second game of the twin bill, Johnson was required to make an emergency appearance in the opener. Senators starter Joe Boehling cruised through eight innings and began the ninth with a 3-0 lead, then fell apart, surrendering two runs and loading the bases with no outs. In came Johnson, who defused the situation on four pitches. Pinch-hitter Ray Caldwell hit a fly to deep left field, which Joe Gedeon caught, then hurled a "remarkable throw," gushed sportswriter J. Ed. Grillo of the *Evening Star*, to catcher Eddie Ainsmith, who tagged out the sliding Frank Gilhooley for a crushing twin killing. Johnson fanned Fritz Maisel on three pitches to end the game.

Sufficiently warmed up after his first-game heroics, Johnson took the mound in the second game in search of his 30th victory. "Unlike most managers in the Ban Johnson circuit," suggested the *Washington Herald*, "[Yankees] skipper Frank Chance refused to put in a dub pitcher against the Nationals with Walter Johnson on the job and ordered Russell Ford to go to work."[3] The 30-year-old right-handed spitballer burst on the scene in 1910, winning 26 games as a rookie; so far in 1913, he sported a 12-13 slate and a 73-51 lifetime record.

"The Chancemen simply walked to the plate," gushed sportswriter William Peet of the *Washington Herald*, "sniffed at Walter's smoke, and trekked back to the bench."[4] The Big Train was dominant, as he had been in almost every game that season. He faced just 29 batters, yielding three hits and a walk, and only one batter reached second. In the first he issued a free pass to Harry Wolter, who was caught stealing; three innings later Wolter reached on a single and was gunned down again by Ainsmith attempting to swipe second. The two other hits were by, of all batters, the pitcher. Ford, who collected 32 hits in '12, led off the third with a single and swiped second, and singled again in the ninth. Johnson fanned eight, including Birdie Cree three times, and was never in trouble. Newspapers also praised the Senators fielders. "The Nationals gave a splendid demonstration of their defensive strengths," opined J. Ed. Grillo of the *Evening Star*,[5] while the *Times* added that "senatorial speed marveled during the game."[6]

Despite Johnson's dominance and his fielders' brilliance, the game unfolded as an unlikely pitching duel. An average offensive team, finishing fifth in the league in runs scored, averaging 3.8 runs per game, the Senators were perplexed by Ford's wet ones. Through eight frames, the Senators had a man in scoring position only twice. In the second Frank LaPorte singled over short and stole second, but Ford punched out Ainsmith and George McBride. Johnson singled with one out in the sixth and moved to third on a groundout and passed ball, but was left stranded when Clyde Milan grounded out. Ainsmith led off the eighth with a single, but was caught stealing.

The Yankees "never had a chance" against Johnson, the *New York Times* sadly recounted.[7] Nonetheless Ford was in "fine fettle," noted the *Washington Times*, yielding only five hits and walking one through eight innings;[8] while the *Herald* suggested that the game "would have gone into extra innings" or would have been "terminated by darkness" if not for an inopportune defensive miscue by the visitors that gave the Senators the victory.[9]

Ford dispatched the Big Train on a popup to third to begin the ninth. Danny Moeller followed with a single, which newspapers in the nation's capital and New York considered only the Nationals' second hard-hit ball of the game. After Moeller swiped second, Milan hit a routine grounder to second baseman Roy Hartzell. The eight-year veteran fumbled the ball (no error was charged) and Moeller reached third. Eddie Foster followed with what would have been the final out of the game, a fly to left fielder Cree. Moeller scored easily to tally the only run of the game and give the Senators a dramatic 1-0 victory in 1 hour and 45 minutes.

The Big Train's 30th victory was also his 10th shutout of the season and commenced an awe-inspiring stretch to end what was surely his best season and one of the best by any hurler in baseball history. Including both games on September 5, Johnson closed out the season by winning seven straight decisions and posting a 0.62 ERA in 57⅔ innings before an ill-fated relief outing in the season's last game. He captured the Triple Crown of pitching, leading the majors with 36 wins, a 1.14 ERA, and 243 strikeouts. He also led the big leagues with 29 complete games, 11 shutouts, and 346 innings pitched.

SOURCES

In addition to the sources cited in the Notes, the author accessed Retrosheet.org, Baseball-Reference.com, SABR.org, and *The Sporting News* archive via Paper of Record.

NOTES

1 "Johnson Saves One Game, Wins Another," *New York Times*, September 5, 1913: 8.

2 "Johnson Is Star of Close Battle," *Washington Times*, September 6, 1913: 14.

3 William Peet, "Nationals Won Both Ends of Double Bill from Yankees," *Washington Herald*, September 6, 1913: 10.

4 Peet.

5 J. Ed. Grillo, "Johnson Saves Boehling's Game, Then Wins His Own," *Evening Star* (Washington), September 6, 1913: 6.

6 "Johnson Save One Game, Wins Another."

7 "Johnson Save One Game, Wins Another."

8 "Johnson Is Star of Close Battle."

9 Peet.

WALTER JOHNSON TOSSES 11TH SHUTOUT FOR 36TH VICTORY

SEPTEMBER 28, 1913
WASHINGTON SENATORS 1, PHILADELPHIA ATHLETICS 0

by Gregory H. Wolf

Walter Johnson was on a roll of historic proportions as he prepared for his final start of the season. Beginning with his three-hit shutout against the New York Yankees in the second game of a doubleheader on September 5 for his 30th victory of the season, the Washington Senators hurler had yielded only two earned runs in his last 47⅔ innings, and won all six decisions. His 36th victory seemed a foregone conclusion when Connie Mack, owner-manager of the Philadelphia Athletics, trotted out a "kindergarten brood," noted the *Philadelphia Inquirer*, instead of his regulars.[1] Perhaps taking the group of ragtag green recruits for granted, the Big Train "did not exert himself," opined Washington sportswriter J. Ed. Grillo in the *Evening Star*. "He loafed most of the day, and did not use a single curve ball." Nonetheless Johnson was no ordinary pitcher and "hitting and scoring on him are two entirely different propositions," continued the scribe.[2]

The second-place Senators (85-63) had no chance to catch the front-running A's (95-52) in the final six games of their last homestand of the season. A Monday afternoon affair at National Park, the club's two-year-old steel-and-concrete ballpark, drew a robust crowd of 15,000 spectators, with boys under 12 admitted free, to celebrate George McBride Day.[3] (National Park was renamed Griffith Stadium to begin the 1920 season.) The captain of the club, McBride was widely considered the AL's best fielding shortstop, a position he had held down for the Senators since 1908, his first season with the team. In a pregame ceremony at home plate, McBride was presented a diamond-studded watch fob from fans and US Vice President Thomas Marshall gave a short speech praising the hard-nosed, scrappy player. Described as McBride's closest friend on the team, Johnson requested to pitch this game. Baseball's most dominant pitcher, the 25-year-old sidewinder entered the game leading the major leagues with 35 wins, 10 shutouts, and a 1.12 ERA.

With the A's third pennant in four years wrapped up, the Tall Tactician gave his starters the day off against Johnson's heater. The club's vaunted "$100,000 Infield" (Stuffy McInnis, Eddie Collins,

Jack Barry, and Home Run Baker) were replaced by little-used rookie Billy Orr and three players making their big-league debut, Press Cruthers, Monte Pfeffer, and Harry Fritz.

The game commenced in "emphatic manner," gushed D.C. sportswriter William Peet, when Tom Daly led off with a single and moved to third on Jimmy Walsh's single.[4] Fritz's grounder put Walsh in scoring position before the Big Train buckled down, fanning Cruthers and retiring George Brickley on an infield popup. In the next frame, Orr "hammered a hot one through Johnson's glove" with one out, noted the Washington Times, but Johnson recovered and punched out the next two batters.[5]

"Either Connie Mack has gathered about him a most promising bunch of youngsters," suggested the *Washington Herald*, or the "team produced a feeling bordering on stage fright."[6] At no time was that more evident than in the fourth. Still looking shaky, Johnson served up a "slow ball," which Brickley clubbed over the head of 17-year-old Cuban-born left fielder Merito Acosta, making his first big-league start, and scampered to third with a one-out triple.[7] In a rare bout of wildness, the Big Train loaded the bases by grazing the sleeve of Pfeffer's uniform with a pitch and then walking Orr. Another player making his major-league debut, Wickey McAvoy, grounded to McBride, who initiated a 6-4-3 inning-ending twin killing. Johnson must have decided he was done toying around after his second rough inning and held the A's' newbies hitless over the last 5⅔ innings. Sportswriter Stanley Milliken of the *Washington Post* noted that Nationals second baseman Ray Morgan "pulled the feature of the afternoon," robbing Pfeffer of a hit by snaring his screeching liner in the sixth.[8]

Johnson's uninspired pitching early in the game might not have been newsworthy had the Senators managed any semblance of offense against rookie Weldon Wyckoff (2-2, 5.10 ERA). The 22-year-old right-hander was coming off a bizarre complete-game victory, 10-9, over the Boston Red Sox at Fenway Park five days earlier, despite yielding 24 baserunners on 12 walks, 11 hits, and a hit batter. In this game, however, Wykoff did his best Big Train impersonation and held the Senators hitless for 5⅓ innings until McBride connected squarely for a single that left fielder Walsh misplayed, allowing the ball to go through his legs while the captain reached second.

Walsh's miscue was symptomatic for the A's fielding woes, including five errors, all afternoon in a game that Wyckoff deserved to win. Two innings earlier, an errant throw by Fritz and a flubbed grounder by Pfeffer put runners on first and third with two outs, but both were left stranded.

"In thrills the game was lacking in many respects and at times dragged considerably," lamented the Post.[9] Thankfully for the *Post*, the game was completed in a swift 1 hour and 25 minutes, with the sole run scored in a sloppy seventh. Chick Gandil led off with a single, the second hit Wyckoff surrendered, and then raced to third when Morgan beat out a slow roller to third base that Fritz probably did not charge. Rip Williams, making just his fifth start of the season as a catcher, hit a tailor-made double-play grounder to Pfeffer at short; however, keystone sacker Cruthers' relay throw to first baseman Orr was high and pulled him off the bag as Gandil crossed the plate. Poor baserunning by the Griffithmen led to the next two outs: Williams was picked off first and Acosta was caught stealing after drawing a walk.

Washington's 1-0 victory improved Johnson's record to 36-7 and lowered his ERA to 1.09. The Big Train had a disastrous relief appearance in the season's last game and was charged with two earned runs without retiring a batter, pushing his ERA to 1.14. It was by all accounts one of the greatest seasons by a pitcher in baseball history. Johnson led the majors in wins, complete games (29), shutouts (11), innings (346), strikeouts (243), and ERA. Johnson was awarded the third annual Chalmers Award, bestowed by baseball writers as an MVP-type award, which was discontinued after the next season.

Connie Mack placed little value on the outcome of this game, nor the next two against the Senators, both shutout losses, while he rested his starters so that they could be fresh for the World Series. His strategy paid off: The A's defeated the New York Giants in five games for their third championship in four seasons.

SOURCES

In addition to the sources cited in the Notes, the author accessed Retrosheet.org, Baseball-Reference.com, SABR.org, and *The Sporting News* archive via Paper of Record.

NOTES

1 "Johnson Had No Cinch Winning," *Philadelphia Inquirer*, September 30, 1913: 12.

2 J. Ed. Grillo, "Doc Ayres to Face Mack's Rookies in Game Today," *Evening Star* (Washington), September 30, 1913: 16.

3 "Johnson Is to Pitch in 'McBride Day' Game," *Washington Post*, September 9, 1913: 5.

4 William Peet, "Connie Mack's Recruits Bow to Walter Johnson," *Washington Herald*, September 30, 1913: 10.

5 "Mack's Uniforms Played Fine Ball," *Washington Times*, September 30, 1913: 12.

6 "Mack's Uniforms Played Fine Ball."

7 "Mack's Uniforms Played Fine Ball."

8 Stanley Milliken, "Nationals Defeat Athletic Youngsters 1 to 0 - Ayres to Pitch Today," *Washington Post*, September 30, 1913: 8.

9 Milliken.

JIM SCOTT TOSSES NO-HITTER THROUGH NINE, LOSES IN TENTH

MAY 14, 1914
WASHINGTON SENATORS 1, CHICAGO WHITE SOX 0

by Derek Blair

The year 1914 is defined by the beginning of World War I as well as the completion of the Panama Canal. It was also the third year that Griffith Stadium had been open, and on May 14, 1914, the stadium was host to one of the most amazing games in the history of baseball. The Washington Senators, led by Clark Griffith, played host to the Chicago White Sox, who were managed by Jimmy Callahan. It's no surprise that a game between these two teams finished with such a low score. In that season both the Senators and White Sox had excellent pitching staffs. Chicago had the fourth-best team ERA of the 24 big-league teams (including the eight in the inaugural season of the Federal League) and the Senators were just one spot behind them. A lot of the Senators' pitching success was due to Walter Johnson. He earned his nickname, the Big Train, for being one of the most dominating pitchers of his era, earning two MVP awards as well as the ERA title in five seasons. In 1936 he was a part of the inaugural class of inductees into the Hall of Fame.

However, on May 14, 1914, the fans at Griffith Stadium were treated to a pair of stellar pitching performances not from Johnson, but from the opposing moundsmen. The starting pitcher for the visiting Chicago White Sox, Jim Scott. Scott pitched a no-hitter for nine innings, but gave up two hits in the 10th and lost the game, 1-0. Scott, who grew up in Wyoming and acquired the nickname Death Valley Jim, was a hard-luck pitcher. Each year of his major-league career he posted an ERA well under 3.00, and at 2.30 is ranked 19th all-time in lowest career ERA, but he had a winning record in only two of his nine seasons in the big leagues and finished with a 107-114 slate. Scott's major-league career ended when he enlisted in the military to fight in World War I after the 1917 season.[1] Scott had an astonishing career but somehow never received any form of recognition for his performance. After returning from the war, Scott had a nine-year career in the minors, winning 125 games, but with markedly higher ERAs.

The Senators starter, Doc Ayers, didn't disappoint either that day, giving up just three hits in 10 innings pitched. Ayers, who picked up his nickname because he had been a medical student in Virginia, won 64 games and lost 78 in a nine-season career with the Senators and the Detroit Tigers, and had a career ERA of 2.84.

The *Washington Post* wrote of the Scott-Ayers pitching duel, "There has never been a greater ball game staged in this city."[2]

After pitching nine brilliant innings, Scott had a disastrous 10th. He surrendered a leadoff single to Chick Gandil. Then on a 1-and-2 count, Howie Shanks smacked a ball into right field where Ray Demmitt made a diving attempt, only to miss the ball. Gandil scored and the game was over. Sportswriter Stanley Milliken of the *Washington Post* described Shanks's hit as "like a thunderbolt out of clear sky."[3] The game had changed so quickly. Scott went from not allowing a hit for nine innings to surrendering two hits that dealt him the loss. It was a marvelous performance, but an unfortunate ending. The *Chicago Livestock World* described Scott's experience as "only to be robbed of the fame and the feel of victory because the White Sox could not make one little run for him out of several good chances."[4]

As for Ayers, he gave up a two-out triple in the first inning to first baseman Hal Chase, but then retired the side. In the second inning Chicago's Ping Bodie led off with a single and Scotty Alcock reached on an error by Senators second baseman Ray Morgan. Ayers escaped the jam by getting a double-play ball. After that no one reached base until the sixth inning when Demmitt hit the ball to center field. The *Post's* Milliken wrote, "Then came one of the best plays of the contest. [Clyde] Milan sprinted toward the scoreboard in right-center and picked up Demmitt's drive with one hand. The runner tried to go to second but his life was snuffed out."[5]

In the White Sox' 10th, Senators third baseman Eddie Foster made a wild throw on a ball hit by Ping Bodie. Ayers walked the next batter, Alcock (the only walk he gave up). But Ayers escaped a jam yet again, and Scott was undone in the bottom of the inning.

Each pitcher struck out two batters. Scott walked two Senators; Ayers walked one. Milliken noted that the game "was replete with sensational plays not only in the infield but the outfield as well."[6]

This game was the highlight, so to speak for both teams, in their 1914 season. The White Sox (70-84) ended up in seventh place while the Senators (81-73) took third place, though 19 games behind the Philadelphia Athletics. Washington's bright spots were 28-game winner Johnson and Foster, who finished seventh in MVP voting. This game is one to be remembered as one of the greatest pitching duels ever to be hosted at Griffith Stadium.

SOURCES

In addition to the sources cited in the Notes, the author accessed Retrosheet.org, Baseball-Reference.com, SABR.org, and *The Sporting News* archive via Paper of Record.

NOTES

1 Stanley Milliken, "Nationals Lone Two Hits in Tenth Bring Victory Over White Sox, 1-0," *Washington Post*, May 15, 1914.

2 Milliken.

3 Milliken.

4 *Chicago Live Stock World*, May 15, 1914.

5 Milliken.

6 Milliken.

RIP WILLIAMS DELIVERS CAREER PERFORMANCE DURING SENATORS' SLUGFEST

SEPTEMBER 29, 1915
WASHINGTON SENATORS 20, PHILADELPHIA ATHLETICS 5
(SECOND GAME OF DOUBLEHEADER)

by Gordon Gattie

As October 1915 approached in the nation's capital, 20,000 Civil War veterans were marching through Washington city streets as veterans and residents alike reflected upon events from 50 years earlier.[1] Across the city, the Washington Senators and Philadelphia Athletics were nearly finished with their disappointing 1915 seasons. The fourth-place Senators (81-65) were 18½ games behind the eventual pennant-winning Boston Red Sox with one week remaining. Washington had finished third in the American League the previous season, and second in 1912 and 1913. The Senators finished the 1915 season strong; but though they earned a 21-9 September record, they never overcame their rough May and early July swoon.[2]

Washington's best player was future Hall of Famer Walter Johnson, now finishing his ninth season. The veteran staff ace led the AL in wins, innings pitched, strikeouts, and shutouts the previous two seasons. He was complemented by pitchers Bert Gallia and Doc Ayers, third baseman Eddie Foster, and outfielder Clyde Milan. When the season opened, Clark Griffith, Washington's manager, planned on returning his entire infield: first baseman Chick Gandil, second baseman Ray Morgan, shortstop George McBride, and Foster; however, concerns existed about their low offensive production.[3] The 1916 Reach Guide labeled the 1915 Washington squad as the "chief disappointment of the season" based on its slow start, lackluster pitching, and little offensive prowess from the Senators' outfield.[4]

By comparison, Philadelphia was faring even worse. From 1909 through 1914 the Athletics won three World Series titles and at least 90 games each season. Though Philadelphia won the pennant by 8½ games over the Red Sox in 1914, the Athletics were swept by the Boston "Miracle Braves" during the 1914 World Series. The famed "$100,000 Infield," which consisted of Hall of Famers second baseman Eddie Collins and third baseman Frank "Home Run" Baker, perennial Chalmers Award vote-getter first baseman Stuffy McInnis, and stalwart veteran shortstop Jack Berry,[5] and identified as the top infield in baseball history, according to Bill James's Win Shares methodology,[6] played together

Deadball Era style: Clark Griffith managing the Senators 1915. In a baseball career that spanned 70 years, the Old Fox won 237 big-league games as a pitcher, managed for 20 seasons, including the Senators for nine years (1912-1920), became the largest stockholder in the club in 1911, and owned the Nats until his death in 1955. (Photo by Bettmann/Getty Images)

from 1911 to 1914 while forming the nucleus of Philadelphia's championship teams. After the 1914 season, part-owner and manager Connie Mack disassembled his first Athletics dynasty,[7] including the $100,000 Infield. Though Mack retained McInnis another three seasons, he sold 1914 Chalmers Award winner Collins to the Chicago White Sox in December and Barry to the Red Sox the following summer; Baker was sold to the Yankees in February 1916. Mack also gutted his pitching staff, releasing Hall of Fame hurlers Chief Bender and Eddie Plank. Mounting financial pressures, combined with the threat of players jumping to the Federal League, had forced Mack to dismantle his ballclub.[8] Expectations were extremely low for the 1915 season,[9] and the Athletics were solidly occupying the cellar by July. Philadelphia had compiled a dreadful 4-25 September record entering the doubleheader.

Earlier that afternoon, the Nationals[10] defeated the Athletics 10-2 in the first game. Philadelphia scored first when Amos Strunk and Rube Oldring came home on Napoleon Lajoie's two-run double. Washington responded with three first-inning runs and scored seven unanswered runs to easily defeat the Mackmen. Washington right fielder Turner Barber enjoyed a career day, scoring three runs and delivering five hits in six plate appearances.[11]

For the nightcap, Griffith tapped Bert Gallia for the start. Gallia was concluding his first full year with Washington and was arguably the staff's second-best starter behind Johnson. He compiled a 16-11 record and 2.39 ERA over 248⅔ innings. Gallia expected to join the rotation as a backline starter, though during spring training one writer noted, "Gallia, the former 'firecracker,' seems to have developed into a 42-centimeter Krupp cannon now."[12]

Rookie Tom Sheehan started for Philadelphia. The 21-year-old joined the Athletics in July, debuting against Chicago by pitching three scoreless innings.[13] Sheehan had initially faced Washington three weeks earlier and allowed five runs on 11 hits in a complete-game loss. The Senators had quickly jumped on Sheehan, scoring one run each in the first and second innings.[14] Since his Washington outing, Sheehan had shut out Boston but lost his next two starts. Still, one writer noted that Sheehan was "probably the most promising of Mack's young twirlers."[15]

Gallia walked Philadelphia leadoff hitter Wally Schang to start the second game. Schang stole second base and scored the game's first run when Washington center fielder Clyde Milan's throw to the plate sailed over catcher Rip Williams's head. The Senators evened the score in the bottom half when Foster and Milan singled, rookie Joe Judge – playing in just the sixth game of a 20-year, 2,171-game career – walked to load the bases, and Barber's sacrifice fly scored Foster. In the next inning the Senators inched ahead when Williams tripled and Tom Connolly singled, providing Washington with the lead it never relinquished. Neither team scored in the third inning so Philadelphia led 2-1 after three innings.

Gallia maintained his effectiveness during the middle innings, but Sheehan was ineffective and didn't receive the same defensive support. In the fourth the Senators extended their lead when two doubles, Foster's triple, a single, and a sacrifice fly, plus some poor fielding by the Athletics gave the Senators five runs and increased their lead to 7-1. The Senators' fifth was scoreless as Washington runners took a quick breather from the basepaths.

In the sixth inning a mixture of three singles, a double, a walk, and multiple errors resulted in Washington's second five-run inning. Their third came in the next inning on four singles, a double, and errors, making the score a laughable 17-1.

After the errant throw that gave Philadelphia the initial lead, the Athletics were scoreless until they rallied for four eighth-inning runs. While one Washington sportswriter suggested that the four runs were due to Washington errors,[16] another observed that that Washington "took advantage of everything until late in the second encounter, when 'Bert' Gallia started to toss them over to stir up a little enthusiasm. As a result, the visitors were handed four runs."[17] Philadelphia scored those four runs on a walk, two errors, and two hits, and the score was a slightly more respectable 17-5.

The Nationals scored their final three runs in the eighth inning on two walks, two hits, and an error. Mercifully blanking Philadelphia in the ninth and ending the slugfest, Washington won 20-5. Gallia pitched the complete game, allowing only five hits; all five Philadelphia runs were unearned.

Although the Senators scored 20 runs, only 12 were earned.[18] One sportswriter commented, "[Mack's fielders] ... played in a half-hearted manner typical of a team that is hopelessly last, with nothing to gain in battle. They ran circles around fly balls, stepped on their own feet in going after grounders, and never exerted themselves on the base paths."[19] Washington's 20 runs and 23 hits represented the highest offensive output in the major leagues that season, topping the 20 runs and 22 hits set by the Boston Braves when they walloped the St. Louis Cardinals 20-1 on September 18.[20] Washington's team record for 20 runs scored in a single game lasted until August 5, 1929, when the Senators defeated the Detroit Tigers 21-5 at Griffith Stadium. Joe Judge, the only Senator who played in both the 1915 and 1929 slugfests, hit in the leadoff spot in the latter game and went 1-for-2 with two runs, two RBIs, and two sacrifice hits.

Rip Williams recorded a career-high four runs and five consecutive hits in six plate appearances, including a triple and double; he popped out to the catcher for his lone recorded out.[21] Light-hitting Washington rookie leadoff hitter Charlie Jamieson, who was hitting a miserable .143 entering the game, went 3-for-5 and scored three times. Jamieson hit safely over the next five games, raising his average to .288 entering the season's final game. Washington shortstop Tom Connolly, who played only one major-league season, also enjoyed the finest offensive day of his career, 3-for-5 with a double and two stolen bases.

Adding salt to the Athletics' wounds was the success of the crosstown Philadelphia Phillies. The same day the Athletics dropped the doubleheader by a combined 30-7 score, the Phillies defeated the 1914 World Series champion Braves 5-0 to capture the NL flag.[22] Pete Alexander fired a one-hitter, striking out four batters and walking one, to earn his 31st victory in dramatic fashion. Phillies manager Pat Moran, in his rookie managerial season, was supported by nearly 3,000 friends in attendance from his nearby hometown of Fitchburg, Massachusetts.[23] The Phillies had moved into first place on July 13 and held off the surging Braves with a 21-10 September.

Washington finished fourth with an 85-68 record, 39 games behind pennant-winning Boston and 7½ games behind third-place Chicago. Gallia finished 17-11 with a 2.29 ERA in 259⅔ innings pitched and remained with the ballclub for another two seasons. The 34-year-old Williams was Washington's backup catcher another season, joining the International League's Baltimore Orioles and ending his career in 1918 with the Cleveland Indians.

SOURCES

Besides the sources cited in the Notes, the author consulted Baseball-Reference.com, Retrosheet.org, Baseball-Almanac.com, and the following books:

James, Bill. *The Bill James Guide to Baseball Managers from 1870 to Today* (New York: Scribner, 1997).

James, Bill, and Jim Henzler. *Win Shares* (Morton Grove, Illinois: STATS, Inc., 2002).

Macht, Norman. *Connie Mack and the Early Years of Baseball* (Lincoln: University of Nebraska Press, 2007).

Mack, Connie. *My 66 Years in the Big Leagues* (Philadelphia: John C. Winston Company, 1950).

Neyer, Rob, and Eddie Epstein. *Baseball Dynasties: The Greatest Teams of All Time* (New York: W.W. Horton & Company, 2000).

Thorn, John, and Pete Palmer, et al. *Total Baseball: The Official Encyclopedia of Major League Baseball* (New York: Viking Press, 2004).

NOTES

1 "Twenty Thousand Veterans, Remnants of Grant's Victorious Army, Retread Triumphal Way of Half Century Ago, in Review Before President Wilson," *Washington Post*, September 30, 1915: 1.

2 *A.G. Spalding & Bros. Spalding's Official Base Ball Guide* (Chicago: A.G. Spalding & Bros., 1915), 161. Accessed at loc.gov/item/spalding.00159/.

3 Louis Dougher, "Dougher Grows in Dubiousness Daily," *The Sporting News*, April 15, 1915: 3.

4 B.B. Johnson, "American League's 1915 Race," In Francis C. Richter, ed., *The Reach Official American League Base Ball Guide 1916*. (Philadelphia: A.J. Reach Company, 1916), 63.

5 Leonard Koppett, *The Man in the Dugout: Baseball's Top Managers and How They Got That Way* (New York: Crown Publishers, 1993), 68-83.

6 Bill James, *The New Bill James Historical Baseball Abstract* (New York: Simon & Schuster, 2001), 548-553.

7 Lew Freedman, *Connie Mack's First Dynasty: The Philadelphia Athletics, 1910-1914* (Jefferson, North Carolina: McFarland & Company), 170-195. Jack Barry benefited from joining another World Series champion with Boston in 1915, his fourth championship team in six years.

8 Bryan Soderholm-Difatte, "Connie Mack's Second Great Athletics Team: Eclipsed by the Ruth-Gehrig Yankees, but Even Better," in Morris Levin, ed., *The National Pastime: From Swampoodle to South Philly*, SABR, 2013; Connie Mack, "'I Broke Up the Athletics to Prevent Baseball Ruin,' Declares Connie Mack," *Philadelphia Evening Ledger*, July 5, 1915: 1.

9 Weart, William, "Eve of Season Finds Unusual Base Ball Situation in Philly," *The Sporting News*, April 15, 1915: 1.

10 *Washington Nationals 2018 Official Media Guide* (Washington: Washington Nationals Baseball Club, 2018), 260-261. The Washington team was known as both the Senators and Nationals from 1905 to 1955. When Washington joined the AL at its inception in 1901, the team was named the Senators. In 1905 the nickname was changed to the Nationals. In 1956 the nickname reverted to the Senators. However, from 1905 through 1955 Senators and Nationals were used interchangeably by fans and sportswriters.

11 William Peet, "Mackmen Badly Beaten; Nationals Sting the Ball," *Washington Herald*, September 30, 1915: 8. A discrepancy exists as to whether Barber hit one or two doubles in the first game of the doubleheader. The game account in the September 30 editions of the *Washington Post* and the *Washington Herald* differ; the *Post* reported one double for Barber while the *Herald* listed two doubles in its box score and game description. Retrosheet and Baseball-Reference credit Barber with one double.

12 Louis A. Dougher, "Rondeau and Hopper Are Promising Looking Lads," *Washington Times*, March 10, 1915: 8.

13 "Athletics Stall but Lose Again," *Camden* (New Jersey) *Courier-Post*, July 15, 1915: 8.

14 Jim Nasium, "Macks Drop Two Without a Murmur," *Philadelphia Inquirer*, September 7, 1915: 13.

15 Stanley T. Milliken, "Pair of Farcical Games to Nationals," *Washington Post*, September 30, 1915: 8.

16 Peet.

17 Milliken.

18 A discrepancy exists regarding the number of errors committed by Philadelphia in the game. The box score in the *Evening Star* reported the Athletics were charged with 10 errors, the *Washington Herald* noted eight errors, and the *Washington Post* stated seven errors. Today's box scores listed on Retrosheet and Baseball-Reference show eight errors on their box scores. The number of Washington hits fluctuates by slightly different numbers.

19 Milliken.

20 W.J. O'Connor, "Bescher Lands on Pitcher Rudolph; Cards Lose Twice," *St. Louis Post-Dispatch*, September 19, 1915: 31.

21 J. Ed. Grillo, "Dumont and Johnson Listed to Face the Red Sox Here," *Washington Evening Star*, September 30, 1915: 22.

22 "Phillies, Beating Braves, Capture National's Flag," *Philadelphia Inquirer*, September 30, 1915: 1.

23 J.C. O'Leary, "Phils Win Pennant," *Boston Globe*, September 30, 1915: 1.

TRENCH WARFARE, DEADBALL STYLE: RED SOX AND SENATORS SLOG TO EXTRA-INNING TIE

SEPTEMBER 12, 1917
BOSTON RED SOX 1, WASHINGTON SENATORS 1 (16 INNINGS)

by Mark S. Sternman

Having won the World Series in both 1915 and 1916, the Boston Red Sox, chasing the idle first-place White Sox, needed to beat Washington to salvage a series split against the mediocre Senators. The game took place in front of only 928 fans in "wartime Washington... an apathetic baseball town"[1] despite a compelling matchup on paper between the two pitchers of record from a memorable game that had occurred only a few months earlier in the 1917 campaign. The reality of a tightly-matched pitching duel greatly exceeded any reasonable expectations.

On June 23 Babe Ruth had started in Boston against the visiting Senators. "After walking the leadoff man, second baseman Ray Morgan, Ruth began jawing with the umpire, Brick Owens."[2] The arbiter ejected Ruth, and Ernie Shore came on in relief. Morgan went out stealing second; Shore retired the next 26 Senators in a 4-0 win over Washington. Doc Ayers took the loss.

More than a century later, Shore's legacy faintly persists due to his connections to Ruth (Shore had also come to the Red Sox in the same transaction in which Boston had secured Ruth from Baltimore of the International League). In 1917, his last of four straight stellar seasons as a stalwart in the Red Sox rotation, Shore would finish with a 13-10 record and a 2.22 ERA. Relying nearly exclusively on a natural sinker and mixing in a few changeups and curveballs, Shore long after his career blamed overwork in the 1917 season for a shoulder injury that essentially ended the effective part of his career.[3]

But even hard-core baseball fans have likely never heard of Ayers in spite of his distinguishing characteristic. According to his SABR biographer, "Among the 17 spitball pitchers exempted when the pitch was banned, Doc Ayers was unique. He was the only one who hurled with an underhand motion."[4]

Only six pitchers started games for Washington in 1917. Walter Johnson led the way with 34, and Ayers brought up the rear with just 15. Besides Johnson, the team featured one other Hall of Famer in the prime of his career, the 27-year-old Sam Rice. For each team, baseball-reference.com ranks players by the retroactively calculated Wins

Above Replacement, often abbreviated as WAR. Surprisingly, sixth starter Doc Ayers ranks second in WAR at 4.0 for the 1917 Senators, far behind the sublime Johnson (8.0) but a bit ahead of the much more renowned Rice (3.7).

Ayers would have a sparkling 2.17 ERA in 1917 yet finish with a record of only 11-10. He had a better ERA but a worse winning percentage than Shore because Washington provided its spitballer with insufficient support at the plate and in the field. On August 26, just a few weeks before his re-engagement with Shore, Ayers yielded only one earned run but dropped a 2-1 decision in a game captured by Jim Bagby of Cleveland. According to *The Sporting News*, "Ayers outpitched Bagby ... but lost, because Bagby got faultless support, while two errors of commission and one of omission gave Cleveland its two runs."[5]

In contrast to the June 23 game, both Ayers and Shore would start and star in the September 12 contest. A game report in the *Boston Globe* praised Ayers, who "never had shown any better form than that which he displayed today. Although his slants were touched for 13 safe clouts he was master of the situation at all times and time and again pulled himself out of what looked to be ticklish positions."[6]

Neither team scored a run until the bottom of the fifth inning. Shore walked Eddie Foster. Morgan hit a groundball to Boston shortstop Everett Scott, who "stood inanimate ... thus losing a fine chance for a double [play.]"[7] Morgan reached on the fielder's choice. Trying to advance the runners, Joe Leonard beat out a bunt to load the bases with none out. Eddie Ainsmith drove in Foster on a fly ball to Harry Hooper to give the Senators a 1-0 lead. Hooper must have made a fine catch as he not only threw out Morgan at second for a double play but almost contributed to a rare 9-4-2 triple play.[8] Alas for the Red Sox, Jack Barry's relay nearly nipped but did not quite get Morgan at the plate as he scored the lone Washington run.

The Red Sox rapidly responded in the top of the sixth thanks to a big hit from a most unlikely source. Playing in only his 14th game of the season, Hick Cady doubled for his first extra-base hit of 1917 and his first two-bagger since August 24, 1916. Shore singled his batterymate to third. Playing key roles in the two runs scored in the game, Hooper singled in Cady to tie the score and snap a career-best 27-inning scoreless streak by Ayers.

Boston looked poised to take the lead with runners on the corners and none out before Washington catcher Ainsmith "made a fine throw to Foster to catch Shore off third. ... Had he not been put out of the way the pitcher could have scored on [Dick] Hoblitzell's fly to [Sam] Rice."[9]

"In the seventh inning each side filled the bases with one out, but neither could score."[10] Before darkness descended, the game would conclude with 10 straight scoreless innings, a slight but not severe surprise given the lack of punch of both teams. (The Red Sox hit 14 home runs in 1917, a titanic total compared with the four struck by Washington, which finished last in the AL in home runs, slugging percentage, and total bases.)

The Senators did threaten in the 15th with a walk, a stolen base, and an intentional walk to get to the pitcher's spot. Given the rally, the amount that Ayers had already pitched, and the lateness of the hour, one might have expected a pinch-hitter, but Ayers went to the plate before futilely "fouling out to Cady."[11] Both Ayers and Shore finished the final inning and both set career marks for innings pitched in a game.

Washington's second 16-inning tie of the season[12] meant little for the Senators, but the failure of the Red Sox to win more than a single game in a four-game set against Washington lengthened the already long odds against a third consecutive pennant in 1917. The game represented some measure of revenge for Ayers After losing to Shore and bottoming out at 1-6 after June 23, Ayers as part of a season-closing run that saw him take 10 of his last 14 decisions, matched the more heralded Shore frame-for-frame in this game.

SOURCES

In addition to the sources cited in the Notes, the author accessed Retrosheet.org, Baseball-Reference.com, SABR.org, and *The Sporting News* archive via Paper of Record.

NOTES

1 Shirley Povich, *The Washington Senators* (Kent, Ohio: Kent State University Press, 2010), 94. Washington would draw a franchise-low 89,682 fans in 1917.

2 Michael Clair, "Ernie Shore Once Threw a Quasi-Perfect Game ... After Babe Ruth Punched an Umpire," mlb.com/cut4/ernie-shore-threw-quasi-perfect-game-after-babe-ruth-ejection/c-132245176, June 23, 2015 (accessed August 13, 2018).

3 Roger Birtwell, "Ernie Shore's Greatest Thrill Not Perfect Game," *Boston Globe*, December 13, 1959: 187. From 1914 to 1917, Shore went 58-33 with a 2.12 ERA for the Red Sox. After serving in the Navy in 1918, Shore pitched two more seasons for the Yankees and went 7-10 with a 4.39 ERA. He last appeared in a game in the majors at the age of 29.

4 Charles F. Faber, "Doc Ayers," sabr.org/bioproj/person/95ee682f (accessed August 13, 2018).

5 "Rain Halts Griffith on His Upward Way," *The Sporting News*, September 6, 1917: 3.

6 "Red Sox Play a 16-Inning Tie," *Boston Globe*, September 13, 1917: 9.

7 "Notes of Red Sox Game," *Boston Globe*, September 13, 1917: 9. Another reporter thought that Scott (and his Washington counterpart Howie Shanks) played well defensively in this game: "Both teams gave a fine fielding exhibition, the works of Shanks and Scott, the opposing shortstops, standing out prominently." *The Sporting News*, September 20, 1917: 6.

8 Hooper in 1917 finished second in the American League in assists by a right fielder with 20 and holds the career mark (for players since 1908) for right fielders by a comfortable margin with 332 baserunner kills.

9 "Ayers and Shore Pitch Superbly When in Trouble in Contest Ended by Darkness," *Washington Post*, September 13, 1917: 8.

10 Paul W. Eaton, "Griffmen Making a Belated Splurge," *The Sporting News*, September 20, 1917: 3.

11 J.V. Fitz Gerald, "Nationals and Red Sox in a 16-Inning 1-1 Tie Game," *Washington Post*, September 13, 1917: 8.

12 The *Washington Post* reported that the Senators tied 2-2 on June 11, but baseball-reference.com lists that game as taking place on June 12. "Second 16-Inning Game This Year for Griffs," *Washington Post*, September 13, 1917: 8.

WALTER JOHNSON AND LEFTY WILLIAMS SPAR FOR 18 INNINGS

MAY 15, 1918
WASHINGTON SENATORS 1, CHICAGO WHITE SOX 0 (18 INNINGS)

by Michael Huber

Had there been room, the Griffin Stadium scoreboard would have shown 35 zeroes going into the bottom of the 18th inning. Neither team had scored a run. The same starting nine players were still holding their positions, even as both squads were completing twice the length of a regulation game. Claude "Lefty" Williams, "Chicago's diminutive southpaw, pitched Walter Johnson, Washington's giant northpaw, to an absolute standstill." In what the *Washington Post* called "the greatest game ever played here and one of the classiest of the national pastime,"[1] the hometown Senators defeated the defending world champion White Sox in the pitchers' duel of the season, 1-0, with the game's only run scoring on Williams's wild pitch. The game set a record for the longest American League 1-0 match, and it tied the National League record, set 36 years before.[2]

The American League standings were jumbled a month into the season. Only three games separated five teams from the first-place Boston Red Sox. Chicago sat out a game in fourth place with an 11-9 record, placing the White Sox two games ahead of the 10-12 Senators, who were tied for fifth position with the St. Louis Browns, while the Yankees and Indians were tied for second place, each a half-game back.

Johnson's only real trouble came in the first and final innings. As the game opened, the White Sox got to him for two hits, by Eddie Murphy and Buck Weaver, but neither runner scored. Johnson's counterpart Williams was cruising with a perfect game and allowed his first hit in the seventh inning. With two outs, "Milan [pulled] a drive over [Swede] Risberg's head for the swat that wrecked the chance of a no hit game."[3]

In the eighth, Williams hit Ray Morgan with a pitch to start the inning and Eddie Foster followed with a single. Two outs later, Burt Shotton beat out a grounder to short, loading the bases, but Williams worked his way out of the jam. The game kept going with little to no offensive action. Each team put a runner at second base in the 12th inning, only to strand him there.

The Senators had a chance in the bottom of the 17th. With one down, Clyde Milan hit a looping fly ball past second base that dropped between center fielder Shano Collins, right fielder Murphy, and second baseman Risberg, who managed to get a glove on the ball but could not hold on. Howie Shanks singled and again the Senators had a rally, but again Williams killed it. Joe Judge hit a ball up the middle, but "Williams stabbed Judge's bounder and forced Milan at third brilliantly."[4] Morgan then fouled out to end the inning.

In "the first half of the fatal eighteenth,"[5] Risberg stroked a one-out double. After Fred McMullin flied out, Johnson's wild pitch let Risberg advance to third. Ray Schalk worked Johnson to a full count and, according to the *Chicago Tribune*, "Johnson tried to pass him intentionally with a fourth ball."[6] However, Schalk reached out with his bat and made contact, attempting to drive the ball into right field. He "hit a mean grounder to Morgan, but not too hot for Ray to stop and hand the ball"[7] to first baseman Judge to get the third out of the inning.

With one down in the bottom half, Eddie Ainsmith singled past second base. That brought up Johnson, who was "so tired he could hardly drag his feet to the plate,"[8] yet the pitcher drove the ball for a single into left-center, sending his batterymate Ainsmith to third. With Shotton now in the batter's box looking at a two-strike count, Williams "heaved the ball far over [catcher] Schalk's head to the grandstand and Ainsmith romped across the plate, sending the small crowd home rejoicing."[9] The walk-off wild pitch ended the game.

Johnson and Williams had earned five wins apiece before this game. Johnson had lost his first three decisions of the season, while Williams had won his first four. Both pitchers had almost perfect control in this matchup. Each "let slip one wild pitch in that last inning, but Walter's came with a runner on second, while Claude's happened with a man at third."[10]

Neither team made an error in the game, and a total of 125 batters stepped up to home plate. The time of the game was 2 hours and 50 minutes, and according to the *Chicago Tribune*, "it would have been possible to play at least two more rounds before dark."[11] The crowd was small (the attendance was not recorded), but according to the *Washington Times*, "hardly a handful left the park until the end. They sat and rooted for the home boys, but did not keep back their applause for clever fielding plays by the champions."[12]

Johnson struck out nine batters, including his counterpart Williams "five times in succession."[13] Washington's ace yielded 10 hits (eight singles and two doubles) with only one walk. In earning his sixth win of the season, en route to a league-high 23 victories, he had 11 three-up, three-down innings. The Big Train's earned-run average dropped from 1.25 to 0.98. He ran his scoreless streak to 31 innings, dating back to May 7. He pitched another complete-game shutout against the Detroit Tigers on May 26 (*only* nine innings), and then allowed three earned runs in a loss to the Boston Red Sox on May 29. For the season, Johnson allowed no earned runs in 20 of his 39 appearances, and he finished the 1918 campaign with a 1.27 ERA and 162 strikeouts, which, with the 23 wins, gave him his second pitching Triple Crown.

For Chicago, Williams held the Senators to just eight singles and two bases on balls (he also hit a batter), and he struck out three. Despite the earned run, his ERA dropped from 2.49 to 1.96 in this, his fifth complete game of the season. Williams used his defense, especially his outfield. The *Chicago Tribune* reported, "All told the Nationals hit the ball into the air for 35 outs."[14] The outfielders had made 22 putouts and the rest were by the infield. Chicago's Eddie Murphy had the best offensive day for either team, getting a double, two singles, and a walk in seven plate appearances.

Although this was the longest outing in his career, Johnson twice pitched a 15-inning shutout; first against the Boston Red Sox on July 3, 1913, and then against the Philadelphia Athletics on April 13, 1926 (Opening Day for the 1926 season). In 1918 Johnson led the American League with eight shutouts, which also gave him the best career mark (with 79).[15] Johnson retired as the career shutout leader with 110.

SOURCES

In addition to the sources mentioned in the notes, the author consulted baseball-reference.com and retrosheet.org.

NOTES

1. W.H. Hottel, "18-Inning Game to Nationals, 1 to 0," Washington Post, May 16, 1918: 10.
2. Louis A. Dougher, "Griffmen Make New League Record When They Win, 1 to 0, in 18 Innings," Washington Times, May 16, 1918: 18. According to the Washington Times, the National League record for the longest 1-0 contest was set on August 17, 1882, when it took 18 innings for the Providence Grays to defeat the Detroit Wolverines. The previously longest 1-0 game in the American League was played on August 14, 1903, as the Senators defeated the St. Louis Browns in 15 innings in the first game of a doubleheader.
3. Dougher.
4. Dougher.
5. Dougher.
6. Dougher.
7. Hottel.
8. I.E. Sanborn, "Williams' Wild Pitch Loses 18 Inning Battle for Sox, 1-0," Chicago Tribune, May 15, 1918: 11.
9. Hottel.
10. Sanborn. According to both Retrosheet and the Tribune's own box score, Johnson did not throw a wild pitch. Instead, his catcher Ainsmith was charged with a passed ball.
11. "Notes," Chicago Tribune, May 15, 1918: 11.
12. Dougher.
13. "Washington Wins 18-Inning Game," Philadelphia Inquirer, May 15, 1918: 12.
14. Hottel.
15. Johnson shared the career mark of 79 shutouts with Christy Mathewson until the 1919 season, when he added seven more to his total and became the outright leader. As of 2018, his tally of 110 career shutouts has led the major leagues since 1927.

FIRST SUNDAY GAME DRAWS RECORD CROWD IN WASHINGTON

MAY 19, 1918
WASHINGTON SENATORS 1, CLEVELAND INDIANS 0 (12 INNINGS)

by Jack Zerby

Paid-admission Sunday baseball came with relative ease to the District of Columbia. On May 14, 1918, "the District Commissioners, after careful consideration of the needs of the Capital, lifted the [Sunday] ban on professional sports."[1] Without the extensive legal, referendum, and legislative maneuvering that was ultimately necessary to bring Sunday baseball to New York, Massachusetts and Pennsylvania,[2] "the action of the Commissioners [was] not in response to any request or demand by outside parties. They were not consulted, nor or even informed that the new rule was to be issued until its announcement."[3]

The United States had entered World War I in April 1917, two years and nine months after the conflict erupted in Europe. Nearly a year into US participation, the national capital was consequently filled with soldiers and civilian military workers – the commission determined "baseball will be beneficial to the thousands of war workers here."[4] Washington was already permitting movie theaters to operate on Sundays; additional public-amusement options like baseball were also cited as a possible deterrent to increases in sales of illicit liquor in the District.

Because the Yankees' game scheduled for April 18 in Washington had been rained out,[5] sportswriters expected the New Yorkers to play the first Sunday game against the Senators on May 19, just five days after Sunday games were authorized. But American League czar Ban Johnson asked the Cleveland Indians to play the game, "as a return favor for all the one-game road trips the Senators made to Cleveland for Sunday games since 1911 when Sunday games were legalized there."[6] This scheduling also provided a convenient makeup, as the Indians had themselves been rained out in Washington on May 13. Cleveland, on an Eastern road swing, was relatively close by in Philadelphia the day before the first-ever Sunday game in Washington.[7]

On May 11 the Senators' ace, Walter Johnson, had outdueled Cleveland's Jim Bagby Sr. 1-0 at Washington's American League Park.[8] Then, four days later, he went 18 innings against Lefty Williams of the White Sox in another 1-0 win. Johnson was reported to have "caught cold and felt the effects of the grueling struggle"[9] but the assumption was that he would pitch this watershed game, and even the early editions of the game-day newspapers reported that he was still expected to start for Washington.

He didn't. Senators manager Clark Griffith gave 27-year-old right-hander Doc Ayers the starting assignment against Stan Coveleski, Cleveland's ace,[10] as 15,352 civilians and 2,000 soldiers from military camps near Washington settled in for the 3:30 P.M. first pitch, pushed back a half-hour to allow for the expected attendance surge.[11] This included "[s]enators, representatives, diplomats, officers from practically all the allied armies, society folk rubbing elbows with Mr. Average man and his wife or sweetheart [as well as] a justice of the Supreme Court," and constituted "the biggest crowd that ever saw a ball game in the District of Columbia."[12] The thinking of the District Commission about Sunday entertainment had been verified.

The assemblage was treated to a back-and-forth pitchers' duel replete with defensive gems and lapses. Clyde Milan got the game's first hit with two outs in the Washington first when he legged out an infield roller toward Cleveland second baseman Ray Chapman. He reached base again in the third when Coveleski botched his comebacker; Doc Lavan, who had singled ahead of Milan, advanced to second on the play but was forced at third base on Howie Shanks' groundball. The next batter, Joe Judge, hit a ball that Chapman couldn't handle in the infield, but the Indians got out of the inning when he recovered to throw Milan out at the plate.[13]

Washington collected two more hits in its fourth inning, but efficient infield force-out work by the Indians kept the game scoreless.

Meanwhile, Ayers and his submarine[14] spitball rolled along for the Senators without allowing a hit until, with one out in the Cleveland fifth inning, Terry Turner reached on an error by Lavan and Steve O'Neill singled to right field, moving Turner to third base. But what had looked like a good scoring opportunity ended when Coveleski's dribbler forced O'Neill at second base. as Turner stayed at third on the play; Ayers bore down and ended the

One of the best defensive first basemen of his era, Joe Judge was an overlooked hitter, regularly batting over .300, including .324 for the World Series champion 1924 Senators. In parts of 18 seasons with the Nats (1915-1933), he collected 2,291 hits, including 157 triples, second to Sam Rice (183) in franchise history. (Photo by Sporting News and Rogers Photo Archive via Getty Images)

inning, getting Smoky Joe Wood[15] to foul out to Eddie Ainsmith.

Each spitballer[16] recorded one-two-three innings in the sixth to keep the game scoreless. The crowd was apparently getting restless, as the writer who recorded the *Washington Herald's* play-by-play account[17] noted "[they] stood up in the wrong half of the seventh." In its half of the inning, Cleveland managed two more hits separated by a pair of outs, but Coveleski popped out to second base to thwart a rally.

The Senators advanced Burt Shotton as far as third base with two outs in their seventh; Coveleski got Milan to roll out to Chapman to keep the plate unsullied. The only double play in the game – Lavan to Ray Morgan to Judge – ended a mild Indians' threat in the eighth fueled by a walk and a Washington error. Coveleski responded with a one-two-three eighth against the Senators.

Some nifty fielding by Lavan for Washington and Cleveland first baseman Rip Williams in the ninth inning carried both pitchers through regulation with the game still scoreless.

The Senators looked to be in business in the bottom of the 10th when a bobble and throwing error by Williams left leadoff hitter Shotton on second base. But yet another force out at third base, a force at second, and Coveleski's sure handling of a hot comebacker by Shanks erased the threat.

Ayers had to deal with two Indians baserunners in the top of the 11th inning on an error and a walk but got O'Neill on a popup to third base to wiggle out of the jam. This time, Coveleski cruised through Judge, Morgan, and Eddie Foster when Washington batted in the bottom half.

Coveleski's teammates nearly broke the deadlock in the top of the 12th. With two outs Chapman legged out a roller to shortstop. Tris Speaker singled him to third, then stole second base. Cleanup hitter Braggo Roth stood in, but Ayers, equal to the challenge, retired him on a groundball to second base.

It had been five innings since the crowd had enjoyed its early stretch but the Senators got them to their feet again quickly in their half of the inning. Frank "Wildfire" Schulte led off pinch-hitting for Ainsmith and beat out an infield hit. Ayers bounced back to Coveleski, but a would-be double play dissolved when he threw wildly to second base. With no outs and runners on first and second, Cleveland cut down Schulte at third on Shotton's comebacker to Coveleski, then got Lavan as Ayers moved to third and Shotton to second.

The stage was set yet again, and this time Milan "furnished the big thrill. He sent a sizzling hit over the third-base bag that gave the [Senators] a 1-0 victory."[18] Ayers, who had pitched around errors all day, scored the only run he needed to get his third win against two losses in the young season. Coveleski had also pitched masterfully given his teammates' errors; it was his own error that did him in.

This was still May, fewer than 30 games into the season, and both teams were bouncing around .500. Cleveland went on to finish 73-54 and 2½ games behind the American League pennant-winning Boston Red Sox. The Senators, 72-56, were another game and a half back in third place.

Including this first-ever game, Washington played 12 Sunday home games in 1918. They adapted well to this new concept, giving their fans wins in nine of the 12. Those wins included a doubleheader sweep of the White Sox on August 25.

SOURCES

In addition to the sources cited in the Notes, I used Baseball-Reference.com and Retrosheet.org for box scores, team and player pages, and schedule logs for the 1918 season. The detailed play-by-play appearing as a sidebar to the game story in the May 20, 1918, *Washington Herald*, accessed through Newspapers.com, was especially useful.

baseball-reference.com/boxes/WS1/WS1191805190.shtml

retrosheet.org/boxesetc/1918/B05190WS11918.htm

NOTES

1 "Sabbath Ban Lifted on Own Initiative by Commission," *Washington Times*, May 14, 1918: 1, 19.

2 The first legally sanctioned Sunday games were played in New York City in 1919, Boston in 1932 and in Philadelphia and Pittsburgh in 1934. Charlie Bevis, *Sunday Baseball* (Jefferson, North Carolina: McFarland & Co., Inc., 2003), 272.

3 "Sabbath Ban Lifted."

4 "Soldiers to Be Favored as Sabbath Ban Is Lifted," *Washington Post*, May 15, 1918: 10.

5 Baseball Results and Standings, *Boston Post*, April 19, 1918: 11.

6 Bevis, 193.

7 The Yankees were at home in New York, playing a series with St. Louis. With Sunday games not permitted in New York until 1919, the Yankees had an open date on May 19, 1918.

8 Opened in 1911, the ballpark was located at 7th Street and Florida Avenue. In 1918 newspaper coverage it was referred to either as American League Park or as the Florida Avenue grounds. Although Clark Griffith managed the Senators in 1918 and the team was routinely referred to as the "Griffmen," Griffith did not have a controlling ownership interest in the team until 1920; only then did the ballpark become known as Griffith Stadium. Griffith Stadium entry, AndrewClem.com, accessed September 14, 2018.

9 Denman Thompson, "Record Crowd Is Expected at Base Ball Park Today," *Washington Evening Star*, May 19, 1918: 43.

10 Coveleski went on to win 22 games for the 1918 Indians, starting a string of four straight seasons with 20-plus wins. In December 1924 he was traded to Washington, where he won 20 games for the 1925 pennant-winning Senators. Coveleski was voted into the Baseball Hall of Fame in 1969 by the Veterans Committee.

11 The soldiers received complimentary tickets. Temporary seating had been installed "in front of the grandstand and pavilions, where the men in uniform will get a close-up view of the proceedings." Thompson, "Record Crowd."

12 J.V. Fitz Gerald, "Milan Hits Nationals to Victory in Twelfth as More Than 17,000 Look On," *Washington Post*, May 20, 1918: 8.

13 Errors were definitely a feature of this game, which took 2 hours 29 minutes, an eternity in the Deadball Era, to complete. Each team had six miscues. Because the teams totaled only six walks and strikeouts between them, the ball was usually in play, most often in the infield. Several force outs at third base resulted - something rarely seen in today's "three true events" (home runs, strikeouts, walks) baseball.

14 A submarine pitch is delivered from an even lower angle than a side-arm pitch. In the Deadball Era (1901-20) writers often referred to it as "underhand." As of 2020, there were several submarine pitchers active in the major leagues, but, presumably, no spitball pitchers. The spitball was legislated out of baseball in 1920 when Cleveland's Ray Chapman died after being hit in the head by a spitball from New York Yankees' submarine pitcher Carl Mays. By way of a "grandfather" provision, baseball allowed all spitball pitchers who had been active in 1920 to continue to use the pitch until their retirement.

15 Smoky Joe Wood won 117 games as a pitcher with the Boston Red Sox from 1908 through 1915. In February 1917 Boston sold his contract to Cleveland, where, at age 27, he became an outfielder and utility player. He hit .297 in six seasons with Cleveland.

16 Coveleski also threw a spitball. See Daniel R. Leavitt, "Stan Coveleski," SABR Biography Project, sabr.org, accessed September 24, 2018.

17 *Washington Herald*, May 20, 1918: 8.

18 J.V. Fitz Gerald, "Milan Hits Nationals to Victory."

AS RELIEVER, BIG TRAIN WINS NUMBER 300 WITH ARM AND BAT

MAY 14, 1920
WASHINGTON SENATORS 9, DETROIT TIGERS 8

by Gregory H. Wolf

It was cold, windy, dreary, and damp in the nation's capital when the cellar-dwelling Detroit Tigers (5-16) and fifth-place Washington Senators (10-11) arrived at Griffith Stadium to see if they could salvage the final contest of an originally-scheduled four-game series. Rain had canceled the previous two games and probably should have wiped out this game, given what sportswriter Louis A. Dougher of the *Washington Times* described as a "small crowd shivering here and there in the capacious stands, biting breeze sweeping cross the field, slow running and rotten pitching" and declaring that "the afternoon was not exactly a howling success."[1] The threat of yet another double-header later in the season, opined the *Washington Post,* encouraged Clark Griffith, the Senators owner-skipper, and Bengals pilot Hughie Jennings to play despite the ragged conditions on the field.[2]

The players' pent-up energy was released in the initial frame, which foreshadowed how the game would unfold. The Tigers missed a shot for the first run when Ty Cobb (on first via a fielder's choice), was thrown out at home on a "perfect relay" from right field on Bobby Veach's double.[3]

The Nationals, as the team was often called by sportswriters, wasted no time taking advantage of John Glaiser, whose big-league experience consisted of six innings and who was making what proved to be his first and only start in the majors. Joe Judge led off by drawing a walk but was caught in a rundown between third and home on Sam Rice's one-out grounder. After Braggo Roth walked, Bucky Harris doubled home both runners. Frank Ellerbe also caught the "pedestrian fever," noted the *Washington Post,* and then in Deadball-Era style, Harris stole third, and subsequently home in a daring double steal for the Senators' third run.[4] Red Shannon drew yet another free pass from Glaiser, but was forced at second.

The Senators' pitching "staff suffered from inaction," opined Dougher, who described starter Tom Zachary as "look[ing] like a busher."[5] The 24-year-old didn't resemble the southpaw who had blanked the New York Yankees on five hits six days earlier for his fifth big-league victory. Harry

Heilmann led off the second with a single, took second on Sammy Hale's single, stole third, and then sped home on Oscar Stanage's fly to left field. According to Nationals beat writer J.V. Fitz Gerald, home-plate umpire George Hildebrand called Heilmann out but reversed his call when Patsy Gharrity dropped the ball.[6] The Tigers tied the game, 3-3, in the fourth on Stanage's two-run double, plating Veach (who had led off with a two-bagger) and Ira Flagstead.

The Senators stormed back in the fifth, loading the bases on singles by Clyde Milan and Rice and a walk to Roth. Milan was tagged at home on Harris's squeeze bunt, but Ellerbe and Shannon followed with run-scoring singles and Gharrity with a sacrifice fly for a 6-3 lead.

Swedish-born Eric Erickson had taken over for Zachary and pitched a scoreless fifth. "He was Olaf when he strode to the mound," wrote the acerbic Dougher, and "was Oh Laugh within two innings."[7] Flagstead beat out a roller to lead off the seventh and Stanage and Chick Shorten, pinch-hitting for Glaiser, drew one-out walks to load the bases. Castigated by Dougher for his "ludicrous lack of control," Erickson's third straight walk, to Ralph Young, forced in a run and sent the hurler to the showers.[8]

To the rescue with the bags bursting came Walter Johnson, sitting on 299 career victories. The 32-year-old right-hander had finished the decade of the teens by winning at least 20 games each season, 265 in all, including 74 shutouts. He led the AL victories five times during that stretch and posted a career-best 36 in 1913. Vying with Grover Cleveland Alexander as the decade's best hurler (at least until Old Pete was debilitated from serving in the Great War), Johnson relieved regularly, and 20 percent of his appearances in the 1910s were in relief.[9]

Johnson had been uncharacteristically hit hard in his last two outings, both complete-game losses, yielding 24 hits and 12 runs (8 earned), and seemed confused when the first batter he faced, Donie Bush, hit a tapper back to the mound. According to sportswriter Jack Nye of the *Washington Herald*, the Big Train threw late to home and Babe Pinelli, pinch-running for Stanage, scored.[10] Johnson was on the verge of putting out the fire, but the Georgia Peach, coming off his 12th AL batting crown in 13 seasons, yet batting just .243 in 1920, belted a line drive that center fielder Sam Rice handled "as if it was a chunk of TNT," quipped Fitz Gerald.[11] Cobb cleared the bases (credited with two RBIs on Rice's error) to give the Bengals an 8-6 lead.

Despite that rough inning, allowing three inherited runners to score (charged to Erickson's slate) and yielding an unearned run, Johnson "brought a semblance of order out of a wild and woolly game," wrote the *Herald*.[12] He held the Bengals scoreless over the last three frames, and helped lead the Senators' comeback with his bat.

The Senators rallied in the seventh off reliever Ray Oldham, back in the big leagues after a four-year absence. Roth led off by walking, and Ellerbe beat out a one-out grounder. Shannon's grounder forced Ellerbe but second baseman's Ralph Young's relay throw to first was wide, enabling Roth to scamper home and Shannon to advance to second. After Gharrity walked, Johnson blasted a single to drive in Shannon and tie the score, 8-8. No slouch with the bludgeon, Johnson was a robust .235 career hitter and regularly pinch-hit. Manager Jennings, seemingly out of patience with his hurler, took a page out of Griffith's playbook and called on his ace, Hooks Dauss, to stop the bleeding. A longtime workhorse who was coming off 21 victories in 1919, Dauss retired Judge to end the frame and then hurled a scoreless eighth.

The Senators put on their "big shillalah act in the ninth," cooed the *Post*.[13] Singles by Ellerbe, Shannon, and Johnson loaded the bases against Dauss. With the outfield drawn in for a play at the plate, Joe Judge came to bat. Mostly forgotten by modern baseball historians, Judge was a productive hitter throughout his 20-year career (1915-1934), collecting 2,352 hits and batting .298. He blasted a ball to center field, where "Tyrus made no effort to chase after it," reported the *Post*, and was credited with a single, giving the Senators a 9-8 victory in 2 hours and 35 minutes.[14]

Johnson earned his 300th career victory, becoming just the 10th pitcher to reach that milestone and the first since Eddie Plank in 1915, and also joined Plank and Christy Mathewson as the only members of that fraternity who started their careers in the twentieth century.[15] Despite the importance contemporary sportswriters and fans place on statistics and cumulative accomplishments, Johnson's achievement was apparently lost on contemporaneous sportswriters. Neither the *Herald*, *Post*, nor *Times* mentioned his 300th victory in its game summary.

The biggest story about Johnson in May focused on his uncharacteristic struggles. Two days after his win in relief, the Big Train was shelled for 12 hits in a complete-game 4-2 loss to the St. Louis Browns. On May 20 he was hammered for nine hits and 10 runs, though only two were earned, in a disastrous six-inning relief appearance resulting in another loss and dropping his record to 3-5. Washington scribes wondered if Barney was washed up, and those sentiments grew louder when Johnson was tagged for four runs in four innings of relief in his next outing. For the first time in his career, Johnson was suffering from an injury, to his shoulder. Given extra time between starts, Johnson was inconsistent. On July 1 he tossed arguably the best game of his career, holding the Boston Red Sox hitless and fanning 10 while walking none at Fenway Park. Fifteen days later, his season was over (8-10, 3.13 ERA) as pain made pitching impossible.

SOURCES

In addition to the sources cvited in the Notes, the author accessed Retrosheet.org, Baseball-Reference.com, Newspapers.com, and SABR.org.

NOTES

1 Louis A. Dougher, "Looking 'Em Over," *Washington Times*, May 15, 1920: 17.

2 J. V. Fitz Gerald, "Judge's Hit Yields Victory Over Tigers," *Washington Post*, May 15, 1920: 12.

3 Harry Bullion, "Washington Beats Tigers in the Ninth Inning, 9 to 8," *Detroit Free Press*, May 15, 1920: 13.

4 Fitz Gerald.

5 Dougher.

6 J.V. Fitz Gerald, "In the Wake of the Game," *Washington Post*, May 15, 1920: 12.

7 Dougher.

8 Dougher.

9 In the decade of the teens, Johnson started 361 of 454 appearances (79.5 percent); in his career, he started 666 of 802 appearances (83.0 percent).

10 Jack Nye, "Joe Judge's Timely Drive Over Ty Cobb's Head in Ninth Wins Game for Nationals," *Washington Herald*, May 15, 1920: 12.

11 Fitz Gerald.

12 Nye.

13 Fitz Gerald.

14 Fitz Gerald.

15 The leaders in wins at the time were Cy Young (511), Christy Mathewson (373), Pud Galvin (365), Kid Nichols (361), Tim Keefe (342), John Clarkson (328), Eddie Plank (326), Old Hoss Radbourn (309), and Mickey Welch (307).

MEUSEL HITS FOR THE CYCLE AS RUTH WALLOPS LONGEST HOME RUN EVER AT GRIFFITH STADIUM

MAY 7, 1921
NEW YORK YANKEES 6, WASHINGTON SENATORS 5

by Mike Huber

In the second of a two-game series at Griffith Stadium, Bob Meusel and the Yankees "brought about the downfall of the Nationals"[1] with the use of the long ball. Former President Woodrow Wilson "drove out to the game and witnessed the contest from the shelter of his automobile, which was parked near the right field fence."[2] He and the rest of the approximately 15,000 spectators were treated to a slugfest that featured a colossal Babe Ruth home run and a cycle by Meusel.

Jack Quinn, "[Miller] Huggins's veteran spitballer,"[3] started on the mound for New York (8-7) which stood in fourth place in the American League. Quinn had spent much of his 10-year career as a starter, but in 1921 he was also used as a reliever in 20 of his 33 appearances. For the second-place Senators (11-7), Walter Johnson toed the rubber. The Big Train was coming off a poor season in 1920, when he registered only eight wins due to "a combination of a bad cold, a sore arm, and pulled leg muscles,"[4] halting a 10-year consecutive streak of garnering at least 20 wins per season. The 33-year-old right-hander had already surpassed the 300-win plateau and entered this contest seeking win number three for the season and 308 for his career.

Washington grabbed an early lead in the bottom of the second inning. With one out, "a barrage of singles by Howie Shanks, Frank O'Rourke and Val Picinich, coming in rapid-fire order,"[5] resulted in a run and put runners on the corners. Johnson then helped his own cause when he "walloped a long one over Meusel's head against the right field fence for two bases"[6] to bring home O'Rourke (Picinich had stopped at third base). Joe Judge lifted a fly ball to center for the second out, but the fly brought in Picinich for the third tally. On the play, Johnson was caught in a rundown between second and third and was tagged out by Yankees second baseman Aaron Ward for the final out.

Back on the mound, Johnson retired the first two New York batters in the third, but then Wally Pipp worked a walk. Meusel, who had singled in the first inning, sent Johnson's offering beyond the scoreboard for a two-run homer, hit in the same position where teammate Ruth had launched a home run the day before.

Washington's four straight hits in the second "convinced Manager Huggins it was not Quinn's day,"[7] and he stayed in the dugout when his team took the field in the bottom of the third, as "Waite Hoyt took up the burden."[8] Hoyt retired Clyde Milan and then Sam Rice skied a ball between shortstop and left field. Roger Peckinpaugh backed up and Ruth came in, calling for the ball. Instead, Ruth "stood still and let it drop to the ground"[9] and Rice ended up at second with a double. Frank Brower singled up the middle, advancing Rice to third. Bucky Harris then smashed a deep fly ball to Roth in center for the second out, and Rice trotted home with Washington's fourth run.

Scoring then ceased until the eighth inning. At one point, Johnson had retired 11 Yankees in a row, until Hoyt and Braggo Roth hit back-to-back singles in the seventh. Now, in the eighth, Ruth led off and "with the count 2 and 2, Johnson rifled one of his fast ones plateward; the great Babe took a vicious cut and the sphere sailed by yards clear of the new high fence recently erected in center field."[10] In just his 16th game of the season, this was Ruth's eighth home run. In 1920, when the three-time-reigning home-run king swatted a record 54 home runs, he had only two at this point of the season. According to several newspaper accounts, Ruth's "volcanic clout"[11] was the "longest hit ever made"[12] at Griffith Stadium. Just the day before, reporters were in awe of Ruth's seventh round-tripper, which was said to have traveled farther than any other previously-hit ball. However, Number Eight "exceeded the terrific seventh home run by many yards."[13] The *New York Times* reported that it was a "full fifty yards further."[14] The ball cleared the signboard well beyond the deep center field wall. Had it not been hit so high, the papers claim, "it would have dented the red 'Hahn's Shoe' sign."[15] Instead, it cleared that sign, coming to rest where no other ball had ever gone. The *Washington Herald* described the phenomenon of Ruth: "Ol' Bam marched up in the eighth with fire in his eyes. The fans were 'booing' as usual. They 'boo' before he hits and cheer afterward."[16]

After Pipp was retired, Meusel doubled to left and Baker walked. Ward sent a "screaming double"[17] into right field, scoring Meusel and sending Baker to third. Johnson then walked pinch-hitter Wally Schang intentionally, loading the bases for Hoyt, who delivered a pitcher's best friend, a double play, started by Johnson. However, the Yankees had tied the score, 4-4.

The Senators "came right back in their half of the eighth."[18] Harris reached first on a hit-by-pitch but was forced out at second when Pipp made a great throw after fielding Shanks's sacrifice bunt attempt. O'Rourke singled to right, and Meusel's throw to third base skipped into the dugout, "rolling to the edge of the players' bench, where a kid stopped it,"[19] allowing Shanks to come home with the Senators' fifth run.

In the final frame, the Yankees "treated Walter Johnson to a pasting which only ended when two runs had been added to the New York string and the lead regained."[20] There was also a controversial play. Roth led off with an infield single to the left side. Peckinpaugh followed with a hit down the left-field line and when third-base umpire Frank Wilson "called it foul a small sized riot was loose."[21] Players from both teams stormed the field, some to the home-plate umpire Bill Dinneen and others to the spot where the ball landed. The Yankees claimed the ball was fair, but "when the excitement died down the situation was just what might have been expected."[22] Roth retreated to first and Peckinpaugh re-entered the batter's box, where he proceeded to pop out to short. Ruth also popped out (to second), but then Pipp singled up the middle. With runners on first and second, Meusel drove a "wicked clout to right"[23] for a two-run triple which "spelled defeat for the Nationals."[24] In giving the Yankees the lead, Meusel had hit for the cycle.

The Yankees prevailed, 6-5, as Carl Mays came in to pitch a 1-2-3 ninth inning and save the win for New York. The game featured 11 extra-base hits and 27 total safeties. Johnson had offered up the two round-trippers to Meusel and Ruth and had walked four New Yorkers. His earned-run average soared to 3.73. He pitched in six more games before finally earning a victory (on June 1 against the Yankees).

Meusel "continued his remarkable stickwork,"[25] appearing to be a one-man nemesis of the Nationals. In the two-game series with Washington, New York's right fielder had eight hits (four for extra bases) in 10 at-bats, with seven runs batted in and three runs scored. He raised his batting average from .255 to .338 and his slugging percentage from .491 to .646.

The 24-year-old Meusel was in just his second major-league season, and he became only the second New York Yankees player to hit for the cycle (after Bert Daniels on July 25, 1912). In his career, Meusel shared the major-league record of hitting for the cycle three times. This game was his first. A year later, on July 3, 1922, Meusel accomplished the rare feat against the Philadelphia Athletics, and on July 26, 1928, against the Detroit Tigers, Meusel hit for the cycle for the third time.

This was also the first cycle of the 1921 season. Three more players went on to hit a single, double, triple, and home run in the same game that year: the New York Giants' Dave Bancroft (June 1 against the Philadelphia Phillies), the St. Louis Browns' George Sisler (August 13 against the Detroit Tigers), and the Pittsburgh Pirates' Dave Robertson (August 30 against the Brooklyn Robins). Sisler's accomplishment was the second of his Hall of Fame career.

Ruth kept up his slugging. By the end of May, he had 15 homers. He swatted seven in a five-game span from June 10 to 14, and finished the campaign with a record 59 round-trippers, breaking his own mark. Ruth tagged Johnson for another home run (his 26th of the season) on June 25.

SOURCES

In addition to the sources mentioned in the Notes, the author consulted baseball-reference.com, mlb.com, and retrosheet.org.

baseball-reference.com/boxes/WS1/WS1192105070.shtml

retrosheet.org/boxesetc/1921/B05070WS11921.htm

NOTES

1 Jack Nye, "Yankee Right Fielder Has Big Day Against Johnson," *Washington Herald*, May 8, 1921: 8.

2 "Babe Ruth Poles Out His Eighth Homer of Season," *New York Daily News*, May 8, 1921: 22.

3 "Two Late Rallies Win for Yankees," *New York Times*, May 8, 1921: 97.

4 Charles Carey, "Walter Johnson," sabr.org/bioproj/person/0e5ca45c.

5 *New York Times*.

6 Nye.

7 *New York Times*.

8 *New York Times*.

9 *New York Daily News*.

10 John A. Dugan, "Home Runs Factor in Gotham Victory," *Washington Post*, May 8, 1921: 25.

11 *New York Times*.

12 *New York Times*.

13 *New York Times*.

14 *New York Times*.

15 Nye.

16 Nye.

17 *New York Daily News*.

18 *New York Times*.

19 *New York Times*.

20 *New York Times*.

21 *New York Daily News*.

22 *New York Daily News*.

23 *New York Times*.

24 Dugan.

25 *New York Times*.

WHISTLING DIXIE IN THE NATION'S CAPITAL: DAVIS GOES ALL 19 FOR IRONMAN VICTORY

AUGUST 9, 1921
ST. LOUIS BROWNS 8, WASHINGTON SENATORS 6 (19 INNINGS)

by Gregory H. Wolf

It was a "marvelous exhibition of skill and stamina," gushed D.C. sportswriter Denman Thompson about the St. Louis Browns Dixie Davis's 19-inning complete-game victory over the Washington Senators.[1] Another capital city scribe, Jack Nye, suggested that "Davis appeared to gain strength as the game proceeded," overcoming six initial shaky frames to settle down and hold the hometown squad hitless over the last nine.[2] The game was "a thrilling battle," exclaimed the *Washington Herald*.[3]

The Senators and Browns were in the midst of their most competitive stretch of ball all season as they prepared for the third game of a four-game set. Skipper George McBride's Nationals (59-50) were firmly ensconced in third place, propelled by a recent 11-game winning streak, all but one of those victories coming on their current 17-game homestand. Manager Lee Fohl's fourth-place Brownies (49-54) had won 14 of their last 20.

Toeing the rubber for the home team was 32-year-old left-hander George Mogridge, a former swingman acquired from the New York Yankees in the offseason, whose surprising 13-8 slate (2.59 ERA) pushed his career record to 64-71. His opponent was Dixie Davis, a slightly built 30-year-old right-hander, who was "supposed to be a physical weakling," claimed sportswriter Louis Dougher in the *Washington Times*.[4] The 5-foot-11, 150-pound twirler had failed in cups of coffee with three different teams in the 1910s before sticking with the Browns in 1920, going 18-12 and completing 22 games, proving that he was anything but fragile. The North Carolinian had struggled somewhat thus far in '21, posting a 5.17 ERA and splitting his 20 decisions.

A sparse crowd of 3,138 paid spectators was on hand at National Park (renamed Griffith Stadium in honor of the club's owner and longtime pilot Clark Griffith in 1920) on a Tuesday afternoon between first-division aspirants.[5]

This game was a synthesis of Deadball and Liveball Era tactics. It combined daring baserunning, double steals, and attempted steals of home with the increased offense and contact of the modern game. The teams combined for 36 hits (23 by the Browns), including nine triples, but no home runs. The early innings suggested that neither hurler would last long. The Browns tallied in the opening frame when Frank Ellerbe tripled and scored on George Sisler's single.[6] The Senators responded on Joe Judge's triple and Sam Rice's sacrifice fly and then took the lead, 2-1, in the second on Frank O'Rourke's single to plate Bucky Harris.

The game also featured shoddy defense, including eight errors. Mogridge committed one of the Senators' five miscues to begin the third when he "insisted on taking (Luke Stuart's popup) almost out of Judge's hands," wrote Nye, and let the ball drop.[7] Ellerbe eventually drove in Stuart to tie the game. The Browns took a 4-2 lead moments later when Baby Doll Jacobson blasted a bases-loaded single to drive in Ellerbe and Dixie Davis.[8]

After the Nationals squandered Sam Rice's two-out triple in the third, they began a furious rally in the fifth. Mogridge singled and scored on Judge's second three-bagger. Two batters later, second baseman Marty McManus fielded Rice's grounder and caught Judge in a rundown. The sequence ended when Rice twisted his ankle in an attempt to avoid Ellerbe's whip throw, and he had to leave the game, replaced on the bases by Frank Brower.

The Browns' sloppy fielding resulted in the Senators taking the lead in the sixth. With Howie Shanks on first, Patsy Gharrity hit into a tailor-made 6-4-3 double play, but Sisler could not corral McManus's wild throw to first, resulting in a two-base error. When O'Rourke followed with a single to shallow left, Ken Williams made an ill-advised throw home to nab Gharrity. The ball sailed into the stands and the game was tied. Two batters later, Judge's third triple in as many at-bats plated O'Rourke to give the Senators a 5-4 lead.

Battered and seemingly on the verge of breaking, Davis had yielded 10 hits and five runs (four earned) through six innings, but then found his rhythm, holding the Senators scoreless in the next three frames while his teammates tallied a game-tying run in the top of the ninth, courtesy of slapdash fielding. With McManus on third via a triple, Jack Tobin grounded to short. According to the *Washington Herald*, O'Rourke had an easy play at the plate, but he fumbled the ball and then threw low as McManus slid safely.[9] The Senators escaped defeat in regulation when Brower snared Ellerbe's liner and doubled up Tobin on second to send the game into extra innings.

In what was described as a "nerve-racking battle," it appeared as though the Browns might blow it open in the 10th.[10] Sisler led off with a triple, then scored on Williams's single. After Jacobson sacrificed, Hank Severeid hit a Texas Leaguer to short center, sending Mogridge to the showers. In relief came 30-year-old right-hander Jose Acosta. Standing just 5-feet-6 and weighing 130 pounds, the Cuban-born spot starter almost saved the day for the Nats. The inning ended when Williams was thrown out at home on a daring double steal.

"[T]hings looked gloomy for the Griffs," opined Nye about the bottom of the 10th after Davis registered two quick outs.[11] After Shanks drew a free pass, Gharrity tied the game, 6-6, on a triple.

In the final nine frames, Davis clamped down, holding the Senators hitless, though he did walk three. His only hairy situation occurred in the 16th when O'Rourke led off with a walk and moved to second when Sisler muffed Acosta's bunt. On third with two outs, O'Rourke attempted a daring game-winning steal of home, but was thrown out.

While Davis hung up zeroes in Washington's hit column, Acosta dodged bullets. McManus led off the 11th with a single but was picked off first, prompting a heated protest by Browns coach Lefty Leifield, who was ejected by first base umpire Frank Wilson. Tempers were just beginning to heat up, though. McManus's miscue proved costly when Tobin beat out a two-out roller, followed by Ellerbe's single before Sisler was retired. The Browns squandered Severeid's one-out triple and Tobin's two-out double, in the 12th and 13th respectively.

A "near riot," reported Nye, occurred in the 16th on a baserunning blunder which would have been a heart-wrenching gaffe had the Browns lost.[12] No slouch with the bat, Dixie Davis blasted a deep fly to the jury box in left field. On the relay throw, second baseman Bucky Harris made a "wild heave," according to Nye, to try to nip the hurler sliding into third.[13] The ball sailed over Shanks's head and into the visitors dugout and Dixie ran home to give the Brownies what appeared to be a 7-6 lead. An astute O'Rourke called for the ball and tagged second while making his case to umpire Wilson that Davis had failed to touch with bag. After a short discussion, Wilson called Davis out. The Browns bench erupted, noted Denman Thompson, and the players "protested with such vehemence that for a time physical violence seemed imminent."[14] Eventually ordered was restored.

Contemporaneous newspapers reported that it was getting difficult to see that ball by the beginning of the 17th. After two scoreless frames, the fateful 19th began with Sisler, the reigning big-league batting champ (.407 in 1920), picking up his sixth hit (five singles and a triple). Then Williams drew a walk. Jacobson smashed a single to drive in Sisler, and took second when left fielder Bing Miller fumbled the ball. Acosta intentionally walked Severeid to load the bases and play for an inning-ending twin killing. Wally Gerber hit a grounder to O'Rourke for the force at second, but the latter's throw to first was too late. Williams scored to give the Browns an 8-6 lead.

The game finally ended after 3 hours and 45 minutes when Davis set down the side in order in the 19th.

The next day Davis's name and picture graced the front page of sports sections in newspapers across the country. In 19 complete innings, he faced 74 batters, fanned eight, walked five, and yielded 13 hits, not to mention tossing nine hitless innings to end the game. It was easily the longest game in his eventual 10-year big-league career, during which he went 75-71 and logged 1,318⅔ innings. (He pitched at least 10 innings on seven other occasions.)

The 19-inning contest set a record for the longest game in Senators history in Washington, surpassing the 18 innings on May 15, 1918, when Walter Johnson went the route against the Chicago White Sox' Lefty Williams in a 1-0 victory. It tied the longest game in Senators history, a 5-4 win over the Philadelphia Athletics on September 27, 1912, when Eddie Plank went the route in a tough-luck loss.

SOURCES

In addition to the sources cited in the Notes, the author accessed Retrosheet.org, Baseball-Reference.com, SABR.org, and *The Sporting News* archive via Paper of Record. A partial inning-by-inning summary is found in "Joe Judge Gets Trio of Triples Off 'Dixie' Davis," *St. Louis Star and Times*, August 9, 1921: 13.

NOTES

1. Denman Thompson, "Davis Vanquished Nationals in 19 Innings by Remarkable Display of Skill and Stamina," *Washington Evening Star*, August 10, 1921: 20.
2. Jack Nye, "Dixie Davis in Great Form; Goes Full Route for Browns," *Washington Herald*, August 10, 1921: 6.
3. Nye.
4. Louis Dougher, "Dixie Davis Sticks and Hangs Up Great Victory," *Washington Times*, August 10, 1921: 14.
5. Denman Thompson, "Game Sets a Record in Length for Capital," *Washington Evening Star*, August 10, 1921: 20.
6. According to Nye, Sisler had an RBI single; however, Thompson reported that Ellerbe scored on Mogridge's wild pitch. Neither Retrosheet or BaseballReference provides a play-by-play description of the game.
7. Nye.
8. Davis had executed a sacrifice bunt to the first-base side, but Judge's poor throw to second was late, and both he and Stuart were safe.
9. Nye.
10. Nye.
11. Nye.
12. Nye.
13. Nye.
14. Thompson, "Davis Vanquished Nationals in 19 Innings by Remarkable Display of Skill and Stamina."

A JOHNSON GEM

MAY 23, 1924
WASHINGTON SENATORS 4, CHICAGO WHITE SOX 0

by Thomas E. Schott

Walter Johnson, "The Big Train," one of the most storied and talented pitchers ever to grace a major-league pitcher's mound, threw only a single no-hitter in his 21-year career. If one argues that such a game defines a pitcher's "best game," then certainly the sparkling one-hitter Johnson threw at the Chicago White Sox on May 23, 1924, in Griffith Stadium must rank a close second. Some argued that it was far better than that – "one of the greatest games of baseball ever pitched," one reporter gushed. Even allowing for hyperbole, defending that claim isn't difficult.[1]

The 1924 season was Johnson's 18th in the big leagues, and the glory days of the 19-teens appeared to be fading into the past. It had been a "rejuvenating" year for him. Indeed, since 1920, Johnson's numbers compared with what had preceded them were for him "just OK." For example, he went 57-52 in the four-year stretch; his average number of strikeouts, innings pitched, and number of shutouts fell off, while his ERA, WHIP, walks, and hits allowed all crept higher.[2]

At the start of the 1924 season, Washington fans were widely bemoaning Johnson's decline. The 36-year-old right-hander had apparently reached his inevitable final slide out of the game. "Poor old Walter Johnson," they said. "He's almost in, down and out." They could not have been more mistaken. The Big Train that left the station in 1924 resembled the earlier models. And the cars it pulled had improved as well. Johnson's Senators would win their first-ever pennant that year, and the World Series, too. Johnson led the AL in a raft of pitching categories: number of wins (23), ERA and ERA+ (2.72/149), strikeouts (158), WHIP (1.116), strikeouts per 9 innings (5.1), and K/BB ratio (2.05). A pitching triple crown winner for the last of three times in his career –1913, '18, and '24 – he was unquestionably the league's most valuable player.[3]

The game Johnson won on this pleasant spring day in the nation's capital was his eighth start of the year. With his team in sixth place (12-16), he was 4-3 coming in, on his way to 19 more wins and only 4 more losses. His opponents, the White Sox, stood one place above the Nats in the standings, but they were headed to a dismal last-place finish, 25½ games behind these same Senators. Johnson's striking out 14 opponents, a marvel in 1924, has been surpassed over 200 times by major-league pitchers since then.[4] Another Johnson feat that day was fanning six consecutive hitters, which tied the AL record at the time. This, too, has been bettered several times.[5]

Employing what the writers referred to as "his shoots, slow balls, and fast" and "his smoke ball with great control," Johnson's side-arm deliveries baffled the White Sox the entire game. Still in the decades-long backwash of the team's decimation in the wake of the Black Sox scandal, Chicago was but a shadow of the dominant club of 1919-20. The lineup, though studded with three future Hall of Famers – not counting two pitchers on the bench – rose to the level of barely competent in comparison to the rest of the league.[6]

The Senators of 1924, however, were one of the best teams ever to represent the nation's capital. Besides the Big Train, the team had three additional Hall of Fame members on the field: Bucky Harris at second, Sam Rice and Goose Goslin in the outfield. And the team was nothing less than solid at every other position, from Joe Judge at first base to veterans Nemo Leibold in right field and Roger Peckinpaugh at short.

Johnson made swift work of the White Sox in the first inning. As if to preview coming events, he struck out the leadoff hitter Johnny Mostil, and then, in an odd spot to do it, he walked Harry Hooper, the only base on balls he'd surrender in the game. But Hooper was immediately erased when Eddie Collins lined a hot shot to Bucky Harris, who threw to Judge for a snappy double play. The pitcher the Senators faced this afternoon, 30-year-old Texan Dixie Leverett, was on the mound for the third of only 11 starts in the season. In his third season with the White Sox, Leverett had evinced little promise thus far, a course he would continue for the rest of the season.

The hometown boys didn't waste any time putting up a run for themselves. White Sox catcher Ray Schalk misplayed a bunt by leadoff hitter Leibold for an error. Leibold advanced to third on a sharp single to left by Harris and scored an unearned run on another single by Sam Rice. Three hitters into the game, Walter Johnson had all the runs he would need.[7]

The game settled into its more or less unrelenting groove for the next eight innings as Chicago came to bat in the second. Johnson faced three hitters: One flied out to center and the next two struck out. The Senators picked up another run in their half of the inning on Muddy Ruel's double, a sacrifice, and an infield out. Three up and three down for Chicago in the third, all strikeouts. That made five in a row for the Big Train. Again, the Nats scored a run in their half of the inning: Leibold bunted his way on and advanced on a sacrifice. He then scored on singles by Rice and Goslin.

The White Sox managed to get their lone hit in the top of the fourth inning. After Mostil fanned, Johnson's sixth consecutive K, Harry Hooper lined a clean line-drive single to right, getting the only hit for the visitors and halting Johnson's strikeout streak at six. Washington failed to score in the bottom of the fourth, and in the top of the next inning Johnson fanned three more White Sox. He now had a total of 10. The Senators scored their fourth and final run in the bottom of the inning. Leibold stroked a double to the left-field wall, went to third on a sacrifice by Harris, and then scored on a fly to right by Sam Rice.[8]

Johnson went on to strike out four more hitters, one in each of the following innings: Mostil, for the third time, in the sixth, then Hooper, then Willie Kamm in the eighth – also for the third time, and pinch-hitter Maurice Archdeacon (for Mostil) in the ninth to end the game. Only a pair of White Sox had reached base during this masterpiece of a game, and nobody had got any farther than first base. Reporters couldn't resist playing up the "comeback" aspect of game for Johnson. "Folks said he was losing his power," wrote a New York newsman. "To which Mr. Johnson and all the rest of us say 'Ha Ha.'" It's tempting to imagine that the Big Train himself might have entertained a similar thought.[9]

SOURCES

All statistics and play-by-play information are from Baseball-Reference.com/ and Retrosheet.org/boxesetc/1924/B05230WS11924.htm.

NOTES

1 "Walter Johnson Works Greatest Game of Career," *Fremont* [Ohio] *News-Messenger*, August 24, 1929.

2 Joe MacKay, *The Great Shutout Pitchers: Twenty Profiles of a Dying Breed* (Jefferson, North Carolina: Mcfarland & Company, 2003), 12. Any statements about the statistics Johnson posted from the "off" years 1920-23 must be seen in the context of the seasons that preceded them, which were by any measure stupendous. But his seasons from 1920 to '23 could hardly be described as shabby. Indeed, Johnson led the league in strikeouts and was among the league's most valuable players for two of those four "off" years.

3 "Walter Johnson Works Greatest Game of Career."

4 Readers interested in the list of these pitchers can find it at baseball-reference.com/tiny/gqjQP.

5 "Walter Johnson Ties League Record by Fanning Six in Row," *Chicago Tribune*, May 24, 1924. Johnson joined a pair of other hurlers who shared the record: T.J. O'Brien of the Boston Red Sox (April 26, 1913) and Jim Scott of the White Sox (June 22, 1913). On September 25, 2013, two pitchers for the Red Sox combined to strike out 11 consecutive Tampa Bay batters; see Adam Gilfix, "Red Sox Pitchers Set MLB Record with 11 Consecutive Strikeouts," HSAC, September 25, 2016, accessed Jul 14, 2019, harvardsportsanalysis.org/2016/09/red-sox-pitchers-set-mlb-record-with-11-consecutive-strikeouts/. The individual mark belongs to Tom Seaver of the New York Mets, who fanned 10 consecutive San Diego Padres on April 24, 1970.

6 *Philadelphia Inquirer*, August 24, 1924; "Walter Johnson Works Greatest Game of Career." The White Sox did not finish in the first division again until 1936, and from 1921 to 1935 they finished either seventh or in the cellar eight times. As of 2020 they have won only two pennants since 1919, and only a single World Series. The three future Hall of Famers on the field for the White Sox were Harry Hooper in right field, Eddie Collins at second base, and Ray Schalk, catcher; the pitchers were Ted Lyons and Red Faber. Modern analysts consider only Lyons and Collins as top-tier members of the HOF; the others are all either marginal or questionable to some degree. See Jay Jaffe, *The Cooperstown Casebook: Who's in the Baseball Hall of Fame, Who Should be in, and Who Should Pack Their Plaques* (New York: St. Martin's Press, 2017) and Bill James, *Whatever Happened to the Hall of Fame? Baseball, Cooperstown, and the Politics of Glory* (New York: Simon & Schuster, 1994).

7 Leverett had a distinctly awful year in 1924, finishing the season with a 2-3 won-lost record in 99 innings pitched and a 5.82 ERA to accompany a frightful 1.657 WHIP.

8 *Danville* (Virginia) *Bee*, August 24, 1924.

9 "Walter Johnson Yesterday's Hero," *New York Daily News*, August 24, 1924.

SURPRISING SLUGFEST ENDS IN NEAR-RIOT

JULY 13, 1924
WASHINGTON SENATORS 15, CLEVELAND INDIANS 11

by Steven D. Schmitt

Sunday, July 13, 1924, was a typical hot, humid midsummer day in Washington.[1] As the mercury climbed to 88 degrees, hot bats and hot tempers marked a surprising and memorable 15-11 slugfest between the Washington Senators and the visiting Cleveland Indians, who had won seven of the first nine meetings between the two teams. Washington and Cleveland combined for 30 hits, though they finished the season sixth and fifth in the American League in runs scored. The Senators had the league's best pitching but blew two early leads The Indians started George "The Bull" Uhle, who won 26 games in 1923 and 200 in a 17-year career, but did not last two innings. The offensive show, wrote Frank H. Young in the *Washington Post*, "set most of the 8,000 fans crazy."[2]

A bevy of bases on balls added to the scoring frenzy. Two Washington pitchers issued 11 free passes. Paul Zahniser walked six in three innings, allowed eight hits, and was charged with six runs. His three consecutive walks with two outs in the ninth inning resulted in the ejection of Washington manager Bucky Harris. which sparked postgame fisticuffs. A fan struck home-plate umpire Howard "Ducky" Holmes. A Cleveland player cold-cocked a fan who wanted to do the same. Police restored order but the fan escaped police and disappeared into the crowd.

The pennant race itself had become roasting hot for the Senators. They led the powerful New York Yankees by 3½ games on July 2, then lost four of five in Yankee Stadium – two by shutout. Next, they managed only a win and a tie in a five-game home series with the Detroit Tigers (including two morning/afternoon doubleheaders) that drew 89,000 fans to Griffith Stadium.[3]

Washington owner Clark C. Griffith still hoped that his longtime lovable losers would finally make the World Series. In December 1923 Griffith named Harris, his second baseman, as the Senators' manager. Harris took the job intending to lead the Senators to the pennant.[4] After a slow start that had fans and writers calling Harris's hiring "Griffith's Folly," Washington won 21 of 30 games in June, reaching first place on June 24. Over a nine-day stretch leading up to the July 13 contest, the Senators lost eight games and scored three or fewer runs seven times.[5] "If Manager Stanley Harris and his crew are serious about their pennant contentions," Frank H. Young wrote in the July 10 *Washington Post*, "they certainly have to put their bats to better use."[6] The offense failed American League Most Valuable Player Walter Johnson in two bids for his 11th win. The Big Train's 4-3 loss to Detroit on July 11 put the Senators in second place. (The *Post* titled the box score "Going Down!")[7] Splitting a July 12 twin bill with Cleveland put Washington 1½ games back of New York. Washington fans, who became known for loud whistling to distract opposing players, enjoyed watching their team's bats get hot from the start.[8] The Senators jumped on Uhle with their customary offensive attack of doubles and triples to take a 5-0 lead in the first two innings. Goose Goslin — who led the league in RBIs with 129 — laced a 3-and-0 pitch to right field for a two-out double to score Harris, who had doubled.[9] First baseman Joe Judge singled and Goslin scored. Right fielder Sam Rice's two-run triple and center fielder Nemo Leibold's single finished Uhle, who had not pitched in 22 days because of a badly sprained ankle that limited him to three or four workouts going into the game.[10]

Cleveland manager and center fielder Tris Speaker brought in rookie lefty Watty Clark, the eventual losing pitcher, who earned one victory for Cleveland that season but revived his career with a 19 victories for the Class B Terre Haute Tots. (From 1927 to 1937, Clark won 110 games, mostly with the Brooklyn Dodgers, posting 20 victories in 1932.[11]) Firpo Marberry saved 15 games for the Senators in 1924 as one of the game's first true relief pitchers. Pressed into service because of the Senators' grueling schedule of seven games in four days, Marberry started and worked two scoreless innings but walked three batters in the third to force in a run, then served up a two-run single to Cleveland catcher Glenn Myatt. In the fifth, Speaker drilled a two-run homer, the only circuit shot in the entire American League that day, to tie the score, 5-5. Speaker also singled, doubled, and drew three walks.[12] Goslin's two-run double broke the tie in the bottom of the fifth but he was out trying to stretch the hit into a triple.

Enter Paul Vernon Zahniser, whose 5-0 shutout of the Boston Red Sox gave the Senators their three-game lead on July 2. Pitching with a wrenched right wrist heavily bandaged, the second-year pitcher walked first baseman Turkey Brower and Chick Fewster Third baseman Rube Lutzke bunted them into scoring position and Clark singled to center to tie the game again, 7-7. The Senators answered with an eight-run eruption against Clark, rookie Luther Roy, and ex-Chicago Cub Virgil Cheeves. Shortstop Roger Peckinpaugh and third baseman Ossie Bluege placed bunt singles and Zahniser walked with the bases loaded. Judge doubled twice in the inning, the second time off Cheeves with the bases loaded, clearing the sacks. "Calling on Cheeves to pitch is an unpardonable sin," wrote Stuart M. Bell in the *Cleveland Plain Dealer*. "He has little 'stuff' and bad control." A "disgusted" Speaker went to Brower, who finished the game facing 10 batters without allowing a run. Bell lamented that Speaker "could win more ball games if he used better judgment in handling the few pitchers he has at his disposal."[13] Cleveland came back in the seventh, rapping Zahniser for four singles and three runs. Speaker – baseball's all-time leader with 792 two-baggers – cracked another of his specialties in the eighth and scored on Myatt's single.

Washington's four-run lead seemed safe when Zahniser got the first two outs in the ninth. Then Holmes gave leadoff batter Pat McNulty and left fielder Charlie Jamieson free passes. Speaker followed and worked the count to two balls and one strike. That was enough for Harris, who lost his cool, and Holmes ejected the rookie skipper for arguing balls and strikes and trying to "show him up."[14] Speaker walked and Cleveland shortstop and RBI leader Joe Sewell came up. Washington interim manager Joe Judge brought in a weary Allen Russell – one of the select group of pitchers still allowed to throw a spitball – who had worked in both ends of a doubleheader on July 9. Sewell flied to right field to end the game.

Suddenly "a hot-headed fan leaped from the (right-field) grandstand near the local dugout" and struck Holmes, prompting several hundred fans to surround the two men.[15] "Immediately players of both teams and Umpires George Moriarity and George Hildebrand rushed to Holmes' assistance," Bell reported. Fewster leaped on Holmes's assailant, who had struck the umpire in the temple and started to flee when Cleveland backup catcher Luke Sewell grabbed him. "Umpire Moriarity struck the fan with such force as to send him reeling from Sewell's grasp." Another fan tried to take a whack at Holmes but Lutzke delivered a knockout punch.[16] Eighth Precinct Police Captain Doyle and several officers responded and hauled the fan toward the exit between the grandstand and right-field pavilion, where the fan jerked himself loose and got away in the crowd. Police led the remaining fans to the exits while the players milled through the fans to their clubhouses.[17]

League President Ban Johnson suspended Harris indefinitely, apparently for calling Holmes a "fat head."[18] Harris watched from the stands while Peckinpaugh led the Senators to two victories, 12-0 and 4-2. The same umpiring crew worked both games. Blue-coated police officers occupied two boxes of the right-field pavilion for the first game and the *Washington Post* reported that the 3,500 fans who saw the Monday afternoon game under a threatening sky were "meek as lambs."[19] Harris returned to the dugout the next day.

The Senators also had their offense back. In mid-August, Walter Johnson told Harris that he wanted the ball every third day.[20] Washington went on to win its only World Series championship. Cleveland entered the game seven games behind the Yankees but remained in sixth place, the 1920 World Series title a fading memory. In all, six members of the Hall of Fame, including charter inductee Tris Speaker, played in this wild slugfest that really got the fans into the game.

Meanwhile Holmes's umpiring career ended after the season. He had been victim of another assault outside Sportsman's Park in St. Louis on June 24 when a fan, Paul Farina, struck him in reaction to Holmes's ejection of Browns manager George Sisler in a game against Detroit. "I was excited and I did it in the heat of passion," Farina told Court of Criminal Correction Judge Calvin Miller, who fined Farina $25.[21] Holmes had denied the Browns a putout because a pinch-runner for Ty Cobb who took off for second base had not been announced to the crowd. Sisler argued that the runner had, according to baseball rules, been engaged in the game and was out. Holmes held that play had not officially resumed and tossed Sisler.[22] A St. Louis Cardinals catcher in 1906, Holmes was a manager and owner of various minor-league teams, notably the Western League Sioux City Packers, during a 36-year baseball career.

SOURCES

In addition to the sources mentioned in the Notes, the author consulted Baseball-Reference.com and Retrosheet.org.

NOTES

1 "Weather by Telegraph," Washington, D.C., *Baltimore Sun,* July 14, 1924: 10.

2 Frank H. Young, "Fan Hits Umpire, Gets Hit, Escapes," *Washington Post,* July 14, 1924, Sports: 1.

3 baseball-reference.com/teams/WSH/1924-schedule-scores.shtml. Accessed November 27, 2018.

4 Mark Gauvreau Judge, *Damn Senators* (San Francisco: Encounter Books, 2003), 72.

5 baseball-reference.com/teams/WSH/1924-schedule-scores.shtml. Accessed November 27, 2018.

6 Frank H. Young, "Washington Gets Even Break with Ty Cobb's Tigers," *Washington Post,* July 10, 1924, Sports: 1.

7 Young, *Washington Post,* July 12, 1924, Sports: 1.

8 Judge, 86.

9 "Notes on the Nationals," *Washington Post*, July 16, 1924, Sports: 3.

10 Stuart M. Bell, "Indians Lose Slugfest to Senators," *Cleveland Plain Dealer,* July 14, 1924: 1.

11 baseball-reference.com/players/c/clarkwa02.shtml. Accessed November 19, 2018.

12 "Yesterday's Homers," *Cincinnati Enquirer,* July 14, 1924: 9; "Notes on the Nationals."

13 Bell: 12.

14 Young, "Fan Hits Umpire."

15 Young, "Fan Hits Umpire."

16 Bell, "Umpire Holmes Struck by Fan," *Cleveland Plain Dealer,* July 14, 1924: 12.

17 Young, "Fan Hits Umpire."

18 "Notes on the Nationals."

19 Young, "Ogden Blanks Indians with Harris in Stands," *Washington Post,* July 15, 1924: 2.

20 Tom Deveaux, *The Washington Senators, 1901-1971* (Jefferson, North Carolina: McFarland & Company, 1971), 65.

21 "Assailant of Umpire Holmes Is Fined $25," *St. Louis Post-Dispatch,* July 28, 1924: 18.

22 Herman Wecke, "Double Victory Puts Browns Within Two Games of First Position," *St. Louis Post-Dispatch,* June 25, 1924: 22.

THE BIG TRAIN TOSSES RAIN-SHORTENED NO-NO

AUGUST 25, 1924
WASHINGTON SENATORS 2, ST. LOUIS BROWNS 0
(7 INNINGS)

by Gregory H. Wolf

"Although Father Time has tried to mock the dean of pitchers in either major leagues," opined a sportswriter poetically about 36-year-old Walter Johnson in 1924, "the old man with the scythe could not have the cunning and strength from that great arm today."[1] The Washington Senators hurler continued his season-long resurgence by holding the St. Louis Browns hitless in a rain-shortened seven-inning contest.

Player-manager Bucky Harris's Senators were on a roll as they prepared to kick off a four-game series again the Brownies to conclude a 15-game homestand. The Nationals, as the team was often known, had won the first nine of those games to push their record to 69-52 and into a tie for first place with the New York Yankees. An AL charter member, the Senators had finished as high as second place just twice (1912, 1913) since 1901. The Browns, on the other hand were going in the opposite direction. Gorgeous George Sisler, who like Harris was juggling the duties as player and skipper for the first time in his illustrious career, had seen his club drop 11 of their last 17 and fall to 61-58 and fourth place.

One of the major reasons for the Senators' unexpected success was Johnson. In his 18th season, the Big Train "shook off the shackles of age" and was enjoying his best season in the Live Ball Era.[2] After posting a pedestrian 57-52 combined slate in his previous four campaigns – granted, for mediocre clubs – Johnson entered this game having won his last five starts (with a minuscule 1.43 ERA) to push his record to 16-6 and his career mark to 370-249. He was leading the AL in games started (29), shutouts (5), and strikeouts (121). His mound opponent was Frank "Dixie" Davis, a tall and lanky 33-year-old right-hander whose 150-pound stature was at least 50 pounds lighter than Johnson's. Davis was 8-8 (3.98 ERA) and 57-51 in his career, which spanned parts of eight seasons.

Despite threatening skies, the scheduled twin bill on a Monday afternoon in the nation's capital drew 7,000 patrons to Griffith Stadium. Johnson had tossed 103 career shutouts, easily the most in big-league history, and came out blazing his famous fastball and his dropping his knee-buckling curveball. Though his control was not what it was in his halcyon days more than a decade earlier, the robust 6-foot-1 hurler from Kansas still had enough heat to lead the AL in punchouts in 1923 for the 11th time in his career. After issuing a one-out free pass to Gene Robertson in the first, the Big Train dispatched the next 19 consecutive batters, though only two by strikeout, before walking dangerous cleanup slugger Ken Williams with two outs in the seventh.

Davis was shaky from the start, but didn't break. In the second Joe Judge led off by clubbing a double off the right-field wall, according to the *St. Louis Post-Dispatch*. Two batters later, Muddy Ruel blooped a Texas Leaguer to shallow center that might have led to the first run had not Baby Doll Jacobson raced in and slid to make a nifty catch. Roger Peckinpaugh followed with a line-drive single to left-field, but Williams fielded it cleanly and hurled a strike to nail a sliding Judge at home plate.

Johnson helped his own cause in the third by leading off with a single. (Adept with the bat his entire career, Johnson batted .235 and knocked in 255 runs in his career, including 20 twice.) He advanced a station on a passed ball by catcher Hank Severeid and then to third on Sam Rice's two-out single. Davis's bugaboo was his control; he had led the AL in walks in 1920 (149) and 1921 (123), and his wildness bit him in this situation. He walked Goose Goslin to load the bases, then walked Judge to push Johnson home, before Ossie Bluege's grounder forced Judge to end the frame.

The Nats had another leadoff hitter on base in the fourth when Ruel beat out a bunt back to Davis, whose wild throw to first enabled the slow-footed catcher to reach second. Peckinpaugh laid down a sacrifice bunt back to Davis, who was apparently indecisive about which base to throw to and ultimately threw late to first, and Peck was safe (no error charged). Johnson's perfectly placed bunt advanced both runners, but Davis once again extracted himself from danger by inducing popups by Earl McNeely and Harris.

Save for Judge's two-out double in the fifth, there was little action until the fateful seventh. McNeely

Regarded as one of the greatest pitchers in baseball history, Walter Johnson (pictured in 1917) won 417 games, including a record 110 shutouts, and led the Senators to their only World Series title, in 1924, and to the pennant the following season. (Photo by Sporting News and Rogers Photo Archive via Getty Images)

led off with a single and moved up on Harris's sacrifice. Rain began falling as Goslin stepped to the plate, but the eventual 1924 American League RBI champion shrugged off the weather and laced a triple down the right-field line to drive in McNeely with the second run of the game.

With the rain still coming down hard as the Browns prepared to bat in the eighth, home-plate umpire Dick Nallin sent both teams off the field. After a 30-minute wait, he called the game, giving the Senators a 2-0 victory in 1 hour and 25 minutes. The second game was also postponed and was rescheduled for the next day as part of a double-header.

Rain robbed Johnson of the chance to record his second official no-hitter (which according to MLB rules must be a complete game of at least nine innings). He had authored the first and at the time the only no-hitter in Senators history on July 1, 1920, when he beat the Boston Red Sox, 1-0, at Fenway Park. Despite its cavernous dimensions, Griffith Stadium had not been the site of an official no-hitter by either the Senators or an opponent, though two games deserve mention. Carl Cashion tossed an abbreviated six-inning no-hitter in the second game of a doubleheader on August 20, 1912, beating the Cleveland Naps, 2-0, in a game that was called so that the Naps could catch a train to Boston for a game the next day. In the first game of that twin bill, the Big Train set an AL record by winning his 15th straight decision, beating the Naps, 4-2. The Chicago White Sox' Jim Scott suffered a heartbreaker on May 14, 1914, when he held the Senators hitless through nine innings, then yielded two hits and a run in the 10th to lose, 1-0. In its entire existence, from 1911 through 1961, Griffith Stadium experienced only one no-hitter and it came from an unlikely source: Bobby Burke, a 6-foot, 150-pound swingman who tossed only four shutouts in his career. Burke turned the trick on August 8, 1931, beating the Red Sox, 5-0.

According to one report, Johnson threw only 67 pitches, consisting of 16 called strikes (all on curves), 12 swinging strikes, and 11 foul balls; 19 were hit for outs, giving the Big Train a 58/9 strike/ball count.[3]

It was indeed a magical season for Johnson and the Senators in 1924. He won his next five starts after his no-hitter and extended his winning streak to 12 games by beating the Chicago White Sox on September 22. In season for the ages, the Big Train won the pitching triple crown by pacing the junior circuit in victories (23), ERA (2.72), and strikeouts (158); he also led the AL in shutouts (6) and games started (38), and fewest hits per nine innings (7.6), and was named American League MVP. More importantly, he led the Nationals to the pennant and ultimately the World Series title over the New York Giants. Johnson emerged as one of the heroes by pitching four innings of scoreless relief in Game Seven and picked up the win when McNeely's double in the 12th inning drove in Ruel for the dramatic game-winning and Series-clinching run.

SOURCES

In addition to the sources cited in the Notes, the author accessed Retrosheet.org, Baseball-Reference.com, SABR.org, and *The Sporting News* archive via Papetr of Record.

Complete-play-by-play accounts were supplied by two newspapers:

"No-Hit Pitching of Walter Johnson Beats Browns, 2-0, in 7 Innings," *St. Louis Post-Dispatch*, August 25, 1924: 18.

Roy J. Gillespie, "Johnson Gives No Hits in Game Stopped in 7th by Rain," *St. Louis Star and Times*, August 25, 1924: 15.

NOTES

1 "Veteran Washington Twirler Blanks His Foes Without Hit or Run," *Philadelphia Inquirer*, August 26, 1924: 19.

2 "Veteran Washington Twirler Blanks His Foes Without Hit or Run."

3 "Veteran Washington Twirler Blanks His Foes Without Hit or Run."

ART NEHF OUTDUELS BIG TRAIN IN WORLD SERIES OPENER

OCTOBER 4, 1924
NEW YORK GIANTS 4, WASHINGTON SENATORS 3 (12 INNINGS)

GAME ONE OF THE WORLD SERIES

by Mike Lynch

The 1924 World Series pitted the National League's New York Giants, a team that had won 10 pennants since the inception of the American League's Washington Senators in 1901, against a team that had finally won its first pennant after a winning a franchise-best 92 games. Not only was that a mark the Giants had equaled or topped 13 times in 21 seasons since their first pennant in 1904, but John McGraw's men had *averaged* 92 wins over those 21 campaigns. Still, the Senators were not to be taken lightly.

New York Daily News writer Marshall Hunt predicted a Senators victory on the strength of a "flexible" and "strong" pitching staff, an infield "like a stone wall," a "heady catcher," a "good outfield," and "above all, an unquenchable and indomitable spirit to win."[1] The pitching staff was led by 36-year-old veteran Walter Johnson who had just recorded his 11th 20-win season with a league-leading 23 wins. He also topped the circuit in ERA at 2.72, and in starts, shutouts, and strikeouts en route to his second Most Valuable Player award.

His "heady" catcher was Muddy Ruel, who had thrown out 50 percent of would-be basestealers and was considered to be the class backstop of the American League;[2] the infield comprised first baseman Joe Judge, one of the top three offensive players on the team,[3] manager and second baseman Bucky Harris, third baseman Ossie Bluege, and Roger Peckinpaugh, the best defensive shortstop in the junior circuit. The outfield boasted two of the game's greats in Goose Goslin and Sam Rice, and a center field tandem of veteran Nemo Leibold and rookie Earl McNeely, who combined to hit .308 and scored 72 runs.

But Hunt's counterpart at the *Daily News*, Harry Schumacher, was convinced the Giants were too strong for Washington even despite injuries to starting third baseman Heinie Groh and second baseman Frankie Frisch. "The Giants are strong in every department of play," he wrote. "They can hit and field and run the bases and always have been able to score more runs on a given number of hits than their senatorial rivals."[4]

Johnson got the start for the Senators while McGraw countered with southpaw Art Nehf, a

14-game winner with an ERA of 2.01 in seven prior World Series starts. In the three previous World Series (1921-23), Nehf had tossed 58⅓ innings against the powerful New York Yankees and allowed only one home run. Johnson was making his first fall classic start since breaking into the big leagues in 1907.

President Calvin Coolidge threw out the first pitch to home-plate umpire Tommy Connolly and the Senators took their positions to "roars of applause" from the hometown fans.[5] The Giants went down easily in the first on a fly out by Freddie Lindstrom, a popout on a bunt attempt by Frisch and a called third strike on Ross Youngs.[6] Washington was equally ineffective, but the Giants almost suffered yet another injury when Harris collided with first baseman Bill Terry after grounding to shortstop Travis Jackson. Terry remained in the game and the Senators went down in order.

New York took an early 1-0 lead when George "High Pockets" Kelly belted a home run into the left-field seats to lead off the top of the second. Terry followed with a single over second base before Johnson fanned Hack Wilson for the first out. Jackson drew a walk to put Giants at first and second, and that brought 35-year-old backstop and 1914 World Series hero Hank Gowdy to the plate.[7] Gowdy lined a shot to Peckinpaugh, who caught the drive and threw to second to double off Terry and end the threat.

Judge drew a free pass in the bottom of the second but nothing came of it when Bluege struck out and Peck flied out to Wilson. Frisch started a two-out rally in the Giants' third with a double to center, but Ruel picked him off. Ruel walked to lead off the bottom of the inning and the crowd came to life with Johnson at the plate, but he quieted them with a double-play grounder, Jackson to Frisch to Terry. McNeely drew a base on balls before the frame ended on a Harris popout to short.

The throng was abuzz again when Johnson fanned Youngs and Kelly to begin the fourth, but Terry spoiled the mood with a homer to left to give the Giants a 2-0 lead. Then Johnson whiffed Wilson for his sixth strikeout of the contest. In the bottom of the fourth Nehf continued to confound Senators batters with a wide curveball and left Judge stranded after his two-out single. The left-hander was carving up Washington's lineup with the precision of a surgeon; Johnson's weapon of choice was a sledgehammer.

The Senators legend began the fifth inning with a four-pitch strikeout of Jackson before surrendering a single to Gowdy. He then retired Nehf and Lindstrom on three pitches, and the game stayed 2-0 in favor of New York. Nehf continued his dominance and set down Peckinpaugh, Ruel, and Johnson on only six pitches. Through five, the only hit Nehf surrendered was Judge's single in the fourth. Frisch walked to lead off the top of the sixth, but Johnson fanned Youngs for the third time in three at-bats, then retired Kelly and Terry on a fly out and popout, respectively.

Washington finally reached Nehf in the bottom of the sixth when McNeely ripped a two-bagger to left, went to third on a groundout by Harris, and came home when Rice grounded to Frisch for the second out of the inning. Goslin then singled but was caught stealing with Judge at the plate, and New York held a slim 2-1 lead going to the seventh. The Giants had a chance to extend their lead when they put runners at second and third on a walk to Gowdy, Nehf's bloop hit to right, and a passed ball, but Johnson got out of the jam by coaxing Lindstrom to ground to Jackson.[8]

Johnson almost cut into New York's lead in the seventh when he smoked a liner with Peckinpaugh and Ruel on base, but his drive was speared by a leaping Frisch and the game went into the eighth with the Giants still up 2-1. New York threatened in the eighth when Youngs doubled and moved to third on a groundout by Kelly, but he was foolishly picked off by Ruel to end the inning. The Senators made some noise in their half of the frame when Rice got a two-out walk and stole second, but Nehf struck out Goslin to end the brief threat.

New York had a chance to extend its lead in the top of the ninth when Wilson lined to right for his second hit of the game, then moved to second on a sacrifice. But when he tried to score on Nehf's two-out hit to Rice, the latter threw him out at the plate to keep the score at 2-1.

In the bottom of the ninth, Bluege shot a one-out hit past Jackson and into left, then scored the tying run on a "snorting" double to left-center by Peckinpaugh that set off a wild celebration.[9]

"Washingtonians were fit to be tied," reported Will Murphy in the *New York Daily News*. "Only a town that has never had a pennant winner could loose such a blast of joy. They threw cushions, they climbed down onto the field – someone even fired a pistol."[10] Play was suspended to remove the cushions from the field before Ruel and Johnson were retired to end the inning and send the game to the 10th.

Both teams threatened to score in the first extra frame – Frisch singled and stole second but was stranded; Harris and Rice poled out consecutive one-out singles, and Judge just missed winning the game when his bid for a homer hooked just past the right-field pavilion for a foul ball, then his fly to deep center was hauled in by Youngs. Johnson and Nehf were perfect in the 11th inning and that set up the climactic finish.

"The crushing break came in the twelfth inning," wrote Murphy. "The Giants had little enough to do. It was the eighteen years of pitching that beat Johnson, not the efforts of the New Yorkers, determined fighters though they were."[11] Gowdy walked to lead off and Nehf followed with a fly to center that fell just in front of McNeely, who attempted a shoestring catch before bobbling the ball, then fired it into the Giants' dugout to put runners and second and third with no outs. Jack Bentley hit for Lindstrom and walked to load the bases.

Bentley was replaced at first by Billy Southworth, who moved to second on a force out at the plate, Frisch grounding to Harris for the first out. Youngs dropped a single in front of McNeely to plate Nehf and give the Giants a 3-2 lead, and Kelly flied out to deep left field to score Southworth. Terry singled to load the bases again, but Goslin pulled in Wilson's liner to end the inning.

Little-used first baseman Mule Shirley hit for Johnson to lead off the bottom of the 12th and reached second when Jackson muffed his easy pop fly. McNeely flied out to center, then Harris cut the lead to 4-3 with a single to center that scored Shirley. Rice rapped a hit to center that sent Harris to third, but Rice was erased at second when he attempted to stretch his hit on Southworth's fumble. With two outs, Goslin tapped a slow roller toward second and was thrown out to end the game and give the Giants a one-game advantage in the best-of-seven Series.

SOURCES

In addition to the sources cited in the Notes, the author also accessed Retrosheet.org, Baseball-Reference.com, and SABR.org.

NOTES

1 Marshall Hunt, "News Experts Differ in Choice for Series," *New York Daily News*, October 4, 1924: 22.

2 Hunt.

3 Judge's 119 OPS+ was second to Goose Goslin's 143 and his Offensive Wins Above Replacement (oWAR) of 3.2 was third behind Goslin's 5.3 and Sam Rice's 3.3.

4 Harry Schumacher, "News Experts Differ in Choice for Series," *New York Daily News*, October 4, 1924: 22.

5 "Giants Leading Senators," *Elmira Star-Gazette*, October 4, 1924: 1.

6 Newspapers often referred to Youngs as "Young" and that was the case in the play-by-play from the October 4, 1924, *Elmira Star-Gazette*.

7 Gowdy's 1914 World Series slash line of .545/.688/.1273 ranks among the top five batters in World Series history (minimum 15 plate appearances).

8 Earlier in his at-bat, Gowdy insisted a Johnson pitch had hit him on the hand, but umpire Connolly wasn't buying it. Gowdy ended up at first anyway when Johnson walked him on his eighth pitch of the at-bat.

9 Will Murphy, "Giants Win Game of Games," *New York Daily News*, October 5, 1924: 2.

10 Murphy.

11 Murphy.

SENATORS BLOW NINTH-INNING LEAD, RECOVER TO EVEN SERIES AT ONE GAME APIECE

OCTOBER 5, 1924
WASHINGTON SENATORS 4, NEW YORK GIANTS 3

GAME TWO OF THE WORLD SERIES

by Mike Lynch

After a hard-fought Game One of the 1924 World Series in which Washington fell to the New York Giants, 4-3 in 12 innings, it was thought the Senators had shaken their jitters off and were more confident going into Game Two.

Senators skipper Bucky Harris called on 28-year-old left-hander Tom Zachary, a 15-game winner who had pitched to a then-career-best 2.75 ERA in 33 games. Giants manager John McGraw countered with his second straight southpaw starter, journeyman hurler Jack Bentley, who went 16-5 with a 3.78 ERA in 28 games.[1]

For the second straight day, Griffith Stadium hosted an overflow crowd and tickets were hard to come by. A ballpark that held 32,000 fans had seen crowds of 35,760 and 35,922, respectively, but those without tickets were determined to follow along on radio, and sales of radio "apparatus" jumped 50 percent in the Washington area.[2]

The Giants came out fast in the top of the first and loaded the bases on consecutive singles by Freddie Lindstrom and Frankie Frisch, and a one-out error by Harris on a grounder by High Pockets Kelly. But Zachary was able to get out of the jam with some help from catcher Muddy Ruel and a trio of infielders. Zachary had strike three on Irish Meusel, but Ruel couldn't hold on to the foul tip and Meusel had new life only to ground to third baseman Ossie Bluege, who started an around-the-horn double play to end the inning.

The Senators roared back in their half of the frame when Sam Rice singled over second with two outs, stole second with Goose Goslin at the plate, and came home on Goslin's blast into the right-field bleachers for a 2-0 lead. Joe Judge tapped a slow roller down the first-base line for another hit, but was forced at second on Bluege's grounder to end the threat.

"Yesterday the novelty of being league champions and participants in a world series was worn down a bit," wrote Eddie Trantor in the *Buffalo Enquirer*, "and the Senators displayed greater pep and agility on the field."[3]

Zachary settled in nicely in the second and retired the Giants in order on groundouts by Hack Wilson, Travis Jackson, and Hank Gowdy that

Arguably the best hitter in Senators history, Hall of Famer Goose Goslin batted .344 with an AL-best 129 RBIs and led the Senators to the World Series title in 1924, belting three home runs. A member of all three Senators pennant winners, the Goose batted .323 in parts of 12 seasons with the team. (Photo by Sporting News and Rogers Photo Archive via Getty Images)

went to Harris, Roger Peckinpaugh, and Bluege, respectively. Bentley was almost as effective and set down three of the four men he faced, the only blemish being a walk to Zachary.

Zachary continued his fine pitching and went to the sixth inning having allowed no hits since Ross Youngs' fourth-inning single. Bentley walked a tightrope in the third but came out unscathed. He walked Harris to lead off the inning and the Senators skipper went to second on Rice's sacrifice, then advanced to third when Gowdy dropped a third strike to Goslin and had to fire to first for the out. Bentley issued a free pass to Judge, but the latter was too eager to steal second and was thrown out at second base by the Giants hurler.

Bentley was more effective in the fourth and retired Bluege, Peckinpaugh, and Ruel in order, then set down Zachary and Earl McNeely to start the fifth before Harris extended Washington's lead to 3-0 with a home run into the left-field seats. Rice followed with a single to short right-center field, but Goslin fanned again to end the inning.

Zachary's run of success finally ended when he walked Lindstrom with one out in the top of the sixth. Harris ordered veteran right-hander Allen Russell to warm up, but Zachary quickly recovered and retired Frisch and Youngs to send the game to the bottom of the sixth with Washington clinging to a 3-0 lead.

Bentley wrapped groundouts by Judge and Peckinpaugh around a Bluege whiff, and Zachary took the hill again to start the seventh. New York finally broke through with a run when Kelly walked, went to third on Meusel's base hit past Peckinpaugh, and scored when Wilson grounded into a "lightning" double play that went from Bluege to Harris to Judge.[4]

That was all New York could muster and things looked bleak for the Giants when Zachary followed Bentley's perfect seventh with a perfect eighth. "The Washington pitcher was working like a well-oiled machine," reported the *New York Times*. But he needed some help from Peckinpaugh, who made a "brilliant play on Lindstrom's grounder and got the youngster at first by a step" to end the inning.[5]

Bentley was also in a groove and coaxed three straight groundouts off the bats of Harris, Rice, and Goslin in the bottom of the eighth, dispatching his 10th straight Senator without a hit since Rice's safety in the fifth. The top of the ninth saw Zachary go back out to finish what he started, but Harris was taking no chances and had pitchers warming up, including Firpo Marberry, who had set a new major-league single-season record for saves with 15.[6]

Zachary walked Frisch on four pitches, then threw a fifth straight ball to Youngs, prompting Ruel to confer with his pitcher in front of the plate. Youngs popped out to Peckinpaugh, then Kelly shot a liner to right-center field that Rice fielded brilliantly before firing a strike to Harris, who threw home but a hair too late to get Frisch, and Washington's lead was cut to 3-2. Zachary retired Meusel on a grounder that was headed to right before Harris snared it and threw to first for the second out. Kelly went to second and he and Wilson teamed up to tie the game when the latter punched a hit to right and the former went head-first over a crouching Ruel to knot the game at 3-3.

Marberry was called upon to end the threat and did so in quick fashion, firing three strikes past Travis Jackson, including a curve that Jackson "missed by at least a foot."[7] Judge led off the bottom of the ninth and drove one to left, but it went just foul. He followed with a shot down the first-base line that also went foul, then coaxed a walk out of Bentley. "The crowd gave vent to a big cheer," wrote the *New York Times*.[8] The Giants infield surrounded the hurler to give words of encouragement. Then Bleuge's sacrifice bunt sent Judge to second. "They yelled some more and now Peckinpaugh was at bat."[9]

As Peckinpaugh approached the plate swinging two bats, the crowd spurred him on. Frisch wanted an intentional walk to set up a possible double play, but McGraw overruled his captain and ordered Bentley to pitch to the Senators shortstop. Bentley's first pitch was a ball, then Peck fouled the next two off to go down 1-and-2 in the count before smashing a hit to left. "Peck hit the ball a mile a minute between Lindstrom and Jackson," wrote the *Times*. "Meusel fielded the ball well and threw swiftly, but there was no chance of catching Judge. He was over the plate in a great leap before Gowdy had the ball."[10]

Washington's 4-3 win tied the Series at one game apiece going into Game Three at the Polo Grounds in New York.

SOURCES

In addition to the sources cited in the Notes, the author also accessed Retrosheet.org, Baseball-Reference.com, and SABR.org.

NOTES

1. Bentley made his major-league debut with the Senators in 1913 and was with them until 1916, although he spent most of his time in the minors. Before landing with the Giants in 1923, Bentley starred for Baltimore of the International League and went 41-6 with a 2.07 ERA in 395 innings from 1920 through 1922.
2. "Thousands of Fans, Ticketless, Hear of Series Over Radio," Washington Post, October 5, 1924: 10.
3. Eddie Trantor, "Eddie Says," Buffalo Enquirer, October 6, 1924: 6.
4. "Senators Tie Series, Beat Giants, 4-3; To Play Here Today," New York Times, October 6, 1924: 1.
5. "Senators Tie Series."
6. The save scoring rule wasn't adopted until 1969 and saves were retroactively calculated by researchers for every season that came before. It's because of them that we know that Marberry passed Mordecai "Three Finger" Brown (13 saves in 1911) and Chief Bender (13 in 1913) on the single-season saves list when he recorded his 14th "save" on September 19, 1924, then pushed his total to 15 four days later.
7. "Senators Tie Series."
8. "Senators Tie Series."
9. "Senators Tie Series."
10. "Senators Tie Series."

PECKINPAUGH AND SENATORS FORCE GAME SEVEN

OCTOBER 9, 1924
WASHINGTON SENATORS 2, NEW YORK GIANTS 1

GAME SIX OF THE WORLD SERIES

by Don Zminda

As they prepared for Game Six of the 1924 World Series on the morning of October 9, the Washington Senators had reason to feel confident of a victory that would force a decisive Game Seven the next day. Although the Senators trailed the New York Giants, three games to two, the clubs had alternated victories thus far in the Series, with the Giants taking Games One, Three, and Five and the Senators winning Games Two and Four. The Senators would also be sending left-hander Tom Zachary, the winning pitcher in Game Two, to the mound for Game Six. Both of Washington's wins thus far in the Series had been recorded by lefties – in addition to Zachary's Game Two victory, George Mogridge had started and won Game Four. Over the first five games of the Series, Giants hitters had batted .356 (42-for-118) and slugged .517 against the Senators' right-handed pitchers; against Washington's lefties, the Giants were hitting .158 (9-for-57) and slugging .175. A southpaw on the hill also meant that Giants rookie Bill Terry — a left-handed hitter who was being platooned at first base with George Kelly — would probably not be in the lineup. Thus far in the series, Terry was batting .500 (6-for-12) against Washington pitching.

The Senators' Game Six lineup featured the return of shortstop Roger Peckinpaugh. A 33-year-old veteran who had missed only one game during the regular season, Peckinpaugh had been hurt legging out a game-winning double in Game Two, and hadn't played since being removed from the lineup in the third inning of Game Three. "As Harris' club took the field for the game's start," wrote Shirley Povich about Game Six, "a thunderous cheer acclaimed the figure of Roger Peckinpaugh limping toward the shortstop position. He was back in the Series after missing the fourth and fifth games, pain-wracked for three days with hemorrhages in his left thigh from an ugly Charley horse. Peck was strapped from ankle to waist to keep him upright, and had announced he'd be in the lineup 'if I have to break a leg to get in there.'"[1]

The Senators had one more thing going for them as Game Six started: President and Mrs. Calvin Coolidge were in the Griffith Stadium stands to root for the Senators. Only the second sitting president to attend a World Series game — Woodrow Wilson had been the first in 1915 — Coolidge had thrown out the first pitch on Opening Day of the 1924 season; the Senators had gone on to win the American League pennant for the first time in club history, so his presence was considered a good omen. He had also thrown out the first pitch before the start of Game One of the Series. In truth President Coolidge was neither much of a fan nor much of a ballplayer – syndicated columnist Westbrook Pegler wrote that Coolidge had thrown out the first pitch "with a windup and delivery like that of a lady throwing away a soiled glove"[2] — but First Lady Grace Coolidge was a passionate baseball fan who attended numerous games, faithfully recording the events on a scorecard. Senators player-manager Bucky Harris described Mrs. Coolidge as "the most rabid baseball fan I ever knew in the White House."[3] When Harris was married in October of 1926, the Coolidges would be among the guests.

Despite the presence of Zachary, Peckinpaugh, and the Coolidges, Game Six did not start well for the Senators. Giants second baseman Frankie Frisch doubled with one out in the top of the first. Frisch was caught in a rundown between second and third when Ross Youngs hit a bouncer to Zachary, but Youngs was able to make it to second while Frisch was being tagged out. Long George Kelly then singled to center, plating Youngs with the first run of the game.

New York's starting pitcher was left-hander Art Nehf, a veteran who was appearing in the World Series for the fourth consecutive year and who was making his ninth career Series start. Nehf had worked all 12 innings while defeating Senators immortal Walter Johnson, 4-3, in Game One, and he was sharp again in Game Six. After permitting a walk and a single in the first inning and another single (by Peckinpaugh) with one out in the second, Nehf settled down and retired the next eight hitters. But Washington broke through in the fifth. Peckinpaugh (described as "the limping veteran" by the *New York Times*) led off the inning with a single to left; according to the *Times*, "[Giants left fielder Irish] Meusel played the ball timidly and might have caught it with a bit more dash and daring." Peckinpaugh advanced to second on Muddy Ruel's sacrifice, and moved to third when Zachary grounded out. Senators leadoff man Earl McNeely then walked on four pitches and stole second ("helped," wrote the *Times*, 'by [catcher Hank] Gowdy's slowness in getting away his throw and by Frisch's failure to put the ball on the runner."[4]) Both Peckinpaugh and McNeely raced home when manager Harris singled to right.

Meanwhile the Giants were failing to score again off Zachary, despite putting runners on base in several innings. New York hitters recorded hits in the second, third, fourth, and seventh innings, but failed to capitalize each time. Then in the ninth, more heroics from Peckinpaugh helped preserve the Washington victory. Kelly singled for the Giants with one out, and Billy Southworth ran for him. Irish Meusel was the next hitter. According to the *Times*:

> *Meusel, the next man at bat, smashed a hard grounder to the right of second base. Peckinpaugh, limping badly from the effects of a sprint around the bases in the ninth, tore madly for the ball. It looked like a hit until Peck, forgetting his sore leg, forgetting everything except the duties of an old-time shortstop, managed to get his hands on the ball.*
>
> *Even then the hardest part of the play was still to come. Kelly [actually Southworth] was dashing madly for second base and Peckinpaugh was not in position to throw. Half turned away from the bag, he had to twist around swiftly and make a backhand toss to Harris. In getting the ball he had wrenched his leg severely and the second part of the play finished him. Turning quickly for the throw he tore a ligament behind the knee and his leg buckled up under him.*[5]

"Had that smash gone through," wrote Irving Vaughan, "there is no telling what might have happened. But it didn't get through, and Peck, knowing that he had met the big test when it came, stood on the spot from where he had thrown and smiled."[6]

Peckinpaugh needed to be helped from the field, with third baseman Ozzie Bluege moving to shortstop and Tommy Taylor taking over at third base. "35,000 folks, President Calvin Coolidge among them," wrote Vaughan, "rose up and noisily acclaimed [Peckinpaugh] the hero of a battle that will go down in the books because of its sheer brilliance."[7] Zachary struck out Hack Wilson on four pitches to finish the 2-1 win. "He held the Giants to a total of seven hits all day," wrote Shirley Povich of Zachary's performance, "and only one Giant reached second base after the first inning. Never did Zachary have a count worse than two balls against any hitter. He threw only ninety-seven pitches and kept the Senators in the ball game until they won it."[8]

Peckinpaugh's injury made him unavailable for Game Seven the next day. But with President and Mrs. Coolidge in attendance once more and Senators immortal Walter Johnson finishing the game in relief, Washington defeated the Giants, 4-3 in 12 innings for the franchise's first – and as it turned out, only – World Series championship during its 60 seasons in Washington.

SOURCES

Baseball-Reference box score and play-by-play baseball-reference.com/boxes/NY1/NY1192410060.shtml; accessed 9-27-2018.

David Pietrusza, "Grace Coolidge: First Lady of Baseball," davidpietrusza.com/coolidge-grace.html; accessed 9-26-2018.

"President Calvin Coolidge Baseball Game Attendance Log," baseball-almanac.com/prz_ccc.shtml; accessed 9-26-2018.

NOTES

1 Shirley Povich, *The Washington Senators: An Informal History* (New York: G.P. Putnam's Sons, 1954), 127.

2 Michal Beschloss, "The President Attends the World Series," *New York Times*, October 24, 2014.

3 William Bushong, "The First Fan: Mrs. Coolidge's Passion for the Game," whitehousehistory.org/the-coolidges-and-baseball; accessed 9-26-2018.

4 "Senators Win, 2-1; World Series Hinges on 7th Game Today," *New York Times*, October 10, 1924.

5 "Senators Win, 2-1."

6 Irving Vaughan, "Peck the Hero as Griffs Win from Giants," *Chicago Tribune*, October 10, 1924.

7 Vaughan.

8 Povich, 127.

BIG TRAIN FINALLY WINS THE BIGGEST ONE OF ALL

OCTOBER 10, 1924
WASHINGTON SENATORS 4, NEW YORK GIANTS 3 (12 INNINGS)

GAME SEVEN OF THE WORLD SERIES

by Stew Thornley

The 1924 World Series marked the fourth straight post-season appearance for the New York Giants and the first for the Washington Senators. Despite having Walter Johnson, who is still regarded today as one of the greatest pitchers of all time, the Senators had experienced limited success since the American League became a major league in 1901.

John McGraw, now 51 years old and completing his 23rd season with the team, managed the Giants. The Senators had a skipper known as the "Boy Manager." Bucky Harris was 27 years old when given the job of manager to go with his duties at second base at the beginning of the 1924 season.

Controversy shrouded the World Series on its eve. On October 1, Commissioner Kenesaw Mountain Landis placed New York outfielder Jimmy O'Connell and coach Cozy Dolan on the ineligible list for trying to bribe Philadelphia shortstop Heinie Sand to "not bear down too hard" in a September 27 game between the Giants and Phillies. The Giants won that game, 5-1, clinching the National League pennant as second-place Brooklyn lost to Boston. Sand reported the incident to his manager, who passed it on to league president John Heydler. Three other Giants — Frankie Frisch, Ross Youngs, and George Kelly — were implicated but cleared by the commissioner.

Nevertheless, a cloud hung over the New York team for its attempt to get preferential treatment from another team during the pennant race. Two days before the opening game, a rumor circulated that the Senators would not be playing the Giants, that New York had been disqualified and Brooklyn would instead represent the National League in the World Series.[1] The series went on as planned, with the Giants meeting the Senators, but American League President Ban Johnson, who had demanded the series be called off because of the scandal, refused to attend any of the games.

While the American League president was absent, the president of the United States, Calvin Coolidge, was on hand for the games played in Washington's Griffith Stadium. The normally laconic Coolidge was as excited as any of the Senators fans about their team playing for the championship. Many were even happier about the 36-year-old Johnson, who hinted at retiring from baseball at the end of the season,[2] finally getting his chance. Washington fans were even advised to not be "too vigorous" in shaking Johnson's hand in order to protect his right arm.[3]

However, Johnson—who had won 23 games during the regular season—was the losing pitcher in the 12-inning opener. He lost the fifth game as well, just two days before. It looked like he wouldn't get the World Series win so many were hoping for.

With Johnson unavailable, Bucky Harris had no obvious choice to pitch Game Seven. So he tried to deke McGraw. He started right-hander Curly Ogden, but planned to replace the 23-year-old in the first inning with the veteran George Mogridge, a lefty. Harris's goal was to neutralize Bill Terry, the Giants' left-handed first baseman, who was 6 for 12 in the series with a home run and a triple.

Although Terry later became one of baseball's best hitters, in 1924 McGraw was benching him against left-handed pitching. Harris hoped Terry would start the game, and then McGraw would pinch-hit for him when Mogridge came in. McGraw bit, putting Terry in a starting lineup that included seven future Hall of Famers.

The strategy worked—sort of. McGraw did not replace Terry immediately after Harris made his switch. Harris even stuck with his ersatz starter longer than he had intended after Ogden struck out Fred Lindstrom on three pitches to start the game. It was here that Harris had planned to call for Mogridge, and Ogden even started walking off the mound. However, his manager called him back and told him to try another batter. This one—Frankie Frisch—walked, getting Harris to finally signal for Mogridge, the man he had really wanted all along. Mogridge retired Ross Youngs and George Kelly to end the inning and kept the Giants off the scoreboard for the next four innings.

New York starter Virgil Barnes did even better in the early innings. Barnes retired the first 10 batters, five on strikeouts, when Bucky Harris stepped in with one out in the last of the fourth. On a 3-2 pitch, Harris hit a long fly that just cleared the low wooden fence in left field. Even Cal Coolidge rose and joined in on the prolonged applause that serenaded Harris as he trotted around the bases.

Giants left-fielder Hack Wilson was shaken up on the play as he tumbled into the left-field pavilion in pursuit of the ball. Wilson stayed in the game and got to a liner from Sam Rice, the next batter, snaring it with a diving grab and hanging on as he slid on his stomach for another few feet.

The Washington lead held into the sixth when Mogridge walked Ross Youngs to start the inning. Youngs was running on a 3-ball, 1-strike pitch to Kelly, who singled to center with Youngs going to third on the play. Bill Terry was up next, and at this point McGraw finally made his move by sending Irish Meusel up to hit for him. Harris countered by calling for right-hander Firpo Marberry.

Who won this battle of managerial maneuvers can be debated, but McGraw was pleased with the final result as Meusel hit Marberry's first pitch deep enough to right to bring in Youngs with the tying run. Wilson sent Kelly to third with another single to center. Travis Jackson then rolled a soft grounder to Joe Judge at first. Normally a sure-handed fielder, Judge bobbled the ball. Kelly had held up at third, but raced for the plate and scored when he saw Judge fumbling the ball. Jackson reached first safely on the error as the Giants took the lead. Things got worse for Washington when Hank Gowdy hit a grounder to shortstop Ossie Bluege. Rather than turning a double play to end the inning, Bluege had the ball roll through his legs. Wilson scored from second.

Barnes, now with a 3-1 lead, continued to mow down the Senators. After Harris's home run in the fourth, Barnes didn't allow another baserunner for the Senators until Harris came to bat again three innings later. Harris opened the seventh with an infield hit but was wiped out when Rice grounded into a reverse-force double play. Goose Goslin followed with a single but was left at first when Judge flied out to end the inning.

Art Nehf and Hugh McQuillan began warming up as the Senators came to bat in the last of the eighth, although it looked like they wouldn't be needed as Bluege popped out to start the inning. But pinch-hitter Nemo Leibold pushed a fastball off the end of his bat. The ball grazed third base on its way down the left-field line, and Leibold hustled into second with a double. Muddy Ruel, who was hitless in the series, punched a grounder toward right. Kelly, now playing first, got his glove on the ball, but Ruel had a single and the Senators had runners at the corners. Bennie Tate hit for Marberry and walked to load the bases with one out. Barnes retired Earl McNeely a low liner to left as the runners held, and it looked as if he had worked his way out of the jam when he got Harris to hit a ground ball toward Lindstrom at third. "Harris didn't hit the ball hard," reported the *New York Times*, "but just as the grounder hit in front of Lindstrom, the pellet took a sudden leap, cleared the fielder's head by a foot and rolled out to left field."[4] The bad-hop hit scored two runs.

After Nehf relieved Barnes and Rice grounded out to end the inning, the Washington fans roared for two reasons. One was the game-tying rally. The other was for Walter Johnson, who was on his way to the mound for the ninth inning. The Big Train would again get a shot at a World Series win, one that would give his team the championship.

However, Johnson quickly found himself in trouble, giving up a one-out triple to Frisch. He got out of it, though, by intentionally walking Youngs and then striking out Kelly on three pitches. Meusel then hit a grounder to third baseman Ralph Miller, who was saved by a great stretching catch of his erratic throw by Joe Judge.

Like the Giants, the Senators threatened in the last of the ninth. Judge singled with one out. Bluege grounded to Kelly, who threw to second to try and force Judge. Shortstop Travis Jackson was late in covering, then dropped the throw and had it roll away as Judge made it all the way to third on the error.

With Washington needing only a long fly to win, McGraw went to his bullpen, bringing in McQuillan to face Miller. After taking a ball, Miller hit a sharp grounder. It was right at Jackson, though, who made up for his error by starting an inning-ending double play and preventing the winning run from scoring.

A dramatic inning had failed to produce runs, and the game went into extra innings. The Giants continued to put runners on against Johnson, who continued to work his way out of jams. He walked Wilson to open the tenth, then struck out Jackson and got Gowdy to ground into a double play. In the top of the eleventh, a single and sacrifice gave the Giants a runner at second with one out. Johnson then struck out Frisch and, after an intentional walk, fanned Kelly – as he had two innings before -- with the go-ahead run in scoring position. Irish Meusel led off the twelfth with a single, but the Giants could advance no farther than first base in the inning.

As for the Senators, they went down in order in the tenth—although Johnson had sent a drive to deep center that was hauled in by Wilson—and got a two-out double by Goslin, followed by an intentional walk, in the eleventh off Jack Bentley, New York's fourth pitcher of the game. Bluege grounded into a force out to end that threat. With the game still tied in the last of the twelfth, Miller led off for the Senators with a soft ground ball toward second. Frisch charged in, gloved it, and threw to Kelly in time for the out.

Muddy Ruel lifted a pop fly behind the plate. Giants catcher Hank Gowdy had trouble with the ball from the start. He circled under it, then flung his mask away as he seemed to figure out the spot it would drop. However, at the last instant, Gowdy had to lunge to his right. He might have still made the catch if he hadn't stumbled over his mask. Nearly falling to one knee, Gowdy dropped the ball.

The error gave another chance to Ruel, who ripped a pitch inside third base and into left field for a double. The Giants missed a chance for the second out of the inning when Jackson booted Johnson's grounder to short, although Ruel had to hold on the play. With one out and the winning run on second base, Earl McNeely—hitless in five at-bats in the game—stepped to the plate and hit a sharp grounder toward Lindstrom.

News reports vary on exactly how the ball ended up past the Giants' third baseman, allowing the winning run to score. Most retrospective accounts describe it as a similar play to Harris's hit in the eighth, which took a bad hop over Lindstrom's head. Stories from the time, however, provide other details, some of them contradictory. *Washington Post* sports editor N. W. Baxter wrote, "The Pacific coast youth [McNeely] met a ball from Bentley. Down the third base line it sped. A momentary shout and then a hush for it was just the sort of ball on which Lindstrom had made a brilliant play and out when the game opened. This time it was not to be. Fortune evidently considered she had done enough for this boy who humbled Walter Johnson and played a real man's role throughout the series. His outstretched hands missed the ball completely, despite a marvelous dive. Muddy Ruel was in, standing up, with the winning run."[5]

The *New York Times*, on the other hand, went with the bad-hop version in one account—"Earl McNeely hit another hopper over Lindstrom that was twin brother to Harris's hit of the eighth, except that it was a little harder and, therefore, a more legitimate hit"[6] —in addition to adding another twist to the tale in a story elsewhere on the same page: "Around went the bat, and down the third base line, straight for Lindstrom, scurried the ball, going fast and bounding viciously. As Lindstrom crouched, the sun blinded him. He threw out his hands but the ball hopped like a thing possessed, shot up and over his head and never stopped."[7]

However it got by, through, or over Lindstrom, the ball made it out to left-fielder Irish Meusel, who held the ball, declining to make even the gesture of an attempt to head off Ruel with a throw home.

The Senators had their championship, Walter Johnson had his victory, and the citizens of Washington rejoiced on Pennsylvania Avenue and elsewhere through the night.

SOURCES

In addition to the sources cited in the Notes, the author also accessed Retrosheet.org, Baseball-Reference.com, and SABR.org.

NOTES

1. "Baseball Scandal Will Not Interfere with World's Series," *New York Times*, October 3, 1924: 1.
2. "Senators Win World Championship, Johnson Pitching Them to Victory over Giants, 4 to 3, in 12-Inning Battle," *New York Times*, October 11, 1924: 9.
3. "Handshakers Urged to Save Johnson's Arm for the Giants," *New York Times*, October 2, 1924: 18.
4. "Senators Win World Championship, Johnson Pitching Them to Victory over Giants, 4 to 3, in 12-Inning Battle," *New York Times*, October 11, 1924: 9.
5. N. W. Baxter, "Johnson Is Hero as Nationals Win Decisive Game of World Series, City in Carnival, Celebrates Victory," *Washington Post*, October 11, 1924: 5.
6. "The Johnson of Old Too Much for Giants," *New York Times*, October 11, 1924: 9.
7. Senators Win World Championship, Johnson Pitching Them to Victory over Giants, 4 to 3, in 12-Inning Battle," *New York Times*, October 11, 1924, p. 9

JOHNSON WINS 20TH FOR 12TH AND FINAL TIME

SEPTEMBER 11, 1925
WASHINGTON SENATORS 5, BOSTON RED SOX 4

by Gregory H. Wolf

"Many base ball critics have been trying to pass [him] out of the picture for the past several seasons," mused D.C. sportswriter John. M. Keller, but Walter Johnson continued to forestall the effects of age.[1] The 37-year-old Big Train went the distance to lead the Washington Senators to a 5-4 victory over the Boston Red Sox, thus reaching the 20-win plateau for the 12th and what would prove to be last time in his remarkable career.

Player-manager Bucky Harris's defending World Series champion Senators (85-48) occupied first place with a comfortable seven-game lead over the Philadelphia Athletics as the club prepared for its last home stand of the season. Coming off losses in three of their last five contests, the Senators began the 16-game stretch in the nation's capital with a two-game series against the lowly, last-place Boston Red Sox (39-94).

In a game between teams with the best and worst records in the big leagues, each club sent its ace to the mound. Skipper Lee Fohl called on 31-year-old rubber-armed submariner Howard Ehmke, who had followed up his 20-win, 316 ⅔-inning campaign in 1923 with 19 wins and a league-best 315 innings in 1924. His record thus far in '25, just 8-17, reflected his team's woes and dropped his career slate under .500 (122-128). In the twilight of his career, Johnson was at the top of his game. He was coming off an MVP season, having captured the AL pitching crown (23 wins, 2.72 ERA, and 158 strikeouts). It marked the first time in five seasons that Barney had reached the 20-win plateau. Despite missing a month of the '25 campaign with leg miseries, Johnson entered the game with 19 wins, second-most in the AL, a 396-256 lifetime record, and was pacing the junior circuit with a 2.96 ERA. Johnson "has baffled all opposing clubs," gushed Keller, and the writer wondered if he might equal his record from the previous campaign.[2]

It was a sweltering Friday afternoon with temperatures reaching the low 90s as the Nationals and Red Sox took the field for the 3 P.M. start time at Griffith Stadium.[3] The champions started in "brisk manner," noted the *Boston Globe*, as Sam Rice led off with a double.[4] After Bucky Harris popped up in an attempt to lay down a sacrifice, Goose Goslin walked, leading to a series of wild events.[5] The team's primary long-ball threat, Goslin was also dangerous on the basepaths and finished the season with a team-high 27 thefts. Goslin's presence on first bothered Ehmke, whose third throw over to keep him close "hit [him] in the head and bounced all the way to right field," according the beat reporter Frank H. Young of the *Washington Post*.[6] While Rice crossed the plate, first sacker Phil Todt retrieved the ball and threw wildly out of third baseman Doc Prothro's reach. The ball "hit one of the camera men's 'boxes,'" continued Young, and bounded back to Prothro, who then threw the ball to the plate erase Goslin.

The Senators tacked on another run in the fifth inning. Coming off an AL-most 216 hits and en route to a career-high 227 safeties in '25, Rice beat out a single "off Prothro's glove" with one out and stole second.[7] The 28-year-old boy wonder, player-skipper Harris laced an RBI single and moved up a station on left fielder Sy Rosenthal's throw home, but was left stranded on the keystone sack.[8]

Johnson looked strong in the early going, yielding only three baserunners in the first four frames. He worked around consecutive one-out singles by Jack Rothrock and Val Picinich in the fifth,[9] then was attacked savagely in the sixth. Rookie Roy Carlyle, whom the Senators had traded to the Red Sox on April 29 for Joe Harris, clouted a one-out home run over the right-field wall to cut the lead in half. After Todt doubled to the left-field corner, Prothro smashed a triple in almost the same spot to tie the game. Pitching on three days' rest, Johnson looked wobbly, but retired Bill Wambsganss on a grounder and then left fielder Goslin made what the *Boston Herald* described as a "brilliant running catch" on Rothrock's fly to left to end the threat.[10]

The resilient Nats took the lead in the seventh. After Bucky Harris reached on a bunt past Ehmke, Goslin lofted a deep shot, his 14th round-tripper of the season, over the right-field wall for a 4-2 lead. Coming off an AL-high 129 RBIs in 1924, the Goose knocked 113 in '25, the second of 11 times he reached the 100-RBI plateau.

A Senators victory seemed imminent after the Big Train rolled through the seventh and eighth innings without yielding a baserunner and began the final frame with a 4-2 lead. The "Sox become obstreperous in the ninth," declared the *Herald*.[11] Prothro led off by beating out a bunt when Johnson made no effort to cover first. Wambsganss lofted a routine fly to center fielder Ed McNeely, who had entered the game to begin the eighth as a defensive replacement for Bobby Veach, shifting Rice from center field to right.[12] According to Keller of the *Evening Star*, McNeely "misjudged the ball," recovered to catch it, then muffed it.[13] Boston and D.C. papers were miffed that the miscue was ruled a single for Wamby, putting runners on first and second. Two batters later, Denny Williams, pinch-hitting for Ehmke, hit a lazy grounder to first baseman Joe Judge that should have ended the game; however, Judge "found no one at any of the bases to take a heave for an out," reported Keller, and the bases were loaded.[14] Rookie Sy Rosenthal, who debuted three days earlier, singled to drive in the first two runs of his brief career, to tie the game, 4-4. An exhausted Johnson punched out Ira Flagstead for the third out.

Fohl sent Oscar Fuhr to the rubber in the bottom of the ninth. Not only were the Red Sox the league's lowest-scoring team, they also possessed the circuit's highest ERA. A southpaw, Fuhr was winless in five decisions with a bloated 6.54 ERA. "His arrival," opined Young, "took all the pep out of the party."[15] Goslin led off with a double. Judge executed a perfect sacrifice bunt which Todt fielded but then threw late to Prothro at third base.[16] Veteran Hank Severeid, a consistent .300 hitter acquired in a midseason trade with the St. Louis Browns, batted for McNeely and was walked intentionally to load the bases, then ceded to pinch-runner Nemo Leibold.[17] Needing a play at the plate to stave off defeat, the Senators got one, but not necessarily what they expected. Fuhr had a 3-and-2 count on Ossie Bluege, who took a low offering for ball four, thus pushing across Goslin for the winning run, ending the game in 2 hours and 14 minutes.

The Senators' comeback gave Johnson his 20th victory of the season, though it was far from one of his stellar games. He surrendered 11 hits, walked one, and registered just five punchouts. He reached the 20-win plateau for the 12th and final time, moving one ahead of Kid Nichols and trailing Cy Young (who accomplished it 16 times between 1891 and 1908) and Christy Mathewson (13 times between 1901 and 1914).

Johnson's victory proved to be his last of the 1925 regular season. He made only two more starts during the regular season, suffering from back pain, and finished with a 20-7 slate and a 3.07 ERA in 229 innings. The Big Train almost led the Senators to a second straight title, tossing consecutive complete game victories in Games One and Four in the World Series against the Pittsburgh Pirates, before losing Game Seven, 9-7, on a muddy field on a cold, wet, and miserable day in Pittsburgh, when the game should probably not have taken place.

SOURCES

In addition to the sources cited in the Notes, the author accessed Retrosheet.org, Baseball-Reference.com, and SABR.org.

NOTES

1 John M. Keller, "Johnson May Exceed His 1924 Record; Three American League Clubs in Hot Race," *Evening Star* (Washington), September 12, 1925: 13.

2 Keller.

3 "The Weather," *Evening Star*, September 12, 1925: 7.

4 "Pass in Ninth Beats Red Sox," *Boston Globe*, September 12, 1925: 6.

5 As of January 1, 2020, neither Baseball-Reference.com nor Retrosheet.org had a play-by-play account for this game. The events of this game are pieced together by game reports from the *Boson Globe*, *Boston Herald*, *Washington Post*, and (Washington) *Evening Star*.

6 Frank H. Young, "Nats Defeat Lowly Red Sox, 5-4," *Washington Post*, September 12, 1925: 17.

7 "Fuhr Passes Bluege in Ninth with Sacks Loaded and Senators Defeat Sox," *Boston Herald*, September 12, 1925: 6.

8 *Boston Globe.*

9 *Boston Globe.*

10 *Boston Herald.*

11 *Boston Herald.*

12 "Covey Due to Oppose Ruffing in Last Tilt Here for Red Sox," *Evening Star*, September 12, 1925: 13.

13 Keller.

14 Keller.

15 Young.

16 Keller.

17 "Covey Due to Oppose Ruffing in Last Tilt Here for Red Sox."

STANLEY COVELESKI WINS 20TH AND SECURES ERA TITLE

SEPTEMBER 22, 1925
WASHINGTON SENATORS 3, CLEVELAND INDIANS 2

by Chris Rainey

On August 27 the St. Louis Browns finished a sweep of Washington that allowed the Philadelphia Athletics to creep to within a half-game of first place. Since then the Senators (or Nationals, as many sportswriters called them) were on a torrid pace, posting a 16-5 mark. They were now on the verge of clinching their second consecutive pennant (92-50) when they hosted the Cleveland Indians on September 22.[1]

The Indians were struggling and stood in sixth place with a 67-78 record. They had taken the weekend series from Boston and came to the Capital City for a three-game series. Manager Tris Speaker had expanded the roster and was taking a look at some pitching prospects.

Stan Coveleski took the hill for Washington seeking his 20th victory. He was now 36 years old and was approaching the end of his Hall of Fame career. His primary pitch was the spitball. The pitch had been ruled illegal in 1920, but 17 pitchers who used the pitch were allowed to continue throwing it for the duration of their careers.[2] By September 1925 there were 11 of them still in the majors.

Coveleski would put his fingers to his mouth before every pitch but did not necessarily wet the ball. Making the batter think the spitball was coming could be as effective as actually throwing it. When throwing the spitball, he wet his index and middle fingers. To help generate saliva he would have alum in his mouth. He had a good curveball, a decent fastball, and a changeup to augment the spitter.[3]

Coveleski (nicknamed Covey) had enjoyed his finest seasons with Cleveland. He won 20 games in four consecutive seasons, including 24 wins when they took the 1920 pennant. He concluded that season by winning three games against Brooklyn in the World Series. He posted microscopic ERA (0.67) and WHIP (.630) numbers against the Robins.

But Coveleski's 1924 season was the weakest of his career. He had a losing record and his 4.04 ERA was the highest in his career to that point. In December Cleveland swapped him for two prospects and he was wrapping up his first season with the Senators. Teamed with Walter Johnson and in a pennant race again helped to rejuvenate him. His opponent was 27-year-old Emil "Dutch" Levsen, who had recently been recalled from Rochester and was making his second start in the majors.

The Senators were limping into the final games of the season. Shortstop Roger Peckinpaugh was nursing a foot injury and Walter Johnson was out of action with a charley horse. Coveleski took the hill for the early autumn game and retired the Indians in the top of the first. With one out in the bottom half of the frame Bucky Harris doubled to right field. After a foul out, Harris advanced to third when Joe Judge singled off Levsen's mitt.

Judge attempted to steal second, but the quick throw from catcher Glenn Myatt froze him on the basepath. The play was meant to be a double steal; however, Harris was slow in making his break for home. Both runners were now hung up "with the entire Indians infield and Myatt trying to make an out some place."[4] After five throws, Myatt chased Harris back toward third base and dove and tagged him for the third out.[5] What happened next varies with the newspaper account. The *Washington Evening Star* said that Harris rolled over and Myatt stepped on his hand. The *Cleveland Plain Dealer* wrote that third baseman Johnny Hodapp stepped on Harris, gashing his finger.[6]

Harris had to leave the game with a lacerated digit; Everett Scott replaced him. Harris missed the rest of the regular season but returned to play in the World Series. (The injury hampered him at the plate and he hit a lowly .087 as the Senators lost to Pittsburgh.)

The Indians got on the scoreboard first when Levsen walked to lead off the third. He advanced to second on a grounder and scored on a single to center by right fielder Homer Summa. Washington immediately tied the game in the bottom half of the inning. Sam Rice singled and scampered home on Scott's double. Judge hit an infield single, sending Scott to third. A walk to Joe Harris loaded the bases, but Levsen escaped the predicament by coaxing a popup from Ossie Bluege.

Rice and Scott struck again in the fifth. Rice singled and went to second on Levsen's wild throw.

Best remembered as a four-time 20-game winner who notched three wins in the 1920 World Series to give the Cleveland Indians the title, Hall of Famer Stan Coveleski joined the Senators as a 35-year-old in 1925, winning 20 games with an AL-best 2.84 ERA, to help the club to the pennant. (Photo by Sporting News and Rogers Photo Archive via Getty Images)

Scott drove him home and took second on the throw to the plate. Scott went to third on an infield grounder by Goose Goslin. Scott scored when Freddy Spurgeon "allowed Judge's slow roller to go through the wickets."[7] Washington now led 3-1. The next batter drove the ball into the left-center gap. Judge was given the stop sign at third but overran the bag and was caught by the relay throw.

The Indians staged a threat in the sixth when Summa opened with a Texas League single to center. After a brilliant fielding play by Rice on a line drive, Coveleski issued a walk to Joe Sewell. The next batter, Harvey Hendrick, forced Sewell, putting runners on the corners. Spurgeon beat out a slow infield roller as Summa scored. The inning ended on a fly ball without further scoring.

Both Levsen and Coveleski cruised through the final innings. Levsen retired the last nine with the help of a back-to-the-infield catch by shortstop Sewell. Coveleski had his wet one working brilliantly. Only Sewell reached base in the final three frames.

Coveleski picked up his 20th win of the season with the victory. He lowered his ERA to 2.84 with the performance. His nearest competitor for the ERA title was Herb Pennock, who surrendered nine earned runs in his last three outings. That raised Pennock's ERA to 2.96[8] and gave the title to Coveleski. His .800 winning percentage also topped the circuit with teammates Johnson and Dutch Ruether finishing third and fourth. The two teams were postponed the next day by rain and cold. They met in a doubleheader on the 24th with Washington taking both games and clinching the pennant.

Covey would not pitch any of the remaining regular-season games. Manager Harris gave three newcomers their first big-league starts at the end of the season. Not surprisingly, Washington dropped five of the last six games. Harris's plan was to go into the Series with Walter Johnson well rested and recovered from his injury and Coveleski fresh. Johnson won the opener and Game Four. Coveleski dropped both his starts, in Games Two and Five. The Pirates took the Series in seven games.

Coveleski returned to the Washington rotation in 1926 and won 14 games. The team dropped to fourth place. He returned in 1927 and posted a 2-1 record before being released in June because of a sore arm. He finished his career with the Yankees in 1928, winning five games in May and June. He pitched his last game on August 3 in St. Louis. He enjoyed a long retirement and was in Cooperstown for his enshrinement into the Baseball Hall of Fame in 1969.

NOTES

1. John B. Keller, "Nationals Making Smashing Stretch Drive: Pirates Are Given Edge at Shortstop," *Washington Evening Star*, September 23, 1925: 24.
2. Baseball America baseball-almanac.com/legendary/lispit.shtml on August 1, 2018.
3. Bill James and Rob Neyer, *The Neyer/ James Guide to Pitchers* (New York: Fireside, 2004), 173.
4. James and Neyer.
5. "Scott Races Across with Winning Tally," *Cleveland Plain Dealer*, September 23, 1925: 21.
6. The *Washington Post* coverage attributed the spiking to Myatt.
7. "Scott Races Across."
8. For decades Covey had an ERA of 2.84. In his page on Baseball Reference he is still listed at 2.84 with 76 earned runs allowed. However the Game Logs, also on Baseball Reference, show him allowing 78 earned runs, which account for a 2.91 ERA. Either way, Pennock's late-season woes handed the title to Coveleski. We leave it to the reader whether to accept the traditional 2.84 or the recent 2.91.

SAM RICE MAKES DAZZLING CATCH TO PRESERVE VICTORY, OR DID HE?

OCTOBER 10, 1925
WASHINGTON SENATORS 4, PITTSBURGH PIRATES 3

GAME THREE OF THE WORLD SERIES

by Gregory H. Wolf

The play sparked immediate controversy and remains one of the enduring questions in World Series history. Did Sam Rice catch Earl Smith's deep fly while falling into the stands to preserve the Washington Senators' 4-3 victory in Game Three of the 1925 World Series? Sportswriter Chester L. Smith described Rice's feat as "one of the historic puzzles of sportdom,"[1] while his colleague Charles J. Doyle at the *Pittsburgh Gazette Times* considered it "either good acting or the real thing"[2] and Edward F. Balinger of the *Pittsburgh Post* dismissed it as "one of the most doubtful affairs ever witnessed."[3]

After splitting the first two games of the fall classic in Pittsburgh, the reigning World Series champion Senators returned to the nation's capital. On a Saturday afternoon with temperatures in the high 30s, "wintery zephyrs wheezing,"[4] and a field that "was swept by hurricane blasts that chilled to the marrow,"[5] Griffith Stadium was packed with 36,495 spectators. The huddled masses in heavy coats and blankets, according to Ralph S. Davis of the *Pittsburgh Press*, looked like a "cross between a baseball mob, a football gathering and an assemblage witnessing a boat race."[6] President Calvin Coolidge, who had hosted the Pirates at the White House earlier that day, threw out the ceremonial first pitch, after which a band played the "Star Spangled Banner" and then a bugler performed a rendition of "Taps" in honor of icon Christy Mathewson, who had died three days earlier, before the flag was lowered to half-staff.[7]

Player-manager Bucky Harris sent Alex Ferguson to the mound, a choice many pundits found perplexing. The 28-year-old right-hander, acquired in mid-August from the New York Yankees, was playing for his third team in '25 and went 5-1 down the stretch for the Nationals, with a cumulative record of 9-5 but an unsightly 6.18 ERA. He walked Eddie Moore to lead off the game and then plunked Max Carey to put himself in a hole that was eventually remedied when Clyde Barnhart hit into an inning-ending double play. Pie Traynor led off the second with a liner just out of reach of right fielder Joe Harris's shoestring attempt, according to Ballinger, and the ball rolled to the fence; Traynor was credited with a triple.[8] He scored on Glenn Wright's sacrifice fly to give the Bucs a 1-0 lead.

The Pirates seemed to have an advantage on the hill with their dependable starter, 32-year-old right-hander Ray Kremer, who had posted a 17-8 slate in the regular season. Their defense, however, looked shoddy in the early rounds, committing an error in each of the first three frames. Rice collected the Senators' first hit, leading off the third with a single, and then scored the tying run on Joe Judge's two-out double. A heads-up play by first baseman George Grantham saved a potential run, according to Davis, when he retrieved shortstop Wright's errant throw on Joe Harris's grounder and threw home to nab Judge, who was attempting to score on the miscue.[9]

Ferguson was once again on the ropes in the fourth, when Kiki Cuyler, coming off a phenomenal season, batting .357 and leading the majors with 144 runs scored and 26 triples, led off with a double to deep left-center field that looked as though it would bound over the wall for a home run, but Rice chased the ball down to save a run [According to pre-1931 rules, balls that traveled 250 feet and then bounced into the stands were credited as home runs, not ground-rule doubles].[10] Barnhart grounded through the shortstop hole and left fielder Goose Goslin fired a running throw home, but Cuyler slid under Muddy Ruel's tag while Barnhart moved to second. Traynor followed with a walk, and it looked as if the Pirates might blow it open. But after two infield outs and an intentional walk to Smith to load the bases, Kremer fanned to end the threat.[11]

While Kremer "was brilliant in the early innings," mused Doyle, the high-flying Pirates, who had led the majors with an average of 6.0 runs per game, threatened again in the sixth.[12] On first via shortstop Roger Peckinpaugh's throwing error, Wright scampered to third on Smith's two-out single, just evading Buddy Myer's sweeping tag on a bullet from Joe Harris. Kremer hit what seemed to be a routine inning-ending grounder, but the ball made an awkward bounce out of reach of second baseman Harris and into center field, scoring Wright. After Moore walked to fill the bases for the second time in three innings, catalyst Carey, who had batted .343 and led the NL in stolen bases for the 10th time in the last 13 seasons, fanned swinging.

With the Bucs seemingly in control of the game, yet holding a precarious 3-1 lead, the atmosphere was tense at Griffith Stadium, and it became even more edgy when Goslin, one of the heroes of the Senators '24 title team, led off the sixth by hitting a line drive "on the bound" into the center-field bleachers for a home run.[13]

After Ferguson set down the Pirates in order in the seventh, strategic decisions by Harris led to a two-inning stretch described by Harry Cross of the *New York Times* as "an exhibition of nerve and wonderful spirit."[14] Little used Nemo Leibold, pinch-hitting for Ferguson, drew a walk on four pitches and was replaced by pinch-runner Earl McNeely. Two batters later, the 28-year-old player-manager himself bunted a lazy roller down the third-base line. Catcher Smith "followed the ball, waiting for it to roll into foul territory," reported Cross, but was "too impatient" or too nervous, picked it up before it crossed the line and threw late to first.[15] Surprising the Pirates and none more than Pie Traynor, considered the premier third sacker in the NL, the team's most dangerous slugger Goslin bunted to third to load the bases. After Judge's fly ball tied the game, Joe Harris singled to plate his skipper and give the Senators a 4-3 lead.

Bucky Harris's decisions in the field proved as important as those at the plate. In the bottom of the pivotal eighth inning, Rice moved from center field to right, replacing Judge, whose "stout legs all knotted with muscle carry no speed," opined sportswriter Damon Runyon,[16] while McNeely took over center field. To the mound came right-handed Firpo Marberry, whom Mark Armour described in his SABR biography as "the first great hurler to be used primarily as a reliever."[17] Marberry fanned Wright and Grantham, then Smith connected on a hard-hit blast to right field. Playing back, "Rice and the ball reached the bleachers rail at the same instant,"

One of the premier hitters and right fielders of his generation, Hall of Famer Sam Rice collected at least 200 hits in a season six times and batted .323 in his 19 years with the Senators (1915-1933). His 2,889 hits, 1,466 runs, 479 doubles, and 183 triples rank first in franchise history. (Photo by Sporting News and Rogers Photo Archive via Getty Images)

reported Chester L. Smith. "Sam leaned far into the crowd, with his back to the infield, and, almost hidden from the views of the grandstand."[18] According to Balinger, Rice jumped "into the air and toppled partly over a small fence in front of a low tier of circus seats."[19] By the time Rice got up with the ball in tow, Smith was rounding third, and veteran NL umpire Cy Rigler, signaled a catch, despite manning second base approximately 250 feet away from the action.[20] It was an "astounding, one-handed catch," exclaimed Runyon.[21] Pirates players, led by skipper Bill McKechnie, had a different view and poured out of the dugout in protest as the scene teetered on the verge of a melee. Generally soft-spoken, an enraged McKechnie subsequently went to the box seat occupied by Commissioner Kenesaw Landis and stated that he would lodge a formal protest if the Pirates lost. Landis rejected any protest, declaring the catch the umpire's call.

In the midst of the confusion surrounding Rigler's call, another peculiar scene took place in the bottom of the frame. After Ruel singled, Marberry laid down a sacrifice bunt; however, he should have been out because he batted out of turn, but no one noticed the error.[22] Rice grounded to short to make the point moot.

Rice's catch is the most memorable play of the game, but the Pirates' inability to collect a clutch hit with men in scoring position was the reason for their loss. In the nail-biting ninth inning, the Pirates loaded the bases with one out on singles by Moore and Carey and Cuyler's hit by pitch. Needing just an outfield fly to tie the game, cleanup hitter Barnhart, who batted .325 and knocked in 114 during the regular season, popped up to the catcher. Traynor, whose exploits at the plate (batting .320 with 106 RBIs) almost matched his defensive prowess, drew three consecutive balls, leading Bucky Harris to walk from second to the mound to confer with Marberry. Waiting for his pitch, Traynor took two called strikes before launching a routine popup to McNeely to end the game in 2 hours and 10 minutes and give the Senators a two-games-to-one lead in the Series.

"The Senators won today's game because they were smarter than the dangerous Pirates," opined Cross.[23] Harris's decisions late in the game proved to be pivotal, while the Pirates lacked punch in the crunch, going 2-for-12 with runners in scoring position and leaving 11 men on base, including three times with bases loaded.

After the game, at least two men gave affidavits that a boy handed the ball to Rice; however, those sworn testimonies didn't lead to a reversal of Rigler's call.[24] According to Davis, McKechnie intended to file an official protest, but Pirates owner Barney Dreyfuss did not allow it.[25] Rice himself gave two statements about the play to reporters, one claiming that he had caught the ball and the other stating that he had "momentarily" caught the ball before a fan grabbed it from him.[26] A catch, or no-catch, Rice's play became part of World Series lore.

SOURCES

In addition to the sources cited in the Notes, the author accessed Retrosheet.org, Baseball-Reference.com, SABR.org, and *The Sporting News* archive via Paper of Record.

NOTES

1 Chester L. Smith, "McKechnie Protests Game to Landis, Then Withdraws It - Fans Say Rice Drops Ball," *Pittsburgh Gazette Times*, October 11, 1925: 1.

2 Charles J. Doyle, "Rice Questionable Catch of Smith's Hit Robs Corsairs of Run," *Pittsburgh Gazette Times*, October 11, 1925: III, 1.

3 Edward F. Balinger, "Doubtful Catch of Smith's Hit into the Stands Features," *Pittsburgh Post*, October 11, 1925: 1.

4 Balinger.

5 Doyle.

6 Ralph S. Davis, "Pirates Meet President and Have Big Day - Everywhere Except in Baseball Arena," *Pittsburgh Press*, October 11, 1925: 1.

7 Ralph S. Davis, "Johnson and Yde Slated to Pitch," *Pittsburgh Press*, October 11, 1925: 1. Davis also noted that the band played "Nearer, My God, to Thee" after the bugler performed "Taps."

8 Balinger.

9 Balinger.

10 Doyle.

11 The first of those outs was a bang-bang play. According to Doyle, first baseman Joe Judge's "brilliance" saved a potential run when he saved a bad throw from shortstop Roger Peckinpaugh on Glenn Wright's grounder. "It was apparent to all that he was safe," mused Davis. "Johnson and Yde Slated to Pitch."

12 Doyle.

13 Davis, "Johnson and Yde Slated to Pitch."

14 Harry Cross, "Senators Conquer Pirates By 4 to 3 in Game of Thrills," *New York Times*, October 11, 1925: 1.

15 Cross.

16 Damon Runyon, "Joe Harris Wins Game with Bat, Taken Out, Speedy Outfielder Makes Great Play," *Pittsburgh Gazette Times*, October 11, 1925: 1.

17 Mark Armour, "Firpo Marberry," SABR BioProject, sabr.org. sabr.org/bioproj/person/d7ce09aa.

18 Smith.

19 Balinger.

20 Balinger.

21 Runyon.

22 McNally should have batted in the ninth spot because he was the pinch-runner for Leibold, who had pinch-hit for the pitcher; Marberry was in Joe Harris's batting position.

23 Cross.

24 Smith.

25 Ralph S. Davis, "President Prevented a Protest," *Pittsburgh Press*, October 12, 1925: 24.

26 Davis, "President Prevented a Protest."

THE BIG TRAIN TOSSES SHUTOUT TO PUT SENATORS ON CUSP OF SECOND STRAIGHT TITLE

OCTOBER 11, 1925
WASHINGTON SENATORS 4, PITTSBURGH PIRATES 0

GAME FOUR OF THE WORLD SERIES

by Gregory H. Wolf

The accolades came pouring in after Walter Johnson's resounding six-hit shutout of the Pittsburgh Pirates in Game Four of World Series. "Johnson vindicated the judgement of the world that he is the greatest pitcher of all time," gushed syndicated sportswriter High Fullerton.[1] Though Johnson's performance was not as overpowering as his 10-strikeout, five-hit, 4-1 victory in the Series opener, sportswriters seemed in awe of the Big Train. "The king of pitchers returned to his throne," mused Chester L. Smith of the *Pittsburgh Gazette Times*.[2] Edward F. Balinger of the *Pittsburgh Post* raved about Johnson's "bewildering delivery";[3] "his easy sidearm motion was a delight to watch," cooed Harry Cross of the *New Yok Times*;[4] while Ralph S. Davis of the *Pittsburgh Press* lauded his "clever, heady ball."[5]

Johnson's pitching and what Regis M. Welsh of the *Pittsburgh Post* described as a "relentless attack which combined great pitching, opportune hitting and superior thinking power" put the Washington Senators one win away from capturing their second consecutive title. "The battle along the Potomac has turned into a rout," continued Welsh, whose Pirates were nominal favorites entering the World Series. "The situation looks darker than midnight in a dungeon as far as Pittsburgh's chances are concerned," wrote Balinger poetically.[6]

Skipper Bill McKechnie's NL pennant winners were in disarray as they prepared to play the fourth game of the fall classic. They were still smarting from the controversial call on the Senators' Sam Rice's acrobatic catch while tumbling into the stands, robbing Earl Smith of a potential game-tying home run in the eighth inning of the previous game. Even more concerning was the Bucs' offense, described as "pitiful" by Davis.[7] Featuring seven starters who batted at least .308, and easily leading the major leagues by averaging 6.0 runs per game, the Pirates had managed only 20 hits (in 96 at-bats) and scored seven runs through the first three games of the Series. The vaunted hitters, opined James B. Harrison of the *New York Times*, have shown "nothing like the fast whirling attack which tore the National League open from stem to stern."[8] The Pirates had pitching trepidations, too. Game One starter Lee Meadows, who had led the team with 19 wins, was suffering from a sore elbow, reported Smith, forcing McKechnie to send Emil Yde to the mound, a decision that would eventually be lambasted by Smoky City scribes.[9] A southpaw, Yde (17-8) had made only one start since September 13.

Unlike the previous cold, blustery, and windy day in the nation's capital, the weather was not a factor in this contest. On a sunny, though gradually increasingly cloudy Sunday afternoon with temperatures in the 50s, Griffith Stadium was packed with 38,701 spectators.

"The thrills, the chills and enthusiasm of the Saturday's game," opined Fullerton, "were entirely lacking."[10] Save for one disastrous inning when all of the runs were scored, the game was about the Big Train. The 37-year-old right-hander finished the season with a 20-7 slate, the 12th and final time he reached the 20-win plateau, pushing his career record to 397-257. He had also showed his age, missing a month of the season and also struggling with leg pain down the stretch.

Johnson was in complete control of this game, yielding only six hits, four of them of the scratch variety to the infield, and not a hard-hit ball. His only scare came in the second inning when Pie Traynor led off with a single to third base, the Nationals' weakest link. Regular starting third sacker Ossie Bluege, considered among the best fielders in the AL, missed his second straight game after a beaning in Game Two. In his stead was rookie Buddy Myer, who had played only four games all season. Myer knocked the ball down, but was unable to make the throw. Two batters later, George Grantham hit a high, slow bounder to Myer, whose throw was late. Bluege, opined Davis, "would have turned [those hits] into putouts."[11] Johnny Gooch's two-out grounder pushed runners to second and third, then Yde's grounder ended the inning. It was the only time the Pirates had a runner on third base.

The game was essentially decided in the third inning when the Nationals combined hard hitting with some good luck. The Big Train, who batted .433 and drove in 20 runs in the regular season, led off with a single. He approached first tentatively, then inexplicably, coach Everett Scott waved him to second, where left fielder Clyde Barnhart "nailed him easily."[12] That play subsequently had consequences for Johnson. Rice followed with a tricky bouncer to second baseman Eddie Moore. Moore stopped the ball but slipped and fell, and was unable to make the throw. Grantham fielded player-manager Bucky Harris's routine grounder and threw to Glenn Wright, attempting to retire the lead runner. According to sportswriter Charles L. Doyle of the *Pittsburgh Gazette Times*, the "ball either hit the runner on the shoulder or it crashed against Wright's arm."[13] In a lefty-lefty matchup, Goose Goslin, who led the club with 18 round-trippers, while batting .334 with an AL-most 20 triples, whacked what speared to be an "ordinary long ball" to Barnhart in left field.[14] Bothered by the sun, Barnhart lost track of the ball, which went over his head and bounced into the bleachers for a home run (according to pre-1931 rules, balls that traveled 250 feet and then bounced into the stands were credited as home runs, not ground-rule doubles), giving the Senators a 3-0 lead. It was Goslin's record-breaking fifth home in World Series competition, eclipsing Babe Ruth's mark of four. Joe Harris followed with a prodigious blast that landed almost in the same spot as Goslin's "bounding liner."[15] "Yde looked bad," declared Davis, "lacked good control, and was forced to groove the ball to get it over."[16] He walked Joe Judge before Johnny Morrison was summoned from the bullpen. The Senators kept the pressure on. After Judge was caught stealing, Roger Peckinpaugh singled and stole second and Muddy Ruel walked before Myer's weak grounder ended the inning. In a scathing review of the Pirates, Fullerton opined, "A more subdued and heartless ball team seldom has taken the field and two terrific smashes in the third made them groggy and hopeless."[17]

Johnson proceeded to give a pitching clinic. "Giving Walter Johnson four runs to work with is something like handing Henry Ford a flivver or presenting Germany another debt," joked sportswriter Grantland Rice.[18] Hurling with a severe charley horse since his ill-fated attempt to stretch out a single, the Big Train did not yield a baserunner in the third, fourth, or fifth inning. While Morrison pitched 4⅔ scoreless innings to keep the Pirates close, Bucs hitters continued their Series-long slump. "Pittsburgh's batting power has been throttled," opined Harrison.[19] Johnson's pain was evident when he made no attempt to cover first on Max Carey's swinging bunt in the sixth; and he had a similar play an inning later on Grantham's smash to first.[20] Traynor led off the seventh with the Pirates' first clean hit of the game. Reflective of the luck the Pirates had all afternoon, Wright followed with a bullet right at Bucky Harris, who jumped to snare the ball, then doubled up Traynor.

The Senators rallied in the seventh, leading off with singles by Bucky Harris and Goslin. Joe Harris belted a fly to deep left, but Barnhart made a leaping catch to save a potential home run. Two batters later, with runners on first and third and Peckinpaugh at the plate, the Senators tried a double steal. Grantham took Morrison's throw to first and quickly fired home to nab Harris on a close call that elicited a round of boos from the crowd.[21]

A "thrill seemed to grip both benches," declared the *Pittsburgh Post,* when McKechnie sent Babe Adams to the mound in the bottom of the eighth inning.[22] The 43-year-old right-hander had debuted in 1906 and was the star of the Pirates' only title thus far, when he tossed three complete-game victories over the Detroit Tigers in 1909. After yielding a double and a scratch single, Adams faced Johnson to the delight of fans. Catcher Johnny Gooch picked up Johnson's easy roller in front of the plate and tagged Ruel at home. Adams then retired Sam Rice to end the innings.

Johnson "didn't come near approaching the speed he showed in the series opener," noted Davis, punching out just two batters, but the future Hall of Famer didn't need to overpower hitters.[23] He issued his second walk of the game to lead off the ninth before Traynor hit into a 6-3 twin killing. Wright hit another grounder to Bucky Harris in almost exactly the same spot to end the game in exactly two hours.

Johnson's gem put the Senators on the precipice of another title. In two games against the Pirates, Johnson had yielded just 11 hits, fanned 12, and walked three. Many wondered if the Big Train had yet another miracle in him, yet hoped that the Senators' other future Hall of Famer, 20-game winner and '25 AL ERA-champ (2.84) Stan Coveleski, would make it a moot point in Game Five.

SOURCES

In addition to the sources cited in the Notes, the author accessed Retrosheet.org, Baseball-Reference.com, SABR.org, and *The Sporting News* archive via Paper of Record, as well as:

"'Babe in the Woods," In Nine Acts, by Walter Johnson," *Pittsburgh Post*, October 12, 1925: 12.

NOTES

1 Hugh Fullerton, "Fullerton Says Pirates Were Subdued Before Playing," *Baltimore Sun*, October 12, 1925: 9.

2 Chester L. Smith, "Two Homers Route Yde. Pirates Batters Helpless Before 'Master' - Joe Harris Again Hero," *Pittsburgh Gazette Times*, October 12, 1925: 1.

3 Edward F. Balinger, "Homers by Goslin and Joe Harris Off Yde Win; Bucs Helpless at Bat," *Pittsburgh Post*, October 12, 1925: 1.

4 Harry Cross, "Washington Wins; Johnson Shuts Out Pittsburgh, 4 to 0," *New York Times*, October 12, 1925: 1.

5 Ralph S. Davis, "Pirates Battle Against Odds," *Pittsburgh Press*, October 12, 1925: 1.

6 Balinger.

7 Davis, "Pirates Battle Against Odds."

8 James B. Harrison, "Senators Outclass Pirates All the Way," *New York Times*, October 12, 1925: 25.

9 Chester L. Smith, "Sports Shafts. Bucs in Batting Slump," *Pittsburgh Gazette Times*, October 12, 1925: 11.

10 Fullerton.

11 Davis, "Pirates Battle Against Odds."

12 Ralph S. Davis, "Sport Chats. Pirates Not Down Hearted," *Pittsburgh Press*, October 12, 1925: 14.

13 Charles L. Doyle, "Bucs Hope to Carry Battle to Home Field and to Rally There," *Pittsburgh Gazette Times*, October 12, 1925: 9.

14 Davis, "Sport Chats. Pirates Not Down Hearted."

15 James B. Harrison, "Senators Outclass Pirates All the Way," *New York Times*, October 12, 1925: 26.

16 Davis, "Pirates Battle Against Odds."

17 Fullerton.

18 Grantland Rice, "One More Victory Will Give Crown to Washington," *Baltimore Sun*, October 12, 1925: 1.

19 Harrison.

20 Balinger.

21 Balinger.

22 "Adams Facing Johnson Is Lost in Heat of Battle," *Pittsburgh Post*, October 12, 1925: 9.

23 Davis, "Pirates Battle Against Odds."

BUCS OFFENSE WAKES UP AS ALDRIDGE'S COMPLETE GAME GIVES PIRATES HOPE

OCTOBER 12, 1925
PITTSBURGH PIRATES 6, WASHINGTON SENATORS 3

GAME FIVE OF THE WORLD SERIES

by Gregory H. Wolf

The Pittsburgh Pirates "played headier baseball this afternoon than they have at any time in the series," gushed Smoky City sportswriter Chester L. Smith, as the NL pennant winners beat the Washington Senators, 6-3, in Game Five of the fall classic to stave off elimination.[1] The Bucs' offense, which had scored only seven runs in the first four contests, finally emerged from its Series-long slump. It was "hard to single out the heroes," mused another *Pittsburgh Gazette Times* reporter, Charles J. Doyle, as each of the starting position players hit safely;[2] however, one player stood out: pitcher Vic Aldridge. Praised by Smith for his "cool demeanor," Aldridge tossed his second complete-game victory against the defending World Series champions.[3]

The Senators, led 28-year-old boy wonder player-manager Bucky Harris, were primed to capture consecutive titles in front of their partisan fans in the third and final game in the nation's capital. Playing like a "well-oiled machine,"[4] they were coming off victories in Game Three, preserved by center fielder Sam Rice's eighth-inning tumbling catch into the bleachers and ensuing controversial call, and Walter Johnson's shutout in Game Four. Pirates skipper Bill McKechnie, on the other hand, was searching for answers. The Bucs' vaunted offense, which led the NL with a .307 batting average and 6 runs per game, had managed just 26 hits and a .205 batting average through the first four games. "The Pirates seemed to be whipped, not only in the box score, but in spirit," opined sportswriter Westbrook Pegler.[5] McKechnie shook things up by replacing starting first sacker George Grantham, who batted .326 in the regular season, but had managed just two inconsequential singles in the Series, with a 34-year-old backup and former World Series star with the Philadelphia Athletics and Boston Red Sox, Stuffy McInnis.

The pitching matchup featured a repeat from Game Two. Aldridge, known as the Indiana Schoolmaster because of his former job, had posted a 15-7 slate during the regular season (68-50 career). He owned the Pirates' only Series win, a complete-game eight-hitter, 3-2, over Stan Coveleski. On paper, at least, the Senators had the advantage with their 36-year-old future Hall of Famer, the spitballing

"Covey," considered among the best hurlers of the era with 194 victories at the time. In his first season with the Senators, he won 20 games for the fifth time and led the AL in ERA (2.84) for the second time in three years. Coveleski was also a World Series hero, having tossed three complete-game victories to lead the Cleveland Indians to the title in 1920.

Griffith Stadium was packed with 35,899 spectators, including President Calvin Coolidge, for the 2 P.M. start time on Monday despite the "dull, leaden skies, with rain threatening at any minute," noted syndicated sportswriter Hugh Fullerton.[6] From the outset, the Pirates looked like a different team as they attacked Coveleski. After Max Carey and Kiki Cuyler hit consecutive one-out singles, left fielder Goose Goslin made a "spectacular catch," opined Pirates beat reporter Edward F. Balinger, to rob Clyde Barnhart of a potential extra-base hit.[7] (Goslin repeated the gem the next inning, snaring McInnis's liner on the run.) Pie Traynor walked to load the bases, but the Senators, who had seemingly caught all the breaks in the Series thus far, had more good luck. Glenn Wright's liner back to the mound "almost wrenched the glove from Coveleski," noted scribe Pegler, but the ball caromed to Bucky Harris at second, who made a quick throw to nab Wright at first, ending the threat.[8]

Like his mound mate, Aldridge was battered in the opening frame. Rice led off with a single and moved up a station on Bucky Harris's sacrifice bunt, then scored on Goslin's Texas Leaguer along the foul line in short left field, stretching it to a double. Joe Harris coaxed a two-out walk, but both runners were left stranded.

Coveleski labored in the third. "It was evident from the second pitched ball," mused Fullerton, that he "had nothing;"[9] while sportswriter Harry Cross of the *New York Times* observed that "his wet ones did not have the hop and deception."[10] With one out Carey walked and then stole second, colliding violently with Harris, who was "momentarily injured."[11] The ball was jarred from Bucky's glove and squirted into center field, but Carey was unable to advance. Senators gathered around their skipper, who was rubbing his shoulder, but he remained in the game. After Cuyler drew another walk, Barnhart singled to drive in Carey and tie the game, then Traynor's sacrifice fly gave the Pirates a 2-1 lead.

The Pirates rallied again in the fourth. With two outs and runners on first and third, Senators first baseman Joe Judge produced "one of the most brilliant plays of the series," according to sportswriter Regis M. Welsh of the *Pittsburgh Post*, to save a run.[12] Judge "dove frantically" to snare Carey's hard bounder over the first-base bag, according to Smith, stopped the ball with his glove, then "lying on his stomach" crawled several feet and touched the base with the ball.[13]

In the fourth the Senators pounded Aldridge, who like Coveleski seemed to lack his best stuff at this point. Joe Harris led off with a home run into the left-field bleachers to tie the score. His third round-tripper of the series tied a World Series record set by Babe Ruth (1923) and equaled by his teammate Goslin in 1924. After Muddy Ruel and Ossie Bluege, playing for the first time since he was beaned in Game Two, connected for a single and double, respectively, to move into scoring position with one out. At this critical juncture, McKechnie motioned for reliever Tom Sheehan to start warming up while Harris decided to let the struggling and weak-hitting Coveleski bat; it was a decision roundly castigated by sportswriters the next day. Coveleski fanned and then Rice grounded out, ending the threat.

Coveleski, like Aldridge, hurled a clean fifth and benefited from a double play to end the sixth, but met his demise in a disastrous seventh. With one out, he walked Eddie Moore, Carey singled, and then Cuyler grounded "through Bluege's legs" to give the Pirates the lead again, 3-2.[14] Coveleski was bothered by "fleetest runners in modern baseball" on first and third, according to Welsh.[15] Barnhart followed with another single, driving in Carey and sending Coveleski to the showers. In came rookie reliever Win Ballou, who had logged only 27⅔ innings during the regular season. On his third strike to fan Traynor, Ruel caught Cuyler off third, attempting to steal home.

As they had all Series, the Senators responded to the Pirates' tallies. Pinch-hitting for Ballou, Nemo Leibold led off with a double and then scored on Rice's single. Once again on the ropes, Aldridge "closed in upon the American League champions with a grip of steel," gushed sportswriter Grantland Rice.[16] After Harris executed a sacrifice bunt, Aldridge dispatched the Senators' most dangerous sluggers, Goslin and Joe Harris, sandwiched around a walk to Judge.

The Pirates' offense was a "continual fusillade" in the final two innings, wrote Rice.[17] Wright led off the eighth with a double down the left-field line off Tom Zachary (12-15). A left-hander whose 33 games started tied for the AL lead, Zachary was the odd man out as Harris leaned on his aces, Johnson and Coveleski, in the World Series. Standing out "like a beacon light" for his leadership, according to Doyle, Stuffy McInnis singled home Wright to give the Pirates a 5-3 lead. In the final frame, with Barnhart on second and Traynor on first via a walk and single respectively, Wright greeted Firpo Marberry, the Nationals' fourth reliever of the game, with an RBI single.

Described by Damon Runyon as the "bulldog of baseball," Aldridge cruised through the eighth and ninth innings, retiring all six batters he faced and completing the game in 2 hours and 26 minutes. Aldridge's coolness under pressure was resolutely praised by reporters. In twirling his second complete-game victory of the World Series, Aldridge yielded eight hits, walked four, and struck out five, while permitting only two hits in nine at-bats with men in scoring position. As important as Aldridge's hurling was the re-emergence of the Bucs' offense. The thus-far dormant Pirates batters collected 13 hits, including five in 12 at-bats with runners in scoring position; in a balanced attack, five different players knocked in at least a run and five also scored at least one.

With their 6-3 victory the Pirates rekindled their aspirations for their first World Series championship since 1909. In order to do so, they would have to accomplish what had never been achieved in World Series history to that point: overcome a three-games-to-one deficit. Returning to Pittsburgh for Game Six and a potential Game Seven, the Pirates were suddenly brimming with confidence.

SOURCES

In addition to the sources cited in the Notes, the author also accessed Retrosheet.org, Baseball-Reference.com, SABR.org, and *The Sporting News* archive via Paper of Record, as well as:

"Play-by-Play Story of Aldridge's Second Victory in Series," *Pittsburgh Post-Gazette*, October 13, 1925: 15.

NOTES

1 Chester L. Smith, "Bucs' Victorious Attack Sustained from Start to Finish of Battle," *Pittsburgh Gazette Times*," October 13, 1925: 11.

2 Charles J. Doyle, "Pirates Show Power When Backed to Wall," *Pittsburgh Gazette Times*, October 13, 1925: 11.

3 Smith.

4 Harry Cross, "Washington Wins; Johnson Shuts Outs Pittsburgh, 4 to 0," *New York Times*, October 12, 1925: 1.

5 Westbrook Pegler, "Capital Tearfully Turns Again to Scoreboard as Superstition That Bucs Are Sure Death to Lefthanders Gets Confirmation," *Pittsburgh Post*, October 13, 1925: 11.

6 Hugh Fullerton, "Wrong Tactics Used by Harris," *Baltimore Sun*, October 13, 1925: 14.

7 Edward F. Balinger, "Senators Use Four Pitchers in Vain Effort to Stop Bucs," *Pittsburgh Post*, October 13, 1925: 1.

8 Pegler.

9 Fullerton.

10 Harry Cross, "Pirates Win, 6-3; Washington's Lead Cut to One Game, *New York Times*, October 13, 1925: 1.

11 Smith.

12 Regis M. Welsh, "Pirates Confident After Putting on Surprise of the Series," *Pittsburgh Post*, October 13, 1925: 14.

13 Smith.

14 Smith.

15 Welsh.

16 Grantland Rice, "Pirates Club Way to Victory in Fifth Clash," *Baltimore Sun*, October 13, 1925: 1.

17 Rice.

BIG TRAIN TAKES A LONG JOURNEY TO DEFEAT MACK'S A'S

APRIL 13, 1926
WASHINGTON SENATORS 1, PHILADELPHIA ATHLETICS 0 (15 INNINGS)

by Ken Carrano

Opening Day, at least as far as the Washington Senators were concerned, was Walter Johnson's private domain. Johnson made his first Opening Day start for the Senators in 1910, shutting out the Philadelphia Athletics, 3-0. In the next 15 years, Johnson missed only three Opening Day nods, and won five straight openers between 1913 and 1917. In six Opening Day starts beginning in 1910, the A's were the opponent, and Johnson was 4-2 in those games, with all four wins shutouts. So it was no surprise when Nats manager Bucky Harris named Johnson to start the 1926 season against Connie Mack's men.[1]

Nor should have anyone been surprised to see that Mack considered Slim Harriss to face Johnson on Opening Day. In both the 1923 and 1924 openers, Harriss and Johnson faced off, with Harriss winning the 1923 game, 3-1 and Johnson prevailing, 4-0, in 1924. However, Mack was considering three others to start as well – Sam Gray, Stan Baumgartner, and Eddie Rommel.[2] It would be the knuckleballer Rommel who would get the ball to face the Big Train.

It had been customary in the previous few years for the president of the United States to throw out the opening pitch in Washington to start the baseball season, but President Calvin Coolidge, mourning the death of his father, did not attend. The US Senate adjourned three hours early on this day so that Vice President (and Nobel Peace Prize recipient) Charles Dawes was tasked with throwing out the first pitch in Coolidge's stead.[3] Dawes' throw sailed three feet over the head of Johnson, who was positioned about 30 paces away.[4] It would be one of the few missteps from anyone participating in the nation's capital on this chilly day.

In the first four innings, Johnson gave up two singles, a one-out single to Bill Lamar in the first inning, and a two-out single to Max Bishop in the third. Neither man left first base. Rommel was better, not allowing a baserunner through the first 12 Washington hitters. When Johnson batted with two out in the bottom of the third, Vice President Dawes accompanied 9-year-old Edwin Marshall of Springfield, Illinois, to the plate. Edwin had won a trip to Washington in an essay contest and presented Johnson with a silver cup.[5] Johnson rolled through the top of the fifth, adding his fourth strikeout of the game, and the Senators finally got a man on board in the bottom of the frame when Joe Harris singled to right. A sacrifice by Joe Judge made Harris the first player to get to second base in the game, but he would move no further.

The Senators got runners to second base in the sixth and seventh innings as well but neither could advance. A two-out single to center and steal of second by Sam Rice brought manager Harris to the plate, but his groundout to Rommel ended the sixth. In the seventh, a two-out single by Judge and Rommel's first walk of the game, to Ossie Bluege, again put a runner in scoring position, but again Rommel induced an inning-ending groundout. Both Johnson and Rommel threw perfect eighth innings, and in the top of the ninth, the loneliness of third base ended. Johnson had allowed only one hit since the third, a single by Al Simmons, who was quickly erased in a double play. Now in the ninth, a one-out walk to Bishop, Johnson's first of the game, started a small rally. The free pass was followed by Lamar's grounder to Buddy Myer, whose wide throw to first pulled Judge off the bag, and the A's had two aboard for the first time. Walt French followed with a fly to right that allowed Bishop to get to third. But there he remained as Johnson induced a soft line drive by Simmons to Goose Goslin to end the threat. The Senators followed with a rally of their own that also fell short. Manager Harris walked to start the frame and was sacrificed to second by Goslin. Joe Harris popped out to first, and then Judge was intentionally walked. The strategy worked, as Bluege grounded into a fielder's choice, and the 25,000 in attendance would have to bundle up for further baseball.

Neither pitcher was bothered with a little overtime, as both were perfect in both the 10th and 11th, with Johnson adding four more strikeouts to his major-league-leading career total.[6] In the 12th, however, both teams had a chance to end the proceedings. Lamar's second single of the game started the frame for the A's and a sacrifice and groundout moved him to third. Johnson walked Joe Hauser, bringing up future Hall of Famer Mickey Cochrane, whose long liner was caught by Rice in center. In their half, the Senators loaded the bases with one out on singles by Judge and Bluege and a walk to Myer. Manager Harris had Jack Tobin pinch-hit for catcher Muddy Ruel, but his grounder to short forced Judge at home. Johnson had a chance to end the game but flied out to right, sending the game to the 13th. Johnson pitched around a leadoff single in the top of the inning and then the Senators again loaded the bases without tallying, as Bluege popped up with the winning run on third. Johnson found himself in trouble in the 14th when with one out Walt French had the first extra-base hit of the afternoon, a double to left. A fly ball moved French to third, but after a walk, Cochrane again failed to deliver by flying harmlessly to left.

The Senators sent everyone home to a warm shower in the 15th, when with one out three consecutive hits ended the game. Manager Harris singled to center and moved to third on Goslin's double to right. Joe Harris's single to left drove in Bucky and gave Johnson his 108th career shutout. The winning manager was excited about how the season had started. "I hope I'm not unduly optimistic, but it seems to me that the boys proved that they are not only in good physical condition but have the same old will to win that has meant so much the past two years," Harris said. "They say a good start is half the battle. They'll have to catch us to beat us."[7] The Senators would be caught and unable to defend their crown, finishing fourth in the league. The game was the sixth and last in which Johnson threw 15 innings or more, his first since a 7-6 loss to the Detroit Tigers in August of 1918. It was his ninth Opening Day victory, still a major-league record as of 2019.

For Johnson, in his 20th major-league season, his next start was seven days later against the New York Yankees, who battered him for seven runs in three innings in an 18-5 defeat. Then he won his next five decisions, all but one a complete game. Rommel, 10 years younger than Johnson, threw in relief against the Senators on the 16th, three days after the 15-inning game, then again in Philadelphia on April 21, beating Washington 5-2 on a three-hitter. He pitched more than nine innings only twice more in his career. One of these games was a historic 17-inning relief appearance on July 10, 1932, against the Cleveland Indians, winning 18-17.

SOURCES

In addition to the sources listed in the Notes, the author accessed mlb.com, Retrosheet.org, and Baseball-Reference.com.

retrosheet.org/boxesetc/1926/B04130WS11926.htm

baseball-reference.com/boxes/WS1/WS1192604130.shtml

NOTES

1. Only Tom Seaver (16) has made more Opening Day starts than Johnson. Another Johnson, Randy, and Steve Carlton and Jack Morris are tied with Walter Johnson with 14 openers.
2. James Isaminger, "Lamar Injured, but May Play in Opener," *Philadelphia Inquirer*, April 13, 1926: 22.
3. Paul W. Eaton, "Business as Usual with the Senators," *The Sporting News*, April 22, 1926: 1.
4. James Isaminger, "Athletics Bow to Senators Before Huge Crowd in tFifteen-Inning Diamond Duel," *Philadelphia Inquirer*, April 14, 1926: 27.
5. "Johnson Promises Boy to do His Best and He Does," *Washington Post*, April 14, 1926: 1.
6. At the beginning of the 1926 season, Johnson had 3,336 strikeouts, 533 more than second-place Cy Young.
7. Denman Thompson, "Johnson Brilliant in Blanking Mackmen, 1-0, in 15-Inning Season Inaugural," *Washington Evening Star*, April 14, 1926: 36.

THE TRAIN TRACKS TO HIS 400TH WIN

APRIL 27, 1926
WASHINGTON SENATORS 9, BOSTON RED SOX 1

by Kevin Larkin

Throughout time, superstars in baseball perform extraordinary feats on the diamond. Walter Johnson was one of those superstars. Throwing 110 shutouts, winning 30 games in a season twice, winning 20 or more games for 10 consecutive seasons (1910-1919). All these accomplishments were based on a fastball. The great Ty Cobb once said, "His fastball looked like the size of a watermelon seed, and it hissed at you as it passed."[1]

Johnson, who debuted with the Washington Senators in August of 1907, took the mound on April 27, 1926, at Griffith Stadium in search of his 400th career victory, a figure attained by just one pitcher up to then, Cy Young. He was coming off a 9-5 victory on April 23 over the Philadelphia Athletics. That victory was the 399th of his storied career and the start on April 27 was his first try at number 400.

The Senators were a mediocre team for much of Johnson's career, except for 1924 and 1925, when they appeared in their only two World Series. The 1924 squad won the World Series (for the only time in Johnson's career and the team's history), and in 1925 the team suffered a heartbreaking loss to the Pittsburgh Pirates in Game Seven. Johnson came on in relief in Game Seven in 1924 and was the winning pitcher. In 1925, after winning the first two Series games he pitched, Johnson was the losing pitcher in Game Seven.

Entering the game, Washington had a record of 7 wins 6 losses and was two games behind the New York Yankees. Johnson had a 2-1 record and ended the season with a 15-16 record, just the fifth time in his 20-year career that he failed to produce a winning record.

The Senators were led by their player-manager, second baseman Bucky Harris, and also had outfielders Goose Goslin and Sam Rice and pitcher Stan Coveleski, all of whom eventually joined Johnson in the Hall of Fame.

Washington's opponent was the Boston Red Sox, who were in the midst of a terrible decade after former owner Harry Frazee sold Babe Ruth and other stars to the Yankees. The only player on the team to hit over .300 was outfielder Baby Doll Jacobson, and the only pitcher to finish with double-digit wins was starter/reliever Ted Wingfield (11-16).

Johnson's mound opponent that day was Tony Welzer, who was making his second major-league start in a career that would last just two seasons. He had yet to gain a decision and consequently was 399 wins behind the great Johnson.

Boston took a 1-0 lead in the second inning before an offensive explosion by the Washington nine in the bottom of the third put the game out of reach for the Red Sox.

The Boston run came when Ramon Herrera hit a double that scored Sy Rosenthal. He had walked and gone to second on Topper Rigney's sacrifice.[2]

Before the fateful third inning Welzer had looked good. But in the third he dropped a throw from first baseman Phil Todt on Rice's grounder.[3] Then third baseman Fred Haney and Herrera collided on an easy pop fly by Goslin.[4] Even with those miscues, if Welzer had support from his teammates, there might not have been any scoring.[5]

But Bucky Harris sacrificed, then Joe Harris hit a hot shot to Haney, who let the ball get through and Rice scored.[6] Joe Judge forced Harris, but then Bluege hit a scorching shot down the third-base line that hit the stands and bounced over the head of left fielder Rosenthal for a home run that plated three runs.[7]

The Senators weren't done. Buddy Myer, hitting .178 going into the game, singled. Myer scored when right fielder Roy Carlyle let Muddy Ruel's double get away from him.[8] Johnson, the sixth batter of the inning, flied out to end the inning. Five runs had scored and that was the ballgame.[9]

After the debacle of the third inning, Welzer pitched swimmingly until the sixth inning.[10] He was driven from the mound by a five-hit barrage that netted four runs.[11] Ruel singled and went to third base when Rice beat out a bunt. Another bunt by Bucky Harris caught the Red Sox napping and that scored Ruel.[12] Goslin doubled to right field to score Rice and Joe Harris double in Bucky Harris and Goslin. Welzer was replaced by right-hander Del Lundgren, who succeeded in halting the hit parade.[13] Rudy Sommers pitched the eighth inning, but his pitching along with Lundgren's was wasted as the Red Sox were helpless against the pitching of Johnson.[14]

Goslin led the Washington offense with three hits, including a double. Rice, Joe Harris, and Muddy Ruel each had two hits and Bluege added his home run. Johnson pitched like the Johnson of old, allowing just four hits while walking four and striking out three.

At the end of the game none of the 2,000 to 3,000 fans at Griffith Stadium thought the Red Sox could rally and look like baseball players.[15]

Washington would finish the 1926 season in fourth place while the Red Sox remained mired in last place for the fourth time in five years. As for the Big Train, he finished the year with a record of 15 wins and 16 losses and 412 wins. He would win five more games in 1927 and retire as a player with 417 victories. Johnson's last appearance as a major-league player occurred on September 30, 1927, as a pinch-hitter in the ninth inning for Tom Zachary, who earlier in the game gave up Babe Ruth's 60th home run of the season.

SOURCES

In addition to the sources cited in the Notes, the author accessed Retrosheet.org, Baseball-Reference.com, and the SABR.org websites.

NOTES

1 Baseball-Almanac.com.

2 "Johnson Conquers Red Sox with Ease," *Philadelphia Inquirer,* April 28, 1926: 22.

3 "Senators Win Sloppy Game," *Baltimore Sun,* April 28,1926: 14.

4 "Senators Win Sloppy Game."

5 "Senators Win Sloppy Game."

6 "Red Sox Slump in Their Hitting and Are Beaten," *Boston Globe,* April 28, 1926: 15.

7 "Senators Win Sloppy Game."

8 "Senators Win Sloppy Game."

9 "Senators Win Sloppy Game."

10 Red Sox Slump."

11 Red Sox Slump."

12 Red Sox Slump."

13 Red Sox Slump."

14 Red Sox Slump."

15 N.W. Baxter, "Boston Gets 4 Hits Off Johnson," *Washington Post,* April 28,1926

SENATORS EXPLODE FOR 12 RUNS IN INNING

JULY 10, 1926
WASHINGTON SENATORS 19, ST. LOUIS BROWNS 4

by Doug Schoppert

On Saturday July 10, 1926, the temperature in Washington reached 99 degrees, the hottest day of the year. In the late afternoon and evening, heavy storms rumbled through the city, downing trees and blowing glass from windows. The next morning, the *Washington Post* reported the storm's toll in graphic headlines — "ARTERY OF WOMAN'S ARM IS SEVERED AT HER HOME BY FLYING GLASS."[1] Farther north, in northern New Jersey, a bolt of lightning struck the Picatinny Arsenal and set off a chain of explosions that destroyed more than 200 buildings.

Earlier that day, at Griffith Stadium, 7,000 spectators witnessed another explosion. The Senators' bats pounded out 12 runs in a single inning against the St. Louis Browns. The outburst exceeded the team's single-inning scoring record — 11 runs — set just a few weeks earlier, on May 25 at Philadelphia's Shibe Park.[2]

The run explosion provided some solace to Washington fans who feared the Nationals would fall short of a third consecutive AL pennant. With a lineup nearly identical to that which had captured the flag in 1925 with 96 wins, the Nats had begun well with an Opening Day 15-inning shutout of the Athletics by the ageless Walter Johnson. As late as May 9, they clung to a slender lead over the Yankees. But after losing 11 of 15 games on an early June road trip, the team was languishing in fourth place.

As a result, the Nationals, who had led the AL on this date the last two years, entered play on July 10 in fifth place, 11½ games behind the Yankees. The Browns had had a more consistent if less satisfying season. After losing the first five games of the year, they had risen to seventh place on May 29 and there they remained. Despite their lowly status, the Browns had gained a 5-4 edge in the season series with Washington with a 4-3 victory on July 9. The loss was made even more bitter by the fact that the winning pitcher, Win Ballou, had been dealt by Washington to St. Louis in the offseason. Moreover, the winning runs had scored thanks to an error by Nationals shortstop Buddy Myer — his 17th of the season.

As a result of the loss, the Senators had just three wins more to their credit than the Browns. But Nats' bats continued to generate runs. Earl McNeely, Sam Rice, and Goose Goslin were all hitting over .300 and McNeely and Goslin owned on-base percentages over .400. In eight July contests, the team had plated more than five runs per game. The pitching was the Achilles heel of the 1926 Senators.

On July 10, Stan Coveleski was pitching on six days' rest. With a 3.06 ERA, he was no Achilles heel. But Coveleski had lost his last three decisions, evening his record at 6-6. In his last outing against St. Louis, on June 19, he had lasted just three innings after allowing five runs (only one earned) on six hits. On the hill for the Browns this hot July day was Milt Gaston. He boasted a 3.82 ERA. It had earned him but eight victories.

The Nats started the scoring in the second inning when a double-play groundball drove Myer home. The home team added another run in the third and forced Gaston off the mound. He was replaced by Dixie Davis with runners on second and third and no outs. Davis induced a groundout from Bucky Harris but a fly ball by Rice plated Coveleski to give the Nats a two-run lead.

It was to be short-lived. In the top of the fourth, Coveleski allowed singles to Marty McManus and Harry Rice and loaded the bases with a walk to Wally Gerber. Davis then helped himself with a single that plated two runs when Harry Rice kicked the ball from Muddy Ruel's glove as he crossed the plate. In the next inning, the Browns took the lead when George Sisler scored from first on a double by McManus.

The Nats fought back with a fifth inning rally. Ruel led off with a single and manager Harris had Dutch Ruether pinch-hit for Coveleski. Ruether was a proto-Shohei Ohtani — a pitcher who in 1925 delivered a 3.87 ERA and an .816 OPS. He drew a walk. McNeely bunted to Davis, who helped the Nats by tossing the ball into the outfield, scoring Ruel. Now with runners on second and third, Davis retired Bucky Harris but allowed a single to Sam Rice that brought both runners home. After Rice stole second and Myer walked, they advanced on a wild pitch by Davis, who was lifted for Elam Vangilder.

Vangilder was a 30-year-old veteran of seven seasons with the Browns. He notched 14 wins for the Browns in 1925, second only to Gaston. He had debuted in the majors against the Senators in 1919. That day the Nats scored 12 runs. Now they would tally as many in a single frame.

Vangilder's day started inauspiciously as he walked Goslin to load the bases. Joe "Moon" Harris then delivered a two-run single to give the Senators a 7-3 advantage.

In the top of the sixth, the Browns got back on the scoreboard. Harry Rice led off with a double and Leo Dixon moved him to third with a groundout. Gerber got him home. The score was 7-4, Washington, and all was quiet until the fateful eighth.

Vangilder was still on the hill when the Nats came to bat in the bottom of that frame. Ossie Bluege led off with a triple. Bennie Tate, who had replaced Ruel as catcher, grounded out. That brought up Firpo Marberry.

Marberry had entered the game after the fifth inning. A pioneer reliever who, like Johnson, relied heavily on his fastball, Marberry would be retroactively credited with 22 saves in the 1926 season. He was a decent hitter who batted .263 in 1925 and was credited with four RBIs in 22 plate appearances. On this day, he singled home Bluege. McNeely followed with a double that moved Marberry to third. Manager Harris doubled him home and sent McNeely to third. Vangilder's day was done.

Out trotted Chet Falk. He had pitched to an 8.28 ERA in 1925 at the tender age of 20. Now he was pitching on 13 days' rest. He might have wished for a little more rest before the inning was done.

It wasn't all Falk's fault. He got Sam Rice to hit a groundball to Ski Melillo at second base. Melillo threw home but McNeely scampered back to third and catcher Wally Schang threw to second to nail Rice. His throw wound up in center field. McNeely scored and Harris and Rice were on second and third.

That seemed to deflate Falk. He served up a triple to Myer that plated two more runs. Goslin singled Myer home. Joe Harris, who had replaced the other Joe (Judge) after the latter was ejected by umpire Red Ormsby in the fourth inning, walked. That brought up Bluege for the second time in the inning. He singled, scoring Goslin for the seventh run of the frame. Tate got his first hit of the inning — a double that plated Joe Harris and Bluege. Marberry was unable to collect his second hit but advanced Tate to third.

By now the shadows must have been deepening and perhaps storm clouds were gathering. But the Nats were not deterred. McNeely singled to drive home Tate. Bucky Harris collected his second hit of the inning. He replaced himself at first with pinch-runner Stuffy Stewart. Adding insult to injury, Stewart and McNeely pulled off a double steal that scored the latter. Stewart scored the 12th and final run of the inning when Rice reached on an error by Falk. Myer grounded out to shortstop to stop the bleeding.

Add it all up. Sixteen batters, four singles, three doubles, two triples, one walk, two errors, and three stolen bases (including home). No homers, no strikeouts. Just one true outcome — and a perfect one for Nats fans.

Remarkably, Marberry had enough in the tank to retire the demoralized Browns in a scoreless ninth. The game totals are a thing of wonder: 29 hits, 23 runs, 8 walks, 3 strikeouts. Time of game — 2 hours 15 minutes. Home before the storm.[3]

SOURCES

In addition to the sources cited in the Notes, the author accessed Retrosheet.org, Baseball-Reference.com, SABR.org, and the *Washington Evening Star*.

NOTES

1 "3 Hurt in Storm Ending Hot Wave; 3 Are Prostrated," *Washington Post*, July 11, 1926: 1.

2 The Nats had twice scored 10 runs in an inning. On July 28, 1902, they did it at American League Park against the White Sox. On July 8, 1910, they accomplished the feat for a second time at American League Park II against the Browns.

3 Frank H. Young, "12-Run Inning Gives Nats Easy Win," *Washington Post*, July 11, 1926: M17.

RED BARNES FIRST SENATOR TO HIT TWO HOME RUNS IN CAVERNOUS GRIFFITH STADIUM

JUNE 26, 1928
WASHINGTON SENATORS 4, PHILADELPHIA ATHLETICS 1

by Luis A. Blandon Jr.

Griffith Stadium was death to home runs, yet inside-the-park home runs dictated the results in a game between the hometown Washington Senators and the Philadelphia Athletics.

Ty Cobb, playing with the A's at age 41 in what was his final year, batted second, going 0-for-4 and showing his liability in right field. Cobb hit 46 inside-the-park home runs in his career, the third-most by a player since 1898.[1] On a warm Tuesday afternoon, with temperatures in the low 80s, he played in a game in which Red Barnes became the first Senators player to hit two home runs in a game in the spacious ballpark in the nation's capital. But they were not the garden-variety home run; rather, Barnes hit two "interior homers," something Cobb himself accomplished on July 15, 1909, in a game coincidentally against the Senators.[2]

The Athletics were on the cusp of greatness. Connie Mack had built his team with young players like Mickey Cochrane, Lefty Grove, Al Simmons, Jimmie Foxx, and Mule Haas, paired with veterans like Cobb, Tris Speaker, and Eddie Collins. The Athletics were 37-25 and in second place, 9½ games behind the Yankees. In 1929 they overtook the Yankees, to win the first of three consecutive pennants.

Under player-manager Bucky Harris, the Senators were in a decline from their days as American League champions in 1924 and 1925. The core of the 1924 World Series champions, however — Harris, Sam Rice, Goose Goslin, and Joe Judge — were still producing. To fill holes, the team brought in veterans like George Sisler and young prospects like Joe Cronin. The Senators were 29-33, mired in fourth place and 17½ games behind the first-place Yankees.

For the Senators to win, Goslin had to be in the lineup but Harris "had secret fears that (Goslin's) days were numbered."[3] Goslin was leading the AL in batting but his right arm hurt. Long-term rest was prescribed. He tried "baking, massages and the violet ray,"[4] to no avail. The pain affected his outfield play so much that he practiced throwing the baseball with his left arm.[5] When the team was in Detroit, Goslin traveled to Battle Creek to Bonesetter Sweet, a chiropractor who had supposedly alleviated Babe Ruth's aching wrist. Goslin came away with worse pain.[6] He was done babying the arm. Prior to June 26, he threw in practice with pain but decided he could deal with it. In the game, Goslin made two putouts, batting cleanup and going 1-for-3 with a "screaming double to right."[7] In the bottom of the second, "the fans broke into a cheer when [Goslin] made a short, but direct throw" back to the infield after Bing Miller singled.[8] By the end of the game, Harris was likely relieved that Goslin was back in action.

Playing center field and batting third for the Senators, Barnes was a difference maker as "a new Napoleon of the bat, [who] unloosed two fiery interior home runs,"[9] each with Harris on base, driving in all the runs in a 4-1 victory.

The day's starting pitchers, Milt Gaston of the Senators and Eddie Rommel for Philadelphia, both pitched well enough to win. One did. Gaston "went through the scorched Macks like an elephant through a Main Line garden."[10] The description of Gaston's performance belied his dominance: "knocked 'em off with such cyclic regularity that only thirty-three gray-garbed bat carriers faced him. ..."[11]

Gaston had a complete game, with three hits, two walks, and three strikeouts, giving up an unearned run for his second win against five losses. However, Gaston did not pitch to the Senators' expectations that season. He finished 6-12 with a 5.51 ERA in 22 starts with three shutouts. In 1928, Rommel was a spot starter, going 13-5 with a 3.06 ERA. In an eight-inning complete game, he gave up five hits and four runs, three earned, with a walk and a strikeout for his third loss against three wins. It was not enough.

Starting off the game, Gaston faced Jimmy Dykes, who flied out to Goslin in left field. Cobb popped out to the shortstop. Gaston walked Cochrane but forced Simmons to pop out to second baseman Harris. In the bottom of the first, the Senators scored all the runs needed to win the game, aided by shoddy Philadelphia defense. Rice led off, grounding to second. Harris reached base on a poorly played line drive to Simmons, who dropped the ball "after staggering like an inebriate to make the catch."[12] Barnes followed, delivering "a virile liner" down the edge of the stands in left that Simmons misplayed, bouncing into the pocket in left for "an interior home run."[13] The score was 2-0 and Rommel efficiently dispatched Goslin and Bobby Reeves to finish the inning.

The A's scored an unearned run in the top of the seventh. Sammy Hale reached base via an error by the shortstop Reeves, and ended up reaching third on Miller's double to center field. Joe Boley's fly ball drove Miller home, enabling the A's "to score a shady run ... the only Pennsylvania visitation to the pentagon."[14] The score was 2-1. In the bottom of the eighth, an almost exact replay from the first inning occurred. With two outs, Harris roped a single to left. Then Barnes "lofted the ball" to Cobb in right field "who made a desperate try for a one-hand grab. He barely missed the sphere" as the ball rolled "between the field boxes and pavilion."[15] Barnes was rounding third when Cobb picked up the ball. It was 4-1, with Gaston quietly putting away Simmons, Foxx, and Hale in the top of the ninth. The entire game was over in 1 hour and 12 minutes. The first six innings were played in 43 minutes.[16]

Frank Young of the *Washington Post* highlighted Barnes's day: "[B]eing a newly wed, the three suits of clothes which Red Barnes won himself with homers since he joined the 'matrimonial league' will come in mighty handy."[17] For the *Post's* Shirley Povich, the game was decided by Gaston's great pitching and Barnes's hits that were made homers by Cobb's "aging legs" and Simmons's "lamentable outfielding."[18] However, the errors were not deserving: "[B]oth balls took educated hops off (Simmons and Cobb's) immediate reach."[19]

Jimmie "The Beast" Foxx started at first for the A's and was a year away from his breakthrough season. His power became legendary, as Lefty Gomez later noted: "When Neil Armstrong first set foot on the moon, he and all the space scientists were puzzled by an unidentifiable white object. I knew immediately what it was. That was a home-run ball hit off me in 1937 by Jimmie Foxx."[20] Foxx entered the game with a 15-game hitting streak. Gaston silenced the streak. Going 0-for-4, "the Prince of Wales of swat was denied admittance to the hit column today."[21]

Defense let Rommel down. The knuckleballing Rommel pitched a game worthy of a win but "was beaten by the superb art of Gaston"[22] and "[S]ave for the two home runs, Rommel might have had a shutout and a 1-0 victory."[23] He deserved a better result "as four runs were woefully tainted."[24] Rommel was an AL umpire from 1938 to 1959, becoming the third man to appear in the World Series as both a player and an umpire. In 1956 he became the first umpire to wear glasses.[25]

Emile "Red" Barnes achieved an unique accomplishment with his two "interior homers." Well-known from his time on the 1925 and 1926 Alabama University football teams as captain, quarterback, defensive lineman, and punter, he led Alabama to its third consecutive Southern League championship and its second consecutive Rose Bowl appearance, a 7-7 tie with Stanford.[26] Barnes had a short major-league career with the Senators and Chicago White Sox, from 1927 through 1930. His 1928 rookie year was his best season, and on June 26, Barnes hit two of his eight career homers and drove in four of his 97 career RBIs. Barnes would later play and manage in the minors, and after that served as the postmaster in Suggsville, Alabama, until his death at 55 on July 3, 1959.[27] Who else can boast he was the starting quarterback in the Rose Bowl and also hit two inside-the-park home runs in a major-league baseball game?

SOURCES

In addition to the sources cited in the Notes, the author consulted Baseball-Reference.com, Retrosheet.org, and MLB.com.

NOTES

1 "Inside The Park Home Run Records," Baseball Almanac, baseball-almanac.com/recbooks/rb_isphr.shtml, (accessed August 14, 2019).

2 "Marse Joe's Get Two Bumps," *Washington Evening Star*, July 16, 1909: 15.

3 Frank H. Young, "Series in Hub Next Test of Nats," *Washington Post*, June 26, 1928: 13.

4 John B. Keller, "Goose's Ailing Arm Nearly O.K. Again," *Washington Evening Star*, June 27, 1928: 30.

5 Frank H. Young, "Goslin Shifts to Left-Hand Throwing on Outfield Balls," *Washington Post*, June 29, 1928: 13.

6 Keller.

7 Shirley L. Povich, "2 Cheap Home Runs By Barnes Decisive in Duel of Pitchers," *Washington Post*, June 27, 1928: 11.

8 Frank H. Young, "Goslin Shifts to Left-Hand Throwing on Outfield Balls."

9 James Isaminger, "Red Barnes Drives 2 Interior Homers and Mackman Droop," *Philadelphia Inquirer*, June 27, 1928: 24.

10 Isaminger.

11 Isaminger.

12 Isaminger.

13 Isaminger.

14 Isaminger.

15 Keller.

16 Isaminger.

17 Frank H. Young, "Nats Facing Strenuous Week," *Washington Post*, June 27, 1928: 11.

18 Povich.

19 Povich.

20 "Jimmie Foxx," Baseball Hall of Fame, baseballhall.org/hall-of-famers/foxx-jimmie, accessed August 16, 2019.

21 Isaminger.

22 Isaminger.

23 Povich.

24 Povich.

25 "Rites Planned for Rommel, Baseball Pitcher, Umpire" *Baltimore Sun*, August 28, 1970: C-20.

26 "Pasadena Clash Has a National Grid Flavor," *Ogden* (Utah) *Standard-Examiner*, December 26, 1926: 13; "Stanford and Alabama Play to Tie," *Florence* (South Carolina) *Morning News*, January 2, 1927: 5.

27 "Ex-Tides Barnes Dies in Mobile," *Birmingham News*, July 5, 1959: 51.

NATIONAL FIREWORKS IN RECORD-SETTING GAME

AUGUST 5, 1929
WASHINGTON SENATORS 21, DETROIT TIGERS 5

by Gary Sarnoff

On Monday, August 5, 1929, a mild day during the dog days of summer, the Senators and Detroit Tigers prepared to resume their series at Washington's Georgia Avenue ballpark. With the season nearing the two-thirds mark, both teams, lodged in the second division in the American League standings, were hopeful of a strong finish that would place them in the first division.

Before the season the consensus among sportswriters was that the Tigers, with a stern but fair manager in Bucky Harris, would finish fourth. After sweeping a doubleheader from Washington the day before, Detroit was in fifth place with a 49-52 record. "Shortstop has been our greatest weakness this season," said Harris. "We thought (Heinie) Schuble would do, but he proved to be too unsteady."[1]

Hopes had been high for the Senators during spring training. Walter Johnson was rewarded for his 21 years of service in Washington by being named the Senators' manager. Although Johnson had no experience as a major-league manager, Washington fans were excited over his getting the job. Ironically, the man Johnson replaced was the current pilot of the Tigers.

In 1924 Bucky Harris was the Senators' Boy Wonder manager at the ripe age of 27. In that season, as the manager and starting second baseman, Harris led the Senators to a surprising American League pennant and World Series championship. The following season, Harris's Senators repeated as AL champions, but lost the World Series. Then the Senators began to decline, as did Harris's popularity. The Boy Wonder became the scapegoat for the Senators' deterioration and was ridiculed for hastily trading away popular infielder Buddy Myer and pitcher General Crowder. While Myer and Crowder starred in their new surroundings, the Senators posted a losing record in 1928, and Harris was fired.

Senators President Clark Griffith went to work on rebuilding the team by naming the popular Johnson as manager and trading five players to the Boston Red Sox to bring Buddy Myer back to Washington. With Myer's return and a new spirit injected into the Senators, hopes were strong for

1929. But those expectations crashed into a cruel reality after the season began. On August 5 the Senators were in sixth place.

Washington's disappointing season was fueled by several reasons, but mostly a lack of offensive production. The statistics in the August 4 Sunday newspapers showed that the Senators were sixth in team batting average and runs scored.[2] Another chief factor was Walter Johnson, who most believed was too nice to manage. "I had my doubts about him as a manager," admitted Senators coach Al Schacht. "I was afraid that the players might take advantage of him. That's just what happened."[3]

After a good turnout of over 15,000 for a twin bill on Sunday,[4] this game's attendance was sparse,[5] unsurprising for a Monday and with two of the league's lower-tier teams in action. The small crowd saw the Senators' starter, left-handed hurler Lloyd Brown, retire the first two Tigers before Detroit second baseman Charlie Gehringer smacked one off the right-field scoreboard for a triple and outfielder Fatty Fothergill drill one into the gap in left-center field for an RBI double. Washington answered in the bottom of the first when leadoff batter Joe Judge walked and moved to third when he and Sam Rice executed a hit-and-run. After Goose Goslin, hitting 78 points lower than his league-leading .379 batting average in 1928, popped out, Buddy Myer hit a long out to left field, far enough to allow Judge to tag and score from third.

After Detroit failed to score in the top of the second, the Senators went to work against Tigers pitcher George Uhle. With one out in the bottom of the second, Joe Cronin tripled, and third baseman Jackie Hayes and Lloyd Brown walked, loading the bases. Judge followed with a fly ball to score Cronin from third and allow Hayes to take third. Hayes scored when Tigers catcher Eddie Phillips was charged with a passed ball. Rice followed with a walk, and then Goslin and Myer followed with RBI singles to tally the third and fourth runs of the inning.

With the score now 5-1, and with two runners on base with only one out, Harris replaced Uhle with Josh Billings. Washington center fielder Sam West greeted Billings with a drive down the right-field line for a two-run double. Catcher Bennie Tate singled to score West, and when Detroit center fielder Harry Rice booted the ball, Tate took second base. After Cronin walked, Tigers catcher Phillips thought he could catch a baserunner napping. He threw to first base, and might have had a pickoff, but first baseman Dale Alexander whiffed on the catch. As the ball rolled down the right-field line, Tate took off from second, rounded third and scored the eighth run of the inning. An error was charged to Alexander, but the catcher received the blame. Manager Harris immediately replaced Phillips.

With the game moving into the top of the third, and with the Senators owning a seemingly safe 9-1 lead, Washington fans were unsure. The day before the Nats squandered an 8-0 lead in a loss that capped their doubleheader sweep. Could the home team hold the early lead today? In the top of the third, Gehringer smacked his second three-bagger of the day and scored when Fothergill followed with a fly out. The home crowd must have worried when the next two batters singled, but Brown retired the next two to end the threat. The Senators scored two more in the bottom of the inning for an 11-2 lead. Lloyd Brown tripled and scored on Judge's fly out. Rice, Goslin, and Myer followed with singles for the other run. That was enough to convince Harris to replace Billings with Augie Prudhomme, the third Detroit pitcher of the day.

No runs were scored in the fourth inning. The Tigers scored one on the top of the fifth. In the bottom of the fifth, Goslin singled and Myer walked. They scored when West and Tate singled. With runners now on first and third, the Senators attempted a double steal. After Cronin swung and missed for strike three on the play, Catcher Merv Shea threw wildly to second base for another Detroit error. Sam West, the runner on third, scored to make it 14-3.

Hoping to avoid humiliation and make the final score respectable, the Tigers put two on base with two outs in the top of the sixth. Gehringer then came through with his third triple of the day to score both runners. In the bottom of the sixth, Brown, Judge, and Rice singled in succession to load the bases with nobody out. When Augie Prudhomme threw wide on the first pitch to Goslin, manager Harris sent Emil Yde in to pitch, a decision that made Prudhomme unhappy. In the dugout he confronted Harris, claiming he was not given a fair chance. "If you think you haven't a square deal, you can take the train back to Detroit and tell Mr. Navin (Tigers owner)," replied Harris. The angry pitcher took his manager's advice.[6]

With the bases loaded, no outs, and a new pitcher in the game, Goslin grounded out, scoring Brown. Myer then connected and drove one to the deepest point of the ballpark in right-center field for his third hit of the day. Two runs easily scored and Myer, one of the fastest in the American League, completed the circuit for a home run to give Washington 18 runs (two shy of Washington's American League franchise record).[7]

Washington's offense wasn't finished. Harley Boss, sent in to take Judge's place at first base, singled in the bottom of the eighth. Sam Rice followed with a grounder to Heinie Schuble, the Detroit shortstop whom Harris had considered disappointing. Schuble's throw to first was wide for his 40th error of the season. Myer then slapped another hit to complete a 4-for-4 batting performance. Boss and Rice scored on the hit to give Myer seven RBIs in the game and the Senators a 20-5 lead. Then, to pad his stats, or perhaps to get revenge against Harris for trading him from Washington to the lowly Red Sox in 1927, Myer stole second. Sam West followed with a grounder to Schuble, who threw out West at first. Myer broke for third after the throw, and first baseman Alexander's throw to cut him down was wild, the fifth Tigers error of the game. Myer got up from his slide and headed home to cap his great day and make it a 21-5 score.[8] Myer, however, was just warming up. The next day in New York he would get four hits in his first four at-bats. Combined with a hit in his last at-bat on Sunday and his 4-for-4 on Monday, Myer's four hits at Yankee Stadium gave him nine hits in nine consecutive at-bats.

SOURCES

Besides the sources cited in the Notes, the author consulted Baseball-Reference.com and Retrosheet.org.

NOTES

1. Frank H. Young, "Nats and Tigers in doubleheader here today," *Washington Post*, August 4, 1929.
2. Major-league team and individual statistics in sports section, *Washington Post*, August 4, 1929.
3. Al Schacht, *My Own Particular Screwball* (New York: Doubleday, 1955), 190-191
4. Frank H. Young, "15,000 See Nats Lose Two," *Washington Post*, August 5, 1929.
5. Frank H. Young, "Nats on Hitting Spree, Trounce Tigers, 21-5," *Washington Post*, August 6, 1929.
6. "Prudhomme Argues, and He's Sent Home," *Detroit News*, August 6, 1929.
7. baseball-reference.com.
8. Baseball game account from John B. Keller, "Nationals Weak against West at Home," *Washington Times*, August 6, 1929.

AN UNMATCHABLE FEAT: BOBBY BURKE FIRST AND ONLY WASHINGTON SENATOR TO TOSS NO-HITTER IN GRIFFITH STADIUM

AUGUST 8, 1931
WASHINGTON SENATORS 5, BOSTON RED SOX 0

by Gregory H. Wolf

Griffith Stadium was the home of the Washington Senators from 1911 until the club relocated to Minneapolis-St. Paul after the 1960 season, and then for the inaugural campaign of the expansion Senators in 1961; but only one Senators hurler ever fired in a no-hitter in that mammoth steel and concrete structure. The author of that gem was spot starter and reliever Bobby Burke, described by the Associated Press as an "in-an-outer,"[1] who fashioned a record of 38-46 and made just 88 starts in his 10-year big-league career (1927-1935, 1937), all but the last of those with Washington.

As Washington prepared to take the field on August 8, 1931, against the lowly Boston Red Sox, their third-year manager and the greatest former player in franchise history, Walter Johnson, probably recognized that his second-place club (64-39) had just a slim chance to catch the two-time reigning World Series champion Philadelphia Athletics , whom they trailed by 11 games. Sixth-place Boston (41-63), skippered by rookie pilot Shano Collins, was battling the Chicago White Sox and Detroit Tigers for the worst record in the league, and trailed the eventual pennant-winning A's by 34½ games.

Toeing the rubber for Boston was 34-year-old Wilcy Moore, who had made national headlines in 1926 by winning 30 games for the Greenville (South Carolina) Spinners in the Class-B South Atlantic League. The following season, he won 19 games and led the AL in ERA for the world-champion New York Yankees. Acquired by Boston prior to the '31 campaign from the St. Paul Saints in the Rule 5 draft, the right-handed sinker-ball pitcher known as "Cy" sported a career record of 38-23, including 9-8 thus far in '31.

Described by sportswriter Ronald Valentine as a "tall and bashful youngster, his name not outstanding in the minds of baseball fans,"[2] the 24-year-old left-handed Burke had been the eighth pitcher on Washington's eight-man staff since the rail-thin, 6-foot, 150-pounder debuted with the club in 1927. The fifth-year hurler seemed to reach his stride earlier in the '31 season, winning five straight decisions in June to improve his record to 7-1, but had been hit hard since. A most unlikely candidate to join his manager as the only Senators to pitch no-hitters (the Big Train turned the trick on July 1, 1920, against Boston at Fenway Park), Burke was making his first start since a disastrous outing against the St. Louis Browns on July 2 in which he yielded four runs and walked five in just 2⅓ innings, and had been victimized for 16 runs (all earned) in his last 26 innings. If that weren't cause for concern, the United Press reported that Burke was "working under a handicap" after he supposedly fell on an exhaust pipe the previous day while boating, and suffered a serious burn on his back.[3]

Only 5,000 spectators braved "depressing summer heat" to take in a Saturday afternoon of baseball and witness history.[4] After Burke retired leadoff hitter Jack Rothrock, Hal Rhyne smashed what the *Boston Globe* considered the Red Sox' only hard-hit ball of the game, a sharp liner that center fielder Sam West snared in "handy fashion" for the second out.[5] Burke "frequently had himself in trouble," reported the Associated Press, and struggled at times with control for the remainder of the game;[6] however, the Joliet, Illinois, native mesmerized the Red Sox hitters with what the *Boston Herald* called a "barrel of stuff."[7]

Wilcy Moore's hope to replicate his success from his previous outing, a career-best three-hit shutout against the Yankees on August 2 at Fenway Park, was dashed in the first inning. Sam Rice, a 41-year-old with 2,715 hits in his 17-year career, executed a one-out bunt. Former AL batting champ Heinie Manush, who had entered the season with a .340 batting average in eight seasons, lined to short for what seemed to be a routine double-play ball.[8] According to the *Boston Herald*, shortstop Hal Rhyne broke too soon to cover second base, and the ball went through the gap, enabling Rice to scamper to third.[9] He subsequently scored Washington's first run on Joe Cronin's force out.

A "broad grin from Dame Fortune," opined the *Herald*, led to Washington's second run, in the third inning.[10] Buddy Myer walloped a high fly ball under which, according to the *Globe*, left-fielder Rothrock "camped almost directly."[11] Blinded by

In the long history of Griffith Stadium, only one pitcher threw a nine-inning no-hitter: Bobby Burke, an occasional starter and reliever. Burke went 38-46 in parts of nine seasons with the Senators, posting a 4.28 ERA in 918 ⅔ innings. (Photo by National Baseball Hall of Fame Library/MLB via Getty Images)

the sun, Rothrock lost sight of the ball, which hit the ground and bounced. By the time he retrieved it, Myer was on his way to third. No error was charged to Rothrock. Rice followed with a whistling single (his 10th hit in his last 19 at-bats) past the pitcher to drive in Myer.

Both teams threatened in the fourth inning. With a "tendency toward unsteadiness," Burke issued free passes to rookie Urbane Pickering and Bill Sweeney, but escaped unscathed.[12] It was the only time Boston had two runners on base. After Washington's Joe Kuhel belted a two-out double, Moore intentionally walked Roy Spencer to play the percentages against his hurling counterpart. Burke obliged by making the third out.

Save for two scratch safeties in the first and a fluke hit in the third, Moore pitched well enough to keep Boston in the game. He escaped a scare in the seventh, stranding Kuhel at third after he had reached on a one-out single. But the stout, 6-foot, 200-pound Moore seemed to be wilting in the heat and humidity in the nation's capital. The Nationals, as Washington was affectionately called by both sportswriters and fans, broke the game open in the eighth when Rice, Manush, Cronin, and West connected for four consecutive singles resulting in two runs; Cronin and West were each credited with an RBI. Kuhel knocked in Cronin on a force play to give Washington a 5-0 lead.

Burke took the mound in the ninth with the Washington faithful on their feet cheering him on. He was in unusual territory. The softspoken hurler had completed only 11 of his 41 starts in his career thus far, and had only one shutout to his credit – a seven-hitter against Boston on June 22, 1928. Wiping the sweat from his brow, Burke quickly retired Rothrock on a routine liner to center fielder Sam West, and then dispatched Rhyne on a weak roller to shortstop Joe Cronin.

Club owner Clark Griffith supposedly had a soft spot in his heart for Burke, yet was concerned that the southpaw's frail frame and stamina would keep him from becoming a bona-fide big-league starter. But on this day, Burke was just one out away from baseball immortality. Nonetheless, both the players and fans had to endure a few minutes of suspense before the game concluded. Undoubtedly feeling a rush of adrenaline and perhaps some jitters, Burke issued his fifth walk of the game – and third to Pickering – to prolong the game. Boston's most dangerous hitter, Earl Webb, who set a major-league record with 67 doubles that season, took two strikes and a ball as Pickering strolled unmolested to second and third. (No stolen bases were credited.) Needing one more strike, Burke heaved a fastball; Webb kept the bat on his left shoulder as he watched the ball rocket over the plate. Home-plate umpire George Moriarty yelled strike three to end the game in just one hour and 39 minutes.

Mobbed by his teammates on the mound, Burke finished with a career-high eight punchouts while becoming, in the words of the *Boston Herald*, "one of the heroes of the national pastime."[13] Burke's gem earned him another shot as a starter, but success proved to be elusive. In his subsequent five starts, he surrendered 30 hits, 19 walks, and 19 earned runs in just 23⅓ innings. Winless after his no-hitter, Burke finished the season with an 8-3 record and 4.27 ERA in 128⅔ innings.

Major-league baseball was played for another 30 years in Griffith Stadium, but only Bobby Burke can lay claim to be the sole Senators hurler to toss a no-hitter in the history of that park. The next no-hitter by a Washington pitcher in the nation's capital came 83 years later, when 28-year-old All-Star right-hander Jordan Zimmerman of the Washington Nationals turned the trick on September 28, 2014, against the Miami Marlins in the club's last game of the season.

SOURCES

In addition to the sources cited in the Notes, the author accessed Retrosheet.org, Baseball-Reference.com, and SABR.org.

NOTES

1 Associated Press, "Bobby Burke, an In and Outer With Washington for 4 Years, Pitches No-Hit, No-Run Game," *Jacksonville* (Illinois) *Daily Journal*, August 9, 1931: 10.

2 Ronald Valentine (Associated Press), "No-Hit, No-Run Gem Pitched by Youngster," *Anniston* (Alabama) *Star*, August 9, 1931: 12.

3 Ibid.

4 Ibid.

5 "No Hit for Red Sox Against Burke," *Boston Globe*, August 9, 1931: A1.

6 Associated Press, "Bobby Burke, an In and Outer With Washington for 4 Years, Pitches No-Hit, No-Run Game," *Jacksonville* (Illinois) *Daily Journal*.

7 "Senators Bunch Hits to Emerge Victorious, 5-0," *Boston Herald*, August 9, 1931: 1.

8 As a member of the Detroit Tigers, the 24-year-old Manush led the majors with a .378 batting average in 1926.

9 "Senators Bunch Hits to Emerge Victorious, 5-0," *Boston Herald*.

10 Ibid.

11 No Hit for Red Sox Against Burke."

12 Ibid.

13 "Senators Bunch Hits to Emerge Victorious, 5-0." Burke also had eight strikeouts against the St. Louis Browns in an eight-inning relief outing on May 12, 1934, at Griffith Stadium.

SENATORS ERASE SEVEN-RUN DEFICIT THANKS TO EIGHT WHITE SOX ERRORS

JULY 12, 1932
WASHINGTON SENATORS 13, CHICAGO WHITE SOX 12 (10 INNINGS)

by Ken Carrano

The Washington Senators had a good year in 1932 – their final season tally shows them with 93 wins, good enough for third place in a New York Yankees-dominated American League. The Senators got to their 93 wins in the traditional way – playing OK against the better teams in the league and beating the bottom-dwellers. They were the only team not to have a losing record against the Yankees in 1932, going 11-11 against New York. And if there was the term "Sox" in your name, the Senators would have your number. They went a combined 35-9 against the Boston Red Sox (17-5) and Chicago White Sox (18-4). The White Sox should have done one better than that but couldn't get out of their own way on July 12 at Griffith Stadium.

The game couldn't have started any better for the struggling White Sox. Bob Seeds led off the game against Senators hurler Bobby Burke with a triple and scored on an infield grounder off the bat of Billy Sullivan. Burke survived the first inning but didn't record an out in the second. Lu Blue started the White Sox' big inning with a single, which was followed by another single by Luke Appling, who had an interesting day. Frank Grube followed with a grounder to first base, but Joe Kuhel slipped and couldn't get to the bag for the putout, loading the bases. Sad Sam Jones helped his own cause by singling home Blue and Appling. Seeds followed with his second extra-base hit in as many innings, a double that scored Grube and Jones. At this point Senators manager Walter Johnson, a man who knew something about pitching, knew enough to replace the ineffective Burke with Dick Coffman. Coffman was just marginally better: Jackie Hayes beat out a bunt, then was forced at second on a Sullivan grounder with Seeds scoring. Red Kress brought Sullivan home with a triple, but was stranded at third, leaving the White Sox with a 7-0 advantage after an inning and a half.

The Senators started chipping away at the lead immediately, as the White Sox decided to keep their gloves in the dugout for safekeeping the balance of the game. Joe Cronin led off the Senators' second with a clean single. Dave Harris followed with a bouncer to third baseman Sullivan, who bobbled it. (The official scorer credited Harris with a hit.) After Sam West struck out, Grube tried to pick Harris off first, but Blue could not hold the throw. The mistake seemed to rattle Jones, who proceeded to walk Ossie Bluege, Roy Spencer, and pinch-hitter Sam Rice, plating two runs. Kuhel followed with a fly ball that scored Bluege, and the Senators now trailed 7-3.

The Senators got two more across in the third, thanks to more White Sox blunders. Heinie Manush bunted for a hit as Sullivan watched the ball roll, hoping it would go foul. Sullivan then bobbled Cronin's grounder that would have probably been a double-play ball. After a fly out, West walked to load the bases. Another potential double play was lost when Appling dropped a flip from Hayes on Bluege's grounder and Manush scored. Cronin followed him home on Spencer's fly, and the deficit was cut to two runs.

The White Sox tried to right the ship in the fifth when Blue's single, two infield outs, and another RBI single by Jones stretched the lead back to three runs, and it became four after another double by Seeds scored Jones. But the White Sox couldn't clean up their fielding – again. Doubles by Cronin and West in the bottom of the inning brought the score to 9-6, and after Jones walked Roy Spencer, White Sox manager Lew Fonseca replaced him with Urban "Red" Faber. Faber did his job, getting the Nats' third pitcher, Firpo Marberry, to pop up, but shortstop Appling collided with left fielder Seeds and dropped the ball, allowing West to score: 9-7, White Sox.

The roller-coaster game moved back in favor of the White Sox in the sixth when singles by Sullivan and Blue and a triple by Appling restored their four-run advantage at 11-7, but in the bottom of the sixth, Buddy Myer beat out a bunt, got to third when catcher Grube's wild pickoff throw to first sailed into right field for Chicago's fifth error of the game, and scored on Cronin's fly ball. The sixth White Sox error, in the seventh inning, reduced the Senators deficit to one run. Spencer scratched out a hit, Hayes made a wild throw on Marberry's grounder, and Kuhel's single drove in both runners, and the Senators trailed 11-10.

The White Sox added a run in the eighth to make their lead 12-10, but Hayes' second error (and the White Sox' seventh) was responsible for the Senators tying the game in the ninth. With the Senators down to their last out and Bluege on second after a walk, Kuhel's sharp single scored Bluege and brought the score to 12-11. On Myer's potential game-ending grounder, Hayes made a nice stop but threw wild to first. Cronin then lashed a single off new third baseman Carey Selph's glove (no error), and the game was tied.

The Senators finished off the defensively challenged White Sox in the 10th, again with two out. Spencer singled, bringing up General Crowder, who had come in to pitch in the top of the inning. Crowder's grounder went to Appling, who attempted to force Spencer at second. His aim was off, however, and the throw went to right field. Spencer never stopped running and easily scored the winning run. Crowder picked up the win, one of his league-leading 26 for the season.

Appling's game on this day was decidedly uneven. He went 4-for-4 (for the first time in his career)[1] with a triple and two RBIs, but his three errors resulted in three runs for the Senators, including the game-winner. For the White Sox, it was the second time in 1932 that they had 18 hits in a game and lost.[2] The Senators gave up 18 or more hits four times in 1932, but this was the only game they won, thanks to nine unearned runs, easily their highest total of the season.

Hall of Famer Heinie Manush batted .328 in parts of six seasons with the Senators (1930-1935), helping them to the pennant in 1933. He collected 2,524 hits, including a career-best and AL-most 241 in 1928 with the St. Louis Browns, and compiled a .330 average in his 17-year career. (Photo by Sporting News and Rogers Photo Archive via Getty Images)

SOURCES

In addition to the sources listed in the Notes, the author accessed mlb.com, Retrosheet.org, Baseball-Reference.com, *The Sporting News* via Paper of Record, the *Chicago Tribune* via newspapers.com, the *Washington Post* via ProQuest, and the *Washington Evening Star* via geneologybank.com.

baseball-reference.com/boxes/WS1/WS1193207120.shtml

retrosheet.org/boxesetc/1932/B07120WS11932.htm

NOTES

1 Appling had 34 career four-hit games, second to Nellie Fox, who leads the team with 41.

2 The White Sox had 18 hits against the Philadelphia A's on June 20 and lost 18-11, and had 18 against the Boston Red Sox on August 26 and lost 11-8.

MICKEY'S CYCLE PACES THE MACKMEN

JULY 22, 1932
PHILADELPHIA ATHLETICS 8, WASHINGTON SENATORS 4

by John Bauer

There are many long-standing myths about Washington, one of which asserts that the city was originally built on a swamp. The myth perhaps explains the misery inflicted on its residents through unbearable heat and humidity on many midsummer days. In the summer of 1932, there was much to be miserable about and not just the weather. The Great Depression caused much social and economic dislocation throughout the country. Resulting homelessness led to the sprouting throughout the country of so-called Hoovervilles, shantytowns named in "honor" of President Herbert Hoover and his ineffectiveness in dealing with the Depression. Washington was home of one of the largest Hoovervilles as the World War I-era Bonus Army sought expedited payment of bonus certificates. Their demands were refused and, within the week, General Douglas MacArthur forcibly cleared the Bonus Army from several sites around the capital.

July 22, 1932, was "a blistering hot day that made ovens of the sidewalks."[1] This was the setting for a game between the Philadelphia Athletics and Washington Senators. The three-time defending American League champ Athletics arrived the morning of the contest in second place despite just having achieved a six-game winning streak (snapped by the St. Louis Browns, 5-3, the day before at Shibe Park). The hometown Senators defeated the Detroit Tigers the previous day, 5-4, improving to 51-41, three games behind the Athletics. Amid the headlines about the general effects of the Depression, there were reminders of its effects on the national game. The major leagues were in a rough state, but the minor leagues were suffering and seeking help from the big leagues. Newspapers reported that Commissioner Kenesaw Mountain Landis could only acknowledge the problem but did not see the major leagues as providing the solution. The commissioner suggested, "It would take an act of Congress and the United States Treasury to pull them out."[2] If neither would act for the Bonus Army, it was difficult to imagine federal relief for minor-league baseball.

There remained the game scheduled at Griffith Stadium on July 22, with two baseball legends managing affairs in the dugouts: Philadelphia's Connie Mack and Washington's Walter Johnson. The pitching matchup featured two veterans with Washington's 33-year-old righty Al "General" Crowder facing Philadelphia's 35-year-old lefty Rube Walberg. In his most recent start, on July 18, Crowder went the distance but dropped a 2-1 decision to Detroit, evening his record at 11-11. What Crowder could not have known is that when the calendar turned to August, he would win his final 15 decisions and lead the junior circuit in wins for the season. That streak, however, would not begin this afternoon. Walberg entered the contest with a mark of 9-8 and an ERA north of five (5.10). He would pitch on only two days' rest after a complete-game 16-6 win over St. Louis in the back half of a July 19 doubleheader.

Leading off for the Mackmen, Max Bishop rapped a single to right. Doc Cramer's subsequent at-bat provided an early fielding thrill. From his shortstop position, Joe Cronin "raced back of second for a fancy backhand stop of Cramer's scorcher and slipped the ball to [second baseman Buddy] Myer to force out Bishop."[3] Cramer stood on first as Mickey Cochrane strode to the plate; he would complete the remaining 270 feet around the bases when Cochrane tripled on a drive to right. Al Simmons grounded to Cronin, and the shortstop took the fielder's choice to throw out Cochrane at home. Cronin also factored into the third out when he snared Jimmie Foxx's liner.

Joe Kuhel held the leadoff spot in the Senators batting order. The 26-year-old Ohioan had experienced a circuitous journey to his spot in the lineup. Going back to preparations for the 1931 season, Kuhel and veteran Joe Judge had been locked in a battle to hold down first base. Judge had been the Senators' regular first baseman since World War I, but Kuhel overtook the veteran for the 1931 season. When Kuhel injured his hand before the 1932 season, Judge reclaimed his old spot; however, Judge pulled a leg muscle running out an infield rap on July 8, allowing the younger Kuhel another opportunity.[4] Kuhel rose to the occasion, evidenced by his batting average rising from .136 to .253 in just two weeks. Backstory aside, Kuhel grounded out to Bishop. Myer lined to Cramer in center field for the second out, but Heinie Manush's single kept the inning alive. Cronin followed Manush with a triple to center that plated the latter and evened the score at 1-1. Dave Harris flied out to end an eventful opening frame.

In the second inning Philadelphia's Jimmy Dykes hit a two-out single of little consequence. The home half of the inning, however, witnessed a lot of consequence but nothing that changed the score. Sam West led off with a single and then took a big lead off first base with Ossie Bluege at the plate. West darted for second as Walberg went into his delivery but catcher Cochrane nailed him at second base for the out. Bluege singled into left field, and Moe Berg followed suit. With runners at first and second, Crowder also singled to left. Bluege rounded third but Simmons fielded the ball cleanly and threw "straight on a trolley line"[5] to Cochrane, who tagged Bluege for the out. Four straight singles but nothing to show for it, marking the inning as "one of the oddest of the season"[6] for Washington. Kuhel's inning-ending strikeout confirmed the wasted opportunity.

Philadelphia punished Washington for its profligacy in the top of the third. Bishop opened the inning with a single to center field. After Cramer popped up to third baseman Bluege in foul ground, Cochrane connected with a "herculean wallop that had the carry to escape from the park over the high wall in deep right."[7] The two-run blast was Cochrane's 15th home run of the season and extended Philadelphia's lead to 3-1. Simmons popped up in foul territory, this time on the first-base side of the field, and Foxx flied out to left fielder Manush to end the Athletics' barrage. Crowder seemed to have weathered the early storm and settled into the game as he kept Philadelphia batters from the basepaths in the fourth and fifth. Other than a stray single in each of the same innings, Walberg matched Crowder's effectiveness and allowed the Athletics to maintain their advantage.

Cochrane served again as an offensive spark, hitting a leadoff double in the top of the sixth. Simmons grounded to Bluege, whose errant throw to Kuhel allowed runners at the corners with none out. Foxx popped up to Berg in foul ground behind the plate for the first out. Crowder's free pass to Mule Haas loaded the bases to set up the force, but the tactic proved lacking when Eric McNair's infield single plated Cochrane. With the bases still loaded, Dykes also tapped an infield grounder, but Cronin gathered the ball and flipped it to Myer for the force at second base; Simmons scored from third, however, extending Philadelphia's lead to 5-1. Walberg flied out to West in center field for the third out, then the pitcher made quick work of the Senators in the bottom of the inning.

If the sixth inning hinted at Crowder losing his effectiveness, the seventh confirmed it. The General walked Bishop to start the inning and allowed a single to Cramer that placed runners at the corners. Before this game, Cochrane had sported a mere .185 batting average against the Senators. His single to right completed the cycle, drove in Bishop, and sent Crowder to the showers. Firpo Marberry assumed pitching responsibilities from Crowder and surrendered a single to Simmons that scored Cramer. With his team leading 7-1 and none out, Foxx's grounder to Cronin resulted in a double play; that Cochrane crossed the plate from third provided some consolation. The Athletics enjoyed an 8-1 lead, and Cochrane had played a role in six of the visitors' runs. Haas flied out to West for the final out.

Walberg remained effective in the seventh, permitting only a two-out single by Kuhel. In the eighth, however, the conditions caught up to the pitcher. "[S]uffering from the heat and sweating profusely,"[8] Walberg allowed consecutive singles to Manush, Cronin, Harris, and West to open the Senators' eighth. Unlike events in the second inning, the hits by Harris and West scored Manush and Cronin, respectively, for an 8-3 score. Bluege's grounder to Dykes allowed the Philadelphia third baseman to tap his bag for the force against Harris. Berg's single loaded the bases once again, and manager Johnson tapped Sam Rice to hit for Marberry in hopes of extending the rally. Rice, the honoree of the aptly-named Sam Rice Day on July 19 against Detroit, grounded out to Bishop; West crossed the plate on the play, narrowing the deficit to 8-4. Washington could get no closer as McNair scooped Kuhel's grounder for the third out.

Lloyd Brown took the hill for Washington in the ninth and set down Cramer, Cochrane, and Simmons in order. Despite his wobbles the previous inning, Walberg returned to finish the game. Myer's grounder to Foxx allowed the first baseman to tally an unassisted out. Manush singled to center and Cronin lofted a fly ball to Haas for the second out. Walberg "fell to the grass,"[9] the effects of the heat clearly weighing on the pitcher. Lefty Grove started warming up, but Walberg stayed down for a minute before gathering himself and inducing a Harris groundball to Dykes for the game's final out.

The game itself was not the sort of back-and-forth affair that makes legends of sporting contests. Rather, Mickey Cochrane was the story of the game. His offensive performance, including hitting for the cycle, provided the difference between the two teams. In the end, only one game would separate Philadelphia and Washington in the final 1932 AL standings. Individual performances like Cochrane's provide just such a margin over a 154-game season. What neither team could prevent was a season like the Yankees' 107-47 World Series-winning season. Philadelphia's pennant streak ended, and Washington would have to wait another year for its final pennant in the "swamp."

SOURCES

baseball-reference.com/boxes/WS1/WS1193207220.shtml

retrosheet.org/boxesetc/1932/B07220WS11932.htm

NOTES

1 James C. Isaminger, "Cochrane's Bat Big Factor in Mack Win," *Philadelphia Inquirer*, July 23, 1932: 10.

2 "Majors in No Position to Aid Minor Leagues, Landis Asserts," *Washington Evening Star*, July 22, 1932: A-11.

3 John B. Keller, "Coffman Again Is Seeking First Hill Win: Leading Minor Leagues Appear Safe," *Washington Evening Star*, July 22, 1932: A-8.

4 Denman Thompson, "Kuhel Wins First Base Post Away from Judge," *The Sporting News*, August 4, 1932: 3.

5 Isaminger.

6 Keller.

7 Isaminger.

8 Isaminger.

9 Isaminger.

KLIEG LIGHTS AT GRIFFITH STADIUM: FIRST PROFESSIONAL BASEBALL NIGHT GAME

JULY 25, 1932
PITTSBURGH CRAWFORDS 5, WASHINGTON PILOTS 1

NEGRO NATIONAL LEAGUE

by Gary Sarnoff

"Night baseball will never happen in Washington," said Clark Griffith, the president of the Washington Senators and owner of the team's ballpark. In 1930, Des Moines, Iowa, had hosted the first professional night baseball game. This failed to impress Griffith, who said, "You can make it as strong as you want that I'm opposed to night baseball."[1]

Two years after the Senators president went on record, Washington hosted its first night game, at 8:30 P.M. on July 25, 1932. The game would not involve the Senators, but would be played at their ballpark, Griffith Stadium, with the Washington Pilots hosting the Pittsburgh Crawfords in an East-West Negro League game. Although opposed to night baseball and unfamiliar with the Negro Leagues, Griffith planned to attend the game.

In 1931 a "high-powered"[2] sports promoter named Doug Smith sought to demonstrate that black major-league baseball would be a success in Washington. He asked Baltimore Black Sox owner George Rossiter to shift a Sunday game from Baltimore's Maryland Park to Griffith Stadium. Rossiter agreed, and the Black Sox played the Hilldale Daisies before a crowd of 6,000, more than enough fans to convince officials of the East-West Negro League that black baseball would draw in Washington.

"Washington D.C. will be represented in the East-West Colored League!" sportswriter Lloyd P. Thompson wrote in the *Pittsburgh Courier* in February 1932.[3] John Dykes, owner of Washington's popular Club Prudham, and some associates set about forming a team, which they named the Washington Pilots. They secured a lease at Griffith Stadium for 1932, and demanded that Baltimore owner Rossiter let them hire 35-year-old Negro Leaguer Frank Warfield, highly respected by league officials, players and fans, to manage their team. This request did not sit well with the Black Sox; Warfield was a fan favorite, was a member of Baltimore's 1929 championship team, and currently served as the team's business manager. Dykes insisted that his Pilots must have Warfield, and although Rossiter was reluctant, he bitterly honored the request.[4]

The Pilots owners announced that they hoped to start their home season with a series May 19-21 at Griffith Stadium,[5] when the Senators would be making their first of three extended trips through the Midwest. They also had a vision of drawing more fans by experimenting with night games. As the first half of the season progressed, the talk about night baseball in Washington gained momentum, and before the end of the first half it became official. Night games would begin with a game between the Crawfords and Pilots at Griffith Stadium on Monday night, July 25.

After being awarded a franchise, the Pilots had begun to put a team together. Warfield would manage and playing second base. Among others, the owners obtained Mule Suttles, a power-hitting first baseman who hit 21 home runs for the 1928 St. Louis Stars; pitcher Ted Trent, a 21-game winner for the 1928 Stars; and outfielders Willie O'Bryant and Bill Evans. With time needed to blend into a team, the Pilots started slowly and were in last place for much of the season's first half. Then the team began to jell, and finished the first half in third place. The first half ended on a sour note, though: They were swept by the Pittsburgh Crawfords at Pittsburgh's Greenlee Field.[6]

The two teams then prepared to go to Washington to open the season's second half with a four-game series. On Monday and Wednesday, July 25 and 27, they were to play under temporarily installed klieg lights at Griffith Stadium. On Thursday, July 28, the series would move to Richmond, Virginia, for a day game, and then the series would conclude with a Friday night game at Griffith Stadium. After getting swept by the Crawfords and before leaving Pittsburgh, the Pilots were stunned when their 35-year-old manager Warfield was found dead in his hotel room. The cause of death was not mentioned but was said to be after a brief illness.

As the shocked Pilots team headed to Washington, word of Warfield's death began to spread. "Negro baseball lost one of its outstanding characters and most skilled players," wrote W. Rollo Wilson of the *Pittsburgh Courier*. "His end was sudden and the shock of his going was great, not only to his players, but to fans everywhere."[7]

On July 25 a crowd of nearly 4,000[8] filed into Griffith Stadium. The left-field bleachers were occupied by 1,000 spectators, delighted that this section was minus the usual exposure to the scorching sun.[9] The lights were said to be efficient and bright enough for every play to be clearly viewed from every section in the ballpark.[10]

The newspapers had projected Ted Trent to be the Pilots' starting pitcher. But when the home team took the field in the top of the first, it was 30-year-old right-hander Webster McDonald on the mound. McDonald, who had been named the Pilots' manager to succeed Warfield, had an underhand pitching style, comparable to that of former American League standout Carl Mays and former Senators' pitcher Ad Liska.

The Crawfords had no problems in solving McDonald's unorthodox technique. Ted Page, Chester Williams, and Rap Dixon all reached base to lead off the first, and first baseman Jud Wilson's hit drove in two runs. In the second inning the Crawfords added another run to send McDonald to the showers. Left-hander Leroy Matlock came on in relief, and the 25-year-old rookie held the Crawfords in check through the sixth inning.

Pitching for the Crawfords was veteran William Bell. A black major leaguer for 10 years, Bell was a smart hurler and possessed a wicked curveball. In the bottom of the fourth, the Pilots broke through when center fielder Bill Evans singled to right and stole second and third. Two batters later, Pilots slugger Mule Suttles disappointed the home crowd by striking out. Second baseman Sammy Hughes followed with a walk, but then got trapped between first and second. During the rundown, Evans took off from third and crossed the plate to make the score 3-1.

With the score still 3-1 in the top of the seventh, Rap Dixon of the Crawfords connected with a Matlock pitch. The ball was said to be visible to everyone[11] as it sailed into deep center field before disappearing over the fence for a two-run homer to give Pittsburgh a 5-1 lead. In the bottom of the seventh, Suttles, having his difficulties in measuring

Bell's curves, finally timed his swing perfectly and sent a drive to deep center. Crawfords center fielder Ted Page backed up to the fence to make the catch for a long out. An inning later, Suttles batted again. Bell, pitching carefully to the Pilots slugger, struck him out for the second time. And in the ninth the Crawfords hurler capped the win and an eight-strikeout effort by whiffing Pilots catcher Effie Hamilton for the Crawfords' 17th consecutive win.

Watching the entire game from a front row seat was Clark Griffith. He admitted to a *Washington Times* sportswriter that he was surprised by the caliber of talent of the East-West Negro League.[12] He added that he was now impressed with night baseball.[13] However, it wasn't until 1941, nine years later, that the Senators played their first night game at Griffith Stadium.

SOURCES

Besides the sources cited in the Notes, the author consulted Baseball-Reference.com and Retrosheet.org.

NOTES

1 Frank H. Young, "Johnson rests Nats pitchers today; Brown to pitch tomorrow," *Washington Post*, May 23, 1930

2 Lloyd P. Thompson, "Washington Berth in League Set," *Pittsburgh Courier*, February 13, 1932.

3 Ibid.

4 W. Rollo Wilson, "Craws Win in First Night Game Series in East," *Pittsburgh Courier*, August 6, 1932.

5 Lloyd P. Thompson, "Washington Berth in League Set," *Pittsburgh Courier*, February 13, 1932.

6 The Pilots had the misfortune of running into a red-hot team and the league's best pitching. The Crawfords entered the series riding a 13-game winning streak. They made it 16 straight by holding the Pilots to six runs in the three-game sweep. The Pilots were manhandled by hurlers Satchel Paige and Double Duty Radcliffe in the first two games, then the least known of the Crawfords pitching trio, Willie Gisentaner, allowed the Pilots only four hits to cap the series.

7 W. Rollo Wilson, "Craws Win."

8 "Night Baseball Thrills Griffith," *Washington Times*, July 26, 1932.

9 "4,000 Watch Nocturnal Baseball," *Washington Post*, July 26, 1932.

10 Ibid.

11 Ibid.

12 "Night Baseball Thrills Griffith."

13 Ibid.

GENERAL CROWDER IN COMMAND FOR 15TH STRAIGHT VICTORY

SEPTEMBER 25, 1932
WASHINGTON SENATORS 2, PHILADELPHIA ATHLETICS 1

by Timothy Kearns

As Alvin "General" Crowder took the mound at Griffith Stadium on September 25, the game was of little consequence.

The American League had long been decided. The New York Yankees had clinched the pennant more than two weeks earlier, leaving Connie Mack's Philadelphia Athletics and Walter Johnson's Washington Senators in a fight for second as the teams squared off three times to close out the season.

That drama was dispelled swiftly. Philadelphia claimed an 8-4 win in the series opener, bumping its record to 94-58, ensuring that the Athletics would end the season in second and the Nationals, whose record fell to 91-60, would finish in third.[1] The Senators claimed the second game in Philadelphia's Shibe Park before the teams traveled to Washington to play the season finale.

While the standings were settled, personal glories remained at stake in the contest. Philadelphia first baseman Jimmie Foxx entered the game with 57 home runs, putting Babe Ruth's single-season record potentially within reach[2] and chasing Boston's first sacker Dale Alexander for the batting title.[3]

Standing in Foxx's way, however, was a National who had his own personal statistical achievements at stake in the contest: General Crowder.

The 33-year-old right-hander was amid the most remarkable stretch of his surprisingly young career. Crowder had struggled to find a consistent role in Washington's starting staff after beginning his major-league career at the age of 27, then found greater success with the St. Louis Browns. Crowder hurled 21 wins in 1928 and seemed to be establishing himself as a reliable moundsman. But a rough start to the 1930 campaign landed him back in Washington, traded with Heinie Manush for legendary Senators left fielder Goose Goslin.

The rough start to the season had rendered Crowder's pitching competence almost an afterthought, with his manager, Walter Johnson, offering only the slightest of praise, stating, "Crowder, too, should help us, but I was confident that my pitchers would have delivered without any more help and practically all of my enthusiasm over the trade has to do with the acquisition of Manush."[4]

Even as recently as July 28, Crowder's performance might have done little to cajole greater enthusiasm from the skipper, with Crowder's record an unexceptional 11-13.

But since July 28, Crowder had not lost a game. He had notched 14 straight winning decisions and won all seven of his September appearances, bringing him to a tie with the Athletics' Lefty Grove for the American League lead in wins with 25 and still only 13 losses. With Grove's season over, the job of opposing Crowder fell to Sugar Cain, a rookie right-hander who had made only five career starts. The Athletics' lineup reflected the game's lack of significance, with star catcher Mickey Cochrane on the bench, replaced by Ed Madjeski, a rookie with 31 at-bats in his career.

Crowder began the game effectively, retiring the Athletics in order on two groundouts and an infield popup to the Nationals' budding star shortstop Joe Cronin.

In the bottom half, the Senators' 42-year-old leadoff hitter, Sam Rice, extended his hold on the franchise's all-time hit lead by greeting the Athletics' rookie hurler with a single to center.[5] The future Hall of Famer was erased by the Nats' John Kerr sending a double-play ball to shortstop.[6]

Cain found himself back in trouble, allowing back-to-back singles to center field to Carl Reynolds and Cronin, putting runners on the corners with two outs.[7] First baseman Joe Kuhel then lined a single to left to drive home Reynolds. Cain retired Sam West on a groundout to second, fortunate to have allowed only a single run.

That 1-0 deficit proved significant as the Athletics struggled to muster offense against Crowder. Only Foxx found much success off the righty, reaching in each of his first three plate appearances with two singles and a walk, erasing any real drama over a possible home-run record by reaching only first base in the second inning.

The Nationals nearly scored an unearned run in the sixth. Cronin reached on a two-base throwing error by Athletics shortstop Eric McNair. Kuhel followed with a drive to left, but was "robbed" of a potential run-scoring hit with a "fine catch" by Al Simmons.[8]

Besides Foxx's singlehanded efforts, the Athletics mustered only three baserunners in the second through seventh innings, on singles by Dib Williams, Simmons, and Cain.

The Athletics began the eighth with Williams at the plate, and Foxx, four batters behind him, was assured at least one more plate appearance in the contest.

Crowder's dominance ensured that Foxx's at-bat waited until the ninth. The Athletics failed to even get the ball out of the infield, let alone even the score, with Crowder inducing Athletics batters to pop out to third base, foul out to catcher, and pop out to shortstop.

Cain had bounced back since a rough first, allowing only a pair of singles to West and Roy Spencer after the first. Again, however, Cain struggled with Sam Rice, walking him to lead off the eighth inning. Possibly motivated by the still-narrow score, his earlier double play, or both, Kerr advanced Rice to second with a sacrifice bunt to first base. Reynolds failed to advance him any further, flying out to left.

With Cain nearly evading trouble again, Cronin drove a double to left-center,[9] adding a vital insurance run. Cain closed the eighth by striking out Kuhel.[10]

While Crowder was three outs from the American League's win crown, his task remained formidable, even with the insurance run. The Athletics brought two of the league's best sluggers in Simmons and Foxx against him in the ninth; the pair had already reached base four times against him.

Crowder made quick work of the drama, however, inducing Simmons to fly to right, ensuring that not even the mighty Foxx could tie the game. With the lead no longer on the line, the crowd, an "enthusiastic gathering of about 8000,"[11] offered applause to Foxx as he came to the plate still working toward a possible batting crown.[12]

Foxx drove Crowder's second pitch to him high into the left-field stands for his 58th home run.[13] But it was too little. Crowder retired the next two

Alvin "General" Crowder concluded the 1932 season by winning his last 15 decisions en route to leading the AL in wins (26) and innings (327). He won his 16th straight on Opening Day in 1933 and once again led the AL in victories (24). (Photo by Sporting News and Rogers Photo Archive via Getty Images)

Athletics without incident and brought the 1932 season to a remarkable close.

It was, in many ways, a game of near-misses. The teams landed in second and third, behind the eventual World Series-winning Yankees. Foxx fell just shy of Ruth's record. Crowder's 15th consecutive win ended his season one win shy of the American League record of 16 consecutive victories held by four hurlers, including his own manager.[14] Moreover, the game itself was played at a "near-record" pace, taking only 77 minutes from start to finish.[15]

Crowder's 15 consecutive victories vaulted him to his first American League win crown, although he tied for the lead for the pennant-winning Senators the next season before declining and being dealt to the Tigers in 1934. For his part, Foxx was described both as the junior circuit's batting champ and runner-up, depending on the source.[16] Ultimately, Dale Alexander was named batting champ, while Foxx was voted American League MVP.[17]

The game also ended the 25-year connection between the club and franchise legend Walter Johnson, who was ousted as manager on October 5.[18] Johnson ended his managerial tenure with Washington at a record of 350-264, but faced criticism from hometown fans for not achieving more vaunted success with a talented roster[19] and by critics for lacking "the temperament to fire his men with the same enthusiasm" as former manager Bucky Harris did. Others speculated that the firing was financially motivated, permitting Clark Griffith the opportunity to save Johnson's $20,000 salary by extracting the same work from a player already on the payroll.[20]

Griffith did nothing to dispel this notion by hiring his star shortstop Cronin to manage the club on October 8.[21]

SOURCES

In addition to the articles cited in the notes, the author consulted:

Baseball-Reference.com

Baseball-Almanac.com

Frommer, Frederic J. *You Gotta Have Heart: A History of Washington Baseball from 1859 to the 2012 National League East Champions* (Lanham, Maryland: Taylor Trade Publishing, 2013).

Gauvreau Judge, Mark. *Damn Senators: My Grandfather and the Story of Washington's Only World Series Championship* (New York: Encounter Books, 2003).

NOTES

1 "Hopes of Nats Expire with 8-4 Defeat," *Washington Post*, September 24, 1932. The Athletics would pocket an estimated $400 more per player for their success. Shirley L. Povich, "This Morning with Shirley L. Povich," *Washington Post*, September 23, 1932.

2 Foxx had, on one occasion in 1932, slugged three home runs in a game, though it took him 18 innings to do so.

3 Under the current official baseball rules, Alexander would not have qualified for the title, notching only 454 plate appearances (392 at-bats) over the 154-game season. img.mlbstatic.com/mlb-images/image/upload/mlb/ttajxpedgemiy4sx0cer.pdf.

4 Frank H. Young, "Manager Sees Pennant with New Punch," *Washington Post*, June 15, 1930. Young was slightly more charitable to Crowder, stating "[p]ractically every one with whom the writer has talked agrees that the Nationals would not have gotten any the worst of it had they obtained Manush alone for Goslin and the fact that President Clark Griffith was able to land Crowder, too put the Washington Club owner back in the 'Old Fox' class."

5 "Jimmy's Three Hits Bring Him Unofficial A.L. Swat Crown," *Philadelphia Inquirer*, September 26, 1932.

6 "Senators Defeat Athletics as Foxx Hits 58th Home Run of Season," *Baltimore Sun*, September 26, 1932.

7 "Jimmy's Three Hits Bring Him Unofficial A.L. Swat Crown," *Philadelphia Inquirer*, September 26, 1932.

8 Frank H. Young, "Athletics Escape Shutout on Foxx's 58th Home Run into Stands in 9th Inning," *Washington Post*, September 26, 1932.

9 "Jimmy's Three Hits Bring Him Unofficial A.L. Swat Crown," *Philadelphia Inquirer*, September 26, 1932.

10 "Jimmy's Three Hits."

11 "Jimmy's Three Hits."

12 "Jimmy's Three Hits."

13 Foxx had, in fact, hit 60 home runs over the course of the 1932 season, but two of them were hit in games that were ultimately canceled as a result of rain before the games became official. Tom Deveaux, *The Washington Senators, 1901-1971* (Jefferson, North Carolina: McFarland & Company Inc., 2001).

14 Ronald G. Liebman, "Winning Streaks By Pitchers," research.sabr.org/journals/winning-streaks-by-pitchers.

15 Young, "Athletics Escape Shutout."

16 Philadelphia area newspapers indicated Foxx had the unofficial crown. "Jimmy's Three Hits Bring Him Unofficial A.L. Swat Crown," *Philadelphia Inquirer*, September 26, 1932; Les Conklin, "Foxx-Crowder Star in Final Game of Year," *New Castle* (Pennsylvania) *News*, September 26, 1932. The Associated Press reported that Alexander had the unofficial edge, stating that "[u]nofficial figures credit Alexander with the lead for the year which closed yesterday. ..." "Jimmy Foxx Clouts 58th Homer of Season, Missing Ruth's Record by Pair of Blows," *Los Angeles Times*, September 26, 1932; "Unofficial Figures Put Alexander First," *New York Times*, September 26, 1932.

17 Alan Gould, "Jimmy Foxx Voted Most Valuable Player in American League for 1932," *Baltimore Sun*, October 19, 1932.

18 Frank H. Young, "Griffith Ends Johnson Term as Nats' Pilot," *Washington Post*, October 5, 1932.

19 "Washington Grows Critical of Johnson," *The Sporting News*, September 29, 1932.

20 Frank H. Young, "Club Owner May Assume Pilot's Reins in 'Case of Emergency,' He Declares," *Washington Post*, October 6, 1932.

21 Frank H. Young, "26-Year-Old Shortstop Appointed by Griffith to Succeed Johnson," *Washington Post*, October 9, 1932.

NATS COLLECT 27 HITS TO WIN EXTRA-INNING THRILLER

MAY 16, 1933
WASHINGTON SENATORS 11, CLEVELAND INDIANS 10 (12 INNINGS)

by Doug Skipper

Ending a topsy-turvy, roller-coaster ride, first baseman Joe Kuhel rapped a bases loaded 12th-inning single through the pitcher's box to lift the Washington Senators to an 11-10 victory over the Cleveland Indians at Griffith Stadium. Kuhel's fifth hit of the game capped a 3-hour 34-minute marathon in which the two teams combined to use 11 pitchers, reported at the time as an American League record, and 34 players in all.[1]

The 11 pitchers surrendered 43 hits. Washington lashed out 27, including three singles, a triple, and a home run by Kuhel, five singles by 19-year-old third baseman Cecil Travis, making his major-league debut, and five singles by catcher Luke Sewell. All nine Senators starters collected at least one hit and all eight of Cleveland's position players did the same. Left fielder Joe Vosmik had four of Cleveland's 16 hits.

"Only about 1,000 fans saw the game, which started in a light drizzle on a rain-soaked field, was played in bright sunshine, and ended almost after nightfall," the Associated Press reported, calling the game a "weird twelve-inning slugging battle."[2]

The sparse crowd saw the Senators build a seemingly safe 7-1 lead, but the Indians chipped away and finally grabbed the lead before Washington staged its own late-inning heroics.

It started quietly enough. Senators starting pitcher Walter "Lefty" Stewart surrendered a single in the top of the first, but Sewell gunned down Johnny Burnett trying to steal second. Right fielder Goose Goslin singled against Indians starter Belve Bean in the bottom of the inning, but the Nationals left him stranded.

Cleveland grabbed a 1-0 lead when second baseman Bill Cissell led off the second with a double, moved to third on a groundout, and scored on Vosmik's single to center.

The lead disappeared in the bottom half of the inning. Travis, a spray-hitting left-handed batter, reached on an infield single in his first major-league at-bat, and Sewell slapped a two-out single that Vosmik misplayed, allowing Travis to score and Sewell to scamper into second. Stewart helped his own cause with a single to left to plate Sewell, and Kuhel tripled into the right-field gap to drive in Stewart.

Senators shortstop Joe Cronin committed an error in the top of the third, but Stewart worked through it, and Washington scored four runs in the bottom of the inning. After Bean retired the first two Washington batters, center fielder Fred Schulte beat out an infield single, Travis singled to center, and second baseman Buddy Myer plated Schulte with a single to center. Sewell greeted relief pitcher Sarge Connally with an infield single to score Myer, and Stewart reached again, this time on a walk, to load the bases. Kuhel lined a single to center, driving in Sewell and Myer, and the Senators led, 7-1.

Cleveland whittled away at Washington's lead in the top of the fifth when Connally doubled to left-center field, right fielder Dick Porter tripled to drive him in, and Porter scored on a groundout by Burnett.

Kuhel homered to right field in the bottom of the fifth to extend the lead to 8-3, but Cleveland chiseled away again with three runs in the top of the sixth. First baseman Ed Morgan tripled to left and third baseman Willie Kamm drove him home with a fly ball. Vosmik and catcher Roy Spencer both singled, and after a fly out, Porter's single scored Vosmik and Burnett's single scored Spencer. Cronin, Washington's player-manager, made his first pitching change of the day. Lefty Bobby Burke replaced Stewart and induced center fielder Earl Averill to pop out in foul territory to end the inning.

The Senators could not extend the lead against Cleveland's third pitcher of the day, Howard Craghead, in the bottom of the sixth, and once again Cleveland chipped away, scoring an unearned run when Kamm reached on Cronin's second error and Vosmik doubled him home. Washington's third pitcher, Monte Weaver, came on to end the assault.

Clinging to an 8-7 lead, Washington failed to score in the bottom of the seventh against Cleveland's fourth pitcher, Clint Brown.

The Indians finally reclaimed the lead in the top of the eighth. Center fielder Averill drove in a run with a single, Kamm chased him home with a base hit to left, and Vosmik singled to left – his fourth hit of the day – to drive in a third run. Jack Russell replaced Weaver and recorded the third out.

Down 10-8, it was Washington's turn to chip away, aided by an Indians' error. With one out, Travis reached on a misplay by Cissell, and Myer singled to move Travis to third. After Mel Harder, Cleveland's fifth pitcher, replaced Brown, Sewell singled to left to score Travis.

Cronin called on Washington's fifth pitcher, Bill McAfee, who replaced Harris in the top of the ninth, and retired the Indians in order.

Nursing a one-run lead, Harder retired Kuhel to start the bottom of the ninth inning, but left-fielder Heinie Manush and Goslin both singled to center and Cronin flied to right to score Manush. That was all Washington could muster against Harder, and the game moved to extra innings tied at 10-10.

McAfee worked his second scoreless inning, but not without drama. After he hit Averill to start the 10th inning, home-plate umpire Roy Van Graflan called Cissell out on strikes and then ejected both Cissell and Indians manager Roger Peckinpaugh for arguing the call. McAfee retired the next two hitters, and the game remained tied.

The Senators nearly ended it in their half of the 10th when Travis slapped his fifth single of the day, Myer bunted him to second, and after Sewell grounded out, pinch-hitter Sam Rice singled. Burnett, who had moved from shortstop to second after Cissell's ejection, threw to Sewell, who tagged out the sliding Travis at the plate.

Alvin "General" Crowder, Washington's sixth hurler, replaced McAfee and retired the Indians in order in the 11th. The Senators threatened in the bottom of the inning when Kuhel singled and was sacrificed to second by Manush. Goslin drew an intentional walk. But Harder induced Cronin to ground into a force play and Schulte flied out to center to end the threat.

Crowder set the Indians down in order again in the top of the 12th, and in their half of the inning the Senators cashed in on their chance. With one out, Myer singled to center and took third when

Sewell singled to right. Pinch-hitter Ossie Bluege received an intentional pass to set up Kuhel's game-winning hit.

Bluege had batted for Crowder, and had Kuhel not ended the game, Cronin would have been forced to use his seventh pitcher of the game. Earl Whitehill, a starter, was warming in the bullpen when the game ended, and was Cronin's last available hurler. Alphonse "Tommy" Thomas had been given the day off after getting married that morning.[3]

With the win, Crowder improved to 5-2, in the midst of a highly productive three-game stretch. Two days earlier, he had retired Luke Appling for the final out in an 11-9 win at Chicago in the second game of a doubleheader to preserve a Washington win. After an offday, he pitched the 11th and 12th innings to earn the victory over the Indians on Tuesday, and the next day the "durable righty"[4] who regularly started and relieved in 1933, hurled all nine innings of a 3-2 win over the Indians, scattering eight hits and a walk to outduel Wes Ferrell.

With the win, Washington improved to 17-11 and Cleveland slipped to the same mark, leaving the teams tied for second in the AL. The New York Yankees, who were rained out, remained 15-9, percentage points ahead of the Senators and Indians.

While the Senators went on to win a pennant and represent the AL in the World Series with Kuhel, Crowder, Cronin, Goslin, and Manush playing key roles, Travis enjoyed only a short first major-league stint. The Nationals had rushed the youngster into the lineup because of injuries, including one to Bluege, the team's regular third baseman.

"Cecil Travis, hurriedly recalled from Washington's Chattanooga farm to play third base, turned in two of the most brilliant fielding plays of the game in addition to producing five singles and reaching first by the error route on another try," the Associated Press reported.[5]

After his five-hit effort, he banged out three more hits in his next two games.

"The extent to which Travis made his presence felt in those three games better may be appreciated from the fact that he collected eight hits in 15 times at bat for a percentage of .553 and scored five runs," Denman Thompson wrote in *The Sporting News*. "But his value may not (be) confined to the attacking end, for he handled a total of 18 chances in the field without the semblance of an error, and some were of the most difficult variety.[6] The Indians tried him out with all manner of offensive tactics, including well-placed bunts, yet not once did he fail to perform in the most approved style."[7]

Though he batted.310, the 19-year-old's first stint in the majors lasted barely a week. The Senators sent Travis back to the minors after Washington's May 24 game, when Bluege was able to return to regular play.

Travis did return in September as the Senators cruised to the pennant by seven games over the Yankees, but mustered just four hits in 14 at-bats. He became a regular and batted .314 in 12 big-league seasons, but lost four years of prime playing time to serve in the Army during World War II. Regarded as the best third baseman in the AL when he was drafted in 1942, he suffered frostbite at the Battle of the Bulge that hampered his ability to return to the majors after the war, and earned a Bronze Star.[8]

SOURCES

In addition to the sources cited in the Notes, the author accessed Retrosheet.org, Baseball-Almanac.com, Baseball-Reference.com, SABR.org, *The Sporting News* archive via Paper of Record, dcbaseballhistory.com, and thisdayinbaseball.com, as well as the following:

Deveaux, Tom. *The Washington Senators: 1901-1971* (Jefferson, North Carolina: McFarland, 2005).

Gilbert, Bill. *They Also Served: Baseball and the Home Front, 1941-1945* (New York: Crown Publishers, 1982).

Kieran, John. "Sports of the Times – The Opinions of Bucky Harris," *New York Times*, May 19, 1933: 22.

Sarnoff, Gary. *The Wrecking Crew of '33* (Jefferson, North Carolina: McFarland, 2009).

NOTES

1 *The Sporting News* said the game lasted 3 hours 21 minutes, and that 33 players appeared in it, "coming within two of the record of 35 players utilized by two clubs. "Games of May 16," *The Sporting News*, May 25, 1933: 6. However, the publication's box score, and those of Retrosheet.org, Baseball-Almanac.com, and Baseball-Reference.com list 34 players, 16 for Cleveland and 18 for Washington.

2 Associated Press, "Senators Defeat Indians in 12th: Win, 11-10, Going into Second Place Tie With Rivals - Yanks Now in Lead. Kuhel's 5th Hit Decides - Drives Single With Bases Filled - Teams Collect 43 Safeties and Use 34 Players," *New York Times*, May 17, 1933: 20.

3 "Games of May 16"; "Senators Defeat Indians in 12th."

4 Gregory H. Wolf, "General Crowder," SABR Biography Project, sabr.org/bioproj/person/ab4b0343, SABR.org.

5 "Senators Defeat Indians in 12th."

6 BaseballReference.com says Travis had 19 fielding chances in the three games.

7 Denman Thompson, "Recruit Travis Pulls Nationals Out of Hole," *The Sporting News*, Thursday, May 25: 3.

8 Rob Kirkpatrick's excellent SABR.org biography covers the war service of Cecil Travis. Several other publications about baseball during World War II mention Travis, including Steven Bullock's *Playing for the Nation: Baseball and the American Military During World War II* (Lincoln: University of Nebraska Press, 2004), Bill Gilbert's *They Also Served: Baseball and the Home Front, 1941-1945* (New York: Crown Publishers, 1982), and Gary Bloomfield's *Duty, Honor, Victory: America's Athletes in World War II* (Guilford, Conn.: Lyons Press, 2003).

A PENNANT FOR LADIES' DAY

SEPTEMBER 21, 1933
WASHINGTON SENATORS 2, ST. LOUIS BROWNS 1

by Paul E. Doutrich

September 21, 1933, the last day of summer, was ladies day at Griffith Stadium. A Washington Senators policy since 1929, this ladies day could be special. The Senators came into their final game of the season against the St. Louis Browns needing just one more victory to claim the team's first pennant since 1925.

It had been a remarkable summer for the Senators. The team struggled through the early months of the season but in late June emerged as a legitimate pennant contender. During the next six weeks the Senators battled the Yankees for the league lead. Then in August, Washington began to pull away. Clawing out a 10-game lead, the Senators effectively ended the pennant race by early September. With little more than a week left in the season and the second-place Yankees still 7½ games back, it was a forgone conclusion that Washington would win the pennant. The only question was when. As Senators fans filed into Griffith Stadium on September 21, they hoped this would be the day.

The two teams knew each other well. During the winter three players from each club had been traded to the other. All except one, St. Louis pitcher Lloyd Brown, were in the lineup. Four outfielders, Goose Goslin and Fred Schulte, now with the Senators, and Sam West and Carl Reynolds of the Browns, were also part of the switch. The Senators' starting pitcher, Lefty Stewart, a regular in the St. Louis rotation since 1927, had been the final piece of the trade. The Browns' starting pitcher, Bump Hadley, though not part of the trade, also knew Washington well. He had broken into the major leagues as a Senator and was with them for six seasons prior to 1932 when he was traded to the White Sox and then on to the Browns.

For Leon "Goose" Goslin, the trade brought him back to where he had begun his major-league career 12 years earlier. Acknowledged to be one of the best hitters in baseball but a liability in the field, he had been traded in June 1930 for Heinie Manush and General Crowder. Disappointed with Goslin's play in 1932 season and irritated by his happy-go-lucky approach to the game, Browns manager Bill Killefer was anxious to get rid of the Goose. Clark Griffith was just as anxious to add him to a lineup that already included Joe Cronin and Manush.

The game opened with a leadoff single by Browns third baseman Art Scharein but following Scharein's hit both teams were retired quietly. In the second, after the Browns went down in order, the Senators broke through with a run. Center fielder Fred Schulte knocked a one-out single to center. He went to third on a hit by first baseman Joe Kuhel and scored on Bob Boken's fly ball.

During the next four innings the two pitchers adroitly cut through opposing hitters. Though both teams put together minor threats, neither was able to push across a run. The Browns in the third got their first two hitters on base but, assisted by a poorly placed sacrifice bunt attempt, Stewart quashed the threat. The Senators matched the effort an inning later when, with one out, Joe Cronin walked and Fred Schulte singled to center. From there Hadley easily handled the short-lived threat by getting Kuhel to pop up and striking out Boken.

Bump Hadley was a pitcher who relied almost exclusively on his sizzling fastball but struggled with control. Early in his career, some compared his fastball to that of Walter Johnson. By 1933 he had established himself as a workhorse on the mound. Two years earlier, while still with the Senators, he led the league in pitching appearances and in 1933 he was on his way to leading the league in innings pitched. A year earlier he led the league with 21 losses. It was his second straight 20-loss season. Despite his record, Hadley was a feared pitcher and the closest thing the Browns had to an ace. When he had his control, Hadley could be a very effective hurler, and on this day he appeared to have his control.

In the top of the seventh, the Browns finally got to Stewart for a run. Right fielder Bruce Campbell led off with a walk. Ski Melillo, the Browns' second baseman, followed with a double that scored Campbell. Had it not been for a questionable attempt by Melillo to take third on a ball hit to shortstop Cronin, the Browns might have added to their seventh-inning tally.

Joe Cronin was clearly the heart and soul of the Senators. Only 26, he was already acknowledged to be among the best players in the game. Prior to the start of the 1933 season, team owner Clark Griffith, hoping both to maximize Cronin's talents and economize on salaries, made his star shortstop the team's manager as well. In the grip of the Great Depression, many teams sought ways to cut back expenses. In that sense, Griffith was among the more aggressive owners. Nine years earlier he had made a similar gamble by promoting young Bucky Harris to player-manager status. The move led to a World Series championship. Despite concerns that Cronin might not be up to the dual role, Griffith's experiment again appeared successful. Cronin was having another excellent season as a player and the Senators were about to claim another pennant. Most agreed that "much of the praise for bringing Washington back to the top was directed tonight toward the 26-year-old Cronin."[1]

The Senators wasted no time taking the lead back. In the bottom of the inning, Kuhel laced a one-out single to center field. Boken followed with a walk and catcher Luke Sewell smacked a double to center. Kuhel scored and Boken ended up at third. Had it not been for "some dizzy base running" on the next play, the Senators might have tallied another run.[2] Pitcher Stewart hit a ball to shortstop. Boken broke for the plate but stopped midway down the line and was tagged out in a rundown. Hadley then struck out Buddy Myer to end the inning.

In the top of the eighth inning, Stewart got the first three in order. In the bottom of the inning, with the pennant just six outs away, another potential Senators rally sputtered when Cronin, who had doubled, was picked off second. In the ninth the Browns refused to go easily. Campbell led off with a single but became the front end of a double play, the fourth of the game for the Senators. Down to the last out, Melillo, who had driven in the Browns' only run, launched a shot to deep left-center field. In a flash, Senators left fielder Heinie Manush raced back and "ended the game with a brilliant one-handed catch."[3] The American League pennant was back in Washington.

Even before Manush was in the dugout, thousands of fans, many of them women, rushed onto the field to embrace their heroes. "Hard-bitten big leaguers became broken-field runners as they dodged 10,000 men and women, berserk with joy. ..."[4] Inside the clubhouse, cameras flashed and backs were slapped. Through it all, Heinie Manush tightly grasped the ball he had caught to end the game. Meanwhile, giddy fans waited outside the clubhouse door to collect autographs.

While every Washington player was a target for the adulation, it was Cronin whom most wanted to see. Fans surrounded his car and refused to allow it to be moved until they had gotten a glimpse of the Senators star. Eventually Cronin sent a decoy to his car while he attempted to sneak out through the dugout entrance. The bluff failed. About halfway across the outfield, he was spied by happy fans and chased into a utility room. Eventually a police escort enabled him to leave the ballpark.[5]

Twelve days later the Senators met the New York Giants in the World Series. Back in 1924 the Senators had beaten the Giants in the series. This time the tables would be reversed.

SOURCES

In addition to the sources cited in the Notes, the author accessed Retrosheet.org, Baseball-Reference.com, SABR.org, and *The Sporting News* archive via Paper of Record.

NOTES

1. John F. Chester, "Washington Steps in Charmed Circle," *Newport News* (Virginia) *Daily Press*, September 22, 1933: 9.
2. "Senators Clinch the Pennant," *Baltimore Sun*, September 22, 1933: 15.
3. "Joe Cronin's Club Wins 1933 Pennant in American League" *Newport News* (Virginia) *Daily Press*, September 22, 1933: 9.
4. "Cronin Besieged by Fans as Team Clinches Pennant," *Evening Star (Washington)* September 22, 1933: B-1.
5. Ibid.

WHITEHILL WHITEWASHES GIANTS, MYER IS MIGHTY IN WORLD SERIES WIN

OCTOBER 5, 1933
WASHINGTON SENATORS 4, NEW YORK GIANTS 0

GAME THREE OF THE WORLD SERIES

by Nathan Bierma

With 15 minutes until game time, the tarp was still on the field under dark skies at Griffith Stadium, and the first pitch of Game Three of the World Series was uncertain.

Detaining the 25,727 eager fans braving the elements to witness the return of the World Series to the nation's capital after nine years would be unfortunate, but one of them in particular was on an especially tight schedule: the President of the United States, Franklin D. Roosevelt.

"Word arrived at Griffith Stadium at 1:25 that the president was on his way," wrote Gary Sarnoff. "The start of Game Three would be delayed until the president was comfortably seated in his box, followed by his throwing the ceremonial [first] pitch."[1]

At 1:36 P.M., a door on the right-field wall swung open for the president's motorcade, a band marched onto the field, and the two teams came out of their dugouts and lined up facing the president's box.

"When Roosevelt entered his box, a miracle occurred. The rain stopped, and the sun made its first appearance of the day," Sarnoff wrote. "There is no doubt about the immense influence President Roosevelt wields over affairs in this country," wrote the *New York Times* of the chief executive's apparent meteorological intervention.[2]

The Senators needed all the help they could get, although in their matchup with the Giants Roosevelt was officially neutral, and, as a lifelong New Yorker living in Washington, personally conflicted. Less than 24 hours earlier, the Senators had fallen into a two-games-to-none hole with their second loss at the Polo Grounds. The favored Senators, whom young scribe Shirley Povich nicknamed "the Old Washington Wrecking Crew" for their fearsome threesome of Goose Goslin, Heinie Manush, and Joe Cronin,[3] had no offday to recover. Cronin, in his first season as player-manager after taking over managerial duties from the immortal Walter Johnson, gathered his tired team at the soggy stadium for a pep talk.

"I hope all of you are as ashamed as I am of what happened in the first two series games," Cronin told them. "We're a better ball club than the Giants, and now is the time to show it to a city that has supported us all season."[4]

No one was more motivated than Earl Whitehill, the lefty curveball specialist making his first-ever World Series start after 10 seasons with the Detroit Tigers. Cronin's last-minute decision to start Lefty Stewart over Whitehill in Game One, putting Washington in an early hole, was a head-scratcher, but Bill James writes, "It is generally thought that Whitehill reported to the park that day in no condition to pitch."[5]

Whitehill would not be at full strength for Game Three either. As he warmed up in the rain, he felt a pop in his left elbow. But after a heated conversation with Cronin, Whitehill won the right to start the game, and retired the Giants in order in the first inning. "His injured elbow was swelling by the minute, but he was so focused, he hardly noticed," Sarnoff wrote.[6]

In the bottom of the first, Buddy Myer reached on a single and Goslin doubled. The weather made an impact when Cronin hit a roller toward shortstop and Myer charged for home. Giants starter Freddie Fitzsimmons fielded the ball and prepared to throw Myer out, but his foot slipped on the wet turf and he had to hold onto the ball for an extra split-second. He recovered in time to get Cronin at first but allowed the run to score. The next batter, Fred Schulte, singled to score Goslin, and the Senators suddenly had their largest lead of the series so far, 2-0.

Whitehill had some trouble in the second, with a single and wild pitch followed by a walk, but escaped the inning with a double play on a grounder to Cronin. Ossie Bluege led off the bottom of the second with a double down the left-field line. That brought up Myer.

Myer was coming off a stellar season but a disastrous stint in New York, where he made three errors in Game One. Myer was rattled by a traffic accident that killed a pedestrian, which he observed from a taxi en route to the Polo Grounds. "[I]nstead of focusing on the game, his thoughts were on the tragedy," Sarnoff wrote.[7]

Today Myer was single-minded. In the second inning, he doubled down the right-field line to score Bluege and put Washington in front 3-0. Two innings in, the Senators had equaled their entire offensive output in two games in New York.

The next inning, Myer starred on defense, running down a pop fly by Blondy Ryan with his back to home plate. "[T]he Nat second sacker tore into short center and made a truly sensational play when he snared the ball in his very finger-tips by an over-the-shoulder grab," reported the *Washington Post*.[8]

"After that, Whitehill was in complete command," Sarnoff wrote.[9] He mowed down nine straight Giants over the fifth, sixth, and seventh innings with a total of 15 pitches.

In the bottom of the seventh, the Senators provided an insurance run Whitehill wouldn't even need, once again off the bat of Myer, following a single and stolen base by catcher Luke Sewell. "Myer did not come back to Washington to fail," wrote the *Post*. "His third hit of the day he rocketed into right center field to bring Sewell home with [a] fourth run."

Whitehill endured two baserunners on a single and an error in the eighth, nullifying them on two short outs — a grounder back to the mound by Hughie Critz and a short pop fly by player-manager Bill Terry caught by catcher Sewell.

After the Senators went down in order in the bottom of the eighth, Whitehill walked leadoff batter Mel Ott in the top of the ninth. He then enjoyed two sharp plays by Bleuge on consecutive screaming grounders by Kiddo Davis and Travis Jackson, followed by a fly ball by Gus Mancuso to Manush in left to end the game. The Senators had fended off disaster with a shutout win at home.

"For the first time in the Series we looked like a good ball club," Cronin said afterward. "Our victory was about due. We couldn't go on losing. The tide had to turn."[10]

"This left the National League standard-bearers still leading in the struggle to determine the baseball championship of the universe by a margin of two games to one," the *New York Times* wrote, but added, "The notion that Memphis Bill Terry's team of destiny would gain its objective on a direct line of flight was slightly jarred."[11]

The *Post* praised Whitehill, who held the Giants to five hits (four singles and Travis Jackson's double in the fourth) in the complete-game shutout.

"His wide-sweeping curve slide beyond their bats with eccentric dips all afternoon," the *Post* wrote. "His fast ball left them gasping."[12]

Myer, meanwhile, also earned plaudits.

"Buddy Myer, who had three misplays in the first game, performed so valiantly today that Washington rooters decided those errors in New York must have been made by some stranger who broke into buddy's locker and stole his uniform," joked the *Times*.[13]

Still, Terry presciently realized that even in decisive defeat, the Series was playing out in a way that favored his Giants.

"[T]he Series is still what I have said it is from the start – dominated by pitching," he told the *Times*. "They got it today and we didn't. ... I think we'll have better pitching than they will for the rest of the Series. ... I'll send Hubbell back at them tomorrow."[14]

Sure enough, Washington's wrecking crew would end up doing little damage throughout the Series, humbled by Hubbell and his mound mates.

"What became of Washington's great pitching? New York base hits, that's what it became," the *Post's* Povich wrote. "And what became of Washington's great hitting? Strikeouts, pop-ups and double plays, that's what."[15]

Joe Cronin was a star player, manager, general manager, and league president. The 26-year-old "Boy Wonder" guided the Senators to the AL pennant in 1933 in his first season as player-manager. He batted .301 and recorded at least 100 RBIs in a season eight times in his Hall of Fame career. (Photo by Sporting News and Rogers Photo Archive via Getty Images)

SOURCES

In addition to the sources cited in the Notes, the author accessed Retrosheet.org, Baseball-Reference.com, Newspapers.com, and SABR.org.

NOTES

1 Gary A. Sarnoff, *The Wrecking Crew of '33: The Washington Senators' Last Pennant* (Jefferson, North Carolina: McFarland & Company, 2009), 181.

2 John Kieran, "Whitewashed by Whitehill," *New York Times*, October 6, 1933: 22.

3 Sarnoff, 125.

4 Sarnoff, 180.

5 Bill James, *The Bill James Guide to Baseball Managers* (New York: Diversion Books, 2014).

6 Sarnoff, 181.

7 Sarnoff, 173.

8 "Nats Regain Prestige, Win Over Foe Behind Whitehill," *Washington Post*, October 6, 1933: 1.

9 Sarnoff, 183.

10 "Cronin, Confident, Lauds New Spirit," *New York Times*, October 6, 1933: 22.

11 John Drebinger, "Roosevelt Sees Senators Defeat the Giants by 4-0," *New York Times*, October 6, 1933: 1.

12 "Nats Regain Prestige."

13 Kieran, "Whitewashed by Whitehill."

14 "Cronin, Confident, Lauds New Spirit."

15 "In 1933, Washington Couldn't Overcome Giants, Carl Hubbell," *Washington Post*, October 4, 2012.

KING CARL HURLS 11-INNING GEM TO PUT GIANTS ON VERGE OF TITLE

OCTOBER 6, 1933
NEW YORK GIANTS 2, WASHINGTON SENATORS 1 (11 INNINGS)

GAME FOUR OF THE WORLD SERIES

by Gregory H. Wolf

"There have been few World Series battles in history that carried as much in the way of melodramatic suspense," gushed syndicated sportswriter Grantland Rice about Carl Hubbell's 11-inning complete-game victory over the Washington Senators in Game Four of the World Series to give the New York Giants a seemingly insurmountable three-games-to-one lead.[1] John Drebinger of the *New York Times* described King Carl's second victory in four days as a "tense, nerve-throbbing battle that for thrills and exciting moments far exceeded any of the three previous contests" of the fall classic.[2] "It was bigger than baseball," Giants beat writer Francis Wallace waxed poetically in the *Daily News* about Hubbell's relentless and courageous performance on two days' rest. "[I]t was the triumph of a man over every test of skill, nerve and courage another great ball club could put before him."[3]

The Giants (91-61), led by Bill Terry, who had taken over for legendary skipper John McGraw as player-manager during the previous season, captured an unlikely pennant, their first since four straight from 1921 to 1924. They opened the World Series a 10-7 underdog to the Senators (99-53), piloted by boy-wonder 26-year-old Joe Cronin, in his first season as player-manager.[4] The Nats boasted a high-powered offense that averaged 5.6 runs per game compared with the Giants' 4.1, but they didn't have the Meal Ticket, as Hubbell was called.

"Hubbell is the Giants," proclaimed Wallace without an air of hyperbole.[5] In his sixth season, Hubbell emerged as baseball's best hurler, whose mesmerizing screwball flummoxed batters all season. The lanky 6-foot, 170-pound southpaw led the NL with 23 victories (12 losses) to push his career slate to 100-64, and also with 308⅔ innings, while pacing the majors with 10 shutouts and a microscopic 1.66 ERA, the lowest mark since Walter Johnson's 1.49 in 1919, the last year of the Deadball Era. "When in trouble call on Hubbell," quipped Drebinger, and Terry intended to lean on Hubbell in the fall classic.[6] In the Series opener, on October 3, Hubbell tossed a five-hitter while fanning 10 to beat the Senators 4-2 in the Polo

Grounds; both runs charged to him were unearned. The momentum of the Series shifted when 22-game winner Earl Whitehill shut out the Giants in Game Three at Griffith Stadium to give the Nats their first victory.

Unlike the previous rainy day, Thursday afternoon in the nation's capital was sunny and crisp, with temperatures in the 60s. Nonetheless, the "crowd again failed to live up to expectations," submitted Drebinger, with 26,762 spectators in attendance.[7]

The game unfolded as a pitchers' duel between Hubbell and 27-year-old right-hander Monte Weaver, noted for his "high-powered delivery" and occasional bouts of wildness.[8] A 22-game winner the previous season, his first full campaign in the big leagues, Weaver was plagued by injuries in '33 and posted a 10-5 slate. The only baserunner in the first three innings was the Giants' Jo-Jo Moore, who led off the game with a walk.

The Giants struck in the fourth. Terry at age 34 was no longer the same hitter who led the majors with a .401 average and set an NL-league record with 254 hits in 1930; however, he was still among the most feared hitters in the game. He clubbed a towering one-out home run into the center-field bleachers, clearing "the low three-foot fence in front of the temporary triangular bleachers," reported Drebinger.[9] Mel Ott, team leader in home runs (23) and RBIs (103), walked and Kiddo Davis singled. Suddenly in trouble and pitching to remain in the game, Weaver retired Travis Jackson on a popup and then extinguished the threat by walking Gus Mancuso intentionally to face weak-hitting Blondy Ryan (.238 average), whom he fanned.

Weaver bent, but did not break, yielding one hit per inning in the fifth through the ninth. Ott led off the sixth with a single and was sacrificed a station, but was stranded after Weaver gave Mancuso another free pass and then induced Ryan to tap meekly back to the mound. Moore laced a two-out double in the next frame, but was stranded on third. From the fourth through ninth, the Giants left nine men on.

Despite retiring the first 10 batters he faced, Hubbell was not as sharp as in the Series opener. And like Weaver, he withstood his foes' best shots, yielding one hit in every inning from the fourth through eighth, as the Senators left seven men on. In the fourth Goose Goslin connected for the Senators' first hit then moved to second when Hubbell, known for his impeccable control, walked Heinie Manush.

Tensions flared in the sixth. With Buddy Myer on second with one out, Manush hit what Drebinger described as a "sizzling ground ball well inside the first base line," which eluded the diving Terry at first.[10] Second baseman Hughie Critz made a "miraculous stop" and threw to Hubbell at first.[11] It appeared to be a hit and Drebinger suggested the call "could have been given either way," but first-base umpire Charlie Moran ruled Manush out.[12] A vehement argument ensued; Cronin rushed from the Nationals dugout and it appeared as though Manush would strike at Moran, and apparently did bump him.[13] Holding firm, Moran ejected Manush from the game, while fans pelted the field with bottles in protest. After order was restored a few minutes later, Hubbell fanned Cronin to end the frame.

The fracas was not yet over. Manush, incredulous that he'd been tossed, offered a few choice words to Moran as he defiantly took his position in left field. Moran promptly held up the action again, and ordered him to leave the field and dugout. (After the game, Moran was led off the field by a police escort to ensure his safety.)

The Senators finally caught a break with one out in the seventh. Joe Kuhel hit a routine tapper back to the mound. An excellent fielder who had led the NL pitchers in assists in 1929, 1932, and 1933, Hubbell had his man out by 20 feet, noted Grantland Rice, but the ball slipped out of the hurler's bare hand for a costly error.[14] After Ossie Bluege sacrificed the runner to second, Luke Sewell sent Hubbell's first pitch into center field to tie the game, 1-1.

The Giants squandered leadoff singles in the eighth and ninth innings, while Hubbell seemed wobbly. Myer led off the eighth with a walk the eighth; after and two force outs, Dave Harris advanced to third on Cronin's two-out single. After a one-two-three ninth, Hubbell found himself in trouble again, in the 10th when Myer laced a one-out single and moved to second on Harris's two-out walk. Cronin's feeble grounder ended the threat.

The biggest surprise of the game, arguably the turning point of the entire World Series, came from an unlikely source, a remnant of the Giants dynasty from the early 1920s. Just 30 years old, Travis Jackson was buying time on aching knees. He had lost his starting shortstop position to Ryan, but got a second chance when third baseman Johnny Vergez was sidelined with appendicitis a month earlier. Jackson's shocking bunt to lead off the 11th caught third baseman Ossie Bluege flatfooted. After Mancuso's sacrifice bunt moved Jackson to second, Ryan had a chance to atone for his previous failings with men in scoring position. A popular player who initiated the team's battle cry ("We cannot be beat"),[15] Ryan laced a single to left to drive in Jackson for a 2-1 lead. Hubbell followed with a single to send Weaver to the showers, but veteran Jack Russell recorded two quick outs to end the frame.

Lauded as the "master flinger of his time," Hubbell took the mound in the 11th as intensity mounted.[16] A "silence of death," opined Wallace, spread throughout the ballpark as the Senators came to bat.[17] Fred Schulte's leadoff single revived the crowd, which was on the verge of pandemonium when Terry decided not to play Kuhel's bunt to first thinking it would be foul, but it stayed in fair territory. Bluege's sacrifice put both runners in scoring position, after which Terry called for the infield to huddle around Hubbell on the mound to discuss strategy. Hubbell intentionally walked Sewell to load the bases. A walk or deep fly could tie the game; a single would win it. Cronin called on Cliff Bolton to pinch-hit for Russell. A third-string catcher, Bolton had only 40 at-bats all season (including an unsuccessful punch-hit appearance in Game Two), but had collected 16 hits. On a 2-and-1 pitch, Bolton sent a routine grounder to Ryan at short who initiated a game-ending 6-4-3 twin killing to give the Giants a dramatic 2-1 win in 2 hours and 59 minutes.

"With the bases loaded I wanted to play the infield in," said Terry in the ebullient Giants' clubhouse after the game, "but Blondie suggested that Jackson and myself play in and he and Critz be allowed to play out not to far."[18]

Jackson's bunt and Ryan's single propelled the Giants to victory, but it would not have been possible without yet another yeoman effort from Hubbell, whose screwball the Senators chopped into the dirt all afternoon. He yielded eight hits (all singles) and four walks (two of which were intentional), and fanned five. In 20 combined innings in the fall classic, he had yet to yield an earned run. When asked about his fateful pitch Bolton to end the game, King Carl quipped, "it was a screwball."[19]

SOURCES

In addition to the sources cited in the Notes, the author accessed Retrosheet.org, Baseball-Reference.com, Newspapers.com, and SABR.org.

NOTES

1 Grantland Rice, "Hubbell Stumbles but Comes Through," *Boston Globe*, October 7, 1933: 4.

2 John Drebinger, "Giants Turn Senators by 2-1 in 11-Inning Game," *New York Times*, October 7, 1933: 1.

3 Francis Wallace, "King Hubbell Whips Nats," (New York) *Daily News*, October 7, 1933: 29.

4 The odds are from Drebinger.

5 Wallace.

6 Drebinger.

7 Drebinger.

8 Drebinger.

9 Drebinger.

10 Drebinger.

11 Drebinger.

12 Drebinger.

13 See Debringer; Wallace; and "Ryan, Critz Draw Terry's Acclaim," *New York Times*, October 7, 1933: 9; and Marshall Hunt, "A Great Game, Fans! Here Are the Details," (New York) *Daily News*, October 7, 1933: 26.

14 Rice.

15 The phrase came from Ryan's telegram on July 11 to Terry and the team, informing them he'd rejoin the club after missing a few games due to an injury. See Victor O. Jones, "Ryan's Single Gives Giants Three Games," *Boston Globe*, October 7, 1933: 1.

16 Drebinger.

17 Wallace.

18 "Ryan, Critz Draw Terry's Acclaim."

19 "Ryan, Critz Draw Terry's Acclaim."

MEL OTT'S 10TH-INNING HOMER GIVES GIANTS THE TITLE

OCTOBER 7, 1933
NEW YORK GIANTS 4, WASHINGTON SENATORS 3 (10 INNINGS)

GAME FIVE OF THE WORLD SERIES

by Gregory H. Wolf

It was "one of the most spectacular closing chapters in all World Series history," gushed sportswriter Grantland Rice about Mel Ott's home run in the top of the 10th inning against the Washington Senators in Game Five of the World Series to give the New York Giants a surprising title.[1] It was a stunning turnaround for a team that looked in disarray seven months earlier during spring training in Los Angeles. Many prognosticators had picked the Giants to duplicate their dismal sixth-place (72-82) finish from the previous season, which was marred by legendary manager John McGraw's forced midseason resignation. He was replaced by Bill Terry, the prolific hitter, who suffered a broken bone in his wrist and missed the first month of the 1933 season. The Giants were a "team that nobody knows," quipped Harold C. Burr, and "was ridiculed for awkward misfits in training camp."[2] However, under Memphis Bill's leadership, the team developed a combative spirit and relied on the big leagues' best pitching staff to capture an unlikely pennant.

The Giants were a loose bunch heading into Game Five. Carl Hubbell's extraordinary performance the day before, an 11-inning complete-game, 2-1 victory, his second win in four days, put the club on the verge of its first title since 1922 during a four-year (1921-1924) hold on the NL pennant. The pitching matchup featured age vs. youth and a repeat of Game Two moundsmen. In just his second full season and first as a starter, the Giants' 22-year-old Hal Schumacher emerged as one of most effective hurlers in the NL, posting a 19-12 slate with the league's third-lowest ERA (2.16), and earned a berth in the inaugural All-Star Game. The Senators' 26-year-old boy wonder, player-manager Joe Cronin, called on the "General" to stave off elimination.[3] Rubber-armed staff ace and All-Star Alvin Crowder was a grizzled 34-year-old veteran who had paced the junior circuit in wins the last two seasons (26 and 24 respectively) and boasted an impressive 138-91 slate in parts of eight seasons. Prince Hal had won their first encounter, tossing a complete-game five-hitter to beat the Senators, 6-1, at the Polo Grounds.

On a cloudless, sunny, and seasonably warm Saturday afternoon with temperatures in the mid-70s, Griffith Stadium was packed with 28,454 fans, the biggest attendance of the three games in the nation's capital, though not a sellout. Sportswriter James C. Isaminger opined that the "absence of the usual perpetual buzz among spectators was noticeable," almost as if the outcome of the Series had been foretold.[4] In World Series history, only one team thus far had overcome a three-games-to-one deficit: the Pittsburgh Pirates, who victimized the Senators in 1925.

Crowder was "shaky from the start," noted Isaminger, and was perhaps feeling the effects of pitching in a big-league-leading 52 regular-season games, including 35 starts, not to mention logging 626⅓ innings, easily the most in the majors, over the last two seasons.[5] He yielded a leadoff hit to Jo-Jo Moore and Terry's one-out single, but then doused the fire. He wasn't so lucky the next frame when Travis Jackson and Gus Mancuso led off with a single and walk respectively. Blondy Ryan, who clubbed the game-winning RBI single the day before, surprised everyone by laying down a bunt. That move was "not entirely accepted by baseball's outstanding academic minds," noted sportswriter John Drebinger, given that Schumacher was up next.[6] But the plan made Terry's call look ingenious when Prince Hal hit a lazy single to center field. The ball "float[ed] away like a baked potato," wrote Giants beat writer Jimmy Powers, and both Jackson and Mancuso raced home.[7]

Crowder's afternoon ended in the sixth, just as it had three days earlier in Gotham City. Kiddo Davis whacked a leadoff double over third base and moved to third on Jackson's sacrifice. Mancuso then blasted one to deep center field. Foreshadowing the end of the game, the ball caromed off the glove of an outstretched Fred Schulte, according to Powers.[8] Davis trotted home to give the Giants a 3-0 lead and Mancuso raced to second; the General headed to the showers. Jack Russell, a 27-year-old converted right-handed starter, fanned Ryan and Schumacher to keep the game close.

The first inning gave Senators fans an inkling that Dame Fortune was not on their side. After Goose Goslin laced a one-out single to left-center field, Heinie Manush hit a screeching liner that looked as though it could go for extra bases, but it was right at third baseman Travis Jackson, who snared the ball without moving and doubled Goslin off. There was some debate over whether Manush would play in the game owing to his aggressive confrontation with first-base umpire Charlie Moran in Game Four (Moran was behind the plate in Game Five). Manush bumped and appeared to take a swing at Moran, resulting in his ejection. Commissioner Kenesaw Landis refused to suspend him, given the gravity of this game.[9]

Schumacher rolled through the Nats lineup, encountering a hiccup in the fifth when Schulte and Joe Kuhel led off with singles, but the Senators' bad-luck streak continued. Ossie Bluege fouled out on a crucial bunt attempt. Schulte reached third on a two-out wild pitch to Crowder, who grounded meekly to short to end the threat.

Suddenly and without warning, wrote Drebinger, Schumacher "lost his magic touch" after two outs in the sixth, leading to the Senators' biggest inning in the entire Series.[10] The Senators' stacked lineup, which had led the majors with a .287 batting average, finally awakened from its doldrums. Manush, who had led the team with a .336 average and an AL-most 221 hits and 17 triples, singled with two outs, followed by another by Cronin, whose checked swing blooped the ball over Ryan's head at short. Schulte walloped one to deep left field to tie the game, 3-3. With no one yet warming up in the bullpen, Schumacher yielded a single to Kuhel and Bluege singled to third; Jackson's throw from the hot corner was wild, permitting Kuhel to advance to third. Schumacher's day was over.

With both teams' starters banished by the middle of the sixth inning, the game evolved into an improbable yet noteworthy battle between two relievers. Terry called on a 43-year-old graybeard, Havana-born Dolf Luque, whose "silvery sideburns glinted on a seamed face bronzed by the shade of a panatela wrapper," wrote Powers poetically.[11]

A former workhorse for the Cincinnati Reds, Luque harkened back to the Deadball Era (he debuted in 1914). He was making his first World Series appearance since the infamous Reds-Black Sox encounter in 1919, and had the distinction of leading the NL with 27 victories in 1923, the year after pacing the circuit in losses (23). Using what Grantland Rice called a "fast, jerky motion" and "low, fast breaking curves" to mesmerize the Nats,[12] he retired Luke Sewell to end the sixth, then punched out the side in the seventh. Luque was "chunky, almost fat," according to Rice, who said the pitcher's 5-foot-7 stature belied his ability and competitive spirit.[13] He even got into an argument with his batterymate, Mancuso, over pitch selection shortly after entering the game.[14]

Goslin's right arm saved a potential winning run in the ninth. The Goose narrowly missed a shoestring catch on Ryan's one-out Texas Leaguer to short right, but fielded the ball and fired a strike to erase Ryan at second. Ryan's tactical baserunning error proved costly when Luque followed with a single.

With two out in the 10th, the Giants' most dangerous slugger, Mel Ott, came to the plate. Just 24 years old but in his eighth big-league season, Master Melvin was a squat, 5-foot-9 power coil who had tied the Philadelphia Phillies' Chuck Klein for the NL lead in home runs (38) in 1932. Ott belted 23 of the Giants' NL-most 82 round-trippers in '33, which saw home runs decrease by 21 percent from the previous season.[15] Ott sent a "belt-high curve" deep to center field.[16] Schulte tracked the ball's arc and lurched over the three-foot fence in front of the temporary bleachers in a valiant effort to corral the orb, which "ricocheted off his upflung chocolate glove," wrote Powers.[17] Second-base umpire Cy Pfirman (an NL arbiter) held up two fingers, indicating a ground-rule double; however, the excitement was just beginning. Terry protested the ruling, prompting Pfirman to call a meeting with the other three umpires. After a short discussion, Pfirman reversed the call and signaled a home run. An enraged Jack Russell charged from the mound to confront Pfirman and had to be restrained by Cronin. The call stood. "[I]t was a just decision," said Cronin after the game. "My contention was that Schulte butted the ball over the rail with his knee."[18]

"[T]he crowd sat as badly dazed and stunned as Schulte," wrote Rice about Ott's blast to give the Giants a 4-3 lead.[19]

Luque, who had won 189 games and logged almost 3,200 innings thus far in his career, took the mound in the 10th for the most important three outs in his life. Facing the heart of the order, he retired the Senators' two best hitters, Goslin and Manush, before Cronin brought the crowd to its feet with a single to left. Schulte, who was noticeably limping after the gallant effort on Ott's smash, walked on four pitches and was replaced by pinch-runner John Kerr. A single away from a tie game, Luque emphatically ended the game in 2 hours and 38 minutes by striking out Kuhel to secure the Giants' convincing title.

SOURCES

In addition to the sources cited in the Notes, the author accessed Retrosheet.org, Baseball-Reference.com, Newspapers.com, and SABR.org.

NOTES

1 Grantland Rice, "Unusual Homer by Ott Dazes Capital Fans," *Baltimore Sun*, October 8, 1933: II, 1.

2 Harold C. Burr, "Giants Capture Series, Winning 5th Game, 4-3," *Brooklyn Eagle*, October 8, 1933: A1.

3 The moniker comes from Provost Marshal General Enoch Crowder, head of the Selective Service during World War I.

4 James C. Isaminger, "How the Giants Overcame Senators in Fadeout Fray on Potomac," *Philadelphia Inquirer*, October 8, 1933: 29.

5 Ibid.

6 John Drebinger, "Giants Are Victors in Worlds Series, Four Games to One," *New York Times*, October 8, 1933: III, 1.

7 Jimmy Powers, "Giants Win World Series," (New York) *Daily News*, October 8, 1933: 75.

8 Powers.

9 Associated Press, "Landis Regrets 'Banishment' of Outfielder Heinie Manush," (New York) *Daily News*, October 8, 1933: 76.

10 Drebinger.

11 Powers.

12 Rice.

13 Rice.

14 Rice.

15 In 1932 the 16 big-league teams combined for 1,358 home runs; that number dropped to 1,067 the following season, a decline of 21.4 percent.

16 Powers.

17 Powers.

18 Burr.

19 Rice.

BOBO OUTLASTS LEFTY

SEPTEMBER 1, 1935
WASHINGTON SENATORS 2, BOSTON RED SOX 1

by Jeff Findley

Entering the final month of the 1935 season, a September 1 matchup between the Boston Red Sox and the Washington Senators had little relevance in the eight-team American League. Both teams had long since said goodbye to any possibility of capturing the pennant, with Boston looking upward toward four other teams in the standings, a full 18 games behind the league-leading Detroit Tigers, and Washington, its losses outnumbering its victories by a 52-72 tally, trailing the eventual World Series champions by 28½ games.

Despite the underwhelming season performance of both teams and a constant threat of rain that day, 5,000 fans showed up at Washington's Griffith Stadium to watch Future Hall of Famer Robert Moses "Lefty" Grove go head-to-head with the Senators' Louis Norman "Bobo" Newsom.

Newspaper accounts at the time referred to him as Buck, but the nickname Bobo came about later in Newsom's career because he either could not or would not remember other players' names, instead referring to others as Bobo, and ultimately earning the nickname for himself.[1]

Grove, the Lefty moniker an obvious reference to his pitching arm, had matched up with Newsom just 20 days earlier, with Bobo claiming a 4-2 victory and both hurlers going the distance. Since that matchup, Grove had won two and lost two, and with 16 wins so far, was aiming to again reach the 20-win mark before season's end, something he accomplished seven consecutive times with the Philadelphia Athletics before a lackluster 8-8 record in 1934, his first with the Red Sox.

Despite disparities in their overall career accomplishments, on this day both pitchers showed equal command of their position in the early going. The first three innings were uneventful, as neither team hit safely, the Senators giving Newsom "amazing support in helping him hold the Cronins."[2]

The "Cronins" was a reference to Joe Cronin, acquired by Boston from the Senators in October 1934 for Lyn Lary and $250,000. As a condition of the trade, Cronin signed a five-year deal for $30,000 per season. Boston fans had high expectations, and the mediocre performance of the 1935 Red Sox did little to promote a warm acceptance of the new manager.[3]

In the fourth inning, both offenses got on track.

Third baseman Billy Werber opened the frame for Boston, blasting a line drive down the left-field line. A groundball by Roy Johnson scored Werber. Cronin, the future Hall of Famer, then tripled to left-center when Jake Powell missed on an attempted shoestring catch. But popups by Rick Ferrell and Babe Dahlgren on each side of Dusty Cooke's walk ended the threat.

Boston led 1-0.

For three innings, Grove had held Washington hitless, with only one ball leaving the infield. An error by Dahlgren on Newsom's grounder to first with two out in the third gave the Senators their first baserunner, then Joe Kuhel walked, but Dee Miles popped out to end the inning.

With one out in the bottom of the fourth, Fred Schulte, Cecil Travis, and Jake Powell singled on three successive Grove deliveries, and the game was tied, 1-1.

Boston filled the bases with one out in the top half of the fifth, the result of a free pass to Grove, Mel Almada's single, and Werber's fielder's choice, the result of a late throw in an attempt to force Almada at second. But Johnson hit into a double play, and the score remained even.

The Red Sox advanced runners as far as second base in the sixth, seventh, and eighth, but left them stranded on each occasion. A leadoff single by Ski Melillo in the ninth was wasted when Grove popped up while attempting to bunt, and "Spinach,"[4] a nickname Melillo derived from a kidney ailment known as Bright's disease which forced him to eat nothing but spinach to recover from the affliction,[5] was doubled off first base.

The Senators were ineffective from the fifth through the ninth, with just two runners reaching base. Joe Kuhel advanced as far as second base in the fifth after hitting a single and advancing on a fielder's choice, and Powell beat out a slow roller in the ninth, but Grove shut down the threat on each occasion.

The game moved to extra innings.

With both starters still proving effective, the 10th inning passed with limited action.

Cooke singled in the 11th for his third hit of the game, and Wes Ferrell, hitting for Melillo, was fanned "on a couple of misses by umpire Charley Donnelly."[6]

The Senators again threatened in their half of the 11th, Travis and Powell posting successive singles, but shortstop Red Kress grounded out to end the inning.

With the Red Sox going down in order in the 12th, Newsom singled with one out in the bottom of the inning, only to see Kuhel hit into a double play.

Both starting pitchers remained in the game.

Boston had an excellent chance of putting the Senators away in the 13th. Johnson opened the inning with a walk and Cronin sacrificed him to second. Rick Ferrell flied to right field, pushing Johnson to third. An intentional pass to Cooke was followed by Newsom drilling pinch-hitter Bing Miller, loading the bases. Dib Williams, who earlier replaced Wes Ferrell in the lineup for the Red Sox, worked a 2-and-0 count before Newsom called time and requested a towel to wipe off his hands. He subsequently induced a fly ball to Miles in right, ending the rally.[7]

Washington went down in order in the bottom of the inning.

After Grove flied out to start the 14th inning, Almada hit what looked like a sure extra-base hit to right-center, but Powell made a sensational running catch. Werber walked, but Johnson popped up the first pitch with Werber attempting to swipe second, ending the Red Sox' opportunity.

Newsom had allowed just nine hits in 14 innings, facing 57 batters with four strikeouts and seven walks.

The local news account recognized the stellar performance, but it was more than just Newsom's mound prowess that made the difference. From the *Washington Evening Star*:

"Buck Newsom has been tossed one man's share of orchids for his gameness this season, but to skip over yesterday's 14-inning drama which he won over the Red Sox, 2 to 1, would be an injustice.

"Buck wound up a hero, the out-and-out man of the hour, but were it not for his ability to throw off a stinging jab of fate, Newsom might well have been the 'goat' – and might never have lived down what, from the stands, seemed an out-and-out boner to the 5,000 anxious fans.

"With the bases loaded and one down in the fourteenth frame, Newsom came up to the plate and too late became aware of a daring but smart piece of running by Jake Powell. Starting with Lefty Grove's lazy wind-up, Powell dashed from third base and would have stolen home with ease had not Newsom ticked with ball with a swing. If Buck had held back his bat on that initial pitch, the ball game would have ended there and then.

"In the face of what seemed an unpardonable deed – and which really wasn't, because Powell's daring attempt was prompted by no signal but only by Grove's laxity – Newsom merely hitched up his belt and, with two strikes and no balls, banged a single to center to win the game himself."[8]

Grove's 13⅓-inning effort went unrewarded, but he did reach the 20-win mark by season's end, downing the Philadelphia Athletics on September 24. His 300 career victories earned him a spot in Cooperstown in 1947.

The Senators moved in to sixth place with the win, and would finish the season in that position, 27 games behind the pennant-winning Tigers.

The Red Sox, in Joe Cronin's first season as manager, finished fourth, still 16 games off the pace.

Louis Newsom, then known as Buck later known as Bobo, was left behind on the ensuing trip to Boston, but resumed his place in the rotation five days later against the St. Louis Browns, losing a 10-inning, 2-1 contest. Including the 0-6 early-season record he posted with the Browns before being purchased by Washington on May 21, he finished the year at 11-18.

Bobo won an additional 184 games before his career ended in 1953, six years after Grove's Hall of Fame induction.

SOURCES

In addition to the sources mentioned in the Notes, the author also consulted Baseball-Reference.com and Retrosheet.org.

NOTES

1. Ralph Berger, "Bobo Newsom," SABR BioProject, sabr.org/bioproj/person/b3eeb6d1.
2. Gerry Moore, "Lefty Grove Fails to Collect His 17th Win," *Boston Globe*, September 2, 1935: 24.
3. Mark Armour, "Joe Cronin," SABR BioProject, sabr.org/bioproj/person/572b61e8.
4. Moore.
5. Bill Nowlin, "Ski Melillo," SABR BioProject, sabr.org/bioproj/person/c3d5add1.
6. Moore.
7. Moore.
8. "Rook Catcher, Flashes Rare Fielding Worth in Trio of Plays as Griffs Triumph, *Washington Evening Star*, September 2, 1935: 10.

YANKEES LEAD WAY TO FOURTH AMERICAN LEAGUE VICTORY IN FIVE GAMES

JULY 7, 1937
AMERICAN LEAGUE 8, NATIONAL LEAGUE 3

ALL-STAR GAME

by C. Paul Rogers III

The fifth All-Star Game is remembered chiefly for effectively ending Dizzy Dean's career as a dominating pitcher, thanks to Earl Averill's third inning line drive off ole Diz's toe. It was, however, also the first All-Star Game held in the US capital and the first attended by the sitting president, in this case Franklin Delano Roosevelt.[1] Along the way the American League, after suffering its first loss the year before, reestablished its domination of the National League, winning 8-3 in a game that was never seriously in doubt. The defending champion New York Yankees manned five of the nine starting positions for the American League, leading some to assert that there were now three major leagues: the American, the National, and the Yankees.[2]

Rumors had circulated earlier in the week that the 1937 All-Star Game might be the last because the novelty of the midsummer contest had worn off.[3] An enthusiastic capacity crowd of 31,391 including President Roosevelt and other dignitaries[4] seemingly squelched that concern. Dean had manufactured some pregame drama by announcing that he was going to skip the game, go home, and rest a sore arm during the break. But he flew in from St. Louis for the contest, telling reporters that he was just trying to get out of the long train trip and that he knew eventually someone would foot the bill for an airplane ride.[5]

The All-Star selection process had produced some discord as Commissioner Kenesaw M. Landis and the league presidents disenfranchised the fans and left it up to the two managers, with each having input from the other seven skippers in their respective leagues.[6] The stated reason was for the game to be a real test of baseball ability rather than an exhibition of stars.[7] Hometown Senators fans became upset when American League manager Joe McCarthy selected the Browns' Sam West to replace injured Tigers outfielder Gee Walker instead of their own John Stone, who was batting .332 at the break.[8] McCarthy apparently didn't care about the Senators fans' feelings as he failed to use any of the three Senators who were named to the squad.[9] In fact, all eight position starters played the entire game for the Americans.

FDR made his pregame entrance in an open car escorted by a dozen Eagle Scouts and then proceeded to throw out the first pitch from his box seat to a row of players on the third-base line. After a scramble, Jo-Jo Moore of the Giants emerged with the ball.[10] It turned out to be the National League's only victory of the day.

The pitching matchup was marquee, Dean versus Lefty Gomez, who was starting his fourth All-Star Game, missing only the 1936 game, the one year his league lost. Dean, who was 12-7 at the break, was starting his second game in a row and making his fourth All-Star appearance. Gomez was nearly spotless in his three innings of work, allowing only a first-inning single to Arky Vaughn. Dean, on the other hand, was not as sharp, allowing a walk to Joe DiMaggio in the opening frame and two hard singles in the second to Earl Averill and Bill Dickey before escaping the inning unscathed. In the third, however, he was not as fortunate. After Dean retired Red Rolfe and Charlie Gehringer, DiMaggio sent a line drive past Diz's ear for a single up the middle. Lou Gehrig then excited the crowd by clobbering the second pitch he saw over the right-field roof, but it went well foul. With the count 3-and-2, Lou smashed another drive over the right-field wall, fair this time, to stake the Americans to a 2-0 lead. Averill then ripped a ball off Dean's foot. It caromed to second baseman Billy Herman, who threw Earl out at first. Diz limped off the mound and in the clubhouse after the game it was announced that he had suffered a broken toe.[11]

The National League came back to score a run in the top of the fourth off Tommy Bridges, Gomez's successor, on a single by Herman, who moved to second on a groundout by Vaughn and crossed the plate on Joe Medwick's ringing double over third to bring the score to 2-1. It was the first of four hits, including two doubles, for Medwick, who was in the middle of his Triple Crown season.[12] He came into the game batting a lusty .404 for the regular season.

Carl Hubbell followed Dean to the mound in the bottom of the fourth but didn't last the inning, as the American League got back at him for 1934, when King Carl struck out five American League sluggers in succession. With one out, he nearly beaned Dickey on a 3-and-1 count to put a runner on first. West then blasted a shot through Johnny Mize at first to put runners on first and third. Bridges struck out but Red Rolfe of the Yankees tripled to the scoreboard in right-center to drive in two runs. Gehringer followed by singling past Mize to advance the score to 5-1, leading National League manager Bill Terry to remove his ace in favor of Cy Blanton, who fanned DiMaggio on a full count to end the inning.

Gabby Hartnett of the Cubs led off the National's fifth with a shot through Bridges' legs for a single. With one out, Mel Ott, pinch-hitting for Blanton, ripped a double off the wall in right-center, sending Hartnett to third. Paul Waner then hit a fly ball to West in right to drive in Hartnett and close the score to 5-2, but despite an error by Rolfe on a hot shot by Herman, the National League could do no more damage. Lee Grissom of the Reds pitched the bottom half for the senior circuit and began impressively, fanning Gehrig and Averill. Joe Cronin and Dickey, however, cracked back-to-back doubles to extend the lead to 6-2.

The National League still had some fight in them and scored in the sixth on singles by Medwick and Frank Demaree and Mize's long fly ball to deep center. It could have been worse, but DiMaggio made a terrific throw later in the inning to nail Burgess Whitehead at the plate. Whitehead, running for Hartnett, was attempting to score from second on Ripper Collins's sharp single to right.

Once again, the American League countered in its half of the inning, this time against Van Lingle Mungo, to extend its lead to five. Mungo, apparently nursing a sore back, had made the unfortunate boast before the contest that "I can pitch against American Leaguers with a case of paralysis."[13] With one out, he walked Rolfe and surrendered a single to Gehringer, before striking out DiMaggio. Gehrig then worked the count to 3-and-1 before blasting one in front of the bleachers in center to drive in two runs and make the score 8-3. He was out "by an eyelash" trying to stretch a triple on a snappy relay from Demaree to shortstop Dick Bartell to Vaughn.[14]

That ended the scoring for the day although the National League did threaten against the junior circuit's Mel Harder, who pitched the last three innings. The most acute challenge came in the seventh when he allowed a one-out single by Herman and a two-out double by Medwick to put runners on second and third. But Harder erased the threat by inducing Demaree to ground out to Cronin at shortstop. Meanwhile, Mungo and Bucky Walters held the American League at bay in their last two at-bats, although Walters allowed two-out singles to Rolfe and Gehringer before shutting the door.

Although Harder gave up five hits in his three innings on the mound, he extended his All-Star scoreless streak to 13 innings. He would pitch another 10 seasons for the Cleveland Indians, but never would get a chance to extend his record.

Each team collected 13 hits in what really amounted to a slugfest. Ducky Medwick was the hitting star for the Nationals, while Gehringer led the way for the American League with three hits. Yankees batters, however, drove in seven of the eight runs and Lefty Gomez was the winning pitcher, giving him three All-Star Game victories, a record that still stood as of 2019. The *New York Times* wryly suggested that "perhaps some day they'll inaugurate a three-cornered all-star struggle, with the Yankees batting as a unit."[15]

After the game, Dizzy Dean took responsibility for the home run Gehrig hit off him, saying, "I shook Hartnett off twice and was belted each time. He wanted a curve with Gehrig up there in the third and I shook him off, sending a fast one instead, and Gehrig hit a homer."[16]

Dean did not pitch again for two weeks, losing a tight 2-1 game to the Boston Braves on July 21. But he was ineffective after that and appeared in only six more games in the last half of the season. By coming back too soon from his toe injury, he had altered his motion and hurt his arm. He was just 27 but would win only 17 more games in his major-league career.

On the eve of his induction into the Baseball Hall of Fame in 1975, Earl Averill said, "I batted .378 in 1936. I got over 2,000 hits in my career. But the thing I'll always be most remembered for is breaking a guy's toe."[17]

SOURCES

In addition to the sources cited in the Notes, the author accessed Retrosheet.org, Baseball-Reference.com, and SABR.org.

NOTES

1 James P. Dawson, "All-Star Park's Capacity Forces Return of $125,000 Ticket Bids," *New York Times*, July 7, 1937: 29.

2 David Vincent, Lyle Spatz, and David W. Smith, *The MidSummer Classic: The Complete History of Baseball's All-Star Game* (Lincoln: University of Nebraska Press, 2001), 28.

3 Vincent et al., 28.

4 They included FDR's eldest son, James, Postmaster General Jim Farley, WPA Administrator Harry Hopkins, and the chair of the Reconstruction Finance Corporation, Jesse Jones. "Roosevelt Cheers Americans' Victory," *New York Times*, July 8, 1937: 27.

5 John Drebinger, "All-Star Teams Rated Even in Game at Washington, Baseball Capital for a Day," *New York Times*, July 7, 1937: 29; Vincent et al., 28-29.

6 Drebinger.

7 Vincent et al., 28.

8 West was hitting .347 but Stone's batting average was higher than those of three of the outfielders chosen.

9 They were infielder Buddy Myer, pitcher Wes Ferrell, and his brother, catcher Rick Ferrell.

10 "Roosevelt Cheers Americans' Victory."

11 Donald Honig, *The All-Star Game - A Pictorial History to Present* (St. Louis: The Sporting News Publishing Company, 1987), 28.

12 All four hits were line drives. John Drebinger, "Yankees Drive in Seven Runs as American League Easily Wins All-Star Game," *New York Times*, July 8, 1937: 27.

13 Drebinger, "All-Star Teams Rated Even in Game at Washingtion,":27; Vincent, et.al.,29.

14 James P. Dawson, "Play-by-Play Account of Battle Between Big Leagues at Capital," *New York Times*, July 8, 1937: 27.

15 Drebinger, "Yankees Drive in Seven Runs as American League Easily Wins All-Star Game,":27.

16 "Dean Is Made Butt of Winners' Jibes," *New York Times*, July 8, 1937: 27.

17 Honig, 29.

SLOPPY CLEVELAND DEFENSE OVERSHADOWS ODELL HALE'S CYCLE AGAINST SENATORS

JULY 12, 1938
WASHINGTON SENATORS 9, CLEVELAND INDIANS 8

by Mike Huber

On July 12, 1938, approximately 10,000 fans entered Griffith Stadium to see their Washington Senators take on the league-leading Cleveland Indians. Just six days earlier, the 1938 All-Star Game had been held at Cincinnati's Crosley Field. Washington's third baseman Buddy Lewis and Cleveland's center fielder Earl Averill had started in the midsummer classic for the American League, while Senators catcher Rick Ferrell was named as a reserve to the AL squad, which lost to the National League, 4-1. Neither Averill nor Lewis got a hit in the annual spectacle, and Ferrell did not get into the game at all. Yet on this warm, July afternoon in the nation's capital, Lewis played a key role as the fourth-place Senators won in walk-off fashion over the Indians.

This was the first of a scheduled three-game series. The Indians had just completed a three-game sweep of the St. Louis Browns (all with one-run victories). The Senators had also just completed a series sweep, taking four games from the Philadelphia Athletics, including both ends of a July 10 doubleheader, as they outscored the A's, 31-13.

Senators skipper Bucky Harris handed the ball to Ken Chase for the start. The left-hander was in his second full season in the big leagues and was still splitting time between starting and relieving. This was his ninth start of the season (and 15th appearance), and he brought a 2-5 record and an earned-run average of 6.60 with him. The visiting dugout also had pitching issues. According to the *Tribune* of Coshocton, Ohio, "Despite repeated failures and the subsequent weighty evidence that Denny Galehouse is not good enough to be a starting pitcher, Manager Ossie Vitt sent the big right-hander against the Senators."[1] Although Galehouse's record was 3-3 and his ERA 3.51, this was just his fourth start of the season (and 16th appearance). His previous start, on June 23 against the Yankees, had lasted two innings, when he was tagged for four earned runs and homers by Lou Gehrig and Bill Dickey.

Cleveland scored twice in the opening inning before Chase recorded an out. Skeeter Webb walked and stole second base. Jeff Heath smacked a triple into left, driving in Webb, and then Odell

Hale singled in Heath. Two runs on two hits. However, the lead was short-lived. Washington jumped on Galehouse from the get-go. George Case bunted a single to third. Galehouse then walked both Lewis and Sam West. Al Simmons lifted a fly ball to left that was deep enough for Case to tag and score. Lewis also tagged, moving to third. This proved pivotal, as Buddy Myer grounded out to the right side and Lewis scored the tying run on the play. To add to the Indians' misfortunes, sometime in that first inning, Cleveland coach Johnny Bassler was ejected for "riding"[2] first-base umpire Bill Summers.

With one out in the top of the second, Chase walked Rollie Hemsley and Galehouse, and Pete Appleton was called on to relieve him. However, "he was no roaring success,"[3] serving up a double to Heath and a triple to Hale, and the Indians established a 5-2 lead. It didn't hold, as Galehouse "was hammered off the hill"[4] when the Senators took their swings in the bottom of the second. He faced only one batter. Jimmy Wasdell's leadoff homer sent the Cleveland righty to the showers. This was Wasdell's second home run in his last three games. Earl Whitehill came on to pitch for Cleveland.

In the next inning with one down, West reached on a single to center. An out later, Myer stroked a shot to center and raced around the bases for an inside-the-park home run, making the score 5-5. After that, Whitehill settled down, with no incidents in the fourth and only one run allowed on a triple by Lewis in the fifth inning.

The Cleveland bats would not give up, either. They scored two unearned runs in the fourth off Chief Hogsett. Webb singled with two down and Heath shot a grounder to third, but All-Star Lewis made his 17th miscue of the season, putting runners on the corners. Hale smacked a double to center, driving in both runners and reestablishing the Indians' lead.

In the fifth Lewis atoned somewhat for his two-run error, when he tripled into the right-center gap and scored on West's RBI groundout. The score was now 7-6, still in favor of the visitors.

Whitehill should have escaped the sixth without incident, despite a leadoff walk to Myer. However, with two outs and Travis on third, Ferrell hit a grounder to Hale at second, who fumbled the ball and Travis scored, again knotting the score. Hogsett followed with a triple into the right-field corner, giving the Senators an 8-7 lead. It was Hogsett's first triple of the season and the second (and last) of his 11-year career.

Hale, referred to as Sammy in the papers, was leading his club offensively in the game, with a single, triple, and double in his first three at-bats. He had popped out to second in the seventh, but he had one more chance in the final frame. He swung at the first pitch to lead off the ninth and sent the sphere over Al Simmons' head and into the left-field bleachers. The score was once again tied, now at 8-8.

Shirley Povich[5] of the *Washington Post* characterized Hale's dramatic ninth-inning home run as "a slight delay"[6] in the Senators' effort to achieve their fifth straight victory. After Odell tied the score in top half of the ninth, Washington came back in the bottom half "in a sort of bloodless uprising marked by only one hit, a bunt."[7] Bill Zuber walked Ferrell to start the inning. Vitt jumped out of the dugout and made a pitching change, bringing on Johnny Humphries, another fireballing rookie, from Cleveland's bullpen. Hogsett bunted the ball between Humphries and third baseman Ken Keltner. Humphries lost his footing while trying to field the ball, and both runners were safe. Senators skipper Harris called for the next batter, Case, to sacrifice the runners along, but Humphries walked him, loading the bases with none out. Ossie Bluege was inserted as a pinch-runner for Ferrell. Then, "the 10,000 customers pleaded loudly for Buddy Lewis to produce some kind of a well-hit ball,"[8] but Lewis whiffed at three straight fastballs for the first out. Humphries threw two pitches by West before the left-handed swinging center fielder "swatted a ball into left field."[9] Heath caught it and made a "none-too-capable throw to the plate,"[10] not in time to get the tagging Bluege. With the walk-off sacrifice fly, the Senators' win streak grew to five games.

Washington had scored nine runs on only seven hits. The Indians "contributed four runs to Washington by bad fielding and three more on bases on balls."[11] The Tribe's quartet of pitchers allowed five free passes. Tribe manager Vitt told reporters after the game, "I've been in baseball for nearly 30 years and I've never seen as bad a defensive team as this one – either in the majors or minors."[12] The box score showed only one error, but "atrocious support [and] defensive laxness was extremely costly."[13] Fans and reporters feared that this loss "jolted the precarious pennant chances of the Cleveland Indians."[14] Galehouse did not start again for the Tribe until August 2, when he pitched a complete game against the Boston Red Sox, winning 7-4.

For Washington, a strong case could be made that Hogsett was the hero of the game for the Senators. He "entered the fray in the third inning and allowed but five hits,"[15] earning his third win of the season. He also contributed a single and triple to the offensive attack. Eight different Washington batters had scored a run. Five of them had at least one run batted in, led by Myer's three.

Hale was the only batter in the majors to hit for the cycle in 1938. It was the third such rare feat accomplished in Indians franchise history, coming five years after teammate Averill hit for the cycle (August 17, 1933, against the Philadelphia Athletics) and 35 years after Bill Bradley (September 24, 1903, against the Washington Senators). In a game where Hale stood out offensively, the Cleveland defense stole the show. However, hitting for the cycle extended Hale's hitting streak to four games, and that streak would continue, reaching 19 games on August 2. His batting average rose from .275 to .305 during the streak, and his on-base plus slugging percentage (OPS) jumped from .709 to .796

SOURCES

In addition to the sources mentioned in the Notes, the author consulted baseball-reference.com, mlb.com and retrosheet.org.

baseball-reference.com/boxes/WS1/WS1193807120.shtml

retrosheet.org/boxesetc/1938/B07120WS11938.htm

NOTES

1. "Cleveland is Beaten; Yanks Upset Browns," *Tribune* (Coshocton, Ohio), July 13, 1938: 2.
2. "Senators Nip Tribe, 9-8, For 5th Straight," *Tampa Bay Times* (St. Petersburg, Florida), July 13, 1938: 10.
3. Shirley Povich, "Nats Beat Indians, 9-8, to Win Fifth Game in Row," *Washington Post*, July 13, 1938: 17.
4. "Benches Solters as Indians Lose," *News-Journal* (Mansfield, Ohio), July 13, 1938: 12.
5. In 1975 Povich received the J.G. Taylor Spink Award, the highest award presented to sportswriters by the Baseball Writers' Association of America.
6. Povich.
7. Povich.
8. Povich.
9. Povich.
10. Povich.
11. *Mansfield News-Journal.*
12. *Mansfield News-Journal.*
13. *Coshocton Tribune.*
14. *Coshocton Tribune.*
15. *Tampa Bay Times.*

ROOKIE SENSATION SID HUDSON OUTDUELS LEFTY GROVE IN MARATHON THRILLER

SEPTEMBER 2, 1940
WASHINGTON SENATORS 1, BOSTON RED SOX 0
(13 INNINGS, FIRST GAME OF DOUBLEHEADER)

by John Soroka

The fans had reason to question the wisdom of manager Bucky Harris back in February when the team spent $5,000 for a 22-year-old 6-foot-4 right-handed minor leaguer. He won 24 while losing only 4 but that was for Sanford in the Class D Florida State League. That kid, Sid Hudson, was anything but a sure thing. After a good spring training, manager Harris praised Hudson, calling him "the best looking young pitcher since Schoolboy Rowe broke in with Detroit."[1] The results that followed were uninspiring. Hudson's low point may have been his part in an 18-1 loss to the Cleveland Indians on May 23. He was driven from the mound in the first. His record sank to two wins against three losses. But Bucky retained his faith in Hudson.[2]

It was justified. By August 15, *The Sporting News* referred to Hudson as Cinderella Sid the boy wonder.[3] Hudson had pitched two one-hitters, against the Browns on June 21 (no-hitter broken up in the ninth) and against the Athletics on August 6 (no-hitter broken up in the seventh). In between the one-hitters, he had a string of six straight victories.

An excited crowd of 23,000 filled Griffith Stadium on Labor Day, September 2, when Cinderella Sid was scheduled to pitch the first game of a doubleheader against the Boston Red Sox.

Hudson's opponent, the venerable Robert Moses Grove, came as a surprise. Grove, the legendary lefty who led the great Athletics teams of 1929-1931, was pitching in his 16th major-league season. He had eight 20-win seasons to his credit, including a most impressive 31-4 record for the 1931 Philadelphia Athletics. Entering the game he stood at 292 career victories. The last time Grove faced the Senators, he drove a foul ball off his foot and suffered a broken bone that the Red Sox said had probably finished him for the season.[4] In that August 11 game, Hudson had bested Grove, 2-1, thanks to the ninth-inning heroics of Buddy Lewis, who threw out pinch-runner Tom Carey carrying the tying run.[5] That Grove was making this start with the injured foot was attributed to the slide of the Red Sox in the standings. They had been leading the American League as late as June 19 with a 31-18 record. Their slide had brought them to fourth place by Labor Day, seven games out of first with a 69-58 record. The Senators had spent their season firmly entrenched in the American League's second division and at game time were in sixth place with a 52-73 record.

In the top of the first inning, Doc Cramer tripled to the center-field corner with one out. Hudson pounced on a slow roller by Jimmie Foxx and ran at Foxx for a tag out. Cramer held at third. Hudson then fanned Ted Williams. In the fourth inning, Williams tripled to the center-field corner with two out but Hudson struck out Joe Cronin. In the fifth, George Case misjudged and then failed to catch a long drive by Bobby Doerr, allowing Doerr to reach second with no outs. Doerr moved to third on Lou Finney's groundout. Shortstop Jimmy Pofahl grabbed a ball that third baseman Cecil Travis had muffed, preventing Doerr from scoring. Grove attempted to squeeze the run in with a bunt but Hudson jumped on the ball and Doerr was tagged out in a rundown. Dom DiMaggio made the third out by grounding back to the box. In the seventh, Doerr doubled to left with one out but Hudson easily disposed of Finney on a fly ball to George Case and then whiffed Charlie Gelbert. Catcher Rick Ferrell short-circuited a potential Red Sox rally in the ninth. The 11th inning brought more drama for Hudson. Doc Cramer led off the inning with a single to center. Jimmie Foxx followed with another single to center, sending Cramer to third with no outs. At this point second baseman Jimmy Bloodworth took his turn in the heroics spotlight. After a great play on a grounder by Williams, Bloodworth tagged out Foxx going from first to second, held Cramer on third, and threw out Williams at first for the double play. Cronin then flied harmlessly to Gee Walker for the third out. In the 13th inning, Cramer doubled to center with two out. Harris ordered a walk to Foxx, and Ted Williams grounded into a force play to end the top of what was to be the final inning.

Meanwhile, while Hudson was showing incredible poise for a pitcher with so little experience, Robert Moses Grove was showing what experience could do. No longer the fireballer of old, the 40-year-old veteran used a baffling curve and guile to dominate the Senators. It was not until the ninth inning that the Nats got their first baserunner to third. Through seven innings Grove had allowed only two hits. In the eighth, Ferrell and Case singled with one out but Grove was up to the challenge. In the ninth, Cronin's wild throw put Cecil Travis on base with one out but Travis died on third. The 12th was nearly the end for Lefty. A single by Jack Sanford, a walk to Pofahl, and an infield single by Ferrell loaded the bases with one out. Hudson struck out. Case lifted a fly ball deep to the center-field corner but Dom DiMaggio raced back and made a game-saving catch.

After three hours of great baseball, the climax arrived in the bottom of the 13th. Buddy Lewis led off the inning with a double to right field. The managerial wheels began to turn. Trying to set up a double play, manager Cronin ordered Gee Walker intentionally passed. The strategy was thwarted when Bucky Harris called for Cecil Travis to sacrifice Lewis and Walker to third and second. With the perfect execution of the sacrifice accomplished, Cronin intentionally passed Bloodworth to restore the double play. With the outfielders playing shallow to avoid a score on a fly ball, rookie Jack Sanford, who was hitting only .114 at the time, lined a single over the head of Ted Williams to drive in Lewis with the winning run, ending the marathon matchup between the rookie and the great veteran.

Lefty Grove would start three more games in the 1940 season, winning one and losing two. Two of his starts were complete games. His victory came in another 13-inning complete game in Detroit, on September 10. The 1941 season was Grove's last. He started 21 games and pitched 10 complete games finishing with a 7-7 record. His final win was his career 300th at Cleveland on July 25, 1941. Grove officially retired as an active player on December 9, 1941. Sid Hudson finished his rookie year with three more wins and two losses for a 17-16 record. He followed that up in 1941 with a 13-14 record (an ERA more than a full run lower than his rookie year, 3.46) and an All-Star Game appearance. In

1942, his record slipped to 10-17. Like most players his age, Hudson lost the next three seasons to military service. He never quite regained his pitching effectiveness and finished a 12-year career in 1954 with a won-lost record of 104-152. Hudson finished his career with the Red Sox after being traded in 1952 for Walt Masterson, a teammate on the 1940 Senators.

Jack Sanford's game-winning single was his fifth career hit and his first career run batted in. His career would be limited to parts of three seasons (1941, 1942, 1946), during which he collected 32 hits in 153 at-bats with only 11 RBIs.

SOURCES

In addition to the sources cited in the Notes, the author also accessed Retrosheet.org, Baseball-Reference.com, SABR.org, and the following:

Povich, Shirley. "Boston Drops Brief Second Game, 5-4," *Washington Post*,

September 3, 1940: 16.

NOTES

1 Francis Stann, "'D' Grad Counted In on Nats' Big Four," The Sporting News, March 28, 1940: 2.

2 Denman Thompson, "Senatorial Policies Draw Fire of Critics," The Sporting News, May 23, 1940: 1.

3 Dick Farrington, "Sid Hudson, Nats' One-Hit Specialist, Turned to Hill Two Years Ago, After Failing at Bat as First Sacker," The Sporting News, August 15, 1940: 3.

4 "X-Ray Discloses Lefty Grove Broke Foot Here Sunday," Washington Post, August 18, 1940: SP1.

5 Bill Burnett, "Nats' Rookie Gives Bosox Only 5 Hits," Washington Post, August 12, 1940: SP1

SELKIRK'S GRAND SLAM WINS FOR YANKEES IN THE FIRST NIGHT GAME AT GRIFFITH STADIUM

MAY 28, 1941: NEW YORK YANKEES 6, WASHINGTON SENATORS 5

by C. Paul Rogers III

On the heels of the British navy's sinking of the German battleship Bismarck and President Franklin Roosevelt's "unlimited emergency" speech defying the Germans, the Washington Senators inaugurated night baseball on May 28, 1941, on a sweltering evening in the nation's capital. Senators owner Clark Griffith was following the lead of six other major-league teams and drew 25,000 fans, about 10 times as many as for a weekday afternoon game.[1] Griffith had initially resisted night baseball, calling it 'bush league stuff" after the first major-league night game in Cincinnati in 1935 and stating that baseball was meant to be played "in the Lord's own sunshine."[2] However, buoyed by attendance spikes at other major-league venues that had installed lights, and, according to one veteran writer, by concern that the likely coming war would reduce daytime attendance even more, he had spent $165,000 installing a lighting system that produced 1,140,000 watts.[3] It was said that the Griffith Stadium lights exuded enough power to light 5,000 homes.[4]

The Senators had played their initial night game nearly two years earlier in Philadelphia.[5] Evening baseball was still so new, however, that the Senators had to get permission to raise the flag after sundown to play the national anthem.[6] To turn on the lights for their first home night game, the team trotted out the legendary Walter Johnson to throw a fastball through a projected electric beam that was set on a pedestal over home plate. His first two pitches to catcher Jake Early missed but then the Big Train split the beam, causing the crowd to roar as eight 150-foot light towers lit up.[7]

The game itself was a doozy. It pitted the Senators, struggling in a nine-game losing streak that had landed them in the American League basement, against the third-place New York Yankees. Steve Peek, a 26-year-old rookie from St. Lawrence University recently up from Newark, was making his second major-league start for the Yankees against Sid Hudson, also 26 but in his second full big-league season.[8] Peek was known for his curveball and Yankees manager Joe McCarthy thought breaking pitches would be harder to pick up at night.[9]

The Yankees led off the game with a single to center by Johnny Sturm and a walk to Red Rolfe, but Hudson bore down to retire the heart of order, Tommy Henrich, Joe DiMaggio, and Charlie Keller, on a fly out and two groundballs. It turned out that the Yankees were having trouble with Hudson's hard curve.[10] The Nats struck quickly in the bottom of the first with one-out hits by Buddy Lewis and Doc Cramer, whose ball took a bad hop over Rolfe at third. With two outs, Mickey Vernon drove in Lewis with a sharp single to center to plate the first run of the game. Buddy Myer then beat out an infield hit to Frankie Crosetti at shortstop to score Cramer and make the score 2-0. It could have been worse but Crosetti threw behind Vernon, who had rounded third base too far, for the third out.[11]

The Senators added a third run in the third on an RBI single by Cecil Travis, driving in George Case, who had walked, stolen second, and advanced to third on a groundout. After that inning, Peek got his bearings and was effective in shutting down the Washington attack. Hudson, meanwhile, fairly mowed down the Yankees until the sixth, when Henrich led off with a home run over the right-field wall to bring the score to 3-1.

Neither side seriously threatened until the eighth, when the wheels came off for the home squad. The inning started innocently enough, with Henrich grounding out to Vernon at first unassisted. But DiMaggio, battling a sore throat,[12] blasted one against the right-field fence and motored into third with a triple. Keller then worked Hudson for a walk. Joe Gordon was next and appeared to hit a tailor-made double-play grounder to Travis at shortstop. But Travis fumbled the ball, then kicked it with his foot, and in his haste to salvage a force at second, threw the ball wide of the base and into right field. By the time Buddy Lewis retrieved the baseball, DiMaggio had scored, Keller was standing on third and Gordon was at second. The bases were soon loaded when Washington manager Bucky Harris ordered Bill Dickey intentionally walked.

With the tying and go-head runs in scoring position, Joe McCarthy sent the lefty-swinging George "Twinkletoes" Selkirk[13] to the plate for Crosetti. Selkirk was a 33-year-old veteran who had lost his regular job in right field to the younger Henrich. He worked the count to 2-and-2 and then lifted a blast far into the night sky. It came down well over the right-field wall for a grand slam, suddenly turning the game around and giving the Yankees a 6-3 lead as the Senators fans sat in silence.[14] Hudson recovered to strike out Peek and Sturm, but the damage was done.

The Nats rebounded to get a run back in the bottom of the eighth on a leadoff double by Travis off the right-field wall. With two outs, catcher Early drove him in with a blast to deep right-center, ending up at third base with a triple. Jimmy Bloodworth, however, grounded to Rolfe at third to end further damage.

Alex Carrasquel[15] relieved Hudson in the ninth and retired the New Yorkers in order. In the bottom half, McCarthy brought in Marv Breuer to protect the lead for Peek, who had yielded 10 hits in his eight innings. Breuer proceeded to strike out pinch-hitter Johnny Welaj to open the inning but Case followed with a triple to the left-field corner, showing his considerable speed in getting that far. Buddy Lewis followed by grounding out to Gordon at second for the second out, scoring Case to make it a one-run game. But Breuer retired Cramer on a fly ball to DiMaggio in center to seal the Yankees' 6-5 victory and send the Nats to their 10th straight defeat.[16]

DiMaggio's eighth-inning triple was his only hit of the day and extended his hitting streak to 13 games, which was for the first time getting a mention in the New York papers.[17] He would, of course, eventually make at least one hit in 56 straight games, a record that still stands.

Clark Griffith made back a good deal of his lights' investment that very evening, and, in a complete about-face, became a vocal proponent of night baseball, eventually getting permission during the war years to schedule 21 night contests at home when the rest of the majors were limited to 14.[18]

The Yankees swept to the pennant in 1941 by a resounding 17 games while the Senators finished tied for sixth place with a 70-84 record, 31 games behind New York.

SOURCES

In addition to the sources cited in the Notes, the author accessed Retrosheet.org, Baseball-Reference.com, and SABR.org.

NOTES

1 Michael Seidel, *Streak - Joe DiMaggio and the Summer of '41* (New York: McGraw-Hill, 1988), 72-76.

2 Shirley Povich, *The Washington Senators* (Kent, Ohio: Kent State University Press, 2010, originally published by G.P. Putnam & Sons, 1954), 219. Griffith also said there was no chance that night baseball would catch on in the major leagues. Tom Deveaux, *The Washington Senators, 1901-1971* (Jefferson, North Carolina: McFarland & Co., Inc., 2001), 141.

3 Morris A. Beale, *The Washington Senators - The Story of an Incurable Fandom* (Washington: Columbia Publishing Company, 1947), 164.

4 David Pietrusza, *Lights On! The Wild Century-Long Saga of Night Baseball* (Lanham, Maryland: Scarecrow Press, 1997), 159.

5 Deveaux, 150.

6 Siedel, 76.

7 James P. Dawson, "Homer by Selkirk Tops Senators, 6-5," *New York Times*, May 29, 1941: 22.

8 As a rookie, Hudson had won 17 games against 16 losses after losing 9 of his first 11 decisions in 1940 for the seventh-place Senators.

9 Kostya Kennedy, *56 - Joe DiMaggio and the Last Magic Number in Sports* (New York: Sports Illustrated Books, 2011), 69.

10 Kennedy, 69.

11 Shirley Povich, "Selkirk's 4-Run Homer Beats Nats at Night," *Washington Post*, May 29, 1941: 27.

12 Kennedy, 68.

13 So-called because of his heels-up running style. Kennedy, 69.

14 Dawson; Povich, "Selkirk's 4-Run Homer."

15 Carrasquel was the first Venezuelan player in the major leagues and compiled a 50-39 won-lost record in eight seasons. Lou Hernandez, Alex Carrasquel biography in the SABR BioProject.

16 Peek recorded his second big-league win. He finished his only major-league season with a 4-2 record but a 5.06 earned-run average. Hudson took the loss, finished the season 13-14 and would pitch 12 years in the major leagues, all with mediocre Senators or Red Sox teams.

17 Seidel, 75-76. Strangely, the *New York Times* game story made mention of Sturm's 11-game and Crosetti's 10-game hitting streaks, but did not note DiMaggio's 13-game streak. Dawson.

18 Pietrusza, 164-65; Povich, *The Washington Senators*, 219.

"A VIOLENT BATTING WAR"

SEPTEMBER 8, 1942
WASHINGTON SENATORS 15, BOSTON RED SOX 11

by James Forr

The seventh-place Washington Senators concluded their 1942 Griffith Stadium schedule with what Shirley Povich of the *Washington Post* called, "a violent batting war" against the Boston Red Sox.[1] It was a come-from-behind assault led by two apparently harmless perpetrators.

At one time Jimmy Pofahl was the Senators' future. Clark Griffith paid a hefty $40,000 to acquire the 22-year-old from Minneapolis in August 1939, and it wasn't hard to see why. He led the American Association in batting average for a while that season before injuring his wrist, and still managed to hit .302 with 19 home runs.

Washington's plan for 1940 was to make room for Pofahl by shifting Cecil Travis, a fixture at shortstop, to third base. However, those plans went awry when Pofahl "reported to spring training with a throwing arm more suitable for beanbag than major-league ball," as Povich put it.[2] He did play short that year, but didn't play it particularly well; worse, he couldn't hit at all. Pofahl slugged double-digit home runs in three of his four minor-league seasons. With the Senators, he hit two homers in three years. By the time the home finale rolled around in 1942, the erstwhile next big thing was hitting .215 and had been reduced to a utility role, scavenging scraps of playing time wherever he could.

Jake Early's season had been equally miserable. The witty young man from North Carolina emerged as one of Washington's most lethal hitters in 1941, batting .287 with 10 home runs in 104 games. Over time, he became known more for what he did behind the plate, dutifully handling the cadre of knuckleballers the Senators employed to get them through the war years and distracting batters with his off-key singing and side-splitting imitations of radio announcers and auctioneers. His 1942 performance, though, inspired mostly groans. He entered the game batting .198 with just 15 hits in his last 34 games.

Only about 1,500 people turned out on a Tuesday afternoon, even though it was scheduled to be a doubleheader as the clubs tried to make up a game that had been washed out in August. A glance at the Senators lineup offered no hint of a looming explosion. No one in the bottom half of the order

Exterior of Griffith Stadium in 1958. Originally called National Park and sometimes American League Park, the ballpark was renamed Griffith Stadium, after club owner Clark Griffith, in 1920. (Photo courtesy of Robert E. Wilson)

had an OPS above .635. The fifth-place hitter, John Sullivan, was batting .231 with only 13 extra-base hits, even though he had been the everyday shortstop since mid-June.

Washington manager Bucky Harris turned to rookie Ray Scarborough to make his second career start in the opener. Just five days earlier, Scarborough had blanked the Chicago White Sox on five hits but this outing would unfold much differently. The first five Red Sox reached base against him, with cleanup man Tony Lupien's single scoring Dom DiMaggio and Johnny Pesky. Lou Finney reached on a fielder's choice that scored another run and made it 3-0.

Although it was a rocky start for Scarborough, it was better than the fate that awaited Boston's Oscar Judd. The 34-year-old rookie from Canada entered the game with an 8-9 record and a respectable 3.64 ERA, but his season-long struggles with control proved his doom. Judd surrendered three bases on balls and three singles in the bottom of the first. His bases-loaded walk to Early forced in the tying run and ended his day after just two-thirds of an inning.

Boston tacked on two runs each in the third and fourth innings before the Senators got a couple back in the bottom of the fourth. Mickey Vernon, who entered play with seven multihit games already in the month of September, plated George Case with a single. The light-hitting Sullivan followed with his second RBI of the day, a double down the left-field line that scored Bobby Estalella and brought Washington to within 7-5.

In the top of the sixth inning, with a wobbly Scarborough still on the mound, Boston loaded the bases on an infield hit by pitcher Charlie Wagner and a pair of bunt singles. Ted Williams grounded into a force play to score Wagner, and Finney singled home DiMaggio for a 9-5 lead.

However, the game turned in the bottom of the sixth, as Washington sent 11 men to the plate. Wagner walked the first two batters. One out later Ellis Clary singled to load the bases for Pofahl, who ripped a base hit that drove in two runs and trimmed the lead to 9-7. Joe Cronin summoned his trusty bullpen workhorse Mace Brown to quiet things, but instead Early greeted him with a two-run double to tie the game. A walk to pinch-hitter Bruce Campbell and an infield single by the speedy Case loaded the bases. After Stan Spence tapped back to Brown for a force at home, Estalella dribbled one down the third-base line. Jim Tabor's throw to first was late and wide, as Campbell scored the go-ahead run and Case tore headlong around third. First baseman Lupien hesitated and his throw home was late. The four-run deficit had become an 11-9 Washington lead.

The Senators scored three more off Mike Ryba in the seventh on a run-scoring single by Pofahl and a two-run double by Early, whose five RBIs matched a career high. Pofahl brought home another run on a fly ball in the eighth, giving him a career-best four RBIs. Alex Carrasquel, who took over for Scarborough in the seventh, was not especially effective but he kept Boston off the board until a two-run double by Pesky in the ninth. With men at the corners, Carrasquel induced Finney to ground into a force at second, sealing a wild 15-11 victory.

Scarborough endured quite a beating, allowing 12 hits and nine runs (eight earned) over six innings, but he hung in long enough to sneak away with the victory. Brown fell to 8-3 for the Red Sox. The game took 2 hours 37 minutes. The umpires called the second game at around 5:00 P.M. with the score tied, 1-1, in the fifth inning, so the teams could catch trains out of town to play out the string.

Jimmy Pofahl played only six more major-league games and a year later he was out of baseball for good. He returned to his hometown of Faribault, Minnesota, where he owned a sporting-goods store for 30 years. Jake Early rebounded to become an All-Star in 1943, helping Washington rise from the second division to a surprising second-place finish.

SOURCES

In addition to the sources cited in the Notes, the author used Baseball-Reference.com and Retrosheet.org.

baseball-reference.com/boxes/WS1/WS1194209080.shtml

retrosheet.org/boxesetc/1942/B09080WS11942.htm

The author also reviewed the following sources for play-by-play and other information:

Barry, Fred. "Red Sox' 17 Hits Are Not Enough to Win," Boston Globe, September 9, 1942: 9.

Kirkpatrick, Rob. Cecil Travis of the Washington Senators: The War-Torn Career of an All-Star Shortstop (Lincoln and London: University of Nebraska Press, 2005).

Povich, Shirley. "3-Way Move Depends on Jimmy Pofahl," Washington Post, March 13, 1940: 21.

NOTES

1 Shirley Povich, "Nats Rally and Swamp Bosox in Finale, 15-11," *Washington Post*, September 9, 1942: 11.

2 Shirley Povich, *The Washington Senators* (New York: G.P. Putnam's Sons, 1954), 211.

SATCHEL PAIGE AND THE MONARCHS SHUT OUT THE POWERFUL GRAYS

SEPTEMBER 8, 1942
KANSAS CITY MONARCHS 8, HOMESTEAD GRAYS 0

GAME ONE OF THE NEGRO LEAGUE WORLD SERIES

by Bob LeMoine

"I think I should get a word or two in edgewise about the 1942 Monarchs, who were the best team I ever played with. I do believe we could have given the New York Yankees a run for their money that year."

— Buck O'Neil[1]

The Negro League World Series was reborn in 1942, the first such postseason matchup of the Negro League's best teams since 1927. The Kansas City Monarchs won the Negro American League pennant, their fourth straight. The Homestead Grays, now mostly calling Washington their home instead of Homestead, Pennsylvania, had won their third straight Negro National League pennant and their fifth in six seasons. The series was a much-anticipated matchup in the continuing rivalry between two storied franchises of Negro League baseball. Game One would be played at Washington's Griffith Stadium, the Grays' home park.

The two teams had met three times during the season. The Grays and pitcher Roy Partlow defeated the Monarchs 2-1 in a 10-inning thriller before 26,113 at Griffith Stadium. Partlow later defeated the Monarchs again, 5-4 in 11 innings, in Pittsburgh. Another matchup saw the Grays pull out a 3-2 win before 20,000 at a drizzly Griffith Stadium.[2] Those who avoided the rain that day could catch the game on WWDC radio, a novelty in the Negro Leagues that had begun earlier in the summer.[3] Game One of the World Series was also broadcast by WWDC, allowing African Americans in the region captivated by their team and the rivalry to tune in.[4] The *Washington Post* reported that two previous matchups of the clubs attracted over 48,000 spectators. A ticket to see the highly anticipated matchup could be purchased for $1.10, $1.35, or $1.65.[5]

The *Post* reported that in 10 appearances at Griffith Stadium that season (16 total games including doubleheaders), the Grays drew 102,690 patrons, an average of just over 10,000 per date.[6] One person certainly capable of drawing crowds was the Monarchs' starting pitcher on September 8, the legendary Satchel Paige, who had drawn over 68,000 fans to Griffith Stadium in his three previous appearances.[7] Roy Welmaker, called the "crafty Grays lefthander" by Ric Roberts of the *Baltimore Afro-American*, took the Hill for the Grays.[8] The umpires were John Craig, Ducky Kemp, and Scrip Lee.

Paige set down the first 10 batters in order. In the fourth inning, the Grays finally had a scoring opportunity against him. Sam Bankhead and Tom Easterling scorched singles to right. The legendary Grays catcher Josh Gibson came to the plate. Buck O'Neil, the Kansas City first baseman, remembered the friendly rivalry between the two icons. "In that game," O'Neil recalled, "Satchel rode Josh mercilessly, telling him as he came to bat each time, 'Look at you, you ain't ready to hit. Come on up to the plate. Don't be scared.' But Josh also liked to ride Satchel. They liked to kid each other, and it was funny how they'd go back and forth." Gibson swung, and O'Neil always remembered that crack of the bat. "I can still see that ball streaking across the dark blue sky. But we got a break in that Josh hit it to deep center field, and in Griffith Stadium center field was like the Grand Canyon." It landed innocently in the glove of Willard Brown. "We all let out a big sigh of relief," O'Neil said.[9] Buck Leonard fouled out to catcher Joe Greene, ending the Grays' only scoring opportunity of the day.

Both clubs went scoreless through the first five innings. Paige exited after five innings, having limited the Grays to two hits while striking out five and walking one.

Willie Simms struck out to open the sixth for the Monarchs. Newt Allen lined a single to center and moved to second on Ted Strong's single to center. Brown grounded a double-play ball to second, where Matthew "Lick" Carlisle's underhanded throw was dropped by shortstop Bankhead. Allen dashed home and scored as the throw went past Gibson to the backstop. Strong also tried to score on the miscue but was tagged out. The Monarchs were on the board, 1-0.

Side-arm thrower Jack Matchett replaced Paige and threw the final four innings. The 1-0 deficit was much larger in the minds of the Grays, who "curled up and bust" from that time on, in the words of the *Washington Post*.[10] The Monarchs added three more runs in the seventh. With two out Jesse Williams singled to right. Matchett singled to left and Vic Harris seemed to be in slow motion getting to the ball as Williams raced to third. The runners executed a double steal with Matchett taking second and Williams sprinting home as the return throw was "3 feet short of the plate."[11] Simms nubbed a slow roller toward Jud Wilson at third but the veteran couldn't hold on to it and by the time it was retrieved Matchett had scored from second. Allen doubled home Simms, and while Strong struck out to end the inning, the Monarchs had put three more on the board and led 4-0.

Matchett was unhittable in the final four frames, retiring the side in order in every inning. In the eighth, the Grays' Carlisle booted a grounder that put Brown on first. Greene slammed a double to right to score Brown. O'Neil tripled to the right-field wall to score Greene (the Monarchs' only earned run at that point) and increased the Monarchs' lead to 6-0.

In the ninth the Monarchs punched two more runs on the board. Allen pounded his third hit, a single to right. He was forced at second on Strong's grounder. Brown slammed a deep drive "to the coffin corner in deep center"[12] and Strong scored. Greene singled to score Brown, putting the icing on the cake for the dominating 8-0 win. The huge Griffith Stadium crowd "sat aghast,"[13] watching their stars commit six errors.[14]

The picture of Josh Gibson in the *Baltimore Afro-American* told the story well with the headline "Dejected by Defeat" as the legend sat at his locker "looking forlorn and dejected."[15] The series would continue to be a dejected affair for the Grays, who were swept in four games. The Grays did win Game Four in Kansas City, but the game was officially thrown out over their use of illegal players. The series also dragged out over the entire month as the teams sought to earn extra money between games with exhibition contests in smaller venues. "It might seem odd," O'Neil said decades later, "playing between games of the World Series, but that's the way it was done. World Series or not, there were a lot of folks in those towns who'd pay to see us play."[16]

In the games that counted, however, the one constant was the presence of Paige, who pitched in each of them, and led the Monarchs to the Negro League title.

SOURCES

Seamheads Nego Leagues Database. Seamheads.com/NegroLgs/index.php.

NOTES

1 Buck O'Neil and David Conrads, *I Was Right on Time: My Journey from the Negro Leagues to the Majors* (New York: Fireside, 1997), 119.

2 "Paige's Monarchs Play Here Tuesday Night," *Washington Post*, September 6, 1942: 2; "Grays Beat Monarchs," *Baltimore Afro-American*, August 15, 1942: 27.

3 "Radio Program," *Washington Evening Star*, August 13, 1942: B-22; "Grays-Elite Series to be Broadcast," *Baltimore Afro-American*, August 8, 1942: 25.

4 "Radio Program," *Washington Evening Star*, September 8, 1942: B-18.

5 "Paige's Monarchs Play Here Tuesday Night."

6 "30,000 Fans Expected at Negro 'Series,'" *Washington Post*, September 8, 1942: 18.

7 Ibid.

8 Ric Roberts, "Paige Limits NNL Champs to 2 Hits," *Baltimore Afro-American*, September 11, 1942: 23.

9 O'Neil and Conrads, 129-130.

10 "24,000 See Grays Beaten by Monarchs," *Washington Post*, September 9, 1942: 11.

11 Ibid.

12 Ibid.

13 Roberts.

14 Ibid.

15 *Baltimore Afro-American*, September 11, 1942: 23.

16 O'Neil and Conrads, 130.

POWERFUL GRAYS, UPSTART BLACK BARONS TAKE CENTER STAGE AT GRIFFITH STADIUM

SEPTEMBER 21, 1943
BIRMINGHAM BLACK BARONS 4, HOMESTEAD GRAYS 2

GAME ONE OF THE NEGRO LEAGUE WORLD SERIES

by Bob LeMoine

Griffith Stadium hosted Game One of the 1943 Negro League World Series between the heavily favored Homestead Grays and the underdog Birmingham Black Barons. Game Two was played in Baltimore, followed by a return to Griffith for Game Three. Games Four through Eight would be held in Chicago; Columbus, Ohio; Indianapolis; Birmingham; and Montgomery, Alabama. Game Two ended in a tie, making Game Eight necessary.

Birmingham, managed by Winfield "Gus" Welch, won the first half of the Negro American League season and finished with a 44-34 record overall. The Chicago American Giants, 34-33 for the season, won the second-half title, and the two clubs squared off in a best-of-five playoff series. The series went the limit, with Birmingham winning a Game Five thriller at their home ballpark, Rickwood Field, 1-0. John Huber (4-3, 2.81) pitched a masterful one-hitter over Chicago in the Black Barons' 1-0 win. Huber allowed a leadoff single in the first, but that runner was thrown out attempting to steal. Huber allowed only one walk the rest of the way. The Barons were limited to four hits by Gentry Jessup, but Piper Davis was hit by a pitch and later scored on a fly ball for the lone run.[1]

The Homestead Grays, named for their original home of Homestead, Pennsylvania, a Pittsburgh suburb, now mostly considered Washington their home. But wherever they played, they were a Negro League powerhouse. Candy Jim Taylor's crew went 78-23 in Negro National League competition in 1943, winning the pennant. The Grays had won four straight NNL pennants and seven of the last eight. The Grays had been swept by the Kansas City Monarchs, 4-0, in the 1942 Negro League World Series, the first such postseason series between the two league champions.

The Grays lineup featured Negro League stars aplenty, including some who would one day be inducted into the Baseball Hall of Fame. Third baseman Jud Wilson, outfielder Cool Papa Bell, pitcher Ray Brown, first baseman Buck Leonard, and catcher Josh Gibson were greats among their peers. Gibson batted an astounding .466 with 20 home runs and 109 RBIs in 1943, and seven other starters hit .330 or better.

Birmingham, however, had no such star-studded cast and no future Hall of Famers. Their Negro American League pennant was their first. They were making a name for themselves in Negro League baseball, however, being "the toast of the country with their brilliant and hustling play," wrote the *Pittsburgh Courier.*[2] "This is the best team turned in by any southern city since the days of Satchel Paige, Bill Willis, Harry Salmon, and Sam Streeter," the paper boasted, comparing them to the Birmingham club of 1928 that included the legendary Paige.

The *Courier* writer said of the Barons, "There are no Gibsons or Leonards, but what the Barons lack in distance blasting, they make up in superb pitching."[3] One such pitcher was Alvin Gipson, who had recently struck out 20 in a game.[4] The Grays easily won an earlier matchup, 7-0, but then narrowly defeated the Barons in a later contest, 3-2, in 12 innings.[5]

Logistics in the Negro Leagues were always an obstacle. Cumberland Posey, one of the Grays' owners and a person of influence in the league, described in the *Courier* the issues clubs faced in scheduling since they had to rent stadiums and schedule their games around those of white teams. The series itself might have been played solely in the Midwest, Posey wrote, had it not been for Clark Griffith rearranging the Senators' schedule to accommodate the Negro League games at Griffith Stadium.[6] The Senators' season-ending 14-game homestand was compressed into four single games and five doubleheaders to create open dates for Games One and Three of the Negro League World Series. "That is something to think about," an appreciative Posey said.[7]

Posey also bemoaned the last-minute scheduling. The World Series games "should receive publicity throughout the year. Tentative dates should be agreed upon when schedules are drafted."[8] Another problem was that the Negro American League had a postseason playoff series while the Negro National League pennant was already decided when the Grays won both halves. "The Grays were compelled to remain idle a whole week after the regular season closed waiting to see whom they would play in the world series."[9] Yet the game went on despite the obstacles.

Pitching for Birmingham was Alfred "Greyhound" Saylor (often spelled Sayler), a 31-year-old right-hander from Blytheville, Arkansas, who was 5-3 with a 2.52 ERA. Johnny Wright, who led all Negro League pitchers in wins (20), games (35), games started (26), complete games (17), shutouts (5), innings pitched (212), and strikeouts (118) with a 2.33 ERA, took the hill for the Grays. Wright's numbers, like all Negro League statistics, are certainly nowhere near the accuracy we expect in the modern day. Nevertheless, Wright's season surpassed that of even Paige himself, the greatest of his generation.

Despite "adverse weather conditions," a crowd of 4,000 came out to Griffith Stadium for the 8:30 P.M. start.[10] Francis "Eggie" Greenfield (first base), Fred McCrary (home plate), and Ducky Kemp (second and third) were the umpires.

Felix McLaurin, a .294 hitter in 1943, led off for the Black Barons and lined a scorching double past Leonard at first and down the right-field line. Tommy Sampson followed with a single to right, sending McLaurin home. Sampson was thrown out by Josh Gibson attempting to steal. Clyde "Little Splo" Spearman doubled. Piper Davis singled, sending Spearman to third. Spearman scored on an error by Gibson. The *Washington Post* described the error as a bad throw to second, implying that Davis attempted to steal. The *Baltimore Afro-American* wrote that Gibson missed a low pitch and was sliding in the mud to get it, allowing the run to score. Both events could have happened on the same play, but in any event, the Barons now led 2-0.

The Grays countered with a run in the first. Bell led off with a triple to the left-field wall and scored on Leonard's fly ball to center.

The Barons carried their 2-1 lead into the fourth inning when they struck again. Lester "Buck" Lockett launched a double to left over Bell's head and scored when Leonard "Sloppy" Lindsay singled to left.

Wright survived those two unearned runs in the first and left with a 3-1 deficit after six innings. He had struck out eight, walked four, and danced around the eight hits he allowed. The veteran Ray Brown, 8-1 that season with a 3.54 ERA, took the mound in the seventh. He got into a heap of trouble immediately. Hoss Walker, the Barons' 38-year-old third baseman, singled. Ted "Double Duty" Radcliffe, a 40-year-old catcher on loan to the Barons from Chicago (which resulted in controversy among sportswriters), also singled, and McLaurin was safe on shortstop Sam Bankhead's fielding error. Walker scored on the mishap, and the Barons led 4-1.[11]

Besides those unearned runs in the first, Saylor did not allow another baserunner until the ninth. That was when he seemed to tire; with one out he walked Leonard and Gibson. Howard Easterling singled to score Leonard, and with the score 4-2, the potential winning run would be coming to the plate. However, Easterling tried to stretch his hit into a double and was thrown out. Bankhead, whose ninth-inning error seemed much larger now, couldn't atone for his gaffe and flied out to end the game.

After the Series, Griffith Stadium hosted "A Cavalcade of Negro Music" featuring Billy Eckstine, an event promoted as the "Greatest array of Negro Stars ever Heard Here." Baseball fans had already seen Negro stars at Griffith Stadium, who thrilled fans with a hard-fought World Series.

SOURCES

Besides the sources cited in the Notes, the author also consulted the following:

"At Home Plate Before the Battle," *Baltimore Afro-American*, October 2, 1943: 18.

"Barons Jar Grays, 4-2, in Big Series Opener," *Washington Evening Star*, September 22, 1943: 18.

"Barons Turn Back Grays, 4-2, as 4,000 See Series Opener," *Washington Post*, September 22, 1943: 20.

"Grays and Barons Open Negro World Series Tonight," *Washington Post*, September 21, 1943: 19.

Hauser, Christopher. *The Negro Leagues Chronology: Events in Organized Black Baseball, 1920-1948* (Jefferson, North Carolina: McFarland, 2008), 134.

Hubler, David E., and Joshua H. Drazen. *The Nats and the Grays: How Baseball in the Nation's Capital Survived WWII and Changed the Game Forever* (New York: Rowman & Littlefield, 2015), 130-131.

"Saylor Allows 5 Hits as Barons Win Series Opener," *Afro-American*, October 2, 1943: 18.

Seamheads Negro Leagues Database. seamheads.com/NegroLgs/index.php.

NOTES

1 "Birmingham Nine Wins Negro Baseball Title," *Baltimore Sun*, September 20, 1943: 16; "Birmingham Team Takes Negro Title," *Huntsville* (Alabama) *Times*, September 20, 1943: 6.

2 "Fighting Black Barons Primed for Battles with Eastern Foes," *Pittsburgh Courier*, September 4, 1943: 19.

3 Ibid.

4 "Grays Primed for Series with Birmingham Barons," *Pittsburgh Courier*, September 4, 1943: 19.

5 "Grays Blank Barons, 7-0," *Pittsburgh Post-Gazette*, September 8, 1943: 15; "Grays, Barons Start Negro World Series Tilt Tonight," *Washington Evening Star*, September 21, 1943: 22.

6 Cum Posey, "Posey's Points," *Pittsburgh Courier*, October 2, 1943: 16.

7 Cum Posey, "Posey's Points," *Pittsburgh Courier*, September 18, 1943: 17.

8 "Posey's Points," October 2, 1943.

9 Ibid.

10 Ibid.

11 One such complaint was lodged by Art Carter ("Use of Ineligible Men Belittles World Series") of the *Baltimore Afro-American*, who called the Series a "barnstorming travesty" with "Double Duty" not the only example of inconsistent enforcement of league rules. Carter complained of the "unorganized manner" in which the leagues conducted the series, validating the beliefs of many that the Negro Leagues needed a commissioner. It certainly didn't help when the much-hyped final game of the Series was to be held in New Orleans but had to be moved. Wendell Smith of the *Pittsburgh Courier* blasted, "The entire promotion of the World Series was a farce." *Baltimore African American*, October 9, 1943: 18; "Smitty's Sports Spurts," *Pittsburgh Courier*, October 16, 1943: 16.

COOL PAPA WINS IT

SEPTEMBER 24, 1943
HOMESTEAD GRAYS 4, BIRMINGHAM BLACK BARONS 3 (11 INNINGS)

GAME THREE OF THE NEGRO LEAGUE WORLD SERIES

by Adam Berenbak

Johnny Markham must have looked long and hard at Ted "Double Duty" Radcliffe. He knew what the signal meant and it must have been somewhat of a relief, even though it would load the bases. After all, who would want to pitch to Josh Gibson at all, let alone with freezing hands in Game Three of the Negro League World Series? Markham was a tough veteran from Shreveport, Louisiana, who had been in baseball since he debuted at 21 with the Kansas City Monarchs in 1930, and he was sure to savor the challenge as a competitor.[1] But he had been out there for 11 innings, and his arm must be getting tired. Gibson had been on the bench the entirety of the game, and his appearance so late in the game as a pinch-hitter was most definitely intended to intimidate. Not that bypassing Gibson would ease the pressure – the next spots in the lineup were occupied by the great Raymond Brown and Cool Papa Bell.[2] Nonetheless, Gibson was intentionally walked on four pitches.[3] Like everything else involved with that unorthodox postseason, the odds were stacked against normalcy.

Since 1937 the Homestead Grays had split their home games between Pittsburgh and Washington.[4] During the 1943 campaign they played roughly 22 games on 7th St in Washington, at Griffith Stadium,[5] where local black fans enjoyed both the Grays and the Senators, though the latter only from an "unofficially" segregated right-field section.[6] These were mixed in with dozens of games in Pittsburgh and along the East Coast as the Grays cruised to their second pennant in two years. Led by manager Candy Jim Taylor, they had the best lineup in black baseball, though their star, Josh Gibson, had been in and out of St. Elizabeth's Hospital suffering from varying substance-abuse issues.[7]

The Grays' opponents in the '43 Series, the Birmingham Black Barons, were owned by Tom Hays and booked during the war years by Harlem Globetrotters promoter Abe Saperstein.[8] They were managed by talent scout and former Harlem Globetrotters coach Winfield "Lucky" Welch. The Barons' "hitting and fielding ... blends as perfectly with the expert pitching as a rising sun on a pond of water and with just as picturesque results," wrote an observer.[9]

Beginning in 1937, the annual playoff between the Negro American League and Negro National League champions had been a loose-knit affair arranged and scheduled by the teams themselves instead of a strong central office. Barons catcher Ted "Double Duty" Radcliffe had spent the entire season managing the Chicago American Giants, and had only made the Birmingham roster after regular catcher Paul Hardy had been drafted into military service.[10] This was, according to NNL and NAL bylaws, against the rules. Cum Posey and Wendell Smith, both writing for the *Pittsburgh Courier*, voiced their (somewhat biased) opinion that such flouting of the rules would serve only to hurt the validity and character of the game.[11] Radcliffe's presence on the field only amplified the perception that the Negro Leagues were fit for raiding by the "Majors."

Posey suggested that the converse would be nothing but profitable: "This attendance could be tripled if all those associated with Negro baseball became World Series minded."[12]

Adding to the confusion, the multitude of games played at the end of September led to the September 24 game being referred to as the third or fourth game of the Series in varying press coverage. In fact, if it wasn't for a last minute schedule rearrangement by Clark Griffith of previously booked Griffith Stadium, the entire World Series might have been played outside the East Coast.[13]

No matter, whatever point in the Series it was, the game on the 24th proved to be the most exciting and pivotal of the Series, with reports of anywhere from 7,000 to 9,000 spectators in Griffith Stadium braving the bone-chilling weather to root for the Grays.[14]

Johnny Markham, who had a mean knuckleball,[15] was on the mound for the Barons, and Roy Partlow for the Grays. While Partlow cruised, Markham made it through only one easy inning before things unraveled because of some less than stellar defense.

In the second, with Sam Bankhead and Vic Harris on base, Robert Gaston, who was filling in at backstop for the incapacitated Gibson, hit a sharp liner to center field. The runners both had a good jump and were circling toward home, forcing center fielder Felix McLaurin to force the throw to third in an attempt to catch Harris.[16] The throw sailed over Hoss Walker's head, igniting a scramble for the ball as neither catcher Radcliffe nor pitcher Markham had backed up efficiently.[17] In the confusion, third was left uncovered as Gaston steamed into the base. When the ball arrived at third, no Birmingham player was there to field it and as it careened toward the outfield, Gaston trotted home.[18]

And that would be it, with the exception of a flurry of activity in the top of the sixth. Accounts vary as to when Grays pitcher Partlow injured his finger, with some saying a screamer off the bat of McLaurin in the fifth, and others a ball hit by Spearman doing the damage. Manager Jim Taylor gave his ace the benefit of the doubt and left him in, only to watch as Lester Locket made it on base safely with a single, and a run scored.[19]

Taylor, who had been involved with organized black baseball since 1909 and had played with Rube Foster, was too experienced to take any more chances. Despite a one-walk, five-hit performance, Partlow was replaced by Raymond Brown. Brown seemed destined to live up to his Hall of Fame credentials despite his age, only to watch shortstop Sam Bankhead throw wild and allow two unearned runs to score.[20] After Brown got out of the inning with the score now 3-3, he shut down the Barons without a hit the rest of the game.

Birmingham's ace, Johnny Markham, was equally defiant in the face of the Grays' intimidating lineup.[21] Despite the hiccup in the second inning, Markham had held his own. Birmingham skipper Welch had recognized his stuff and knew that if it weren't for the sloppy fielding of his NAL champs, Markham would already be hitting the showers a winner. Instead he was forced to ask his ace to intentionally walk black baseball's number-one superstar and load the bases in the bottom of the 11th.

Sam Bankhead had opened the inning with a slap single to center field. Vic Harris followed with a dribbler up the first-base line that Sloppy Lindsay threw wild in an attempt to get Bankhead at second. The ball careened into center and the Barons were faced with runners at the corners and no outs.[22]

After Markham walked Gibson, Raymond Brown bunted up the first-base line. Lindsay fielded it cleanly this time and had no choice but to throw home instead of trying for second and an easy two. The ball arrived at the plate on time, but Radcliffe was unable to pivot and throw to first. The tie was preserved, but there was only one out.[23]

The tension was palpable as the fans seemed to momentarily forget the cold in the excitement of Cool Papa striding to the plate. With the infield playing in and all eyes on Vic Harris at third, Harris had options, and the Barons infield knew it – anything they could get their hands on would require quick diligence to hold him at third while getting that precious second out.

Bell, however, never gave them a chance. Markham threw whatever junk he had left, and Bell smacked a clean single between first and second. As the ball settled in right field, Vic Harris strolled home to the screaming cheers of the hometown fans.[24]

It would be a few more days before the Grays clinched the Series, beating the Barons soundly 8-4 in Montgomery, Alabama.[25] As in years past, exhibition games featuring the NAL and NNL champs had been scheduled both during and after the Series – the most contentious being a game in New Orleans that would not be played due to miscommunication between promotor Alan Page and the front office of both Birmingham and the Grays, resulting in an outpouring of anger from organizers and fans alike.[26]

As the fans and sportswriters had made clear, the rising popularity of black baseball was hampered by such disorganization. If things weren't improved in 1944, the whole enterprise would be in jeopardy.

NOTES

1 Johnny Markham Baseball Reference Negro Leagues Page (baseball-reference.com/register/player.fcgi?id=markha000joh), last accessed March 31, 2019.

2 Art Carter, "Grays Win, 4-3, in 11th," *Baltimore Afro-American*, October 2, 1943: 18.

3 Ibid.

4 Brad Snyder, *Beyond the Shadow of the Senators: The Untold Story of the Homestead Grays and the Integration of Baseball* (Chicago: Contemporary Books, 2003), 87.

5 "Record of Games Played by Homestead Grays 1943 Season - Up to and Including September 12th." Undated press release in Art Carter Papers 1932-1988, (Box 170-18, Folder 17), Mooreland-Springarn Research Center, Howard University Libraries, Washington.

6 Snyder, 2.

7 John B. Holway, *Josh and Satch: The Life and Times of Josh Gibson and Satchel Paige* (Westport, Connecticut: Meckler, 1991) 165.

8 Rebecca T. Alpert, *Out of Left Field: Jews and Black Baseball* (New York: Oxford University Press, 2011).

9 "Fighting Black Barons Primed for Battles with Eastern Foes," *Pittsburgh Courier*, September 4, 1943: 19.

10 Cum Posey, "Posey's Points," *Pittsburgh Courier*, October 2, 1943: 16.

11 Wendell Smith, "'Smitty's' Sports Spurts," *Pittsburgh Courier*, October 2, 1943: 16.

12 Posey.

13 Ibid.

14 Fay Young, "Bell's Single in Eleventh Beats Barons," *Chicago Defender* (National Edition), October 2, 1943: 11.

15 Frazier Robinson with Paul Bauer, *Catching Dreams: My Life in the Negro Baseball Leagues* (Syracuse: Syracuse University Press, 1999) 39.

16 Young.

17 Carter.

18 Young.

19 "Grays Beat Barons, 4-3, in World Series: 'Third Tilt Won in 11th on Line Single by Bell," *New York Amsterdam News*, October 2, 1943: 20.

20 Young.

21 Carter.

22 Young.

23 Ibid.

24 Carter.

25 "Washington Grays Win Negro Title," *Washington Daily News*, October 6, 1943: 48.

26 Hayward Jackson, "Failure to Play New Orleans Game Irks Fans," *Pittsburgh Courier*, October 16, 1943: 16.

REPEAT CHAMPIONS

SEPTEMBER 24, 1944
HOMESTEAD GRAYS 4, BIRMINGHAM BLACK BARONS 2
GAME FIVE OF THE NEGRO LEAGUE WORLD SERIES

by Adam Berenbak

"But coming down through that would heighten my sense because I could dig I would soon be standing in that line to get in, with my old man. But lines of all black people! Dressed up like they would for going to the game, in those bright lost summers. Full of noise and identification slapped greetings over and around folks. … [These were] legitimate black heroes. And we were intimate with them in a way and they were extensions of all of us, there, in a way that the Yankees and Dodgers and what not could never be!"

— Amiri Baraka[1]

The heart of U Street in North West Washington stretches from roughly 18th Street to 7th Street, bordered on each side by the corners of Florida Avenue as it's cut off from its original identity as Boundary Road. It was here in the early years of the District's history that the city ended and the rural highlands of DC began. And it was here, most visibly in the first half of the twentieth century, that DC's black culture found its most iconic and accessible avenue. At its heart were the Howard Theatre on 7th, the Republic at 14th and U, and countless other movie houses and entertainment palaces.[2] Culture could be found at every turn. Just to the north was a hub of jazz and classical music at Howard University and the Howard music department.[3]

And it was right there, where 7th met Georgia, that anyone interested in baseball would find themselves on any given summer day, the smell of the Wonder Bread factory several blocks away sweetening the air. Hopping off the Georgia Avenue streetcar, you had only a short walk to the gates of Griffith Stadium. Walking north, past Off Beat Confectionery, the Old Rose Social Club and District Novelty, you passed Little Harlem Café and the old billiard hall next to the Goodwill before turning right toward the gate, the sound of the stadium mingled with the excitement in the air.[4] In 1944 the streets were vibrant, the wartime employment boom affecting all of DC, including the black community in and around U Street. Art Carter, a Howard University alumnus and a journalist with the *Afro American*, had partnered with Clark Griffith and was instrumental in promoting black baseball in DC to the African-American "elite" and middle-class culture, and Griffith Stadium had become the home for black sports fans in DC.[5]

Baseball Commissioner Kenesaw M. Landis was, in September 1944, ill and would soon check himself into the hospital, never to check out. To some, his passing was the final death knell for the color barrier that had long segregated and poisoned the game since the late nineteenth century.[6] Integration was on the horizon. But some of the sportswriters covering Negro League baseball were as worried about what integration might do to the Negro National League and Negro American League as they were eager to capitalize on the growing popularity of black baseball.[7]

In June of 1944 the news of D-Day had burst into headlines, and hope permeated a war-weary populace. Things were looking up. Those sentiments were shared by the Negro League team owners, who had listened to what Cum Posey and Wendell Smith had suggested during the 1943 World Series. After the chaos of 1943, three "Commissioners" had been appointed to oversee the 1944 Negro World Series between the Homestead Grays and Birmingham Black Barons: Frank Young of the *Chicago Defender* (who also ran the press box and served as official scorer); Sam Lacy, a writer for the *Baltimore Afro-American;* and Wendell Smith of the *Pittsburgh Courier.*[8]

Only one game of the 1944 Negro World Series was played in Washington. The first four games were played in Birmingham, New Orleans, and Pittsburgh. It kicked off on September 17 in Birmingham, where the Grays won, 8-3. They also won the next two games, in New Orleans and Birmingham (again). The Barons made a series of it on the 23rd in Pittsburgh, the Grays' other home, with a decisive 6-0 victory, setting up a do-or-die game (for the Barons) in Washington on the 24th.[9]

The Grays had narrowly defeated the Barons in the 1943 Series, but the Birmingham squad had improved upon an already stellar roster for the '44 season. Led by captain Tommy Sampson and All-Star shortstop Artie Wilson, the Barons eyed a triumph over the Grays until a late-season car accident removed Sampson, Pepper Bassett and Leandy Young from competition, and injured Wilson and Johnny Britton, who were able to play in the Series.[10]

Returning for the Grays were most of the championship team of 1943, including a fully healthy Josh Gibson. Starting the game was Grays ace Roy Welmaker, just out of the Army, who took the mound in the bottom of the second with a comfortable 3-0 lead.[11] It had all fallen into place quickly in the bottom of the first for the Grays. Jerry Benjamin and Sam Bankhead came out of the box swinging, each rewarded with a single. Thanks to a bobble by right fielder Ed Steele and a fielder's choice, there was already one run home with just one out. Alfred Saylor, on the mound for the Barons, then intentionally walked Buck Leonard and Gibson and the crowd, estimated to be between 8,000 and 10,000, went wild as Jud Wilson dropped a single into shallow left to score Bankhead and Leonard.[12]

With the Grays up 3-0, the fans, some of whom were the "most passionate" fans of the Senators, were even more excited to see the Grays sweep the series.[13]

Welmaker pitched a masterful game, scattering hits here and there but walking no one. He faced few challenges until the fourth, when John Britton, playing in bandages since the car accident, reached on an error by Jud Wilson at the hot corner. Britton moved around the bases on another error by Wilson and a fielder's choice, giving the Barons their first run. However, Welmaker was too sharp, and if the gloves behind him held, he would prove unbeatable.[14]

And just to prove it, in the bottom of the inning, Welmaker decided to take the run back that had been gifted to Birmingham in the top of the fourth. He ripped a double and one batter later was driven home by Bankhead's sharp single. The score was now 4-1 Grays. Not only had Welmaker singlehandedly taken back control of the game, but had forced the hand of Barons manager Lucky Welsch to remove his dueling partner Saylor. Saylor's replacement, Alonzo Boone, shut down the Grays' vaunted offense.[15]

Only one more run was scored in the contest, by the Barons in the fifth. As if agreeing with Welmaker that the pitchers would control the fate of the game from both the mound and the plate, Boone reached first on an awkward infield bounce. He then advanced around the bases and scored on sloppy play, when Jesse Cannady, who had replaced Jud Wilson at third, committed an error on an easy grounder. Now that both pitchers had satisfied their urge to contribute runs, they both settled in and pitched scoreless ball for the rest of the game.[16]

That's not to say there weren't great moments for the fans. Despite an ailing wrist, Birmingham's Artie Wilson fielded brilliantly. The Grays' second baseman Jelly Jackson did as well, and the fans were treated to a base theft by Cool Papa Bell.[17] But the hometown crowd was hungry for a Grays win, even if it meant the season would end with only one game played in Washington (though the fans would be treated to an exhibition game in the following days).[18]

The final out came on a double play on par with Tinker to Evers to Chance. With one out in the ninth and a runner on first, Johnny Markham hit a slow grounder to back to the mound. "Welmaker to Bankhead to Leonard."[19] Euphoria swelled on U Street as, for the final time, a Washington baseball team would claim a championship on District soil. The next time the Grays were in the Series, in 1948, when they once again faced a formidable Barons team, none of the games were played in Washington. It would not be until 2012 that a deciding postseason game was played in Washington.

About 50,000 saw all five Series games in 1944, proving the naysayers of the disorganized '43 contest right – by appointing commissioners to ensure that all scheduled games, both official series games as well as exhibitions, were played when and where the fans expected them, the turnout was huge. According to Wendell Smith, there were more press requests for the 1944 Negro World Series than any previous major event, including the East-West games.[20]

Yet the end of the '44 Negro World Series was also in some ways the end of an era of great black baseball. Landis died soon after the Series, and World War II ended within a year. Jackie Robinson played his first game in Montreal in April of '46, and Josh Gibson died not too long after that. As many of the sportswriters of the day had feared, the integration of the National and American Leagues would spell the death of the Negro Leagues.

NOTES

1 James Overmyer, *Effa Manley and the Newark Eagles* (Metuchen, New Jersey: Scarecrow Press, Inc., 1993), 63.

2 Blair A. Ruble, "Seventh Street: Black DC's Musical Mecca," in Maurice Jackson and Blair A. Ruble, eds., *DC Jazz: Stories of Jazz Music in Washington, DC* (Washington: Georgetown University Press, 2018).

3 Lauren Sinclair, "No Church Without a Choir: Howard University and Jazz in Washington, DC," in Maurice Jackson and Blair A. Ruble, eds., *DC Jazz: Stories of Jazz Music in Washington, DC* (Washington: Georgetown University Press, 2018).

4 Boyd's District of Columbia Directory, Vol. LXXXVI, 1944 Edition (Washington: R.L. Polk & Co., Publishers 1944).

5 Brad Snyder, *Beyond the Shadow of the Senators: The Untold Story of the Homestead Grays and the Integration of Baseball* (Chicago: Contemporary Books, 2003).

6 Neil Lanctot, *Negro League Baseball: The Rise and Ruin of a Black Institution* (Philadelphia: University of Pennsylvania Press, 2004).

7 Jim Reisler, *Black Writers/Black Baseball: An Anthology of Articles from Black Sportswriters Who Covered the Negro Leagues* (Jefferson, North Carolina: McFarland & Company, Inc., 1994).

8 "Grays Win '44 World Series," *The Negro Baseball Yearbook: 1944 Yearbook*, October 29, 1958: 10.

9 Fay Young, "Summary of 1944: Series Playoffs," *Chicago Defender* (National Edition), September 30, 1944: 9.

10 "Grays Win '44 World Series."

11 Sam Lacy, "Grays Take 4 Out of 5 to Cop World Title: Barons Win but 1 Game in Title Playoff with Negro National League Champs," *Afro-American*, September 30, 1944: 18.

12 Fay Young, "Grays Capture 4 Out of 5 to Win 1944 World Series," *Chicago Defender* (National Edition), September 30, 1944: 9.

13 Snyder, 13.

14 Wendell Smith, "Grays Retain Baseball's Top Banner," *Pittsburgh Courier*, September 30, 1944: 12.

15 Fay Young, "Grays Capture 4 Out of 5 to Win 1944 World Series."

16 Ibid.

17 Wendell Smith, "'Smitty's' Sports Spurts," *Pittsburgh Courier*, September 30, 1944: 12.

18 Fay Young, "Grays Capture 4 Out of 5 to Win 1944 World Series."

19 Ibid.

20 Wendell Smith, "'Smitty's' Sports Spurts."

THE 'CINDERELLA TEAM' OF THE NEGRO LEAGUES PLAYS ROYAL BALL

SEPTEMBER 18, 1945
CLEVELAND BUCKEYES 4, HOMESTEAD GRAYS 0

GAME THREE OF NEGRO LEAGUE WORLD SERIES

by Bob LeMoine

The 1945 Negro League World Series was taking place in a postwar America. Japan had surrendered, World War II was over, and the famous "kiss" of a sailor and nurse in a celebratory Times Square sparkled on the cover of Life magazine. Yet old issues remained. "Jim Crow must go!" African American soldiers demanded, in opposition to the laws in the South that enforced segregation. Wendell Smith of the African-American Pittsburgh Courier had recently reported on a mystery meeting between black star Jackie Robinson and Brooklyn Dodgers President Branch Rickey. Baseball would help guide American society toward the path of desegregation. But we weren't there yet.

"Don't get the idea that baseball was all fun and games for us," George Jefferson said of the Negro Leagues to Dwayne Cheeks of the *Cleveland Plain Dealer* in 1982. "We played a lot of cards and dice to break the monotony of the long bus rides. You saw more trees and bushes than you ever thought existed."[1] There must have been a lot of card playing for Jefferson and the upstart Cleveland Buckeyes as the 1945 Negro League World Series against the champion Homestead Grays was held in Cleveland, Washington, and Philadelphia.

The upstart Buckeyes, winners of the Negro American League pennant, had taken both games in Cleveland: Game One with a tight 2-1 win at Cleveland Stadium, followed by a late-inning comeback to win Game Two, 3-2, at League Park. Both were venues the Buckeyes called "home," although the true home team, the Cleveland Indians, required both teams to use the visitors' locker room.[2] The teams left the wintry weather in Cleveland by train and headed to Pittsburgh for Game Three. Umpire Harry Walker taught rummy to fellow umps Moe Harris and Fred McCleary as they listened to the falling rain as they traveled south. When they reached Forbes Field, one of the Homestead Grays' home parks, they learned the game had been canceled. They proceeded to their next location, Griffith Stadium in Washington, another home of the Grays. The Washington Senators and Detroit Tigers had just finished an afternoon game in muddy conditions. Game Four would be played at

Shibe Park in Philadelphia, and Game Five in New York, if necessary.

The Homestead Grays were a dynasty in Negro League baseball in the 1940s. They had won back-to-back championships in 1943-1944 and seven out of eight consecutive Negro National League pennants. Their roster included several Negro League legends who were getting up in years: Jud Wilson (49 years old), Cool Papa Bell (42), Buck Leonard (37), Ray Brown (37), Jerry Benjamin (35), Bee Jackson (35), Sam Bankhead (34), and a comparatively "young" Josh Gibson (33).

By contrast, the average of the Buckeyes was under 30. They included Sam "The Jet" Jethroe, the speedster who batted .339[3] and would one day be Boston's first black major-league player. Jethroe had been involved in a "tryout" at Fenway Park with Jackie Robinson earlier in the year. The tryout was more of a publicity stunt, but greater days were ahead when the Boston Braves signed Jethroe.

Baseball Commissioner Kenesaw Mountain Landis, an opponent of integration, had died. Happy Chandler, his successor, who would soon take office following his term as Kentucky senator, arrived at Griffith Stadium to watch Game Three.[4] A supporter of integrating the national pastime, Chandler would later throw that support behind Rickey when he signed Jackie Robinson to a contract. "Some of the things he did for Jackie Robinson, Roy Campanella, and Don Newcombe when he was commissioner of baseball," said Newcombe, who would follow Robinson to the integrated major leagues, "those are the kinds of things we never forget." He remembered Chandler as someone who cared about blacks in baseball "when it wasn't fashionable.[5]

Chandler was joined by anywhere from 6,000 to 7,500 fans that night, depending on the account. Wilbur Hayes, the Cleveland sports promoter, who with nightclub owner Ernest Wright had built the Buckeyes from scratch just three years prior, received a telegram from Ohio Senator Harold H. Burton, who sent his best wishes. Earlier that day, Burton was nominated by President Harry S. Truman to the United States Supreme Court. Burton would play a crucial role in the landmark Brown v. Board of Education ruling which declared that segregating public schools according to race was unconstitutional. The presence of Chandler and Burton foreshadowed changes on the horizon.

"Big" George Jefferson (6-feet-2, 185 pounds) was the Game Three starter for Cleveland. His older brother, Willie, was the Game One winner, while Eugene Bremer won Game Two. "We'd get a few hits and then let the pitchers and the defense do the rest," remembered manager Quincy Trouppe.[6] Jefferson was opposed by the Grays "brilliant southpaw" Roy Welmaker, who "has been the mainstay of the Grays' pitching corps," wrote the *Pittsburgh Courier*.[7]

This would be a game of pitching and defense as well, with very little play-by-play detail provided in the weekly black newspapers. The Buckeyes plated all the runs they needed in the third when errors by catcher Gibson and pitcher Welmaker and singles by Parnell Woods and Buddy Armour gave the Buckeyes a solid 3-0 lead. Armour scored an insurance run in the ninth on a grounder to short by Jefferson. Armour was credited with two RBIs, Jefferson and Willie Grace with one each. Armour, Jethroe (who also tripled), Woods and Archie Ware accounted for all the runs scored. Each pitcher struck out three; Jefferson walked three, Welmaker two.

"They hit and fielded all of them; made the crowd shout for joy," Walker wrote. "The Washington fans almost jumped out of their seats when [Johnny] Cowan threw a ball on one knee to retire the side, and [shortstop Avelino] Canizares had them nuts fielding ball after ball that should have been hits," Walker wrote. "The Buckeyes looked like the New York Yankees in their great days."[8]

"Jefferson would turn his body into a windmill and hurl screaming fastballs which broke [a]way from the hitter," Cheeks wrote. "After feeding them a series of fastballs, Jefferson would throw his sneaky curve ball."[9] Jefferson was definitely on his game this day. He allowed only three scattered hits (some accounts gave two or four hits) en route to the victory. His performance was reported as the first shutout of the Grays since Jack Matchett of the Kansas City Monarchs accomplished the feat in 1942.[10] "A pitcher had to get in shape to survive," Jefferson said in 1982. "Teams carried very few relievers, so you knew that most of the time you would be going the distance."[11]

Securing the final out, Jefferson was first greeted by Hayes, the exuberant owner in his "checkered sports shirt which he wore at every game for luck," who ran onto the field to embrace his victorious pitcher.[12]

Smith of the *Pittsburgh Courier* called the Buckeyes a "Cinderella team" who were "fired by determination and youth" and "pulled one of the biggest surprises in baseball history." The legendary Grays, Smith wrote, were "creaking in the joints, in dire need of replacements, and exhausted from that last siege when they had to win nine games in six days to beat out Baltimore and Newark (for the pennant). The Grays just didn't have it in 'em against the inspired, fiery Clevelanders."[13]

The Buckeyes swept the series with a Game Four shutout, a 5-0 gem by Frank Carswell. It was the only title in the history of the Cleveland Buckeyes.

SOURCES

Cincinnati Enquirer (Associated Press). "Series Game Postponed," September 18, 1945: 12.

Seamheads Negro League Database. seamheads.com/NegroLgs/index.php

NOTES

1. Dwayne Cheeks, "The Cleveland Buckeyes Remembered," *Cleveland Plain Dealer*, January 18, 1982: 7-D.
2. Bob Dolgan, "Championship Memories: The Underdog Cleveland Buckeyes Were Negro League Champs in 1945," *Cleveland Plain Dealer*, February 26, 1996: 1C.
3. According to the Seamheads Negro League Database
4. "Buckeyes Win, 4-0; Need 1 More," *Cleveland Plain Dealer*, September 19, 1945: 14.
5. Robert McG. Thomas Jr., "A.B. (Happy) Chandler, 92, Dies; Led Baseball Integration," *New York Times*, June 16, 1991.
6. Cheeks; "Here's Buckeye Pitching Staff, Rated Peerless," *Cleveland Call & Post*, September 15, 1945. Negro League statistics vary from source to source. Bob Williams called this a "sloppy, slipshod method in which official figures are compiled for the league which calls itself bigtime, intelligent baseball business," "Sports Rambler," *Call & Post*, September 8, 1945.
7. "Grays and Cleveland Set for World Series," *Pittsburgh Courier*, September 15, 1945: 12.
8. Harry Walker, "World Series - Dots and Dashes," *Cleveland Call & Post*, September 29, 1945: 6B.
9. Cheeks.
10. "Cleveland Captures 1945 World Baseball Crown," *Baltimore Afro-American*, September 22, 1945: 26.
11. Cheeks.
12. Walker.
13. Wendell Smith, "The Sports Beat," *Pittsburgh Courier*, September 29, 1945: 12.

SENATORS STAY ALIVE IN PENNANT RACE IN TOPSY-TURVY HOME FINALE

SEPTEMBER 18, 1945
WASHINGTON SENATORS 12, DETROIT TIGERS 5

by Nathan Bierma

With two weeks left in the season, the Senators were playing their last scheduled home game at Griffith Stadium. This oddity of the calendar was thanks to owner Clark Griffith, who had rented out the stadium to the NFL's Washington Redskins for the rest of September.[1]

Most years, fans might not have minded missing out on chilly, meaningless late-season games. But the 1945 Senators had come from nowhere to make their first challenge for a pennant in 12 years, staying within three games of the league-leading Detroit Tigers for the entirety of September.

The excitement was out of proportion with the quality of play in the major leagues in 1945. While teams awaited the return of many of their regulars from wartime service, "baseball endured," wrote Rob Neyer, "thanks to rosters stocked with baby-faced rookies, grizzled old minor leaguers, and '4-F' ballplayers (ruled) physically unfit for service."[2]

The Senators faced the team they wanted to play most, the Tigers, to close out their premature final homestand in a five-game series – two doubleheaders, thanks to their penurious owner, followed by a makeup of a rainout in May.

Trailing by 2½ games, the home team crippled its own cause by losing three of the first four to Detroit. Washington absolutely had to win to stay in the race, but in order to win, it needed to play. After the makeup game was itself rained out on Monday, September 17, the Senators would play it Tuesday – come hell, or, as the forecast threatened again, high water.

Griffith, pictured in the *Washington Post* holding an umbrella and lifting a tarp on Monday to inspect what the *Post* called a "chocolate pudding infield," insisted on a Tuesday start time of 2:00 P.M. to accommodate potential rain delays.[3] He had the grounds crew burn oil on the infield to try to dry it out.[4]

Only 5,720 fans showed up in the weekday afternoon gloom, a fraction of the 20,000 or so the Washington Grays expected for their Negro League World Series matchup with the Cleveland Buckeyes later on in a nightcap at Griffith Stadium.[5]

The Senators' do-or-die home finale turned out to be the tale of three games within a game – a blowout, a furious comeback, followed by another runaway.

The Senators enjoyed a thunderous opening inning against Tigers starter Dizzy Trout. After George Case and George Myatt led off with singles, both moved up on a bunt by Buddy Lewis and came home on a triple by Joe Kuhel to give the Senators an instant 2-0 lead.

The Senators kept the pressure on, with Cecil Travis following Kuhel with a double to make it 3-0, and, after advancing on a single by George "Bingo" Binks and a walk to Rick Ferrell, scoring on a base hit by Gil Torres. With the Tigers trailing 4-0, Trout wouldn't finish the first inning. Stubby Overmire came on and retired pitcher Walt Masterson to get the visitors back to the dugout to lick their wounds.

For a few innings Masterson would deny Detroit their revenge, suffering only a leadoff infield single by Roy Cullenbine in the second inning, then twice snuffing out scoring threats of runners reaching third base with one out.

In the top of the third, Joe Hoover walked and hustled to third on Eddie Mayo's single to right, only to watch Doc Cramer pop up to shortstop and slugger Rudy York fly out to center.

Masterson inadvertently helped his cause in the bottom of the third. After Ferrell doubled and moved to third on a fielder's choice, Masterson reached first on an error by Hoover to extend the Senators' lead to a comfy 5-0.

With one out in the fourth, Jimmy Outlaw singled and advanced two more bases on Bob Maier's double. But Masterson struck out Paul Richards and induced an Overmire grounder to second to keep the Tigers off the scoreboard.

But in the sixth, a cruise somehow turned into a crisis for the Senators. "Masterson appeared to be breezing to an easy victory when he folded," wrote Shirley Povich.[6]

Richards had a chance at redemption, at bat again with a runner on third. He ripped a double down the left-field line to score Cullenbine from third and Outlaw from first and make it 5-2.

Hank Greenberg clubbed a pinch-hit double of his own to score Richards, followed by John McHale's pinch hit to bring home Red Borom, who was running for Greenberg. It was a game again at 5-4.

Then home plate seemed to shrink to the size of a fingernail for the Washington pitching staff. After Masterson walked Mayo on four pitches and threw ball one to Cramer, manager Ossie Bluege pulled him, his five flawless innings nearly nullified by this two-out rally.

"[Marino] Pieretti came in and walked Cramer on three more pitches," Povich reported. "York drew four more consecutive balls from Pieretti to force the tying run home and bring Dutch Leonard to the scene. When Leonard's first pitch to Cullenbine was low, it was the thirteenth consecutive ball called against Washington pitchers."

Leonard got Cullenbine to line out to Travis at third on the next pitch, ceasing a bases-loaded threat and ending the unraveling of what Povich called "that uproarious sixth."[7] The game was tied.

After the Senators completely collapsed in the sixth inning, though, they confidently regained command in the seventh. Kuhel led off against reliever George Caster with a single to right field, followed by a fielder's choice and bunt single to load the bases. When Ferrell smacked the ball toward the mound, Caster deflected it off his hand to Skeeter Webb at shortstop.[8] Webb's only play was to first base, recording the out but allowing Kuhel to come home safely.

Desperate, the Tigers brought in Hal Newhouser, in the midst of what would be his second straight MVP season. But after a free pass to pinch-hitter Fred Vaughn, which succeeded by setting up a force out of Travis at home for the second out, Newhouser couldn't get Detroit out of the jam.

"Newhouser's first pitch to [George] Case was the pay-off," Povich wrote. "Case stepped far into the ball and smartly hit a curve into the vast unprotected area of dead right field, and everybody on base scampered home."[9]

The Senators exhaled with a 9-5 lead heading into the eighth inning, in which reliever Roger Wolff toppled the Tigers in order. Zeb Eaton took the hill for Detroit in the bottom of the inning and allowed runners to reach the corners with one out. Binks bonked a base hit to left, scoring one, and Ferrell batted one to right with the same result. Vaughn's fly ball sent Binks home. At 12-5, it wasn't even worth pinch-hitting for Wolff, who fanned to end yet another big inning.

Wolff teased the Tigers in the ninth with a two-out walk of Cullenbine before Outlaw flied out to Cramer to end the game, and with it the regular season at Griffith Stadium. The Senators had survived.

"[T]he Nats kept their pennant hopes faintly alive ... with a last-ditch 12-5 victory at Griffith Stadium," Povich wrote. "It was hectic."[10]

The Senators still had a chance to win the pennant, but it depended on hypothetical, hoped-for losses by their vanquished visitors.

"Washington must now content itself with the meager comfort of mathematical possibilities as far as the 1945 pennant is concerned," Povich wrote.[11] He sized up the situation, figured Washington would need to win out and hope the Tigers faltered, and measured the moral victories in what appeared to be a lost cause.[12]

"The Nats don't figure to win the pennant or tie for it, but for a club that was picked to finish eighth with great unanimity, they did quite a job of it this season," Povich wrote. "No club that failed to win the pennant ever made a better try with what it had."[13]

SOURCES

In addition to the sources cited in the Notes, the author accessed Retrosheet.org, Baseball-Reference.com, and SABR.org.

NOTES

1 "A Cautionary Tale: The 1945 Senators," *Ghosts of DC*, September 13, 2012. Retrieved from ghostsofdc.org/2012/09/13/1945-washington-senators.

2 Rob Neyer, "A Last Great Season: The Senators in 1945," ESPN.com, March 14, 2002. Retrieved from espn.com/page2/wash/s/2002/0314/1351582.html.

3 "Nats, Tigers Hope to End Series Today," *Washington Post*, September 18, 1945:12.

4 James Zerilli, "Nats Whip Tigers, 12-5, to Whittle Game from Lead," *Detroit Free Press*, September 19, 1945: 12.

5 "20,000 Expected to See Grays Meet Buckeyes Tonight," *Washington Post*, September 18, 1945: 13.

6 Shirley Povich, "Nats Blow 5-0 Lead but Rally to Take Tiger Finale, 12-5, in Battle of Pitchers," *Washington Post*, September 19, 1945: 12.

7 Povich, "Nats Blow 5-0 Lead but Rally."

8 Zerilli, "Nats Whip Tigers, 12-5."

9 Povich, "Nats Blow 5-0 Lead but Rally."

10 Povich, "Nats Blow 5-0 Lead but Rally."

11 Povich, "This Morning."

12 The Senators would indeed sag down the stretch, losing three of their last five, but so would the Tigers, dropping four of six before Hank Greenberg's grand slam in the ninth inning of their season finale in St. Louis let them capture the flag.

13 Povich, "This Morning."

DETROIT'S ROOKIE VIC WERTZ CYCLES TIGERS TO 'MAYHEM' VICTORY

SEPTEMBER 14, 1947
DETROIT TIGERS 16, WASHINGTON SENATORS 6
(FIRST GAME OF DOUBLEHEADER)

by Mike Huber

The Detroit Tigers "waited until late in the waning season to unlimber their greatest offensive show of the 1947 season," as they swept a doubleheader from the Washington Senators at Griffith Stadium. A small crowd of 11,170 gathered to watch the double defeat. The *Washington Post* declared, "Defeat is hardly the word to use to describe what happened in the first game. Mayhem comes closer to painting the real picture."[1]

In the first game, the Tigers sent "the clever right-hander"[2] Fred Hutchinson to the mound. He had split time as a starter and reliever for Detroit, but this was his fifth straight start. His last three starts had all been complete games, so manager Steve O'Neill was hoping for lots of innings from Hutchinson, especially with a doubleheader on the schedule. The home team countered with Walt Masterson. He had thrown four consecutive complete games coming into this contest, and he had lowered his ERA to 2.79 while winning three of his last four starts.

The Tigers greeted Masterson by scoring five runs. The *Detroit Free Press* reported that the "explosion came after two were out."[3] Eddie Lake singled to start the game. Vic Wertz walked with one out and Masterson struck out Pat Mullin. Then came consecutive RBI singles by George Kell, Hoot Evers, Roy Cullenbine, and Hal Wagner (who drove in two runs). Hutchinson lined out for the third out, but the Tigers had batted around.

Detroit placed two more men across home plate in the second. Eddie Mayo singled after Lake had fanned. Wertz drove the ball into right field for a triple and Mayo scored the sixth Tigers run. Mullin flied out to left, but it was deep enough to for a sacrifice, bring Wertz home with number seven. Now, with the bases empty and two away, Masterson walked Kell and gave up a single to Evers. Cullenbine grounded out to end the new rally.

Morris Siegel of the *Washington Post* tried for some sarcastic humor in describing the game, writing, "In case you came out to the park late or tuned in on your radio after the second inning you missed him. 'Twould be nice to say that the Tigers did, too, but they didn't."[4] The second inning was the last for Masterson. Senators skipper Ossie Bluege brought

Exterior of Griffith Stadium in 1958. The ballpark was the home of the original Senators from 1911 through 1960, and hosted three World Series and two All-Star Games. (Photo courtesy of Robert E. Wilson)

in rookie Scott Cary to relieve Masterson and start the third, but the young left-hander "was only a slight improvement."[5] Masterson wasn't in the game long enough to get an at-bat, and Cary led off the top of the third.

Hutchinson had allowed one runner to reach in each of the first two frames, but in the third he ran into trouble. After Cary struck out, John Sullivan singled and advanced to third when Buddy Lewis followed with a single to right. Sherry Robertson pulled a grounder to first baseman Cullenbine, who threw to second to force Lewis, but Robertson was safe at first and Sullivan scored.

Wertz singled to lead off the Detroit fourth, and Mullin laid down a sacrifice bunt (with a 7-1 lead!) to advance Wertz into scoring position. This strategy paid off, as Kell drove a single into left field and Wertz came around to score.

In the home half of the fourth, Washington finally gave its fans something to cheer about. Cecil Travis tagged Hutchinson for a double to center. Jerry Priddy followed with an RBI single. Hutchinson retired Rick Ferrell and Cary on groundouts, but that put Priddy on third. Sullivan singled up the middle, plating Priddy. Lewis also singled, and then Robertson hit a grounder "that took a freak hop over Mayo's head"[6] and shot into right field for a double. Sullivan scored and Lewis held up at third, but he and Robertson trotted home when Mickey Vernon singled to center. The inning ended with the score 8-6 in favor of the visitors, but that's as close as the Senators came.

Detroit responded immediately in the fifth. Hutchinson and Mayo each singled, and with two outs, Wertz blasted his sixth homer of the season, giving the Tigers three more runs. They added another in the sixth on a solo shot by Evers, his ninth of the year. The Tigers now led 12-6.

In the seventh the hit parade continued. With one out, Mayo singled and Wertz doubled to left, giving him one of each type of hit. He had hit for the cycle. Mullin tripled into the gap in center, and two more runs scored. Kell singled in Mullin and Evers doubled, driving in Kell. Bluege made his way to the mound, and Buzz Dozier, "the young Texas fireballer, was ushered into the slaughter."[7] He fared much better, getting the Senators out of the inning and limiting the Detroit batters to just one hit and no runs over the final 2⅔ innings of the game.

Wertz's 4-for-5 performance (he grounded out to second in the ninth) with a walk, four runs batted in, and five runs scored was a career day for the rookie, and his batting average rose from .281 to .291. Before this game, he had garnered five hits in a game on August 20, but in that game he had two doubles and a single. He tied his best for RBIs in a game (set August 15 against the Chicago White Sox). Wertz had now hit in five straight games. His hitting streak reached eight games. He "almost licked the Nats single-handed."[8] His five runs scored was only one less than the Senators amassed as a team. For the 1947 season, Wertz batted .333 (7-for-21) at Griffith Stadium, but this was the only game in which he recorded any extra-base hits

The Tigers scored runs in six different innings. Mayo was 3-for-6 with three runs scored. Kell and Evers had identical lines, with 4-for-5 at the plate, plus a walk, three runs driven in and two scored. Evers, though, was a triple shy of hitting for the cycle himself. Every other Tigers batter (including pitcher Hutchinson) contributed a hit. Detroit left nine runners on base, as "the massacre of the Nats served more than just to fatten the Tiger batting averages."[9] Masterson was tagged with the loss, and in his final four games of the season, he allowed 12 earned runs and finished the year with three straight defeats

Despite allowing six earned runs, Hutchinson went the distance for Detroit, picking up his 15th win of the season. Five Washington hitters collected two hits apiece, but they couldn't do any more damage than the fourth-inning outburst. He also earned decisions in his final three starts, but they were all victories for the Tigers, and Hutchinson ended the season with a record of 18-10, arguably his best year in the majors.

Wertz became just the fifth Tiger to hit for the cycle; this performance came eight years after Charlie Gehringer's cycle (May 27, 1939). Three seasons after Wertz's performance, teammates George Kell (June 2, 1950, against the Philadelphia Athletics) and Hoot Evers (September 7, 1950, against the Cleveland Indians) both hit for the cycle. The only player in the majors to hit for the cycle in 1947 besides Wertz was Boston Red Sox star Bobby Doerr, who accomplished the rare feat for the second time in his career on May 13 against the Chicago White Sox.[10]

In the second game, the Tigers put together an 11-hit attack in doubling up the Senators, 8-4. They jumped on starter Milo Candini for two runs in the first inning and scored four more in the second inning, even after Tom Ferrick came in to relieve Candini. Kell had two hits in the game, and Wertz was 1-for-3 with two walks, scoring two runs. The Senators had good swings against Detroit's Dizzy Trout, reaching him for 12 hits in eight innings (Al Benton pitched a scoreless ninth), but Washington stranded nine runners on base. For the Nats, Stan Spence stood out with a 4-for-4 day, but his teammates couldn't capitalize. Masterson pitched the final five innings of the game, allowing two earned runs on five hits and three walks, but at least he did get to bat, getting a hit in his only at-bat.

Since the Chicago White Sox-Boston Red Sox game was called in the seventh inning due to rain (with the score 1-1), the Tigers jumped into second place in the American League pennant race. However, they were still 12½ games out of first. Detroit ended the season with a five-game win streak, but was only 8-4-1 after this game and settled for the runner-up position in the American League.

SOURCES

In addition to the sources mentioned in the Notes, the author consulted Baseball-Reference.com, MLB.com, SABR.org and Retrosheet.org.

baseball-reference.com/boxes/WS1/WS1194709141.shtml

retrosheet.org/boxesetc/1947/B09141WS11947.htm

NOTES

1 Morris Siegel, "Tigers Trounce Nats Twice to Regain 2d," *Washington Post*, September 15, 1947: 11.

2 "Nats Fall Twice as Tigers Lose Control of Bats," *Detroit Free Press*, September 15, 1947: 18.

3 "Nats Fall Twice."

4 Siegel.

5 *Detroit Free Press*.

6 Siegel.

7 Siegel.

8 Siegel.

9 Siegel.

10 Doerr hit for the cycle for the first time on May 17, 1944, against the St. Louis Browns. Both of Doerr's cycles took place at Boston's Fenway Park.

JOE DIMAGGIO HOMERS THREE TIMES

SEPTEMBER 10, 1950
NEW YORK YANKEES 8, WASHINGTON SENATORS 1

by Brian M. Frank

Most players would consider entering an early September game hitting .287 with 24 home runs to be a pretty impressive season. But for Joseph Paul DiMaggio, those numbers were not up to the standard he'd set in his illustrious career. The 35-year-old center fielder, in his 12th major-league season, had hit below .305 only once, in 1946, the year he returned from World War II. The Yankee Clipper's season hit a new low when New York dropped two games in Boston to start a 14-game road trip. Dan Daniel wrote in *The Sporting News* that DiMaggio "looked worse than ever before this season" and that "Once again he appeared tired and jaded."[1] Daniel wrote that DiMaggio struggled at the plate and in the field in Boston: "He did not hit, he dropped a fly ball and gave Boston two runs."[2] *The Brooklyn Daily Eagle* described DiMaggio as "often gloomy and reticent in the recent slump."[3] The Yankees left Boston and headed to the nation's capital to continue their long road trip.

The Yankees entered the first game of their doubleheader at Griffith Stadium on September 10 well rested. The first game of the series had been rained out, and New York had a scheduled offday the day before that. Meanwhile, Detroit had taken a one-game lead over New York to sit atop the American League, while Boston had moved to within a half-game of the idle Yankees. New York tried to right the ship and get back on top by sending Vic Raschi, 18-8 with a 3.99 ERA, to the mound to face Washington's Sid Hudson, a side-arming right-hander, who was 12-12 with a 4.10 ERA.

After Hudson set down the side in order in the first, DiMaggio came to the plate to lead off the top of the second. He certainly didn't look as though he was struggling when he launched the ball into the left-field bleachers for his 25th home run of the season to put the Yankees in front, 1-0.

In the third inning, New York added two more runs. The rally started when Raschi drew a one-out walk. After Phil Rizzuto grounded into a fielder's choice, recently acquired Johnny Hopp collected his first hit as a Yankee, blooping a single to left field that put runners at the corners.[4] Hank Bauer singled home the second run of the game, and DiMaggio walked to load the bases. The Yankees scored another

Third-base grandstand at Griffith Stadium in 1958. (Photo courtesy of Robert E. Wilson)

run on a chaotic play, when Yogi Berra hit a tapper on the first-base side. Hudson came off the mound to field it, but his throw to first nailed Berra in the back. Hopp raced home with the third run of the game, as second baseman Cass Michaels "recovered the ball and threw to shortstop Sam Dente, trapping DiMaggio off second. Bauer then had to race from third to the plate and was caught."[5]

In the sixth inning, DiMaggio deposited another home run into the bleachers beyond Griffith Stadium's spacious left field. The solo shot, his second of the game, put New York on top 4-0. The way Raschi was dealing, the four-run lead must have felt like a mountain to climb for the Senators. The Yankees ace had allowed just a walk and a single through his first five innings. However, in the home half of the sixth, Washington scratched out a run against the right-hander. The mini-rally began when Hudson singled with one out and Eddie Yost drew a walk. Bud Stewart then got the Senators on the scoreboard with an RBI single. Raschi easily retired the next two batters, and the Yankees led at the end of six innings, 4-1.

In the bottom of the seventh, a 28-minute rain delay halted play. The weather continued to be a nuisance for the rest of the day. When the game resumed, Mickey Harris took the mound for the Senators in the eighth after Hudson had been pinch-hit for. DiMaggio, who was already 2-for-2 with two home runs and a walk, greeted the lefty reliever by ripping a "screaming double through Eddie Yost and down the left-field line."[6] Tommy Henrich brought DiMaggio home when he legged out a triple on a ball that hit off the wall in deep right-center field.

After Henrich's hit, the game was delayed for 15 minutes by another cloudburst. Then, as the Yankees took the field for the bottom of the eighth, the skies opened up again, and the game's third rain delay ensued, this time for an hour and 15 minutes. The *New York Times* wrote that the "repeated showers wore a ground crew almost down to exhaustion."[7] When the game finally resumed, Casey Stengel removed Raschi, "Vic's arm having tightened up during the intermission," and replaced him with Tom Ferrick.[8] Ferrick held the Senators down through the final two innings, allowing just two walks, one of which was erased on a double play.

However, DiMaggio and the Yankees weren't done. In the ninth Rizzuto singled with one down and took second on Hopp's groundout to short. Hank Bauer brought the Yankees' sixth run home with a single to center. Up stepped DiMaggio, who once again sent a ball into the distant left-field bleachers. His third home run of the game was described as his longest of the day.[9] The homer was DiMaggio's 27th of the season, and the two runs driven in gave him 101 RBIs, putting him over the century mark for the ninth time in his career. The three-run inning gave the Yankees a commanding 8-1 lead. Ferrick finished off the Senators in the ninth, and the Yankees, after losing three in a row, including the first two games of their road trip, were back to their winning ways.

Raschi ended up winning his 19th game of the season, going seven innings, allowing one run on four hits, striking out five and walking three, and lowering his ERA to 3.91. After the game Casey Stengel gushed over his ace proclaiming him the "best pitcher in the American League, (Bob) Lemon or no Lemon, (Art) Houtteman or no Houtteman."[10]

The rain that hampered the first game continued, and the second game of the twin bill was washed out in the fourth inning before it could become official, with the Senators leading 6-2. DiMaggio blasted a pair of balls that just missed being home runs in the nightcap. "Leaping catches" in front of the left-field wall prevented him from tallying a couple more circuit clouts.[11] The Tigers split a doubleheader with the White Sox, so the Yankees moved to within a half-game of the league leaders, while the Red Sox, who also won, remained a half-game behind New York.

After struggling through a rough patch, DiMaggio was once again the hero for the Yankees. He went 4-for-4, with three home runs, a double, a walk, four runs scored, and four runs driven in. It was the first time a player hit three home runs in a game at Griffith Stadium. The left-field fence at Griffith Stadium was 386 feet down the foul line,[12] and all three of DiMaggio's blasts were reported to have gone over 400 feet. DiMaggio told the *Brooklyn Eagle*: "This Washington Park is a real drive. It's been a jinx for me. You earn every homer you get here."[13] It was the third time in his career that he'd hit three home runs in a game, each time in a road game. (He'd also accomplished the feat in 1937 in a game at Sportsman's Park in St. Louis, and in 1948 at Cleveland Stadium.)

DiMaggio declared, "I guess the two days off we had Friday and Saturday helped me a lot."[14] Stengel echoed his star's comments, saying "Just shows you what rest does for the big fella."[15] Commenting on statements by the aging center fielder's doubters and naysayers, Stengel exclaimed, "Is he through? Hah! I'd like to have a dozen washed-up ballplayers like him."[16]

SOURCES

In addition to the sources cited in the Notes, the author consulted Baseball-Reference.com.

NOTES

1 Dan Daniel, "DiMaggio Gets Into Swing of Yankee Drive," *The Sporting News*, September, 20, 1950: 9.

2 Ibid.

3 United Press, "DiMag Remains Yankee Clipper with Rest Cure," *Brooklyn Daily Eagle*, September 11, 1950: 11.

4 Hopp had been acquired from Pittsburgh in a waiver deal.

5 Joe Trimble, "Yanks Blast Senators, 8-1, as DiMaggio Hits 3 Homers," *New York Daily News*, September 11, 1950: 47.

6 Ed Sinclair, "Yankees Rout Senators, 8-1, Gain as Tigers Split, 1-0, 5-4," *New York Herald Tribune*, September 11, 1950: 19.

7 John Drebinger, "Bombers Triumph at Washington, 8-1," *New York Times*, September 11, 1950: 31.

8 Trimble.

9 United Press, "DiMag Hits Three 400-Foot Homers, Yanks Slug Nats 8-1 - 2d Game Rained Out," *Boston Globe*, September 11, 1950: 6.

10 Daniel.

11 Associated Press, "Has DiMag's Bat Come to Life in Time to Put Yanks on Top?," *Boston Globe*, September 11, 1950: 10.

12 "Griffith Stadium," Baseball-Almanac.com, baseball-almanac.com/stadium/st_griff.shtml, accessed March 22, 2019.

13 United Press, "DiMag Remains Yankee Clipper with Rest Cure."

14 Ibid.

15 Ibid.

16 Ibid.

MANTLE'S MYTHIC BLAST

APRIL 17, 1953
NEW YORK YANKEES 7, WASHINGTON SENATORS 3

by Gregory H. Wolf

It was the "longest home run in the history of baseball," gushed sportswriter Joe Trimble of the *New York Daily News*, about Mickey Mantle's titanic blast over the left-field bleachers and out of Griffith Stadium.[1] Not ready to dismiss the icon who began the sport's love affair with the long ball two generations earlier, *New York Times* reporter Louis Effrat described it as "the longest ball ever hit by anyone except Babe Ruth in the history of major league baseball."[2] Herb Heft of the *Washington Post* called it "the grand daddy of all Griffith Stadium home runs."[3] The Senators' 83-year-old owner, Clark Griffith, who had been around professional baseball since 1888, exclaimed, "No doubt about it, that was the longest home run ever hit in the history of baseball."[4]

Mantle's clout captured the nation's attention, and also imagination – everyone wanted to know just how far it went. Minutes after the ball landed, the first attempt to measure its distance was made, and almost seven decades later scientists and historians are still debating just how far and high the ball could have traveled. As baseball historian Jane Leavy reminded us, Mantle's prodigious blow evoked a new term: the tape-measure home run.[5] Baseball was never the same.

The weather wreaked havoc on the Washington Senators as they tried to inaugurate the 1953 campaign. The season and home opener scheduled for Tuesday, April 14, was rained out, and rescheduled two days later as part of a day-night doubleheader with the New York Yankees.[6] President Dwight D. Eisenhower tossed out the ceremonial first pitch in front of a crowd of 25,112, while a cold front forced the cancellation of the second game.[7]

What a difference a day makes. Gone was the pageantry – and few were the rays of sunshine – as the reigning four-time World Series champion Yankees (2-1) and Senators (0-1) took the field on Friday afternoon. A paltry crowd of 4,206, plus about 3,000 guests on Patrol Boy Day,[8] braved the ominous skies, swirling wind, and threat of even more rain to find their seats in Griffith Stadium, making the cavernous ballpark seem even larger.

Toeing the rubber for the Nats was offseason acquisition Chuck Stobbs, a game-time decision,

Left-field wall at Griffith Stadium with its iconic beer sign and Longines clock. The original Senators averaged more than 10,000 spectators per game five times at Griffith Stadium, where they played from 1911 through 1960, with a season-best of 13,516 in 1946. (Photo courtesy of Robert E. Wilson)

"at practically the last minute," reported Heft.[9] Skipper Bucky Harris felt that the Yankees would have more trouble with a southpaw than with the scheduled starter, righty Walt Masterson. The 23-year-old Stobbs, already in his seventh big-league season, set down the Yankees in order in the first. All eyes were on Mantle as he led off the second. The 21-year-old coil of muscle, however, was hobbling, suffering from a charley horse in his left thigh that required diathermy treatment before the game.[10] Mantle walked, then surprisingly stole second. Joe Collins drew a two-out walk, but both were left stranded.

On the mound for the Yankees was graybeard Eddie Lopat, a favorite of manager Casey Stengel. The 35-year-old "Junkman" boasted a 131-92 career slate but was coming off an injury-riddled 1952 season, limited to just 19 starts. He breezed through the first two innings, yielding just a single.

The teams traded runs in the third. Billy Martin spanked a one-out "wind-blown homer into the left field bleachers" for the Yankees for the game's first run.[11] In the bottom of the frame, Eddie Yost's two-out single plated Wayne Terwilliger to tie the score. The Yankees took the lead in the fourth on Collins's one-out single driving in Hank Bauer, who had led off with a bloop double.

The switch-hitting Mantle came to the plate in the fifth after Yogi Berra drew a two-out walk. In just his third season, Mantle's name was already synonymous with long home runs. Just eight days earlier, in an exhibition game against the Pittsburgh Pirates on April 9, the Commerce Comet duplicated The Babe's last home run by becoming just the third player to clear the right-field roof at Forbes Field.[12] Batting right-handed against the southpaw Stobbs and using a borrowed bat from teammate Loren Babe,[13] Mantle connected squarely with a self-described "chest-high fastball" on a 1-and-0 count.[14] "[H]elped by a brisk tail wind," reported Heft, Mantle's blast sailed over the left-center-field wall, 391 feet from home plate and then over the 55-foot-high left-field bleachers, the first time that had happened since they were built in 1924. The ball clipped the National Bohemia beer advertising sign that sat 15 feet higher, before leaving the ballpark and giving the Yankees a 4-1 lead.

Yankees press secretary Red Patterson immediately recognized that he had a front-page story in the making. He left the press box and looked for the ball. He eventually found a 10-year-old boy, Donald Dunaway, who explained that he had found the ball in the yard at 434 Oakdale Place. By walking 105 feet from the edge of the ballpark, a spot that was 460 feet from home plate, Patterson measured the distance the ball traveled to be 565 feet.

No other home run has been the object of so much deliberation, which is a testimony as much to Mantle's beloved stature as it is to baseball's romantic relationship with the home run. A few days after the blast, a federal judge even declared that Mantle's blast was not wind-aided and was the sole product of his power.[15] Patterson's calculation of the distance was far from scientific and many experts raised questions about it. Among the first was Bill Jenkinson, an authority on the history of long home runs. He estimated that Mantle's blast traveled 510 feet.[16] Alan Nathan, a physicist, baseball historian, and acknowledged expert on Mantle's home run, pointed out that the events after the ball left the park were "unknown and quite likely unknowable."[17] Analyzing launch angles, trajectories, and wind, Nathan argued that the ball traveled at least 538 feet.

The game continued after Mantle's home run, even if sportswriter Louis Effrat quipped that "everything else that occurred in this contest was dwarfed by Mantle's round-tripper."[18] In the bottom of the fifth, Lopat looked "ready to fall apart," wrote Heft. The Senators loaded the bases on two singles and a walk, but Mickey Vernon, who'd go on to win the batting title in '53, grounded out. The Nationals picked up a run in the seventh when Terwilliger led off with a double. Mel Hoderlein, pinch-hitting for Stobbs, lined a one-out single to left to trim the Yankees lead to two runs, 4-2.

The Yankees blew the game open in the eighth inning. Switching sides of the plate against right-handed reliever Julio Moreno, Mantle drew a leadoff walk, but was forced at second on Bauer's grounder. Gene Woodling's double plated Bauer. With two outs Andy Carey, Lopat, and Martin hit consecutive singles, resulting in two more runs (RBIs to Carey and Martin) and extended the lead to 7-2.

Lopat worked around a leadoff walk to Vernon in the eighth by inducing Jackie Jenson to ground back to the mound and helped his own cause by initiating a 1-4-3 twin killing. But Lopat was laboring. After Pete Runnels walked and Ken Wood singled, Terwillger collected his third hit of the afternoon, singling in Runnels.

With the game seemingly decided, Moreno was back on the mound for the Senators in the ninth. With one out, he faced Mantle again. Despite his sore left leg, Mantle attempted a drag bunt. The ball bounced in front of second base and Mantle, considered among the fastest players out of the box to first base batting left-handed, easily reached first on what Effrat quipped was the "longest bunt on record."[19] Bauer followed with a walk, but both were left stranded.

Lopat tossed a few warm-up pitches to begin the ninth, then walked off, too tired to continue, reported the *New York Daily News*.[20] He was replaced by reliever Tom Gorman, who set the Senators down in order to end the game in 2 hours and 27 minutes.

The game featured 22 hits, 12 of those by the Yankees, but none was bigger than Mantle's home run. In the decades since that fateful spring day in Washington, the stature of that clout has grown into mythic proportions, much like Mantle himself.

SOURCES

In addition to the sources cited in the Notes, the autthor accessed Retrosheet.org, Baseball-Reference.com, SABR.org, and *The Sporting News* archive via Paper of Record.

NOTES

1 Joe Trimble, Mantle Clouts Record 562-Ft. Homer," *New York Daily News*, April 18, 1953: 25.

2 Louis Effrat, "Towering Drive by Yankee Slugger Features 7-3 Defeat of Senators," *New York Times*, April 18, 1953: 12.

3 Herb Heft, "Best Swat in History Helps Top Nats, 7-3," *Washington Post*, April 18, 1953: 13.

4 Heft.

5 Jane Leavy, "Out of the Park," janeleavy.com, November 2010. janeleavy.com/out-of-the-park/.

6 Associated Press, "Senator-Yankee Game Washed Out by Rain," *Baltimore Sun*, April 14, 1953: 19.

7 "Yanks Tops Senators, 6-3, in Griffith Stadium Opener," *Baltimore Sun*, April 17, 1953: 19.

8 Leavy.

9 Heft.

10 Louis Effrat, "Mantle Home Run Hit into Hall of Fame," *New York Times*, April 19, 1953: S1.

11 Heft.

12 Jack Hernon, "Bucs Blast World Champion Yankees, 10-5," *Pittsburgh Post-Gazette*, April 10, 1953: 23. Ruth cleared the right-field roof on May 25, 1935, as a member of the Boston Braves; the Pirates' Ted Beard accomplished the feat in 1950.

13 United Press, "Brideweser Called Mantle's Shot," (Binghamton, New York) *Press and Bulletin*, April 19, 1953: 5.

14 "Ruth Never Slugged a Baseball Farther," *Washington Post*, April 18, 1953: 13.

15 US District Judge James R. Kirkland made the bold statement. Associated Press, "No Wind, Declared Judge," Helped Mantle Homer," *New York Times*, April 21, 1953: 4.

16 Bill Jenkinson, "Mickey Mantle's Historic1953 Washington, D.C. Home Run," Bill Jenkinson Baseball: billjenkinsonbaseball.webs.com/mickeymantleshistoric.htm; Jenkinson, *Baseball's Ultimate Power* (Guilford, Connecticut: Lyons Press, 2010).

17 Alan Nathan, "Mantle's Griffith Stadium Home Run Revisited. baseball.physics.illinois.edu/mantle565.htm.

18 Effrat, "Towering Drive by Yankee Slugger Features 7-3 Defeat of Senators."

19 Effrat, "Towering Drive by Yankee Slugger Features 7-3 Defeat of Senators."

20 Trimble.

BOB PORTERFIELD WINS 20TH

SEPTEMBER 12, 1953
WASHINGTON SENATORS 4, CLEVELAND INDIANS 3

by Joseph Wancho

It was all over but the shouting. The pennant race in the American League had just about been decided; the New York Yankees held a commanding 10-game lead over C leveland as the schedule wound down. For the third year in a row, the Indians would be the runner-up to the Yankees.

If there was any drama between the Indians and the Senators, it was the race for the batting championship between Washington's Mickey Vernon and Cleveland's Al Rosen. As the Indians headed to the nation's capital for a two-game series on September 11, Vernon was ahead of Rosen by a slim margin. Vernon was batting .332 to Rosen's .327. Both players were at top of the league when it came to swinging the lumber. Rosen was leading the loop in home runs (40) and RBIs (133), and was tied for the lead in runs (97) with Washington's Eddie Yost and Chicago's Minnie Miñoso. The Triple Crown was within Rosen's grasp, but time was getting short.

Vernon, a left-handed hitter, was ranked second in RBIs (103) and runs (95) in addition to his league-leading batting average. Vernon made his debut in 1939 with Washington, was traded to Cleveland after the 1948 season, then was shipped back to the Senators on June 14, 1950, for pitcher Dick Weik.

While the Indians occupied second place in the AL, the Senators were in fifth place, 23½ games behind the front-running Yankees. In Game One of the series, Washington skipper Bucky Harris sent Spec Shea to the hill to oppose Cleveland's Bob Lemon. Both pitchers went the distance, with Shea getting the win in the 6-4 Nats victory. Rosen and Vernon each went 1-for-3. Going into the second game, and the last time their teams would see each other in the season, Vernon was batting .332 while Rosen posted a .327 average.

The Indians pitcher would be Art Houtteman (9-12, 4.76 ERA). Houtteman had been acquired by Cleveland from Detroit as part of an eight-player deal on June 15. Currently, he was on a four-game winning streak.

Harris countered with Bob Porterfield (19-10, 3.55 ERA). Porterfield was having the best season of his career and was also on a four-game winning streak. Porterfield had also put together two

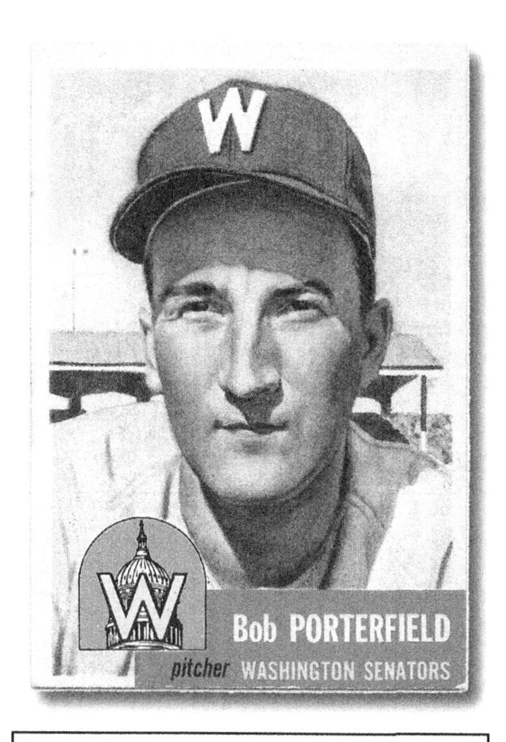

In 1953 Bob Porterfield led the AL with 22 wins, 24 complete games, and nine shutouts, all of which were career bests. The right-hander went 67-64 in parts of five seasons with the Senators (1951-1955) and 87-97 in his 12-year major-league career (1948-1959). (1953 baseball card courtesy of Topps)

five-game winning streaks during the season (April 29-May 22) and (July 26-August 15). He was 4-0 against the Indians thus far in the season.

Apparently, the possibility of Porterfield winning his 20th game, or the hitting exploits was not enough to draw fans to Griffith Stadium. A minuscule crowd of 5,798 attended the afternoon game.

The Senators chipped away at Houtteman and scored single runs in the second, fourth, fifth, and sixth innings to stake Porterfield to a 4-0 lead. Wayne Terwilliger and Vernon each knocked in a run while Ed Fitz Gerald accounted for two RBIs.

Meanwhile, the Indians could not break through against Porterfield. They had runners on base in every inning except the second and seventh. But the Indians could not get the big hit when one was needed most.

In the top of the eighth, Cleveland first baseman Bill Glynn led off with a single to center field. After Dale Mitchell fouled out, Rosen came through with a double to left field. Glynn scored from first and Rosen advanced to third on the throw home. Larry Doby walked and Wally Westlake singled Rosen home to cut the Senators lead in half, 4-2.

Relief pitcher Bill Wight, who was working his second inning, set the Senators down 1-2-3 in the bottom of the eighth. Out of the dugout came Porterfield to attempt to get his 20th victory. But Cleveland did not make it easy on him.

With one out, Cleveland manager Al Lopez sent Luke Easter in to pinch-hit for Wight. Easter came through with a single to center field. Bob Kennedy ran for Easter. Bobby Avila singled, moving Kennedy to second base. After Glynn made the second out with a fly out to center, Mitchell singled to center to plate Kennedy and Avila went to third base. Up came Rosen, who thus far was 3-for-4. But Porterfield struck out the Indians cleanup hitter, preserving the Nats' win and his 20th victory. He was the first pitcher in the AL to reach the 20-win plateau in 1953.

"I left him in against what might have been better judgment," said Harris, "but I had to give him the shot at the white alley. Nobody wanted Bob to win his 20th more than I did, and I was prepared to take the rap if he got licked."[1]

As for the batting race, it came down to the final day on the schedule. Vernon edged out Rosen by one percentage point, .337 to .336, to win the second batting championship in his career. Vernon topped the league in 1946 with a .353 average.

Rosen led the AL in home runs (43), RBIs (145), and runs (115). He was voted American League MVP in 1953. Rosen was the first player to win the award unanimously since the electorate was expanded to three writers from each league city in 1938.

SOURCES

The author accessed Baseball-Reference.com for box scores/play-by-play information and other data, as well as retrosheet.org.

baseball-reference.com/boxes/WS1/WS1195309120.shtml retrosheet.org/boxesetc/1953/B09120WS11953.htm

NOTES

1 Shirley Povich, "Eddie Yost Built Up Big 'Night' Banging Daylights Out of Ball," *The Sporting News*, September 23, 1953: 8

MY MOST MEMORABLE GAME AT GRIFFITH STADIUM

by Clark C. Griffith

I grew up at Griffith Stadium and have great memories of mammoth home runs by Mickey Mantle, Johnny Mize, and Larry Doby, great catches by Mantle and Jim Piersall, and one monumental popup by Ted Williams.

The Griffith Stadium game I remember most was played between the Philadelphia Athletics and the Senators on the last day of the 1953 season, September 27. The game had little significance in the standings but would establish that the Senators first baseman, Mickey Vernon, was the American League Batting Champion by one point over the Indians third baseman Al Rosen, who in the Indians' season finale was playing the Tigers in Cleveland.

As the game between the Athletics and Senators started, the drama was focused on Vernon, who was leading the league with a batting average of .336092175. Rosen was batting .33333333. The difference: .002759382. The batting crown would come down to the last at-bat for both players.

Vernon was batting third for Washington as he did every day; Rosen was leading off for Cleveland to give him a chance for an extra at-bat, and he got it.

The starting pitchers were Joe Coleman, a right-hander, for the Athletics, and Al Aber, a left-hander, for Detroit in Cleveland. As Vernon batted left-handed and Rosen right-handed, they both enjoyed that advantage of facing opposite-handed pitchers and both were playing home games where the backgrounds were friendly and familiar, as was the official scorer.

Rosen led off in the first inning and "singled to second," and the second baseman was given an error on the throw, allowing Rosen to get to second. Maybe a friendly official scorer! Singles to second with a throwing error are very rare as the ball was fielded and thrown. Rosen was not a fast runner. This sort of play is usually a two-base error but rarely a single and an error, but that's how it was scored by the official scorer.

Vernon batted third in the Washington first inning and grounded out to second.

After their first at-bats that day, Rosen was batting .334453782 and Vernon was at .335537190.

The next at-bat for both was in the third inning. After Joe Ginsberg had doubled and Bob Feller popped out to the catcher, Rosen hit a ground-rule double. At Griffith Stadium, after Bunky Stewart had grounded out to second, Eddie Yost walked, and Pete Runnels lined out to short, Vernon executed a perfect bunt for a single. I remember that bunt as being down the third-base line too far from both the third baseman and the catcher.

After both had been to bat twice, Rosen with two hits was at .335570470 and Vernon with one hit was at .336633663.

In the Indians fifth inning, Feller led off and singled. The next batter, Rosen, hit into a fielder's choice with Feller out at second base. In Washington, Bruce Barnes pinch-hit for Stewart and popped up to second, Yost doubled to left, and Runnels singled to center, bringing Vernon to bat. Vernon lined a hit to right, scoring Yost. I remember that perfectly stroked ball, as well.

Three at-bats, two hits for each player, and Rosen was at .335008375 and Vernon at .33726524.

Both players came to bat in the seventh. After Ginsberg flied out to center and Luke Easter struck out, Rosen "singled to the pitcher." This was another questionable hit, but the official scorer gave him one and was at .336120401. In Washington, Vernon led off and lined out to right. and was at .337171053 This is as close as Rosen would get unless he batted and hit safely again.

As both home teams were trailing, the bottom of the ninth would be played. Rosen was seven batters away from hitting again so he needed one Indian to reach base for that to happen. Vernon was the last batter in the seventh and would bat in the ninth if a Senator got on base. Both players were relying on teammates. Rosen needed that last at-bat but Vernon did not.

The Indians went out in order in the eighth; however, there was some theater at Griffith Stadium. The Washington players knew what was at stake and how to act. In the bottom of the eighth inning, Jim Busby grounded out to short and Jerry Snyder hit an easy fly to the center fielder for the second out, bringing light-hitting catcher Mickey Grasso to the plate. He swung and doubled to left! However, as he stood on second, he knew he'd fouled up the "plan" so the Senators players were yelling at him to take a longer lead. Walt Masterson was standing near me waving a towel at Grasso and yelling, "Get off!" Grasso understood the situation and started taking his lead, looking at the ground as it got longer. Coleman took his stretch. He looked at Grasso and paused, then he stepped off the rubber and threw to second, putting Grasso out to end the inning. Grasso had a look of relief when he ran into the dugout. He'd done his job. Vernon would hit fourth in the ninth, if at all.

In the Indians' ninth, Rosen would be the fourth hitter. Owen Friend grounded out, but Aber, leading 7-3, walked the number-eight batter, Joe Ginsberg!! Art Houtteman struck out for the second out, bringing Rosen to bat for the last time in 1953. Rosen hit a groundball to Jerry Priddy at third, a defensive replacement for Ray Boone. Priddy, it is reported, fielded the ball cleanly, took it out of his glove, and appeared to be studying it, maybe checking the league president's name and making sure it was an official American League ball. He then made a soft, looping throw to first that arrived just after Rosen reached the "vicinity" of the bag, but umpire Hank Soar called him out, saying Rosen had "stepped over the bag." There was no argument from Rosen. Game over. I asked Rosen about the call when we met in the late 1980s and he said it was the correct call. Vernon was the leader, but he might have another at-bat.

In the Senators ninth, Kite Thomas batted for Masterson and lined a hit to left fielder Gus Zernial. Recognizing the problem that it caused, Thomas rounded first and kept running. Zernial threw the ball to second baseman Cass Michaels, who was standing on the bag holding the ball and watching Thomas run toward him. Thomas slid early, never actually reaching the bag, and Michaels tagged him out. That was Kite Thomas's last major-league appearance.

The next batter, Senators leadoff hitter Yost, known as the Walking Man for his keen eye and ability to get walks, kept fouling off pitches until he popped up to second on a possible ball four. Yost led the league in walks that year with 123. Two outs.

Runnels then came to bat. He would win two American League batting championships in the ensuing years so he was not an easy out. Vernon was in the on-deck circle, as Runnels fouled off several pitches, then grounded out to second. Game over. Vernon was the batting champion!

Vernon's final average was .337 and Rosen's was .336. The two players were both giants of their times and made hits in the last game to properly challenge the other as neither was content to back into the championship.

The two games had five batting champions playing, Vernon, Runnels, Rosen, Al Kaline, and Harvey Kuenn, and were played before only 3,740 fans in Washington and 9,579 fans in Cleveland. Vernon and Rosen were among 11 players who batted .300 in the eight-team AL that year, as opposed to only 16 (eligible for batting championship) on the 30 major-league teams in 2018. That's an inexplicable decline in batting skill over the years. The average for the AL in 1953 was .264 versus only .248 in both leagues for 2018. The general managers say they don't worry about batting average but only focus on OPS, or On-Base Plus Slugging. If that's the case, note that the AL in 1953 had an OPS of .733 and the OPS in the major leagues was .728 for 2018. Not much of a difference.

Rosen was the American League Most Valuable Player as he led the league in home runs with 43 and RBIs with 145, and dominated other categories. He was trying to win the Triple Crown, but it eluded him. For modern stat fans, his Wins Above Replacement or WAR was 10.1.

Of note for today's game, the game in Washington was played in 2 hours 3 minutes and the game in Cleveland in two hours even. The game in DC had 23 hits, 11 runs, and 11 walks. In Cleveland there were 17 hits, 10 runs, and 5 walks. Today such games would take well over three hours to complete. That's what happens when batters take pitches and swing and miss so much, striking out 41,207 times in 2018.

This was my favorite game at Griffith Stadium and I enjoy sharing that experience with others.

Clark Griffith, the son of former Minnesota Twins owner Calvin Griffith and the great-nephew of former Washington Senators owner Clark C. Griffith, grew up in Washington. He worked for the Twins after graduating from Dartmouth. Griffith served as the Chairman of Major League Properties when it began its marketing/licensing program and was on the Player Relations Committee that developed the player control system that is in force now. Griffith, who lives in Minneapolis, also served as commissioner of the independent Northern League.

ROY SIEVERS KNOCKS IN 7 AS THE SENATORS ROUT THE TIGERS

SEPTEMBER 2, 1954
WASHINGTON SENATORS 16, DETROIT TIGERS 6

by Paul Scimonelli

"BLASTED!" yelled the box score. "Senators Drub Tigers Again, 16-6," lamented the sports page headline of the *Detroit Free Press* on September 3, 1954.[1]

Obviously, the Detroit scribes were miffed that the Tigers were soundly beaten by the Senators the day before, and to make tmatters worse, were swept in a three-game series in September, just as they had been in July. Tigers hurlers were racked for 18 hits in the massacre, three by Roy Sievers and three by All-Star Mickey Vernon. Sievers in particular hustled hard all season to show owner Clark Griffith and manager Bucky Harris that their new faith in him was not unfounded.

"Getting traded to Washington was the best thing that ever happened to me," Sievers said in an interview. "Saved my career!"[2]

And that is exactly what Sievers did in D.C. in 1954.

After a fine 1949 Rookie of the Year season with the St. Louis Browns (.306 BA/16 HR/91 RBIs,) Sievers fell victim to a sophomore slump in 1950, hitting an anemic .238 with 10 homers and 57 RBIs. The slump continued into the 1951 campaign, so much so that he was sent down to the San Antonio Missions of the Texas League for "seasoning." It was there on August 1 that he laid out to catch a low line drive, severely dislocating his right shoulder. Out for the rest of the season, Sievers tried rehabbing on his own, only to dislocate it again in spring training of 1952. Bill Veeck, the Browns new owner, arranged for Sievers to have a very experimental operation to fix the ailing shoulder. He wasn't 100 percent in 1953 but managed a respectable .270 average with 8 homers and 35 RBIs in 92 games, basically hitting with one arm.[3]

Strapped for cash, Veeck was forced to sell the Browns and they moved to Baltimore in 1954. Word of Sievers' busted wing, however, found its way into the hands of Baltimore manager Jimmy Dykes. Considering him "damaged goods," Baltimore traded Sievers to the Senators for Gil Coan. It turned out to be one of Clark Griffith's better trades.[4]

"When I come up to Washington, I asked [manager] Bucky Harris, 'Where am I gonna

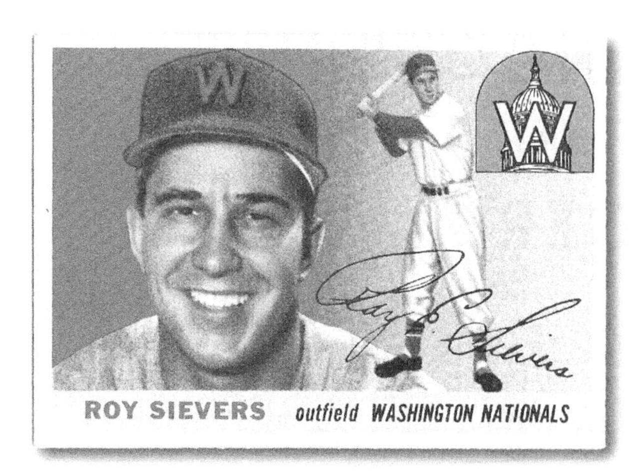

In his six seasons with the Senators (1954-1959), Roy Sievers became one of the American League's most feared home-run hitters, averaging 30 per year. In 1957 he became the first player in major-league history to lead his league in home runs (42) and RBIs (114) while playing for a last-place team. (1955 baseball card courtesy of Topps)

play?' I told him I still couldn't throw too good, so's I couldn't play the outfield. He just said, 'You get rid of the ball quick as you can. I need your bat in the lineup.' So he put me in left field. Back then, I would just kind of loop the ball to the shortstop best as I could."[5]

Nose to the grindstone, Sievers worked diligently to strengthen his arm, under the watchful eye of team doctor George Resta and trainer George "Doc" Lentz. His arm and bat showed great improvement. Playing nearly every game of the 1954 season, Sievers regained most of his power. Although his .232 batting average was subpar by his standards, he still managed 102 RBIs and hit 24 home runs into Griffith Stadium's cavernous 388-foot power alley in left field. He was named Comeback Player of the Year by *The Sporting News*.[6]

On September 2 a meager gathering of 1,260 stalwart Senators fans twirled the Griffith Stadium turnstiles on a balmy, 80-degree Thursday afternoon to watch their Nats make history against the Tigers in the last of a three-game set. If the Senators had a patsy for the year, it was surely the Tigers: They beat Detroit 13 out of their 22 games. Led by veteran two-time AL batting champion Mickey Vernon, Eddie "The Walking Man" Yost, and Sievers, the '54 Senators were a competitive team, despite ending up in sixth place, two games behind the Tigers.

The Senators' Bob Porterfield faced off against the Tigers' Ned Garver. Garver had his career year in 1951, going 20-12 for the hapless St. Louis Browns, where he teamed up with a very young Roy Sievers. Porterfield was coming off of a 22-10 season for the 1953 Senators.

The Tigers struck in the first inning. After Harvey Kuenn flied out, Fred Hatfield and Bob Nieman singled off Porterfield and Ray Boone's fly ball scored Hatfield.

In the bottom of the inning, Yost drew a leadoff walk. Jim Busby flied out, then Vernon singled Yost to third. Sievers, hurting his former Browns teammate Garver, doubled Vernon and Yost home.

With his hit, Vernon became the 95th major leaguer and the ninth Senator with 2,000 hits, joining Joe Cronin, Joe Judge, Joe Kuhel, Heinie Manush, Clyde Milan, Sam Rice, Goose Goslin, and Ed Delahanty.[7] Vernon finished 1954 with career highs in homers (20) and RBIs (97), and led the league with 33 doubles.

The second inning and the top of the third were harmless for Garver and Porterfield. The Senators half of the third was massive. After Yost and Busby singled, Vernon walked to fill the bases. Sievers' double to center field cleared the bases and chased his pal Garver off the mound. Reliever Billy Hoeft fared no better, giving up a triple to Jim Lemon, scoring Sievers, and a double to Ed Fitz Gerald, scoring Lemon, before retiring the side with the Senators ahead 7-1.

The Tigers got two back in the top of the fourth with a triple by Chick King and a single by Hoeft. The Nats responded in kind in the bottom of the inning. Busby led off with his seventh homer of the year and Vernon singled. Sievers chased Hoeft with his 23rd home run of the season. Reliever Dick Marlowe gave up three hits and another run before retiring the side. The Senators were up 11-3.

Sievers' home run broke the team home run record of 22, set by Zeke Bonura in 1938.

Other than Fred Hatfield's single, the fifth inning was pretty much three up-three down for both sides. The Tigers plated a run in the sixth, making the score 11-4. In the bottom of the seventh, Yost singled Jerry Snyder home from second. Jim Busby reached on an error and Mickey Vernon cleared the bases with his 19th homer of the season, setting a team record for left-handed hitters, besting the likes of Goose Goslin, Stan Spence and Eddie Robinson. The Senators now led 15-4.

The Tigers went quietly in the eighth. The Senators plated one more in the eighth when Jerry Snyder singled to score Fitz Gerald. Porterfield gave up four hits and two runs in the top of the ninth, but finished the Senators' 16-6 victory. Sievers ended his day with three hits, seven RBIs, and eight total bases.[8]

Sievers eventually set franchise home-run records in 1954 (24); 1955 (25); 1956 (29); and 1957 (42.) In 1957 he became the first player on a last-place team to lead the league in home runs, and had 114 RBIs and 331 total bases. He hit 39 homers in 1958 and 21 in 1959. In so doing, he set a Senators home-run record with 180, a figure that was bested by Frank Howard's 237 during his years with the expansion Senators.[9]

From 1954 through 1959, Sievers' prodigious home runs made him the Senatotrs' biggest gate attraction since Walter Johnson, increased attendance by over 40 percent, and forced the forever parsimonious Calvin Griffith to rethink a proposed move to Los Angeles or Minnesota in 1957.

A five-time All-Star, Sievers ended his 17-year career with a .267 batting average, 1,703 hits, 318 home runs and 1,147 RBIs. He was only one of five players to hit pinch-hit grand slams in both leagues. (He had 10 grand slams in all.)

Mickey Vernon won a World Series ring as a player-coach for the Pittsburgh Pirates in 1960. A seven-time All-Star, he ended his 20-year career with a .286 batting average, 2,495 hits, 172 home runs and 1,311 RBIs. The two-time AL batting champion (1946, 1953) was the first manager of the expansion Washington Senators (1961-1963).

SOURCES

In addition to the sources cited in the Notes, the author accessed Retrosheet.org, Baseball-Reference.com, Newspapers.com, and SABR.org.

NOTES

1 Hal Middlesworth, "Senators Drub Tigers Again, 16-6," *Detroit Free Press*, September 3, 1954: 24.

2 Author interviews with Roy Sievers, by phone and in person, between 2014 and 2016.

3 Data compiled from Paul Scimonelli, *Roy Sievers: "The Sweetest Right-Handed Swing" in 1950s Baseball* (Jefferson, North Carolina, McFarland Inc. 2017).

4 Ibid.

5 Author interviews with Roy Sievers.

6 Bob Burns, "Highlights and Low Spots of '54 Season," *The Sporting News*, October 6, 1954: 12.

7 Bob Addie, "Nats Pound Tigers 16-6; Vernon hits '2000' Goal," *Washington Post*, September 3, 1954: 31.

8 Game details from baseball-reference.com/boxes/WS1/WS1195409020.shtml, *Detroit News*, *Detroit Free Press*, *Washington Post* and *Washington Evening Star*.

9 Sievers was traded to the White Sox in 1960 and also played for the Phillies. The Senators reacquired him in 1964 and he hit four more home runs, making his total with the team 184.

THE SENATORS INTEGRATE

SEPTEMBER 6, 1954
WASHINGTON SENATORS 8, PHILADELPHIA ATHLETICS 1
(FIRST GAME OF DOUBLEHEADER)

by Paul E. Doutrich

The game appeared to be merely the first in a meaningless, end-of-the-season doubleheader between two teams that many weeks earlier had been eliminated from the 1954 pennant race. The sixth-place Washington Senators trailed the league-leading Cleveland Indians by 39 games and the Philadelphia Athletics were even further out of contention: 51½ games back. However, as the Senators took the field the tiny crowd of 4,865 immediately recognized the significance of the game. Trotting out to left field was Carlos Paula, who was about to become the first Black ballplayer to play for the Senators. Seven years after Jackie Robinson had broken the color barrier in baseball, the Senators on this day became the 12th franchise to do the same.

Paula's appearance in a Senators uniform was the end of a long journey for team owner Clark Griffith. For three decades he had eagerly signed black Cuban players to professional contracts but staunchly opposed allowing them to play major-league baseball. Through the years he had offered numerous rationalizations intended to keep baseball segregated. He argued that black players would be subjected to vicious racist epitaphs and that mixing black and white fans would lead to violence.[1] He also warned that integrating baseball would kill the Negro Leagues, thus significantly reducing the number of African-Americans playing professional baseball. Instead, a vibrant, profitable Negro League would be better for African-Americans.[2]

Underlying Griffith's opposition were concerns about his own revenues. Griffith Stadium was very accessible for the local black community. For years Griffith had leased his ballpark to Negro League teams. He had a particularly profitable relationship with Cum Posey and the Homestead Grays.[3] However, by 1954 Griffith recognized that the Negro Leagues were rapidly losing their viability. He calculated that his long-term revenue interests would be better served by including black players on the Senators roster.

A product of the Cuban leagues, Paula was one of more than three dozen Cubans signed to a Senators contract by legendary scout Joe Cambria. The young Cuban first worked out for Cambria in 1951. By the following spring he was

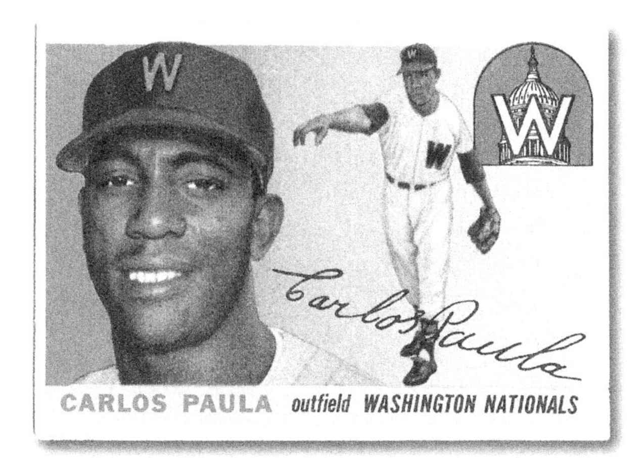

One of more than three dozen Cubans signed to a Senators contract by legendary scout Joe Cambria, Havana-born Carlos Paula was the first Black ballplayer to play in a regular-season game for the Senators. (1955 baseball card courtesy of Topps)

playing in the Senators farm system. Success with the Decatur Commodores in the Mississippi-Ohio Valley League and the Paris Indians in the Big State League brought Paula to the attention of key figures in the Senators organization. By 1954 he was one of two Cubans (Angel Scull was the other) whom many expected to be the first black Senator.

Senators manager Bucky Harris watched Paula intently during spring training in 1954. "He can whack that ball," Harris said. "He has size and gets some beautiful extra leverage to his swing. And he isn't fast simply for a big man. He's fast for a man of any size."[4] Paula had been one of the Senators' last spring-training cuts. Assigning him to Charlotte in the South Atlantic League, Harris wanted him to work on a hitch in his swing and to develop more discipline at the plate. It was his power that particularly impressed Harris. On a team in need of more punch, the big Cuban, who was "the rawest of rookies, but obviously a brute for muscle," might potentially fill a team void.[5]

The day's first game started quietly. In the first inning both teams put a runner on base via a walk but neither was able to do more than that. Philadelphia went in order in the second. Paula led off the second for the Senators. At the plate, he was an imposing figure, 6-feet-3 and "built like a blacksmith."[6] In his first major-league at-bat, he struck out. Then his teammates used two singles and a sacrifice to push across the game's first run.

Two innings later, Paula helped the Senators break the game open. With two outs and a runner on first, the top of the Washington order strung together two singles, a walk, and a three-run triple by first baseman Mickey Vernon. Pete Runnels followed Vernon with a walk, putting runners on first and third for Paula. The Senators first African-American player scorched a double to left-center field, scoring both runners. Paula's first major-league hit also drove the Athletics pitcher, Arnie Portocarrero, from the mound. He was replaced by Marion Fricano, who struck out right-fielder Jim Lemon to end the inning.

Neither team was able to score during the next three innings. The Senators were limited to an infield single and a walk in the fifth. In the sixth Paula collected his second hit, a bases-empty, two-out single to center. Meanwhile the Washington pitcher, Johnny Schmitz, dominated the Athletics, retiring all nine hitters he faced.

In search of his 10th win, Schmitz came into the game with an impressive 2.81 ERA. The 1954 season was a comeback season in many ways for Schmitz. After returning from a stint in the Navy from August 1942 until January 1946, he had been a reliable starting pitcher with an impressive ERA through the 1950 season. Twice during those years, he had been selected to the American League All-Star team. However, the previous three seasons had been a different story. He had some arm problems, his ERA jumped by more than a run per game, he had won a total of only seven games and had been bounced around from team to team through trades. The 1954 season offered a restart for Schmitz. With his ERA back below 3.00, he settled in as one of the Senators' regular starting pitchers. Reaching the 10-win plateau became a notable milestone in Schmitz's comeback journey.

The Athletics finally got to Schmitz in the eighth. Right fielder Joe Taylor walked to open the inning and went to third on a single by Eddie Joost.

One out later Lou Limmer, pinch-hitting for relief pitcher Fricano, lifted a fly to Paula in left field, scoring Taylor. After another walk, Philadelphia's half of the inning ended on a fly ball to Lemon in right field. Schmitz's shutout was gone but his quest for win number 10 was still very much alive.

In the bottom of the inning, the Senators got the run back plus interest. With one out, the new Philadelphia pitcher, Sonny Dixon, walked Tom Umphlett, who had come into the game in the seventh as a defensive replacement for Jim Busby in center field. Mickey Vernon followed with his 20th and last home run of the season. The reigning American League batting champion, Vernon was not known for his power. This season was the only one in which he reached the 20-home-run level.

The ninth inning was another three-up three-down inning for Schmitz. Allowing only three hits and one run, he had one of his better performances of the season.

Despite a 3-2 loss in the second game, for the Senators and several of the team's players, the day was a success. For Johnny Schmitz it was his 10th victory and seemed to confirm his comeback. Mickey Vernon would remember the day because he hit his 20th home run of the season. But far more important was the debut of Carlos Paula in left field. With him in the lineup, the Senators entered a new era in the team's history, becoming the 12th major-league team to open a door to African-American players.

SOURCES

In addition to the sources cited in the Notes, the author accessed Retrosheet.org, Baseball-Reference.com, Newspapers.com, and SABR.org.

NOTES

1. Neil Lanctot, *Negro League Baseball: The Rise and Ruin of a Black Institution* (Philadelphia: University of Pennsylvania Press, 1996), 220.
2. Lanctot, 234.
3. Lanctot, 249, 267.
4. "Harris High on Ex-Paris Indian Paula," *Paris* (Texas) *News*, March 17, 1954: 9.
5. Red Smith, "Views of Sport," *Rocky Mount* (North Carolina) *Telegram*, March 14 1954: 32.
6. "Cuban Rookies May Crack Sen's Roster," *Daily Independent* (Kannapolis, North Carolina), March 12, 1954: 5.

A TALE OF THE KID AND THE MAN AND THE SAY HEY KID AND THE COMMERCE COMET

JULY 10, 1956
NATIONAL LEAGUE 7, AMERICAN LEAGUE 3

MAJOR LEAGUE ALL-STAR GAME

by Alan Cohen

Griffith Stadium played host to the 23rd All-Star Game on July 10, 1956. A sellout crowd of 28,843 saw the National League win its sixth decision in the past seven encounters, 7-3. The overflow crowd filled the seats behind the center-field wall, creating a bad background for the batters, and there were 17 strikeouts in the game. Nevertheless, the game lived up to its billing with home runs being hit by four of the greatest players in the history of the game.

Casey Stengel and Walter Alston led their charges. It was Alston's second turn as manager. He had managed in 1954 after the Dodgers won the NL pennant in 1953. Stengel was no stranger to the leadership role, having already led the AL five times.

Each team had a veteran presence. Ted Williams, selected to his 13th All-Star Game, manned left field for the American League, and St. Louis's popular Stan Musial, also in his 13th trip to the event, started the game in right field for the NL.

Pittsburgh's Bob Friend started on the mound for the National League and stymied the opposition in his three innings. Speaking of his success that day, he said he "had a real good fast ball but didn't use it often on account of their left-handers." He "threw mostly breaking stuff, except when I struck out Mickey Mantle on a fast one."[1] According to Harold Kaese of the *Boston Globe*, Friend threw nine curves and two knuckleballs as Ted Williams struck out and grounded out.[2]

The winners were sparked by the fine defensive play of third baseman Ken Boyer of St. Louis. Boyer, in only his second year in the National League, was playing in his first All-Star Game, and it didn't take him long to start making an impression. In the bottom of the first inning, diving to his left, he grabbed a line drive off the bat of leadoff batter Harvey Kuenn of the Detroit Tigers. It was the beginning of a great day for Boyer.

The starting pitcher for the American League was Billy Pierce of the Chicago White Sox, and he, like Friend, performed well, striking out five batters in his three innings on the mound. He struck out the Redlegs' rookie sensation Frank Robinson twice. However, the National League was able to manufacture a run in the third inning.

After leading the NL with a 2.83 ERA in 1955, the Pittsburgh Pirates Bob Friend started the 1956 All-Star Game at Griffith Stadium. He led the NL with 22 wins in 1958, helped the Bucs to the World Series title in 1960, and posted a 197-230 slate in parts of 16 seasons (1951-1966). (1957 baseball card courtesy of Topps)

Roy McMillan of Cincinnati walked, was sacrificed to second by Friend, and came home on a single by Johnny Temple.

The fans' votes determined the starters and the Redlegs were represented by five players from their league-leading lineup. Robinson was in left field, McMillan and Temple patrolled the middle infield, Ed Bailey was behind the plate, and Gus Bell was the center fielder. Also representing the Redlegs was substitute first baseman Ted Kluszewski. Cincinnati manager Birdie Tebbetts served as one of Alston's coaches.

In the top of the fourth inning, Yankees lefty Whitey Ford came on to pitch. He fanned Musial and then was greeted by Boyer's single. Bell, a left-handed batter, was due up, and manager Alston elected to go to his bench for a right-handed hitter. Pinch-hitter Willie Mays, after swinging through the first pitch, deposited Ford's second pitch into the seats in left-center field, putting his team in front 3-0. After the game, Alston said, "Mays's pinch homer was the turning point. It gave us a comfortable lead and put them on the defensive. After that it was just a matter of getting good pitching from everybody."[3]

The NL extended its lead to 5-0 with runs in the fifth and sixth innings. In the fifth, after righty Jim Wilson had replaced Ford on the mound, Temple led off with a bunt single down the third-base line, took second on a comebacker by Musial, and scored on the third of Boyer's three singles. An inning later, Tom Brewer was on the mound for the AL and was greeted by Kluszewski, pinch-hitting for the NL's starting first baseman, Dale Long. Kluszewski launched the first of his two doubles, went to third when Cincinnati teammate McMillan hit a bloop single to right field, and scored when Brewer uncorked a wild pitch. During his at-bat, Kluszewski fouled a ball off catcher Yogi Berra's right hand. After the side was retired, Berra returned to the dugout and showed his bruised hand to manager Stengel. Yogi's day was over.[4]

In the bottom of the fifth, Boyer, having already made a great defensive play and gone 3-for-3 at the plate, added to his résumé. With two out, Harvey Kuenn scorched a groundball down the third-base line destined for the left-field corner. Diving to his right, Boyer grabbed the ball and threw to first for the inning-ending out.

The AL did all of its scoring in the sixth inning, victimizing Warren Spahn. The Milwaukee ace was the second pitcher to hurl in the game for the National League. He entered the game in the fourth inning. Nellie Fox of the White Sox singled to center off Spahn to open the sixth and two loud swings later, the AL had three runs. Williams sent a towering blast to right, making the score 5-2. Next up was Mickey Mantle of the Yankees. Playing on a bad knee and fighting the glare from the shirts in the center-field bleachers, he had struck out in his first two at-bats. This time, he homered off Spahn for the AL's third run.

The AL got no closer. Manager Alston called on Johnny Antonelli and the Giants' ace extinguished the fire, but not without some drama. Sherman Lollar batted for Berra and singled to center field and Detroit's Al Kaline singled to left. With the tying runs on base and none out, Stengel sent up Vic Power to bat for Mickey Vernon, but Power hit a short fly ball to Musial in left field. Then Cincinnati's tandem of McMillan and Temple converted George Kell's grounder into a 6-4-3 double play, the only DP of the game, to end the threat. Temple, in throwing to first, leapt high to elude the spikes of the hard-sliding Kaline.

Infielders Temple, McMillan, and Boyer were performing so well defensively that manager Alston left them in for the entire game. Reserve infielders Junior Gilliam, Ernie Banks, and Eddie Matthews didn't see action.

The NL, which scored in each inning after breaking the ice in the third, was not about to take its foot off the accelerator, especially with its lead cut to two runs. In the bottom of the seventh inning, after Tom Brewer had struck out Duke Snider, the voice on the press-box loudspeaker announced: "The home run by Ted Williams in the previous inning ties Stan Musial's record for All-Star Games. They now have four apiece."[5] Musial stepped in. He took his distinctive stance at the plate, looking over his right shoulder toward the mound. Brewer, a left-hander, threw a pitch that was moving away from the lefty swinging Musial. Musial sent the pitch toward left-center field and it cleared the fence, extending his team's lead to 6-3. The voice on the loudspeaker came on once again: "Cancel the previous announcement. Musial just took his record back."[6] (Musial extended his record to six with a homer in 1960's second game.)

Willie Mays walked with two outs. Kluszewski hit his second double in as many at-bats and Mays, who was running on the play, didn't stop running. His 270-foot scamper resulted in his team's seventh run, and to nobody's great surprise as related to his readers by Tommy Holmes, "Willie sailed out from under his cap as he slid across the plate."[7]

Boyer, whose perfect day at the plate ended when he grounded out for the second out of the seventh inning, was back to flashing his glove in the bottom of the inning. Detroit's Ray Boone, pinch-hitting for Brewer, sent a liner to third base that was grabbed by the leaping Cardinals third baseman.

Williams began the bottom half of the inning hitting against the shift and launching a fly ball to short left field. Musial charged and caught the ball, colliding with Boyer in the process. Stan came up grabbing his thigh and Alston, choosing to err on the side of the caution, removed his left fielder from the game. Milwaukee's Henry Aaron took over in left field. In his only at-bat, he flied to right field.

In the bottom of the ninth, with one out, Vic Power legged out an infield single. George Kell's single to right field was corralled by Mays, who launched a perfect throw to third base, keeping the runners at first and second.[8] Antonelli got the final two outs and the NL had the win.

SOURCES

In addition to Baseball-Reference.com and the sources shown in the notes, the author used the following:

Bowen, George. "Boyer Is Standout for National Nine," *Bergen* (New Jersey) *Evening Record*, July 11, 1956: 30.

Considine, Bob. "Nationals Tip Americans in All-Star Game, 7-3," *Arizona Republic* (Phoenix), July 11, 1956: 24.

Drebinger, John. "National League Beats American as Mays and Musial Set Pace with Homers," *New York Times*, July 11, 1956: 22.

Lee, Bill. "With Malice Towards None," *Hartford Courant*, July 11, 1956: 17.

NOTES

1 Associated Press, "Walt Alston Picks Boyer as Game's Top Performer," *Hartford Courant*, July 10, 1956: 17.

2 Harold Kaese, "Friend Dazzles Ted , Who Plans 1957 Play," *Boston Globe*, July 11, 1956: 11.

3 Joe Reichler (Associated Press), "Mgr. Walt Alston Praises Redlegs," *Bergen Evening Record*, July 11, 1956: 30.

4 Louis Effrat, "Berra Joins List of injured Stars," *New York Times*, July 11, 1956: 22.

5 Arthur Daley, "Sports of the Times: Sprinkled with Stardust," *New York Times*, July 11, 1956: 23.

6 Ibid.

7 Tommy Holmes, "NL Pitching Halts AL Stars Again, 7-3," *Boston Globe*, July 11, 1956: 11.

8 Gerry de la Ree, "For the Record," *Bergen Evening Record*, July 11, 1956: 30.

JIM LEMON FIRST SENATOR TO HIT THREE HRS IN A GAME AT GRIFFITH STADIUM

AUGUST 31, 1956
NEW YORK YANKEES 6, WASHINGTON SENATORS 4

by Don Zminda

For most of its 51-year history (1911-1961), Washington's Griffith Stadium was considered one of the toughest parks in the major leagues to hit a home run in — if not *the* toughest. To cite one example: In 1924, the year the hometown Senators won their only World Series championship during the club's 60 years in Washington, only eight home runs were hit at Griffith Stadium during the regular season – just one by a Senators player. Entering the 1956 season, the Senators' single-season individual home-run record was a measly 25, by Roy Sievers in 1955 – and Sievers had hit only seven of those 25 home runs at home. Over that 45-year period, only one player had ever had at three-homer game at Griffith: Joe DiMaggio of the visiting New York Yankees, who belted three four-baggers against the Senators on September 10, 1950.

But in October of 1955, Clark Griffith, the Senators' longtime owner, died, and Griffith's nephew Calvin took control of the franchise. "After taking over the team upon the death of his uncle," wrote Gregory H. Wolf, "the cash-strapped owner wanted to sell more tickets by generating more offense. Consequently, the left-field foul pole was reduced from 388 feet to 350 feet..."[1] Said Griffith: "We don't have to apologize for the fact that our distance to left field is only 350 feet. It is still the longest left field in the American League with the exception of Chicago, which is only two feet longer."[2] Righty slugger Sievers, who had hit 24 homers for the Senators in 1954 prior to his (then) record 25 in 1955, was expected to be the main beneficiary of the cozier Griffith Stadium dimensions. But in 1956 Sievers was joined by a powerful right-handed hitter who had spent most of the '55 season in the minor leagues: 6-foot-4 outfielder Jim Lemon.

A Covington, Virginia, native who had begun his professional baseball career as a member of the Cleveland Indians organization in 1947, Lemon had made his major-league debut with the Indians in 1950 but batted just .176 (6-for-34). After spending 1951-52 in the military, Lemon struggled once more in brief action with the Indians in 1953, hitting .174 (8-for-46). He was sold to the Senators in 1954, but entering the 1956 season, had played only 47

An overlooked slugger, Jim Lemon averaged 28 home runs per season over a five-year stretch (1956-1960), finishing third in the AL twice, including with a career-best 38 in 1960. He later managed the second incarnation of the Senators for one season, 1968. (1957 baseball card courtesy of Topps)

games in a Washington uniform, with just three home runs. Lemon made the Senators' Opening Day roster and got off to a hot start, hitting .351 in April. He struck out frequently – his 138 strikeouts in 1956 set a major-league record for the time – but he was also finding the fences. Entering the games of August 31, Lemon's 23 home runs were only three behind Sievers for the team lead, and were tied for fifth-most in the American League.

That night the Senators hosted the New York Yankees, but neither Sievers nor Lemon was the main attraction. The Yankees' Mickey Mantle was mounting a serious challenge to Babe Ruth's single-season home-run record of 60; with 46 homers so far, Mantle was slightly ahead of Ruth's home-run pace in 1927. Mantle and the Yankees drew a crowd of 15,525 to Griffith Stadium for the game, in a year in which the Senators drew a major-league low 431,647 to their home games. It would be Washington's fourth biggest home crowd of the season (the Senators' top six home crowds in 1956 would all be for games against the Yankees).

One of the August 31 attendees was President Dwight D. Eisenhower. A ballplayer during his youth at Abilene (Kansas) High School and West Point, Eisenhower would throw out the first pitch at the Senators' home opener during all but one of the eight years during his presidency. However, the August 31 game was one of the few games attended by the president during his terms of office that was not a special occasion like a World Series game or a Senators' home opener. He made no secret of the fact that he was there to see Mantle. Eisenhower shook hands and posed for pictures with the Yankees slugger before the game. "I hope you hit a home run," he told Mantle. "But I also hope Washington wins."[3]

The game featured a pitching matchup between Yankees left-hander Whitey Ford, a future Hall of Famer having one of the best seasons of his career (19-6 with a league-leading 2.47 ERA) and the Senators Camilo Pascual, a 22-year-old righty who struggled in 1956 (6-18, 5.87) but would go on to win 174 major-league games. The Yankees got to Pascual for five hits (all singles) and three runs in the top of the second, but in the bottom half Lemon homered off Ford into the center-field bleachers. The Yankees got the run back in the third when Mantle walked and Bill Skowron drove him home with a double, but in the fourth Lemon struck again, homering into the new seats in the shortened left field to score behind Roy Sievers, who had walked. Then in the sixth, Lemon became the first Senators player to homer three times in a Washington home game (Goose Goslin had hit three homers in a game at Cleveland's League Park, then known as Dunn Field, in 1925) with another blast off Ford, this one into the Yankees' bullpen in left.

Lemon's third homer tied the game, 4-4, but in the Yankees' next at-bat, Mantle broke the tie – and fulfilled one of Eisenhower's wishes – with "a shot over the high right field wall."[4] It was Mantle's fifth home run off Pascual during the 1956 season; over his career, Mantle would hit 11 homers off Pascual, his third-most off any pitcher behind Early Wynn (13) and Pedro Ramos (12).

The Yankees made it 6-4 with another run in the top of the eighth. Then, in the bottom of the frame, Lemon came to the plate with a chance to become the third player in American League history to hit four homers in a game; Lou Gehrig in 1932 and Pat Seerey (in an 11-inning game) in 1948 were the first two. Lemon had a chance to tie the game with another homer, as Pete Runnels was on first base after singling. However, Yankees manager Casey Stengel took no chances with having Ford face Lemon for a fourth time; he brought in right-hander Tom Morgan to pitch to the Senators' slugger. That may have been a wise move, as Lemon would homer seven times off Ford over the course of his career – the most by Lemon off any major-league pitcher, and the most allowed by Ford to any hitter. To the disappointment of Eisenhower and the Griffith Stadium crowd, Lemon went down on strikes against the Yankees righty. Morgan allowed a single to Karl Olson, the next hitter, but set down the final four Senators hitters to save Ford's 15th victory of the year.

"I hit four in the All-Star Game in the Southern Association in 1955," Lemon remarked later, "but no one ever asks me about that. If they did I wouldn't even be able to tell who I hit them off, though I do remember that it involved four different pitchers and that two were right-handers. But those homers I hit off Ford: I must have answered the question 'What kind of pitches did you hit?' a thousand times. The first was a slow curve, the second a fast curve, the third was a fastball."[5] He would also tell a reporter that "At least a dozen guys have claimed they caught two of the homers."[6]

After the game Eisenhower called Lemon to his box to shake hands. "It was a beaming President Eisenhower who seemed to enjoy every minute of tonight's encounter," wrote John Drebinger. "He rose and led the applause after each of the four homers."[7]

Despite the loss, it was a night that Jim Lemon and Senators fans would never forget. Lemon went on to hit 144 homers in a Washington Senators uniform, second-most for a player during the team's 60 years in the nation's capital behind Roy Sievers' 180.

SOURCES

Boxscore and play-by-play at retrosheet.org/boxesetc/1956/B08310WS11956.htm; accessed 9-28-2018.

"Mickey Hits Homer for Ike, But Lemon Steals the Show," The Sporting News, September 12, 1956: 5.

"President Dwight D. Eisenhower Baseball Game Attendance Log," baseball-almanac.com/prz_cde.shtml; accessed 9-29-2018.

Baseball-Reference.com.

NOTES

1 Gregory H. Wolf, Jim Lemon SABR BioProject biography, sabr.org/bioproj/person/65d8e14b; accessed 9-28-2018.

2 Shirley Povich, "Nats' Shortened Left Field Fence Seen as Gate Aid," *The Sporting News*, December 7, 1955: 4.

3 John Drebinger, "Eisenhower Sees Senators Bow, 6-4," *New York Times*, September 1, 1956: 26.

4 Ibid.

5 Bruce Jacobs, *Baseball Stars of 1957* (New York: Lion Library Editions, 1957), 103.

6 Richard Goldstein, "Jim Lemon, 78, Outfielder, Is Dead; Earned Visit with Eisenhower," *New York Times*, May 17, 2006.

7 Drebinger.

SIEVERS BLASTS SENATORS TO WIN AT END OF LONG HOT AFTERNOON

AUGUST 3, 1957
WASHINGTON SENATORS 4, DETROIT TIGERS 3
(17 INNINGS)

by Alan Cohen

Roy Sievers was the slugging star as the Washington Senators edged the Detroit Tigers 4-3 in a 1957 season-long 17 innings that consumed 4 hours and 24 minutes. His 30th homer of the season, off Detroit's Al Aber in the game's final inning, was the margin of victory, and it was the record-tying sixth consecutive game in which Sievers had homered.[1] The blast tied Sievers for the league home-run lead with Ted Williams, and moved him one ahead of the Yankees Mickey Mantle. Not many of the announced crowd of 7,232 (4,601 paid) were around for the finish, having sought cooler surroundings on a Saturday afternoon when the game-time temperature was 98 degrees.

Billy Hoeft (3-6) started the game on the mound for the Tigers and yielded two first-inning runs to the homestanding Senators. After Bob Usher doubled and Sievers walked, an errant pick-off throw to second by Hoeft went into center field and advanced the runners to second and third. They both scored on a single by Art Schult.

The Tigers broke into the scoring column in the sixth inning. After Frank Bolling flied to center field, Al Kaline hit his seventh homer of the season, off Washington starter Russ Kemmerer. In the next inning, Detroit rallied to tie the game and send Kemmerer to the showers. Red Wilson singled, and went to third on a single by Charlie Maxwell, pinch-hitting for third baseman Jim Finigan. Wilson scored when Hoeft helped his cause with a sacrifice fly. Maxwell, who had injured his arm on July 26 against the Yankees, was making his first appearance in eight games. After a single by Harvey Kuenn, Kemmerer's day was over. Tex Clevenger replaced him and silenced the Tigers bats. He pitched through the ninth inning. Maxwell stayed in the game, replacing Dave Philley in left field, and bonus baby Steve Boros took over at third for the departed Finigan.

Hoeft, who had pitched a complete game in a 15-inning loss against the Yankees the prior Sunday, came out of the game in the eighth inning. With runners on first and third, he was replaced by Duke Maas, who hit pinch-hitter Clint Courtney to load the bases. On the subsequent two plays, grounders to third by Jim Lemon and Sievers, runners were forced out at home. With two out, Detroit manager Jack Tighe summoned Lou Sleater, who retired Julio Becquer on a grounder.

In the bottom of the ninth inning, Milt Bolling doubled and Rocky Bridges was given an intentional pass. Clevenger was due up. Manager Cookie Lavagetto inserted Jerry Snyder as a pinch-hitter and Tigers manager Tighe countered with a pitching change, bringing in right-hander Harry Byrd. Lavagetto's response was to send up Pete Runnels, a lefty hitter, to face Byrd. Byrd retired Runnels and then Eddie Yost, and the game remained tied at 2-2 through the ninth. In the 10th Bud Byerly took over the mound chores for Washington.

In the 14th inning, Washington mounted a threat. Ed Fitz Gerald led off with a double to right field. Pedro Ramos ran for him and this turned out to be an ill-advised move. Milt Bolling sent a fly ball to deep center field that was corralled by Bill Tuttle. Ramos, mistakenly playing it halfway, scurried back to second and tagged up. He was out easily at third, the tag being applied by Boros. The potential winning run went back to the dugout and Bridges' fly ball to deep center field was just that, a deep flyball with the bases empty to end the inning.

Washington's Byerly and Detroit's Byrd were in command from the 10th through the 15th. In the bottom of the 15th Byerly left the game for a pinch-hitter, Herb Plews, but the Senators came up empty. Dick Hyde came in to pitch for Washington in the 16th inning and the Tigers broke through for a run. Leading off the inning, Boros singled and was sacrificed to second by Wilson. A single by Johnny Groth scored Boros, and Groth took second on the throw home. Tigers manager Tighe, although there was a runner in scoring position, let Byrd bat for himself and the pitcher grounded out. Hyde then retired Ron Samford, stranding Groth at second base.

Byrd, who had taken over the pitching chores in the ninth inning with two on and one out, kept Washington from scoring in the next six innings. His fortunes changed in Washington's half of the 16th inning. The Senators quickly tied the score. Sievers, who had been hitless in his first six plate appearances (he had one walk), singled and was bunted to second base by Becquer. Al Aber came in to pitch for Detroit, their fifth hurler of the game, and yielded a single to lefty-batting Lou Berberet that went past Tigers first baseman Ray Boone. Sievers scored the tying run. The Senators loaded the bases, but Aber worked his way out of the jam, striking out Eddie Yost for the third out of the inning, and the game moved into the 17th inning.

Having removed Hyde for pinch-hitter Jerry Schoonmaker in the 16th, Lavagetto called on right-handed side-arm hurler Ted Abernathy to pitch the 17th inning. He quickly dispensed of the Tigers. Aber returned to the mound for Detroit and retired the first two Washington batters. Faye Throneberry flied out and Jim Lemon, who didn't get the ball out of the infield all day, grounded out. Sievers, batting for the eighth time in the marathon, looked at ball one then homered for the 4-3 win.

The victory brought the 24-year-old Abernathy's record to 2-9. (He finished the season at 2-10.) Over the years his side-arm motion evolved into a submarine motion and he had much success after turning 30. From 1963 through 1972, he worked exclusively from the bullpen. He was 55-47 with an ERA of 2.77 and had 149 saves.

Aber took the loss, his record falling to 2-3. Later in August, he was put on waivers and claimed by Kansas City, with whom he made his last three major-league appearances in September.

With the win, the Senators, for the time being, remained out of the cellar. Over the season, they would continue to fight the Kansas City Athletics for the dubious honor of being the worst team in the league. At the end of the season Washington was once again first in war, first in peace, and last in the American League, despite a managerial change 20 games into the season when Lavagetto replaced Chuck Dressen. They were five games behind the seventh-place A's and 43 games, eight seasons, and 1,100 miles removed from first place.

The loss put the Tigers one game below .500. They were in fourth place, 17 games behind the league-leading Yankees. They remained in fourth

Third-base grandstand at Griffith Stadium in 1958. The park was almost devoid of advertisements save for the iconic National Bohemian signs in the outfield. (Photo courtesy of Robert E. Wilson)

place for the balance of a very disappointing season, finishing with a 78-76 record.

Charlie Maxwell, after pinch-hitting in the seventh inning and being a part of the game-tying rally, stayed in the game as the left fielder. He singled in the ninth inning but, still nursing a bad arm, was replaced by pinch-runner Johnny Groth. The injury was unfortunate for the Tigers as Maxwell had enjoyed success at Griffith Stadium, hitting three homers there in 1957. Before Kaline's sixth-inning blast, those three had constituted all of Detroit's homer power in Washington that season.

Detroit's Harvey Kuenn was given the rest of the game off after popping out in the ninth inning. He had singled in the fifth and seventh innings but his batting average was only .255, well off the pace of his prior four seasons. He was replaced at shortstop by Ron Samford. Manager Jack Tighe felt that Kuenn's range at shortstop was limited and had, for a brief time in July, moved Kuenn to third base. The following season, Kuenn was moved to center field.

Kuenn had been up early on August 3 to visit young Christopher Mills at Montgomery County General Hospital in Olney, Maryland, 20 miles north of Washington. The Detroit area lad had been visiting relatives in Maryland when he lost his right leg in a tractor accident. The boy's favorite players, Kuenn and Jim Bunning, came by and brightened his day.

Sievers not only tied for the league lead in homers on August 3, but also set a new home-run record for the Senators, bettering his mark of 29, set the prior season. He was on a home-run binge, having homered in 10 of 17 games. His home-run streak would end at six consecutive games. This 1957 season was his best in the majors. He batted .301 and led the American League in homers (42) RBIs (114), extra-base hits (70), and total bases (331). He finished third in MVP balloting although his team, as so often was the case in those years, finished last in the league.

SOURCES

In addition to Baseball-Reference.com, the author used the following:

Falls, Joe. "Sievers' Record Blast Beats Tigers in 17th," *Detroit Times*, August 4, 1957: 4-1

Hawkins, Burton. "Sievers' 30th Homer in 17th Nips Tigers, 4-3, and Ties AL Record," *Washington Sunday Star,* August 4, 1957: C-1

Middlesworth, Hal. "Sievers' Homer Trips Tigers, 4-3," *Detroit Free Press*, August 4, 1957: E-1.

Middlesworth, Hal. "Tagging the Tigers," *Detroit Free Press*, August 4, 1957: E-3.

NOTES

1 By homering in his sixth consecutive game, Sievers tied for the American League record shared by Lou Gehrig and Ken Williams.

KILLEBREW'S TWO HOMERS AND FIVE RBIS "KILL" TIGERS

MAY 12, 1959
WASHINGTON SENATORS 7, DETROIT TIGERS 4

by Paul Hofmann

The surprising Senators, riding a three-game losing streak, entered the May 12 game tied for fourth place in the American League with a 14-14 record, four games behind the front-running Cleveland Indians. The Tigers, winners of four straight and seven of their last eight under new manager Jimmy Dykes, were 9-16, 6½ games off the pace, and still trying to crawl out of the junior circuit's cellar following a disastrous 2-15 start under second-year manager Bill Norman.

The Tuesday evening game drew a sparse crowd of 4,234. The relatively small turnout was unquestionably attributed to the fact that schools were still in session and rain showers were moving through the area. The high temperature for the day reached a sticky 91 degrees in the late morning before a midday thunderstorm passed through and dropped the temperature more than 20 degrees. The game-time temperature was 70 degrees and remained steady as light rain fell off and on throughout the evening.

Former Tiger Bill Fischer, who was 2-0 with a 1.06 ERA, started for the Senators. The 28-year-old right-hander was coming off back-to-back complete-game victories over the Red Sox and Tigers and in the midst of the finest three-month stretch of his major-league career. He was opposed by 29-year-old Frank Lary, a durable pitcher who had led the American League in innings pitched in 1958. The Tigers right-hander was making his seventh start of the year and entered the game with a record of 3-2 and a 3.46 ERA.

The Tigers opened the game with a pair of runs in the top of the first. Eddie Yost, who had been traded by the Senators to the Tigers during the offseason, led off with a single to center and scored when first baseman Bobo Osborne doubled to right.[1] After Charlie Maxwell was retired on a fly ball to left, Al Kaline singled to left to drive in Osborne. Fischer escaped further damage when he retired Harry Kuenn and Rocky Bridges on fly balls to center.

The game remained 2-0 until the top of the fifth when Tigers second baseman Ted Lepcio hit a one-out solo home run, his second of the year, to left field. In need of some additional infield depth, the Tigers had made an early-season trade that sent

In his first full season (1959), Harmon Killebrew led the AL with 42 home runs, the first of six seasons in which the Killer paced the junior circuit. The 1969 AL MVP with the Minnesota Twins, Killebrew belted 573 round-trippers in his Hall of Fame career. (1960 baseball card courtesy of Topps)

veteran left-handed pitcher Billy Hoeft to the Boston Red Sox in exchange for the 29-year-old utility infielder and pitcher Dave Sisler. Fischer retired the next two Tigers to end the inning. After 4½ innings the Tigers held a 3-0 lead.

The Senators broke through against Lary in the bottom of the sixth. Right fielder Albie Pearson led off with a single and scored when rookie center fielder Bob Allison ripped a double to left. Next up was Harmon Killebrew. The 22-year-old third baseman was the American League's early-season home-run sensation, well on his way to enjoying a breakout season.

Killebrew had hit four of his 10 home runs off Tigers hurlers, so it seemed a wise decision on Lary's part to try to move the young slugger off the plate. After Lary knocked the Senator's big third baseman down, Killebrew "merely got up, brushed off his pants, and tied into the next pitch" for a 420-foot blast into the bleachers in left-center field.[2] The home run was Killebrew's 11th of the season, matching his combined home-run total over his previous five seasons. A 1954 bonus baby, Killebrew was "known as a poor fielding jolter," who until the spring of 1959 sat patiently behind Yost waiting for his chance to play.[3] With the trade of Yost during the offseason, Killebrew was finally getting his chance.

The Tigers retook the lead in the top of the seventh. Kuenn led off with a single to left. Bridges hit back to the box and Fischer threw to shortstop Ron Samford to retire Kuenn. Light-hitting catcher Lou Berberet followed with a double to left to score Bridges and give the Tigers a 4-3 lead. Lepcio reached on an error when he hit a grounder to third and first baseman Julio Becquer failed to gather in Killebrew's throw. With runners at first and third and one down, Fischer escaped further damage when he retired Lary on a popup to second and struck out Yost to end the inning.

Lary came out to start the seventh and preserve the Tigers slim lead, but after he gave up a leadoff double to catcher Jay Porter, Dykes summoned the recently acquired Sisler from the Tigers bullpen. The right-handed Sisler retired pinch-hitter Herb Plews on a fly to left, then walked pinch-hitter Roy Sievers and Pearson to load the bases. The Tigers manager then turned to right-hander Ray Narleski, who had come to Detroit as part of an offseason deal that sent Billy Martin to Cleveland, to extinguish the embers of a potential Senators big inning.[4]

Allison greeted Narleski by lifting a sacrifice fly to center that scored Porter and tied the game, 4-4. It was Allison's second RBI of the game. The red-hot Killebrew then came to the plate and wasted no time as he teed off on Narleski's first-pitch fastball for his second home run in as many innings. This shot to deep left "was just as robust as the other."[5] The three-run homer was Killebrew's league-leading 12th and gave the Senators a 7-4 lead. It was the fourth time in the last 12 games that Killebrew had homered twice, with the Tigers being the victim three times.

Tex Clevenger, a 26-year-old right-handed swing man, was called upon by Senators manager Cookie Lavagetto to preserve the lead. Clevenger threw two perfect innings, striking out three – including Berberet to end the game 2 hours and 14 minutes after it started. The save was Clevenger's fourth of the season.

Fischer, who scattered nine hits over seven innings, earned the victory and improved to 3-0.

After starting the season 8-3, Fischer won only one more game and finished the year with a record of 9-11 and a 4.28 ERA. Strangely enough, Sisler, who pitched to only three hitters, suffered the loss despite earning his first hold of the year. It was his first decision since joining the Tigers 10 days earlier. Used sparingly throughout the year, he finished the season with a record of 1-3 and a 4.32 ERA.

At the end of play on May 12, Killebrew was batting .291 and leading the league in home runs, RBIs (28), and runs scored (26).[6] Despite finishing the season with a .242 batting average, he continued to hit for power and finished tied with Cleveland's Rocky Colavito for the league lead with 42 home runs. Killebrew went on to lead the American League in home runs five more times.

By the end of the season Detroit and Washington would swap places in the standings. The Tigers were six games over .500 for the remainder of the season and finished in fourth place with a record of 76-78, 18 games behind the pennant-winning Chicago White Sox. The Senators' promising start to the 1959 season quickly ended as the team came down to earth and finished last with a record of 63-91, 31 games off the pace.

SOURCES

In addition to the sources cited in the Notes, the author consulted Baseball-Reference.com and Retrosheet.org.

baseball-reference.com/boxes/WS1/WS1195905120.shtml

retrosheet.org/boxesetc/1959/B05120WS11959.htm

NOTES

1 On December 6, 1958, Yost was sent to Detroit as part of a six-player deal that sent Reno Bertoia, Jim Delsing, and Ron Samford to Washington. In return the Tigers received Yost, Rocky Bridges, and Neil Chrisley.

2 Hal Middlesworth, "Killebrew's 2 HRs 'Kills' Tigers," *Detroit Free Press*, May 13, 1959: 33.

3 Ed Wilks (Associated Press), "Harmon Killebrew Setting Red-Hot Batting Pace for Washington Club," *Hagerstown* (Maryland) *Daily Mail*, May 13, 1959: 24.

4 On November 20, 1958, Narleski was traded by Cleveland, along with Ossie Alvarez and Don Mossi, to Detroit for Al Cicotte and Martin.

5 Middlesworth.

6 Wilks.

LEMON AIDS SENATORS' ROUT

SEPTEMBER 5, 1959
WASHINGTON SENATORS 14, BOSTON RED SOX 2

by Joel Rippel

Washington Senators outfielder Jim Lemon struggled offensively over the final five weeks of the 1958 season. In the Senators' final 36 games, he didn't hit a home run and drove in just three runs.

After the season Lemon underwent surgery on his left knee. With his knee repaired and after receiving some advice in the Senators' final series of the 1958 season, Lemon showed improved offensive production in 1959.

After hitting .246 with 26 home runs and 75 RBIs in 1958 and leading the American League in strikeouts for the third consecutive season, Lemon improved to 33 home runs, 100 RBIs, and a .279 batting average in 1959, while cutting his strikeouts from 120 in 1958 to 99 in 1959.

According to the *Washington Post* sportswriter Shirley Povich, the tip Lemon received came from a knowledgeable source.

"Ted Williams had a batting tip for Jim Lemon on his last appearance in Washington (in 1958). He advised Lemon to stop crowding the plate because pitchers were getting him out on offerings that were high and tight."[1]

Lemon's improvement was on display against the Red Sox for the entire 1959 season and especially in the second game of a three-game series in the first week of September. In the 14 games against the Red Sox going into the series, Lemon had hit .360 with six home runs and 16 RBIs.

On September 4 the sixth-place Red Sox and last-place Senators opened a three-game series at Griffith Stadium. On the previous weekend the teams had split a two-game series in Boston, with Boston winning the opener, 4-3 in 10 innings, and the Senators winning the second game, 7-4. After the split, Boston lost twice in Baltimore on September 2 and 3, while the Senators lost two to the Yankees in New York on the same dates.

The Senators won the series opener, 4-3, to hand the Red Sox, their fourth consecutive loss.

Lemon made the second game of the series memorable for the crowd of 4,283. He staked the Senators to a 1-0 lead in the bottom of the first with a run-scoring double off Boston starter Bill Monbouquette.

In the top of the second inning, Lemon prevented the Red Sox from tying the score when he made a leaping catch against the left-field fence to rob Frank Malzone of a home run.

In the top of the third inning, Boston's Pumpsie Green drew a two-out walk off Senators starter Camilo Pascual. Jackie Jensen followed with his 27th home run of the season to give Boston a 2-1 lead. The lead was short-lived.

Monbouquette struck out Senators center fielder Lenny Green to lead off the bottom of the third inning. The Red Sox quickly lost control.

Faye Throneberry singled, bringing Lemon to the plate, and Lemon hit a home run to left-center, giving the Senators a 3-2 lead. Errors by the Red Sox on the next two hitters prolonged the inning. Harmon Killebrew reached second base when center fielder Pumpsie Green dropped his popup in short right field. Red Sox shortstop Don Buddin booted Roy Sievers' routine groundball and Killebrew scored as the ball wound up in left field. Then things got worse for the Red Sox.

Hal Naragon singled, sending Sievers to second. Reno Bertoia's double scored Sievers and sent Naragon to third. Pascual, a good hitting pitcher who batted .302 in 1959, fouled out to first baseman Pete Runnels for the second out. Monbouquette walked Billy Consolo to load the bases and prompt Boston manager Billy Jurges (who had started the season as a Senators coach) to replace Monbouquette with reliever Al Schroll.

Schroll walked Lenny Green and Throneberry on eight pitches to force in two runs. Earl Wilson was brought in to face Lemon with the bases loaded, and Lemon hit Wilson's 2-and-1 pitch into the left-field seats for a grand slam. Killebrew struck out to end the Senators' 10-run inning.

With the two home runs – his 27th and 28th of the season – Lemon tied two major-league records. He became the 13th player to hit two home runs in one inning and became the seventh player since 1901 to drive in six runs in an inning. (On September 23, 1890, Ed Cartwright of the St. Louis Browns of the American Association hit two home runs and drove in seven runs in the Browns' nine-run fifth-inning of a 21-2 victory over the Philadelphia Athletics in St. Louis.)

The most recent major-league player to drive in six runs in an inning was on the Senators bench to witness Lemon's feat. Sam Mele, who became a Senators coach on July 4 when Jurges left to become the Boston manager, drove in six runs in one inning for the Chicago White Sox on June 10, 1952, in a 15-4 victory over the Philadelphia Athletics in Philadelphia. Mele had a three-run home run and bases-loaded triple in Chicago's 12-run fourth inning.

The Senators added a run in the sixth on a run-scoring single by Pascual and closed out the scoring in the eighth inning on a two-run home run by Sievers.

Pascual cruised to the complete-game five-hitter. He walked one and struck out three as he improved to 14-10 for the season.

Nine of the Senators' 14 runs were unearned as Boston made four errors, which prompted a Boston newspaper to declare in a headline over the box score, "Hurry Up Football."[2]

Boston won the series finale, 2-1, as Tom Brewer outdueled Pedro Ramos, and went on to win 13 of their final 18 games. The Red Sox, who were in last place when Jurges succeeded Pinky Higgins as manager, went 18-12 in August and 13-10 in September to finish with a 75-79 record. But the strong finish was quickly forgotten as the Red Sox would not have another winning season until 1967.

After losing the series finale to Red Sox, the Senators went 8-5 over the next two weeks to improve to 63-86 on September 20. But they lost their final five games and at season's end occupied last place for the third consecutive season (and fourth in five). They also reached 90 losses for the fifth consecutive season.

In 1960 Lemon hit .269 with a career-high 38 home runs and 100 RBIs and made an appearance in both All-Star games that season. Between 1956 and 1960, he hit 141 home runs and drove in 435 runs.

Jim Lemon swinging for the left-field fence in a game versus the Baltimore Orioles in 1958. He was the kind of big, lumbering slugger many clubs had in an era defined by powerful hitters. (Photo courtesy of Robert E. Wilson)

SOURCES

In addition to the sources cited in the Notes, the author consulted Baseball-Reference.com, Newspapers.com, and Retrosheet.org.

NOTES

1 Shirley Povich, "Cal Griffith Tosses Topper into 'We Want Billy Ring,'" *The Sporting News*, October 15, 1958: 15.

2 Roger Birtwell, "Lemon Hits Two HRs in 1 inning," *Boston Sunday Globe*, September 6, 1959: 57.

CAMILO PASCUAL SETS OPENING DAY RECORD WITH 15 STRIKEOUTS

APRIL 18, 1960
WASHINGTON SENATORS 10, BOSTON RED SOX 1

by Lou Hernandez

In late December 1959, it was widely published that Senators owner Calvin Griffith "had looked one million dollars in the eye and expressed no interest." It was an offer not for his Washington franchise but merely for two of his ballplayers, first baseman Harmon Killebrew and pitcher Camilo Pascual. One of those published reports further explained the matter as follows: "The bidder was Gabe Paul, vice president of the Cincinnati Reds. 'I offered Griffith $500,000 each for Killebrew and Pascual and it was a firm offer,' Paul said. 'I consider Pascual the best pitcher in the majors.'"[1]

Entering the 1960 season, Pascual had been a pitching machine. Including the Cuban Winter League, during a ten-month period, from mid-April, 1959, and culminating with the Caribbean Series in February, 1960, Pascual threw a stupendous 410.1 innings, recorded 363 strikeouts and compiled a cumulative 34-15 record.

Griffith declined Paul's offer, and on April 18, 1960, Pascual showed why he was such a prized commodity by his owner and such a coveted one by other baseball executives. "Camilo Pascual, the pitching Pearl of the Antilles," read a Washington Post sportswriter's lead the next day, "made the 60th opening day for the Senators a memorable one yesterday when he tossed a three-hitter and set a new club record of 15 strikeouts backed by four Washington home runs, which humiliated the Boston Red Sox, 10-1."[2]

Walter Johnson had first set the Opening Day record for strikeouts with 14 on August 31, 1910. In a scheduling oddity, the American League began its season six days after the National League, with Washington and Boston commencing one day ahead of the rest of the junior circuit. President Dwight D. Eisenhower, who was in attendance, threw out two first pitches. The first was caught by Kansas native (same as Ike) Bob Allison and the second by Senators pitcher Jack Kralick. It was Eisenhower's seventh opening day toss in eight years. Vice-president Richard Nixon had pinch-hit for the Commander-in-Chief in 1959.

The club mark for strikeouts by Pascual also established a major league Opening Day record

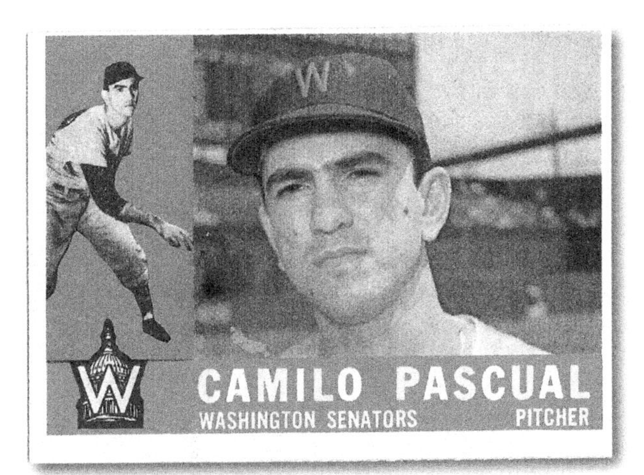

The owner of one of the great curveballs of his era, Cuban-born Camilo Pascual was a seven-time All-Star for the Senators and later Twins, won 20 or more games twice, and averaged 17 wins per season over a six-year period (1959-1964), en route to 174 career victories. (1960 baseball card courtesy of Topps)

for strikeouts by a pitcher that has now stood for a longer period of time than the original set by the Big Train. Pascual's mark has been threatened since, with a number of pitchers, including twice by another Johnson, the "Big Unit" Randy this time, totaling fourteen Opening Day whiffs.

Pascual said after the game that he would have liked to have met the president but his halting English played a role in his backing out at the opportunity. For Red Sox' hitters, it was too late for any of them to back out of the game once the afternoon affair began. Pascual started the contest by retiring the first four Red Sox batters, two by strikeout. The fifth-place hitter, Ted Williams, smashed a 3-2 pitch over the 31-foot high centerfield wall between the 408 and 418 foot markers. It was reported to be the longest home run hit at Griffith Stadium since Mickey Mantle hit two home runs over the same wall on Opening Day, 1956. The home run by Williams was his 493rd lifetime, tying him with Lou Gehrig on the all-time home run list.[3]

Following the home run, Pascual allowed a windblown double to Sox' center fielder Gary Geiger. The Senators' right-hander then struck out the next two Boston hitters to end the inning.

In their half of the second inning, the Senators scored three runs, the final tally being driven home by Pascual himself on a double to right field.

Now pitching with the lead, Pascual retired the Sox in order in the third, with opposing starter Tom Sturdivant his only strikeout victim. In the fourth, Pascual struck out the side for the second time, sandwiched around a walk to Williams.

The Senators scored five times in their half of the inning to take an 8-1 lead. Right fielder Bob Allison and catcher Earl Battey hit home runs against Sturdivant, sending the Red Sox right hander to the showers. Al Worthington relieved and surrendered Washington's fourth round tripper to shortstop Billy Consolo, and another run on an error by third baseman Frank Malzone, before getting out of the inning.

In the fifth frame, Pascual recorded four outs, three officially. The second out of the inning was delayed when first baseman Don Mincher, who was making his major league debut, dropped a pop up in foul territory for an error. Pascual was forced to retire catcher Haywood Sullivan for a "second time" on a fly out to left. Worthington fanned to end the inning on a called strike three by home plate umpire Charlie Berry. In the sixth, showing he was in complete control, Pascual made quick work of three opposition batters. He racked up two more strikeouts, bringing his whiff total to 11.

Gene Stephens led off the seventh with a walk, snapping a string of seven in a row retired by Pascual. In a most unusual occurrence, Ted Williams then attempted to bunt. He was called out on interference when he ran into the batted ball. With one out, Stephens stole second and advanced to third on a throwing error by Battey. Pascual buckled down and struck out Geiger and retired shortstop Don Buddin on a ground out to third. Williams was taken out of the game, and watched from the bench as the Senators scored their final two runs of the contest in the bottom of the seventh inning against Worthington.

Leading off the opening half of the eighth, Sullivan again popped up to first base in foul ground. Mincher this time squeezed the ball for the out, no doubt amid some fretful level of fan derision. Ron Jackson pinch-hit for Worthington and took a called third strike, becoming Pascual's 13th strike out casualty. The next batter, leadoff hitter Pumpsie Greennotched the Red Sox' third hit of the game, singling to right. Pete Runnels followed with a walk but third baseman Frank Malzone swung through a third strike to end the inning.

Stephens led off the ninth and struck out swinging for the third time – Pascual's record-setting 15th punch out. Pascual had fallen behind 2-0, and then threw three straight strikes past the Boston right fielder. The 26-year-old hurler set down the next two hitters to close out the 10-1 victory.

Pascual pitched hitless ball from the third inning through the seventh, using a befuddling mixture of curve and fastballs. Beginning his seventh big league season, Pascual's signature pitch was a rainbow curve, acknowledged as the best in baseball.

Williams and 1960 AL batting champ Pete Runnels were the only Red Sox starters not to succumb to Pascual's strikeout pitch. The Cuban pitcher allowed three hits and walked three. The Senators defense made two errors behind him. "Nobody in this league can compare with that pitcher," said Williams postgame.

AUTHOR'S NOTE

Pascual's fifteen strikeouts established a career high, a total he would reach one other time over his eighteen-year career. Beginning in 1961 he led the American League in strikeouts three consecutive seasons. Pascual also led the AL three times in complete games and shutouts and was a five-time All-Star. He is a member of the Latino Baseball Hall of Fame and was elected to the Minnesota Twins Hall of Fame in 2012.

SOURCES

Figueredo, Jorge, S. *Cuban Baseball A Statistical History 1878-1961.* (Jefferson, North Carolina: McFarland & Co., 2003).

Fogg, Sam. UPI, "Ike Watches as Pascual, Power Pace Senators 10-1 over Bosox." *Mason City Globe Gazette*, April 19, 1960.

Wilks, Ed. AP, "Ike and Pascual Get Nats Away to Good AL Start." *Independent Record*, April 19, 1960.

UPI. "Pascual Sets Whiff Record, 15; Nats Win Opener, 10-1." *Galveston Daily News*, April 19, 1960.

NOTES

1 Shirley Povich, "Reds' Million Offer for Pair Nixed by Nats." *The Sporting News*, December 23, 1959.

2 Bob Addie, "Cuban Fans 15, Aided by 4 Homers." *Washington Post*, April 19, 1960.

3 Shirley Povich, "K-Man Camilo's 15-Whiff Sendoff Lifts Nats Hopes." *The Sporting News*, April 27, 1960.

"ORIGINAL" SENATORS PLAY LAST GAME AT GRIFFITH WITHOUT REALIZING IT

OCTOBER 2, 1960
BALTIMORE ORIOLES 2, WASHINGTON SENATORS 1

by Richard Cuicchi

When the Washington Senators suited up for the final game of the season on October 2, 1960, they didn't know it would be the last one for the storied franchise in the nation's capital. In what appeared to be a hasty action by the American League only a few weeks after the season ended, Senators owner Calvin Griffith received support to relocate his team to the Minneapolis-St. Paul area, where they would become the Twins. In place of the fleeing Senators, a "new" Senators team would literally arise from nowhere to continue the baseball tradition in Washington.

The Senators were one of the original franchises of the American League, dating back to 1901. Their legacy was mostly one of futility, as they won the pennant only three times and the World Series once (in 1924) during their 60-year history. They had posted only four winning seasons since 1934. They won their last pennant in 1933.

The 1960 season was indicative of a more promising future for the Senators: They won over 70 games for the first time since 1953. Going into the final game of the season, they were in fifth place, 23 games behind the league-leading New York Yankees. The Senators had held fourth place as late as September 23, but dropped to fifth when they lost nine of their last 10 games of the month. They suffered a meltdown during September, winning only nine of 25 games. The day after the season ended, the *Washington Post* wrote, "The Nats must have been playing in quicksand for the last three weeks because they kept sinking and sinking."[1] Despite the disastrous end of the season, the team had reason to be optimistic about the next season.

In his fourth season as Senators manager, Cookie Lavagetto appeared to have turned the corner in putting a competitive team on the field. A cadre of young players on the roster included Harmon Killebrew, Bob Allison, Early Battey, Pedro Ramos, and Camilo Pascual. Emerging prospects included Jack Kralick, Don Mincher, Zoilo Versalles, and Jim Kaat.

The Senators' opponent on the last day of the season was the Baltimore Orioles, with a vastly improved team compared with recent years. With

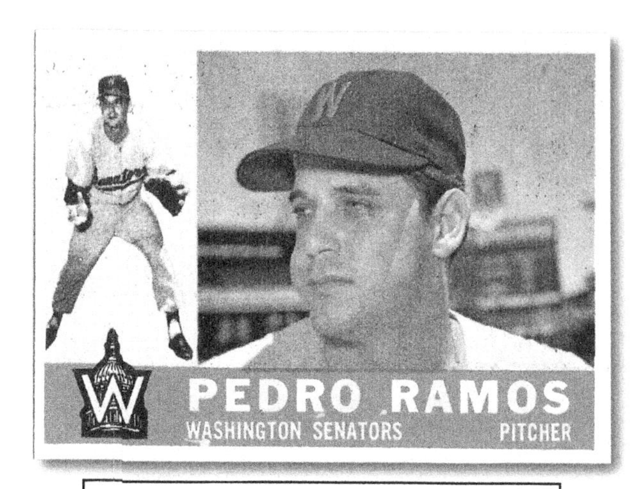

A workhorse on poor Senators and Twins teams, Cuban-born Pedro Ramos became the first pitcher to lead a major league in losses for four consecutive seasons (1958-1961). He went 78-112 in parts of seven seasons with the Senators/Twins and 117-160 in 15 big-league seasons. (1960 baseball card courtesy of Topps)

a second-place finish in the American League, Baltimore became a first-division team for the first time since 1945. (The Orioles franchise had been relocated from St. Louis seven years earlier.)

In front of a crowd of 4,768, a pitchers' duel ensued between the Orioles' Milt Pappas and the Senators' Ramos.

Pappas, 21, had won 14 games coming into the game. After the right-hander made his major-league debut as an 18-year-old in 1957, he had quickly established himself as a regular starter, winning 15 games in 1959. In his last start, on September 25, he had defeated the Senators. Cuban native Ramos was among the American League leaders in games started (35), and had an 11-17 record coming into the game.

The Orioles took advantage of a Senators error in the top of the first inning: Gene Stephens reached first with one out on second baseman Billy Consolo's misplay. After Gene Woodling walked, Jim Gentile hit a grounder to first base that forced Woodling at second. With runners on first and third, Brooks Robinson doubled Stephens home.

The hard-throwing Ramos proceeded to retire the next 18 Orioles batters until Gus Triandos singled in the top of the seventh.

Pappas was having practically the same success as Ramos, except for a triple by Consolo in the bottom of the fifth that scored Hal Naragon, who had singled.

The score remained tied until Baltimore's Jackie Brandt hit a solo homer off Ramos into the left-field bullpen in the top of the eighth inning. Stephens then walked, Woodling singled, and Gentile walked to load the bases. But Ramos ended the inning on a fielder's choice grounder by Robinson.

After Gentile's walk, Ramos retired the final four batters in the game, while Pappas retired the last nine batters he faced. The 2-1 victory was the Orioles' 89th win of the season.

Pappas and Ramos gave up a total of 10 hits in going the distance for their teams. Ramos wound up leading the American League in losses (18) for the third straight year. (He repeated this dubious distinction in 1961.)

The Senators' loss in the final game of the season continued a trend that went back to 1953. Baltimore won five of its last six games to edge the Chicago White Sox for second place.

Baltimore shortstop Ron Hansen, the American League Rookie of the Year in 1960, turned in a hitless performance in four at-bats. Perhaps he was forgiven by Orioles manager Paul Richards, since he was to be married that night after the game.[2]

An interesting development in the game involved Lavagetto watching in the stands with owner Calvin Griffith, while coach Sam Mele managed the team in his place.[3] Was Griffith taking the opportunity to give Lavagetto a sneak preview of his future plans for the franchise?

In any case, Griffith denied rumors that he intended to move the franchise out of Washington. As part of the American League's look at expanding to 10 teams, the word on the street was that Griffith would move his club to Minneapolis to allow Hank Greenberg to bring a new franchise to Washington. However, Griffith was emphatic in his denial, "That's a lot of baloney and sounds like somebody's pipe dream," he said. "It is news to me that the American League will discuss transferring the Washington club elsewhere." He also denied that he was interested in moving his club to Los Angeles.[4]

But a few days later, on October 26, the American League indeed announced its plans for expansion to 10 teams in 1961. The American League owners voted to let Griffith relocate his franchise to Minneapolis-St. Paul and approved a new expansion franchise for Washington. They also approved a 10th franchise in Los Angeles.[5] With only six months until Opening Day in 1961, the actions in late October by the American League seemed a bit impulsive, considering that the two new franchises would need to be organized from scratch. In contrast, the National League had previously announced plans for new franchises in Houston and New York, but they wouldn't begin playing until the 1962 season.[6]

Without knowing it, the Senators had played their last game at Griffith Stadium, providing no opportunity for a formal goodbye to their fans. Washington fans wouldn't get to fully enjoy the fruits of the team's young roster on the verge of a breakout season. They wouldn't get to enjoy Killebrew's Hall of Fame career or see Battey develop into an All-Star catcher. Instead, Minnesota fans became the beneficiary of a vibrant, competitive team that was relevant within two seasons and earned a World Series berth in 1965.

In 1961 Griffith Stadium became the home to a completely new team with a cast of aging veterans and little-known younger players drafted from the other franchises. Washington's on-field futility continued until the franchise moved again 11 years later to become the Texas Rangers in Dallas-Fort Worth.

SOURCES

In addition to the sources cited in the Notes, the author also consulted the following:

baseball-reference.com/boxes/WS1/WS1196010020.shtml.

retrosheet.org/boxesetc/1960/B10020WS11960.htm.

Brandt, Ed. "Orioles Defeat Senators, 2 to 1, and Finish Second," *Baltimore Sun*, October 3, 1960: 17.

NOTES

1 Bob Addie, "Tenacious Orioles Hold Second," *Washington Post*, October 3, 1960: A16.

2 Lou Hatter, "Winter Jobs Await Orioles, *Baltimore Sun*, October 3, 1969: 17.

3 Addie.

4 Shirley Povich, "Cal Punctures New Rumor of Senator Shift," *The Sporting News*, October 26, 1960: 29.

5 Joe King, "A.L. Speeds Expansion - Ten Clubs in '61," *The Sporting News*, November 2, 1960: 3.

6 While it had been rumored that Hank Greenberg would be instrumental in starting the new franchise in Washington, in fact he became president of the new Los Angeles Angels club, the Angels.

"NEW" SENATORS DEFEATED IN FIRST GAME OF EXPANSION ERA

APRIL 10, 1961
CHICAGO WHITE SOX 4, WASHINGTON SENATORS 3

by Richard Cuicci

When the 1960 season ended, Washington Senators fans had good reason to be optimistic about the team for the following season. The Senators narrowly missed out on a fourth-place finish, which would have been their highest since 1946. Losing 11 of their last 12 games of the season scotched hopes for the higher finish. The Senators' roster included a core of young players who seemed to be on the verge of a breakout season. However, the team that suited up for Opening Day of the 1961 season was not the same one that ended the prior season; it wasn't different by just a few players, but by the entire team.

This situation came about over the winter when Senators owner Calvin Griffith moved the franchise to Minneapolis-St. Paul, as part of the American League's expansion to 10 teams for the 1961 season. A new Senators franchise, whose ownership group was led by Pete Quesada, took the place of Griffith's. Los Angeles, already home to the National League Dodgers, would become the home for the 10th franchise as well.

The Griffith family had been entrenched in the franchise since 1912, when Calvin Griffith's stepfather Clark Griffith first took over the club as manager and later became president in 1920. The baseball community was largely surprised by Griffith's defection from Washington, as well as the timeframe the American League set to implement its 10-team league.[1] Griffith was lured to Minneapolis-St. Paul by offers of lucrative radio and TV rights, a guarantee for annual attendance close to a million, and a new ballpark with low rentals and concessions profits.[2]

Former Air Force General Elwood "Pete" Quesada won the bid for ownership of the new Senators franchise in November 1960. A World War II Air Force planner who later became the chief of the Federal Aviation Agency,[3] Quesada had been a baseball fan practically all his life, but had no experience in the business of baseball.[4]

The team's first course of business was to hire a field staff and build a roster. Former Washington Senators first baseman Mickey Vernon was hired as the manager. He had spent the 1960 season as a coach for the Pittsburgh Pirates after a 20-year playing career.

In the first inning of the inaugural game of the expansion Senators in 1961, leadoff hitter Coot Veal collected the first hit and scored the first run in franchise history. The shortstop batted .202 that season and .231 in his six-year big-league career (1958-1963). (1961 baseball card courtesy of Topps)

At the American League expansion draft in Boston on December 14, 1960, the Senators got their two most wanted players, Bobby Shantz (second pick from the pitcher pool) from the New York Yankees and Willie Tasby (first pick from the outfielder pool) from the Boston Red Sox.[5] Other key veterans selected by the Senators included outfielder Gene Woodling, first baseman Dale Long, outfielder Marty Keough, and pitchers Dave Sisler, Dick Donovan, Hal Woodeshick, and Tom Sturdivant. Altogether, the Senators selected 28 players that included a mix of players past their prime years and prospects with little or no major-league experience.[6] Shantz would never play for the Senators; he was dealt shortly after the draft to the Pittsburgh Pirates for three players.

Vernon took an approach in spring training that every starting job was up for grabs. He realized that the new Senators roster would lack power and have to rely on speed, hit-and-run plays, and solid defense to win games. He also knew he would have to be patient with his new team.[7]

The Senators had the best spring-training exhibition-game record of all the American League teams in 1961, so there was hope that the team would be competitive.[8] However, the lineup the Senators put on the field for Opening Day contained only two players, outfielders Woodling and Tasby, who had been regular starters (over 500 at-bats) in 1960.

Opening Day came on April 10 with the type of fanfare expected for a new franchise. Attendance by many dignitaries and entertainment by several bands were part of the festive occasion. The Senators were pitted against the Chicago White Sox in the only major-league game scheduled that day. A crowd of 26,725 showed up at Griffith Stadium, including recently inaugurated President John F. Kennedy, who threw out the ceremonial first pitch. Every president before him since William Howard Taft in 1910 had participated in an Opening Day ceremony.[9] Kennedy spiritedly got into the pregame act and whizzed his official pitch among the gathered Senators and White Sox players, with White Sox outfielder Jim Rivera snagging the throw. White Sox manager Al Lopez offered his assessment of the president's throw: "I'd say the President is sneaky fast. He can really fire that thing."[10]

Donovan got the starting pitcher nod from Vernon. The 33-year-old right-hander had been a member of the White Sox pitching staff of manager Lopez the year before and was miffed at Lopez for limiting his innings throughout the season. Donovan had remarked during spring training about the possibility of drawing the Senators' Opening Day starting assignment, "I want to win for Washington, but I also want to show Al Lopez he should have used me more last year."[11]

The dean of the White Sox staff, 40-year-old Early Wynn, was Donovan's opponent on the mound. He was only 16 wins shy of achieving the 300-win milestone. He had made his major-league debut with the original Senators in 1939.

The Senators jumped out to a 2-0 lead in the bottom of the first on Woodling's triple that scored Coot Veal and Keough, both of whom had singled. White Sox first baseman Roy Sievers, the all-time home-run leader of the Senators, hit a 410-foot solo home run in the top of the second.

In the bottom of the second inning, the Senators pushed across another run on Billy Klaus's sacrifice fly that scored Pete Daley. Then in the third, the White Sox got their second run on back-to-back doubles by Floyd Robinson and Luis Aparicio, cutting the Senators' lead to 3-2.

The Senators held the lead behind Donovan's pitching until the top of the seventh, when Jim Landis hit a triple and scored on a double error by first baseman Long. Long mishandled pinch-hitter Earl Torgeson's groundball and then threw wildly to Donovan, who went to cover first base.

In the eighth inning, Donovan gave up another unearned run initiated when Minnie Miñoso was hit by a pitch. Miñoso stole second and wound up on third base as catcher Daley's throw went into center field. Sievers' sacrifice fly scored Miñoso for a final score of 4-3.

Donovan pitched a complete game, yielding six hits and two walks. However, the jittery Senators fielders made four errors and became his nemesis as much as the White Sox hitters.

Wynn was relieved after two innings and was followed by Russ Kemmerer and Frank Baumann who held the Senators scoreless. Bauman picked up the win. White Sox pitchers gave up nine hits, including Keough's three singles.

The Senators wound up winning only 61 games in 1961, tying the Kansas City A's for last place. Vernon had been correct in his early assessment of the Senators' power potential. They finished as one of the bottom two teams in the AL in runs scored and slugging percentage. They played in a new ballpark in 1963, but the change in venue didn't help their results. The new franchise wouldn't post a winning season until 1969, and three years later it would move again, to the Dallas-Fort Worth area to become the Texas Rangers. The original Senators franchise that became the Minnesota Twins attained a World Series berth in 1965.

SOURCES

In addition to the sources in the Notes, the author also consulted the following:

baseball-reference.com/boxes/WS2/WS2196104100.shtml.

retrosheet.org/boxesetc/1961/B04100WS21961.htm.

Addie, Bob. "Late-Inning Errors Spoil Six-Hitter by Donovan," *Washington Post*, April 11, 1961: C11.

Kates, Maxwell, and Bill Nowlin. *Time for Expansion Baseball* (Phoenix: SABR, 2018), 52.

NOTES

1. Dan Daniel, "Frick 'Disturbed' by A.L. Decision to Expand for '61," *The Sporting News*, November 2, 1960: 4.
2. Shirley Povich, "Cal Promised 'World with a Fence Around It,'" *The Sporting News*, November 2, 1960: 4.
3. In 1967 the Federal Aviation Agency became the Cabinet-level Federal Aviation Administration.
4. Shirley Povich, "'Dream Come True,' Beams New Nat Boss," *The Sporting News*, November 23, 1960: 3.
5. Shirley Povich, "Beaming Nats Land 'Most Wanted Pair' - Shantz and Tasby," *The Sporting News*, December 21, 1960: 5.
6. Hy Hurwitz, "New Clubs Pleased at $4 Million Picks," *The Sporting News*, December 21, 1960: 3.
7. Shirley Povich, "Mickey Using 'Soft Sell' on Nats Players," *The Sporting News*, April 5, 1961: 3.
8. Bob Addie, "New Nats Begin New Era Today," *Washington Post*, April 10, 1961: A13.
9. Ibid.
10. Shirley Povich, "Kennedy Sets Presidential Mark with Fireball Pitch," *The Sporting News*, April 19, 1961: 3.
11. Shirley Povich, "Donovan Aching to 'Show Lopez' in Nats' Opener," *The Sporting News*, March 1, 1961: 11.

WASHINGTON SEES 17 SENATORS WHIFF

MAY 12, 1961
BOSTON RED SOX 2, WASHINGTON SENATORS 1

by Bill Nowlin

It was early in the 1961 season; the Red Sox were 9-12 and the Senators (having played five more games) were 10-16. There was no reason to think either team was going anywhere.[1] It was a Friday night in Washington and the 1961 Senators were a brand-new team, the Angels and Senators having joined the American League in the first year that baseball expanded the number of teams in the league. The Senators of 1960 had decamped to Minnesota and become the Twins. The "new Senators" were 3-9 at home in the young season. Opening Day and a Sunday doubleheader against the Yankees on April 30 had both drawn more than 20,000, but otherwise the team hadn't drawn half that number. There was seemingly nothing special about this Friday night.

Mickey Vernon's Senators started Pete Burnside; his 1960 season for Detroit saw him 7-7 (4.28); it was the first year he'd won more than one game. Back on April 25, Boston had hammered him for four runs in two innings, driving him from the game and dealing him a defeat.

Red Sox manager Pinky Higgins started Bill Monbouquette (1-3). He'd had his first winning season in 1960 (14-11, 3.64).

Neither team did anything in the first couple of innings, other than a double off the right-field wall by Washington's Willie Tasby in the bottom of the second. Burnside had walked one batter in each inning; Monbouquette had struck out one batter in each inning.

Pumpsie Green doubled to lead off the third. Monbouquette laid down a sacrifice bunt, reaching safely on when Burnside's throw pulled first baseman Dale Long off the bag. Chuck Schilling's sacrifice fly to deep right easily scored Green. Rookie Carl Yastrzemski hit into a double play.

Monbouquette struck out the side in the bottom of the third and struck out the two final batters in the fourth. He struck out Burnside in the fifth and two more batters in the sixth. After six, he had 11 strikeouts and was still holding the 1-0 lead.

The Red Sox scored a second run in the top of the seventh. Burnside retired the first two batters but then walked Carroll Hardy, gave up a single to Vic Wertz (Hardy went first to third), and walked

Growing up just a few miles from Fenway Park, four-time All-Star Bill Monbouquette won 96 games over an eight-year stretch with the Boston Red Sox (1958-1965), including 20 in 1963. In parts of 11 major-league seasons, Monbo posted a 114-112 slate. (1962 baseball card courtesy of Topps)

Pumpsie Green. And then he walked Monbouquette, forcing in that second run.

The Senators mounted a threat in the bottom of the seventh. Left fielder Jim King led off with a single. Dale Long reached on an error by Boston first baseman Pete Runnels. Home-plate umpire Bill McKinley called Senators catcher Gene Green out on strikes. Back-to-back pinch-hitters Marty Keough and Harry Bright struck out and walked, respectively. Billy Klaus then struck out swinging. Monbouquette had whiffed 14. The record for strikeouts in a game was 18, set by Bob Feller in October 1938. Sandy Koufax had tied that record on August 31, 1959.

As it happens, in the very last game the Red Sox had played — against the Angels in Los Angeles on May 10, three Angels pitchers had combined to strike out 17 Red Sox. Boston won, nonetheless, 3-2.

Fourteen K's was impressive enough, but Monbouquette would have to strike out five of the final six batters in order to tie Feller, and every one of them to surpass him — and that presumed that the Senators made three outs in the bottom of the ninth. With the score just 2-0, they might yet score three times and win before they made three outs in the ninth.

They didn't. What they did was retire the Red Sox in order in the top of the eighth, and strike out just once in the eighth, still remaining scoreless. Jim King was at the plate with two outs and two strikes. Monbouquette had two strikes on King and threw a pitch that King fouled into the glove of Boston catcher Jim Pagliaroni — but Pagliaroni couldn't hold onto it. What would have been an inning-ending 16th K instead forced Monbouquette to throw another pitch, King grounded out.

In the ninth, the Red Sox couldn't get the ball out of the infield. It remained 2-0, Boston, heading into the bottom of the ninth. If Monbouquette could strike out three Senators he'd not only win the game but tie Feller's record. He struck out Dale Long. Gene Green reached on an error. The tying run was at the plate in the person of Coot Veal. He struck out. Two outs, the game was approaching 2 hours and 30 minutes. The 6,594 fans in attendance awaited his first pitch to pinch-hitter R.C. Stevens. There were several pitches; Monbouquette walked Stevens. Then third baseman Klaus (who'd already struck out three times) swung at the first pitch he saw and singled to center field, driving in Green. Now the tying run was on first base, and the winning run was at the plate – Senators second baseman Danny O'Connell. He was the only batter on the Senators (other than pinch-hitters) whom Monbouquette had not yet struck out. O'Connell could have earned himself a footnote in the history books by striking out, but he was trying to at least tie the game. He hit the first pitch hard. Right fielder Jackie Jensen got a bad jump on the ball, but at the last minute reached high over his head and hauled it in, a "running, one-handed catch."[2]

The Red Sox won, and Monbouquette won, and he set a franchise record for strikeouts that endured 25 years until Roger Clemens struck out 20 in April 1986. The Red Sox record had been 15, shared by three pitchers — Mickey McDermott in 1951, Smoky Joe Wood in 1911, and — most unlikely — Joe Harris in 1906.[3]

For what it's worth, the league record for strikeouts in a night game had been 14.[4] Monbouquette obliterated that.

This 1961 game was remarkable, in that the Senators pitchers, Burnside and Dave Sisler, had held the Red Sox to just two hits. The Red Sox had committed two errors and Monbouquette had walked four Senators. He'd allowed five base hits, two of them doubles, but the strikeouts had helped — the Senators left 10 men on base.

After the game, Pagliaroni said he didn't know whether to smile or to cry. "The ball was half in and half out of my glove. But the webbing was tight and the ball bounced out in front of the plate. If it had bounced high off my glove I could have grabbed it barehanded. I tried, but it stayed low and I couldn't get at it before it hit the ground."[5]

Opinion was reportedly divided over whether Monbouquette's curve or fastball was his better pitch that evening. Red Sox pitching coach Sal Maglie said, "Both pitches were good. It was the way Monbo mixed them up that did the trick."[6]

For his part, Monbouquette was surprised to hear he'd whiffed 17. He said, "I didn't realize I was even close to the record, until they told me just now. I thought I had about 12 or 13, no more."[7] He said that as he'd become increasingly tired in the later innings, his curveball had started to hang so he had gone more often to his fastball.

Monbouquette finished the 1961 season 14-14 (3.39). In 1963, he was 20-10.

SOURCES

In addition to the sources cited in the Notes, the author also consulted Retrosheet.org and accounts in the *Washington Post*, *Boston Record*, and *Boston Traveler*.

NOTES

1 Neither team had finished in the first division since the Red Sox finished third in 1958. Even adding two more teams in 1961, neither team finished in the first division in 1961, either.

2 Bill Fuchs, "Senators Squawking About Grass, But How About Those 17 Whiffs?," *Evening Star* (Washington), May 13, 1961: 12. The reference to grass related to complaints voiced by several Senators that the new sod and grass at Griffith Stadium was "death to hard-hit ground balls," that the weather was bad, and that - in the words of Gene Woodling, "a fly ball won't get you much in this park."

3 In 1906 Harris had a won-lost record of 2-21, but on September 1 he struck out 15 Philadelphia Athletics. That was one of the games he lost, 4-1 … in 24 innings. It had been quite a game, but pitching all 24 innings gave his plenty of extra opportunities to build up his strikeout total. Opposing pitcher Jack Coombs - who also went the distance - struck out 19, but Feller's record of 18 was achieved in a nine-inning game. Mickey McDermott's 15 K's were also in an iron-man performance; he worked all 16 innings of the July 28, 1951, game at Fenway Park. The Indians took a 3-2 lead in the top of the 15th, but the Red Sox tied it. Cleveland took a 4-3 lead in the top of the 16th, but then Ted Williams doubled to tie the score and Clyde Vollmer won the game with a grand slam in the bottom of the 16th.

4 That record had been shared by Feller, Bob Turley, Jim Bunning, and Early Wynn.

5 Larry Claflin, "Pag's Mitt Cost Monbo 18th K," *Boston American*, May 13, 1961: 19.

6 Ibid.

7 Henry McKenna, "Sox Edge Nats, 2-1," *Boston Herald*, May 13, 1961: 11.

ROCKY COLAVITO HITS FOUR HOME RUNS AS TIGERS SWEEP DOUBLEHEADER FROM SENATORS

AUGUST 27, 1961
DETROIT TIGERS 7, WASHINGTON SENATORS 4 (GAME ONE)
DETROIT TIGERS 10, WASHINGTON SENATORS 1 (GAME TWO)

by Thomas J. Brown Jr.

It was hot and humid in Washington when the Detroit Tigers took the field against the Senators for a doubleheader on Sunday, August 27, 1961. They were hoping to make ground on the New York Yankees as they prepared to play a doubleheader. (The second game was a makeup of a rainout on June 21.)

The Tigers were 17-7 so far in August and 81-45 for the season, two games behind the Yankees. The expansion Senators had won just five games in August and were on a seven-game losing streak.

Detroit won the first game on Friday. Jim Bunning pitched eight innings, shutting out the Senators 6-0 before the game was ended in the ninth by rain. Saturday's game was rained out and rescheduled for Monday.

Tigers fans were counting on their pair of sluggers, Rocky Colavito and Norm Cash, to help the team keep pace with the Yankees. While much had been made about the "M and M boys," as Roger Maris and Mickey Mantle were called, the Tigers had their own offensive weapons. "We call them the C and C boys," said one Tigers fan.[1]

Both players were considered MVP candidates. The MVP race was considered as "hot as the current pennant race between the Yankees and Tigers."[2] Cash had 31 home runs and the AL's highest batting average (.364) when the team arrived in Washington. Colavito had 34 home runs and 112 RBIs.

Bennie Daniels started for the Senators. Daniels had been the team's best starter all season. He entered the game with a, 8-7 record and a 3.33 ERA, and was perhaps the Senators' best hope to break their losing streak.

But Daniels stumbled early. With one out in the first, he walked two batters. Colavito flied out but Cash doubled to bring home both runners. Dick McAuliffe tripled, scoring Cash, and the Tigers had a three-run lead.

Don Mossi took the mound for the Tigers. After picking up three complete-game wins at the beginning of August, he had run into a stretch of bad luck. Mossi lost an opportunity for a win on August 19 when he gave up a home run to Boston's Frank Malzone in the top of the ninth. He lost his

A prodigious slugger, Rocky Colavito hit 40-plus home runs three times in a four-year stretch (1958-1961), including a career-best 45 in 1961. Colavito was a nine-time All-Star and hit 374 home runs in his career. (1961 baseball card courtesy of Topps)

next outing, on August 23, and was looking to end the month on a positive note.

The Senators got on the scoreboard in the third inning when Bud Zipfel singled to start the inning, went to third on Chuck Cottier's single, and scored on Daniels' sacrifice fly to left field.

The Tigers added to their lead in the fifth. Frank House led off with a single and went to second on Mossi's sacrifice. Jake Wood's triple brought House home and Bill Bruton's sacrifice fly drove in Wood to give the Tigers a four-run lead.

Colavito added to the lead in the sixth with a leadoff line drive into the front row-seats of the left-field bleachers for homer number 35.

Daniels was removed for a pinch hitter in the seventh. Pete Burnside pitched two perfect innings before Johnny Klippstein took over in the top of the ninth and surrendered McAuliffe's second triple of the game. He scored the Tigers' seventh run when Chico Fernandez singled.

Mossi took the mound in the bottom of the ninth looking to get his 11th complete-game victory of the season. He got into trouble almost immediately when Bob Johnson led off with a double. When Willie Tasby then hit a bouncer down the line at third, McAuliffe threw the ball wide, pulling Cash off the bag. Cash tried to save the play with a tag.

When umpire Harry Schwartz called Tasby safe, Cash kicked the dirt disgustedly. Tigers manager Bob Scheffing came out to question the call, to no avail, and the Senators had runners at the corners.

Johnson scored on Harry Bright's groundball to short. Tasby went to second and came home when Zipfel singled to right field. As Mossi tried to regain his composure, Zipfel stole second. When Cottier singled, Zipfel scampered home and the Senators were now just three runs behind.

Tigers manager Bob Scheffing pulled Mossi and called on Terry Fox to close the deal. Fox surrendered a Senators single to Woodling and was replaced by Gerry Staley. Staley struck out Chuck Hinton for the third out, giving the Tigers a 7-4 win to keep pace with the Yankees.

In the second game, the Tigers faced the Senators' Dave Sisler. Sisler had worked out of the bullpen since 1959 but manager Mickey Vernon called on the reliever for his first start of the season.

Sisler made it unscathed through the first two innings. Mike Roarke singled to lead off the third, went to second on a sacrifice bunt, and scored on Jake Wood's single.

Colavito, leading off the fourth, blasted the ball 400 feet over the left field wall, about halfway up the bleachers. It was home run 36 for the season.

While the Tigers were hammering away at Sisler, Paul Foytack kept the Senators in check. His previous outing was a five-hit, one-run complete-game victory against the Indians. Tigers manager Scheffing said after the game, "When you get good pitching like we've been getting, it gives the whole team a lift."[3]

Detroit broke the game open and sent Sisler to the showers in the fifth. The trouble started after Sisler hit Bruton with a pitch. Bruton suffered a ruptured blood vessel in this right forearm and was pulled from the game. The next batter, Al Kaline, doubled to left field. With two runners in scoring position, Colavito connected and sent the ball sailing over the Tigers' bullpen. The three-run blast, Colavito's 37th home run of the season, gave the Tigers a five-run lead.

When Norm Cash followed Colavito and tripled, Sisler was pulled for Marty Kutyna. Kutyna gave up a double to McAuliffe that brought Cash home to give the Tigers a 6-0 lead.

In the sixth, Woods tripled and scored when shortstop Bob Johnson mishandled a grounder. A single by Kaline brought home one more run and made it 8-0.

Foytack gave up hits in the first three innings before settling down and silencing the Senators bats for the rest of the game, except for the sixth inning, when Washington scored its only run, on singles by Gene Woodling and Gene Green and a double-play grounder by Johnson.

Foytack's pitching motivated the Tigers. Scheffing remarked later, "The batters know that they're going to be in the game even if they don't get any runs in the early innings. They know that they'll have a chance to catch up or break the game open."[4]

After Kutyna was removed for a pinch-hitter, Vernon sent Mike Garcia to pitch the final two innings. The first batter he faced, Bubba Morton, hit "one of his specialties – a half-swing single to right"[5] in the eighth. Colavito came to bat with two outs and hit a drive about eight rows up in the left-field bleachers, close to where his second round-tripper had landed. The home run brought his total to 38 for the season.

"Nobody had more fun, or was more menacing, or received more cheers from the crowd of 10,542 than The Rock. And Rocco Domenico Colavito hit a couple which were almost as long as his name," wrote Joe Falls of Colavito's batting.[6]

This was the second time Colavito hit four home runs in one day. On June 10, 1959, playing for the Cleveland Indians, he hit four home runs against the Baltimore Orioles.

With the score now 10-1, Foytack gave up a leadoff single in the eighth but a double play snuffed out the threat. In the bottom of the ninth, Foytack quickly retired the side on two popups to shortstop and an easy fly ball to right field.

Scheffing lavished praise on Foytack. "Good pitching helps your fielders too," the manager said. "They're always on their toes because they know that the pitchers are keeping the ball around the plate. That's why we've been making so many good plays lately. The guys expect the ball to be hit and when it is, they're ready to get it."[7]

Foytack's win, his ninth of the season, was the 50th complete game by Tigers starters in 1961. (They finished with a league-leading 62.) Delighted with the victory, Scheffing said, "Our guys are playing their best ball of the season. They're running, breaking up plays, getting the hits at the right time – and what pitching!"[8]

The win was the Tigers' ninth victory in 10 games. The sweep extended the Senators' losing streak to nine games. (They would lose five more before a victory over Chicago ended the streak at 14; after the win, they lost another 10 in a row.) Cash and Colavito's exploits continued to give Tigers fans hope that their team might push past the Yankees, but it didn't happen.

The "C and C boys" were the most potent offensive weapons to have worn Tigers uniforms since Hank Greenberg and Rudy York back in the 1930s. Greenberg and York knocked in 91 home runs in 1938 for the Tigers. The four home runs brought Colavito's total to 38 for the season and raised his RBI count to 119, tying him with Maris for the league lead. Cash, who had a single, double and triple, maintained his league-leading batting average.

In his game account, Joe Falls of the *Detroit Free Press* wrote, "The hot-water boiler blew up under the stands at Griffith Stadium Sunday and authorities were wondering what caused the explosion. Was it the heat? Was it the humidity? Or was it Rocky Colavito's bat? All three were blazing hot."[9]

SOURCES

In addition to the sources cited in the Notes, the author used Baseball-Reference.com and Retrosheet.org for boxscore, player, team, and season information as well as pitching and batting game logs, and other pertinent material.

Baseball-Reference.com/boxes/WS2/WS2196108271.shtml

Retrosheet.org/boxesetc/1961/B08271WS21961.htm

Baseball-Reference.com/boxes/WS2/WS2196108272.shtml

Retrosheet.org/boxesetc/1961/B08272WS21961.htm

NOTES

1 Joe Reichler (Associated Press), "Cash and Colavito Just as Good as Maris and Mantle," *Ironwood* (Michigan) *Daily Globe*, August 28, 1961: 5.

2 Steve Snider (Associated Press), "AL Most Valuable Player Race as Close as Tigers vs. Yanks," *Camden* (New Jersey) *Courier-Post*, August 28, 1961: 2.

3 Joe Falls, "Rocky Raises Total to 38," *Detroit Free Press*, August 28, 1961: 1.

4 Ibid

5 Ibid.

6 Ibid.

7 Ibid.

8 Ibid.

9 Ibid.

MEMORIES OF GRIFFITH STADIUM

On July 6, 1958, I drove to Washington from Norristown, Pennsylvania, in my first-ever car, a white 1952 Pontiac convertible with whitewall tires, to see the Orioles play the Senators that afternoon.

One thing I wanted to see was the beer sign that Mantle's famous 1953 home run just missed on the way out. I had seen a diagram of the trajectory, but wanted to see the actual sign. I had witnessed another of his notable distance shots (in Shibe Park, off Frank Fanovich a few months after the one in Washington), so that may have accounted for my interest.

Griffith Stadium was memorable on several counts, one being the small distance from home plate to the stands. It was way, way closer than in any other stadium I know of in O.B. — not quite like sitting on the catcher's shoulders, but it seemed like that. I don't know why more patrons weren't hospitalized by foul balls. Then there was the really big home-run distance to left field — not good for right-handed power hitters! And then the near absence of advertising – just the big National Bohemian beer sign in left field and one sign for the same product over the right-field scoreboard. That was like Shibe Park, back when the A's had it – just the Benrus clock and green walls. Then the wealthy Phillies turned Shibe into gaudy city.

Robert E. Wilson
Gainesville, Florida

Griffith Stadium was the first major league ballpark I had seen outside of New York City. I do not remember the year, except that it was pre-World War II; 1939-1941 I would estimate. I base that on the fact that my father took only me and not my eldest brother, my baseball mentor, who was off to college. I was 10 or 11 at the time. I don't know if my father had some business in Washington that day, or if it was the same day I sat in the public gallery and watched the Senate debate about a military draft; you'll forgive a man if memory dims after 80 years.

It was a midweek day game, maybe against my team the Yankees. I was used to the Polo Grounds and Yankee Stadium, polar opposites as ballparks

— the one U-shaped and dumpy, the other a majestic triple-tiered temple. They had two things in common: The playing field distances were symmetrical though dissimilar, and the crowds when I saw them were invariably large. The Polo Grounds held over 50,000, Yankee Stadium over 70,000.

What struck me about Griffith Stadium that day was its lopsided shape: a rectangle with a taxi ride down the left-field line to the bleachers, a center-field corner deeper than Yankee Stadium but shallower than the Polo Grounds, and a "normal" 326 feet down the right-field line. The other thing I remember was the scant attendance. Even the Yankees might fill only 10 percent of their seats on a weekday. The Browns or Athletics might attract several hundred. General admission entitled us to sit anywhere except the box seats; we sat behind home plate in the lower deck.

Hot dogs were a dime, Cokes a nickel. I'm sure we had a few.

Norman Macht

Escondido, California
normanmacht.com

I was about 15-17 years old when I went to see the Nats (Senators) in Griffith Stadium, from about 1957 to 1960.

Living in Falls Church, Virginia, right outside Washington, I would take the bus to Rosslyn Circle and pick up the streetcar that traveled along M Street, then catch a transfer to the 7th Street streetcar, getting off at U Street. I went to school at George Washington University from 1961 to 1965, so travel there was easier, but money was a problem and going there meant I had to pull funds from something else. I think those later years were at DC Stadium, though.

We didn't have much money, so I got cheap seats in the upper deck just outside third base. I was usually alone, as few wanted to spend the money for this. They were sometimes on TV (Channel 5, WTTG?), and that was good enough for most.

Unfortunately, I had no sense of history and I have no memory of the stars (and future All-Stars) of other teams. I do remember pitchers "Potato" Pasqual and Chuck Stobbs. My father would always make fun of Stobbs as the worst pitcher in baseball, but years later I looked up his record, and it was about major-league average, so my father simply had a selective memory.

The homers of Bobby Allison and Harmon Killebrew flew out to left past me. Allison's were hard line drives that landed 5 to 10 rows up in the bleachers. Killebrew's were lazy fly balls, which seemed like easy outs, except that they just kept going and going, eventually landing farther up the stands than Allison's. An interesting illusion! Roy Sievers, of course, was a real star and I think he was cheered more than the homer hitters!

Finally, my father, Frederick Sperling, was a scientist, a toxicologist, who had a laboratory at Howard University. (He founded their Pharmacology department and their labs were named for him after his death.) His lab looked out through the stadium and had a clear view of the infield, though nothing above or below that. I could have watched a lot of games for free, but I didn't like that restricted view and rarely spent time at the window.

I wish I could remember more, but things that seem important to me now were nothing special then, so 60 years later I have to repeat the few memories I have to preserve them.

Barry Sperling

Alexandria, Virginia

The first games I ever saw were in Griffith Stadium in 1954, when I was 6 or 7. In early 1955 my family moved to upstate New York, but we returned in 1959, and I saw perhaps 10 games in 1959 and 1960 there. Those were exciting years for the Senators thanks to young Harmon Killibrew and Bob Allison, whom I saw hit a number of home runs. By 1960 it was clear that they had the makings of a contending team and we were furious when they departed. I also saw the first game of the expansion 1961 Senators, against the White Sox, in a section filled with Kennedy administration members and children, of which I was one.

My most vivid memory concerns the construction of the park. As pictures show, the upper deck of the grandstand hung over nearly the entire lower deck. The seats near the front of the upper deck along the baselines were better than any seats in any park today. You felt like you were on top of the field. I have been waiting for someone to build a park like that ever since, but they never do.

David Kaiser
Watertown, Massachusetts

I saw my first game (the first baseball game I saw of any kind) at Griffith Stadium in 1959. I was 10 years old, didn't own a baseball glove and had never played in an organized game. I am the Scottish-born son of Scottish immigrants and knew nothing about baseball until I met a couple of classmates in elementary school who were Senators fans and got me interested.

My next-door neighbor, who was three years older, had obtained two tickets to a game through some Tastykake promotion. His father agreed to drive us to the stadium, with enough money for concessions and to pay the streetcar and bus fare home. Simpler times.

Our seats were in the bleachers. I'm not sure who the Senators played or who won, but I recall a home run hit by Harmon Killebrew landing near us.

I made it back to the stadium with my parents in 1961 to see the expansion team play the Cleveland Indians. By this time, I was a devout baseball fan. For this game, we had box seats on the third-base side. The Senators had designated the game as "Beat Mudcat Day," hoping to defeat an old nemesis, Jim "Mudcat" Grant. Thanks to Retrosheet, I know they failed. Grant beat them three times in D.C. that season. The game we attended most likely was on June 7, with the Indians thumping the Nats, 11-0. No wonder I don't recall anything else about it.

Andrew Sharp
Cream Ridge, New Jersey

Yes, I have seen many games at Griffith Stadium.

The Senators had very poor teams and the attendance reflected that fact. It was not difficult to get a seat and spread out most of the times – other than Opening Day. Many times, we would sit out in the bleachers and get a good suntan. Opening Day was always a sellout and the president of the US was usually there to throw out the first ball. The Nats' Opening Day game was usually one day before the rest of the league started. Once I saw Harry Truman walking up a ramp to his seat.

The first game I remember seeing was in June of 1941. Midway through the game, newspaper boys were running through the stands yelling, "Extra, extra! Germany invades Russia!"

In the football season the Washington football team used Griffith Stadium for its home games. My dad had two season tickets and he would take me sometimes. I was at the Washington-Eagles game on December 7, 1941, when the P.A. announcer kept calling admirals and generals to report to their office at once. I was at a party a few years ago and someone there who knew I was at that game said I was probably the last living person who attended that game. Maybe.

David Paulson
Columbia, Maryland

GRIFFITH STADIUM BY THE NUMBERS

by Dan Fields

1

Home run by the Washington Senators at Griffith Stadium in 1917, 1918, 1924, and 1945.

1

Nine-inning complete-game no-hitter thrown at Griffith Stadium, by Bobby Burke of the Senators on August 8, 1931, against the Boston Red Sox. He walked five batters.

1ST

American League player to hit a home run in his first major-league at-bat: Luke Stuart of the St. Louis Browns, on August 8, 1921.

1ST

Major-league hit by Jimmie Foxx, of the Philadelphia Athletics, on May 1, 1925. He was 17 years old.

1ST

Black player in Senators history: Carlos Paula, on September 6, 1954. He hit a two-run double and a single in the first game of a doubleheader against the Philadelphia Athletics and went hitless in the second game.

1ST

Team in major-league history to turn a triple play on Opening Day: the Baltimore Orioles, against the Senators on April 9, 1959.

2

All-Star Games played at Griffith Stadium. On July 7, 1937, the American League beat the National League 8-3 in the fifth-ever All-Star Game. Franklin Delano Roosevelt, who threw the ceremonial first pitch, was the first US president to attend an All-Star Game. On July 10, 1956, the National League beat the American League 7-3.

2

Shutouts by George Dumont of the Senators in this first two starts, on September 14, 1915 (his major-league debut), against the Cleveland Indians and on September 20, 1915, against the St. Louis Browns. In the remaining 33 starts during his five-year career, he threw two more shutouts.

2

Triples by Gil Coan of the Senators in the sixth inning on April 21, 1951, against the New York Yankees.

2

Home runs by Jim Lemon of the Senators in the third inning on September 5, 1959, against the Boston Red Sox.

2

Major-league games in which Hector Maestri appeared. On September 24, 1960, he pitched two innings for the original Senators against the Orioles. On September 17, 1961, he pitched six innings for the expansion Senators against the Kansas City Athletics. The only other players to play for both versions of the Senators at Griffith Stadium were pitchers Rudy Hernandez and Hal Woodeschick.

2.26

ERA of the Senators at Griffith Stadium in 1915, the lowest of any year since 1913 (when ERA became an official statistic in the AL).

3

World Series that the Senators played at Griffith Stadium, in 1924 (vs. the New York Giants), 1925 (vs. the Pittsburgh Pirates), and 1933 (vs. the New York Giants). In Game Seven of the 1924 Series (October 10 at Griffith Stadium), the Senators rallied from a 3-1 deficit in the eighth inning to beat the Giants 4-3 in 12 innings and claim their only World Series championship.

3

Wins in three consecutive days against the St. Louis Browns by Tommy Thomas of the Senators, on July 14, 15, and 16, 1932. The first two wins were in relief, and he threw a shutout in the third game.

5

Players who hit for the cycle at Griffith Stadium: Bob Meusel, New York Yankees, May 7, 1921; Mickey Cochrane, Philadelphia Athletics, July 22, 1932; Pinky Higgins, Philadelphia Athletics, August 6, 1933; Odell Hale, Cleveland Indians, July 12 1938; and Vic Wertz, Detroit Tigers, September 14, 1947 (first game of doubleheader).

5

Consecutive years (1912 to 1916) in which Walter Johnson had at least 15 wins at Griffith Stadium. During that span, he had a record of 81-26 (.757) at the stadium.

5

Strikeouts (in 295 at-bats) by Sam Rice at Griffith Stadium in 1929, for a rate of 1 every 59 at-bats.

5

Hits (in seven at-bats) by Cecil Travis of the Senators in his first major-league game, on May 16, 1933. The Senators beat the Indians 11-10 in 12 innings.

5

Bases stolen by the Senators at home in 1957.

5.55

ERA of the Senators at Griffith Stadium in 1956, the highest of any year.

6

Consecutive games in which Roy Sievers of the Senators hit a home run, from July 28 (second game of doubleheader) to August 3 (in the 17th inning), 1957.

9

Hits in consecutive at-bats by Sam Rice of the Senators from September 17 to 19, 1925.

14

Hits allowed by Milt Gaston of the Senators in a shutout (9-0) of the Indians on July 10, 1928.

16

Consecutive home wins by the Senators from July 30 to September 22 (first game of doubleheader), 1943.

17-2

Record of Walter Johnson at Griffith Stadium in 1915 (.895 winning percentage). He had a record of 10-11 on the road that year.

22-0

Score by which the Yankees led the Senators before the bottom of the eighth inning on August 12, 1953. The Yankees won 22-1.

25

Consecutive games with a hit at Griffith Stadium by Sam Rice from May 18 to July 14, 1920. He had 45 hits in 105 at-bats (.429) during the streak.

26-51

Record of the Senators at home in 1949, for a winning percentage of .338.

46

Extra-base hits by Joe Cronin at Griffith Stadium in 1932. He hit 31 doubles, 13 triples, and 2 home runs. By comparison, he had 21 extra-base hits on the road: 12 doubles, 5 triples, and 4 home runs.

51

Consecutive scoreless innings pitched at Griffith Stadium by Walter Johnson from May 7 to June 30, 1918.

56-21

Record of the Senators at home in 1930, for a winning percentage of .727.

57

Age in years of Nick Altrock of the Senators when he served as a pinch-hitter on October 1, 1933.

83

Home runs by the Senators at Griffith Stadium in 1959, the most in any year.

94

Singles (in 76 games) by Sam Rice at Griffith Stadium in 1925.

147

Bases stolen by the Senators at home in 1913.

185

Total bases by Roy Sievers at Griffith Stadium in 1957. He had 146 total bases on the road.

.237

Batting average of the Senators at Griffith Stadium in 1959, the lowest of any season.

300TH

Career win by Walter Johnson on May 14, 1920.

.315

Batting average of the Senators at Griffith Stadium in 1930, the highest of any season.

400TH

Career win by Walter Johnson on April 27, 1926.

.429

Batting average of Walter Johnson at Griffith Stadium in 1925. He had 21 hits in 49 at-bats.

460

Attendance at a game on September 7, 1954, between the Senators and Philadelphia Athletics.

785-705-15

Regular-season record as manager by Bucky Harris at Griffith Stadium: 729-652-13 with the Senators, 36-41-1 with the Tigers, 13-9 with the Yankees, and 7-3-1 with the Red Sox.

1,923

Total bases by Sam Rice at Griffith Stadium, the most of any player.

2,033-1,874-38

Record of the Senators at Griffith Stadium from April 12, 1911, to September 21, 1961.

4,189TH

And last major-league hit by Ty Cobb of the Philadelphia Athletics, on September 2, 1928.

38,701

Attendance at Game Four of the 1925 World Series between the Senators and the Pirates, the most for a baseball game at Griffith Stadium.

89,682

Regular-season attendance at Griffith Stadium in 1917, the lowest in any year (1,121 per game).

1,027,216

Regular-season attendance at Griffith Stadium in 1946, the highest in any year (13,516 per game).

CAREER LEADERS AT GRIFFITH STADIUM

BATTING

Games

1159	Sam Rice
1093	Joe Judge
927	Ossie Bluege
927	Mickey Vernon
862	Eddie Yost

Plate Appearances

4878	Sam Rice
4592	Joe Judge
3875	Mickey Vernon
3796	Eddie Yost
3551	Ossie Bluege

At-Bats

4391	Sam Rice
3910	Joe Judge
3437	Mickey Vernon
3067	Eddie Yost
3057	Ossie Bluege

Runs

747	Sam Rice
602	Joe Judge
541	Buddy Myer
466	Mickey Vernon
465	Eddie Yost

Hits

1471	Sam Rice
1203	Joe Judge
996	Mickey Vernon
933	Buddy Myer
896	Clyde Milan

Doubles

215	Sam Rice
211	Joe Judge
195	Mickey Vernon
162	Goose Goslin
152	Eddie Yost

Triples

105	Sam Rice
95	Joe Judge
89	Goose Goslin
71	Buddy Myer
66	Mickey Vernon

Home runs

91	Roy Sievers
88	Jim Lemon
41	Harmon Killebrew
38	Goose Goslin
34	Babe Ruth
34	Mickey Vernon

RBIs

567	Sam Rice
513	Joe Judge
478	Goose Goslin
478	Mickey Vernon
421	Ossie Bluege

Walks

628	Eddie Yost
499	Joe Judge
441	Buddy Myer
381	Mickey Vernon
360	Sam Rice

Intentional Walks

40	Mickey Vernon
24	Stan Spence
23	Roy Sievers
15	Ted Williams
13	Joe Kuhel
13	Pete Runnels
13	Eddie Yost

Strikeouts

326	Eddie Yost
310	Jim Lemon
310	Mickey Vernon
231	Joe Judge
222	Ossie Bluege

Hit by Pitch

48	Bucky Harris
44	Ossie Bluege
37	Eddie Yost
33	Joe Judge
28	George McBride
28	Clyde Milan
28	Sam Rice

Hit by Pitch

48	Bucky Harris
44	Ossie Bluege
37	Eddie Yost
33	Joe Judge
28	George McBride
28	Clyde Milan
28	Sam Rice

Batting Average (min. 1,400 at-bats)

.335	Sam Rice
.325	Heinie Manush
.318	Goose Goslin
.313	Buddy Myer
.308	Joe Judge
.308	Sam West

On-base percentage (min. 1,400 at-bats)

.404	Buddy Myer
.393	Muddy Ruel
.391	Joe Judge
.389	Sam Rice
.387	Goose Goslin
.308	Sam West

Slugging percentage (min. 1,400 at-bats)

.524	Jim Lemon
.496	Roy Sievers
.484	Goose Goslin
.471	Heinie Manush
.441	Sam West

OPS (min. 1,400 at-bats)

.871	Goose Goslin
.868	Jim Lemon
.859	Roy Sievers
.839	Heinie Manush
.828	Buddy Myer

Stolen Bases

215	Clyde Milan
179	George Case
176	Sam Rice
117	Joe Judge
103	Bucky Harris

PITCHING

ERA (min. 500 innings)

1.78	Walter Johnson
2.35	Doc Ayers
2.63	Mickey Haefner
2.80	Bob Porterfield
2.81	Dutch Leonard
2.81	George Mogridge

Wins

200	Walter Johnson
66	Dutch Leonard
66	Firpo Marberry
59	General Crowder
54	Early Wynn

Losses

93	Walter Johnson
65	Sid Hudson
55	Early Wynn
54	Tom Zachary
50	Dutch Leonard
50	Pedro Ramos

Winning percentage (min. 40 wins)

.683	Walter Johnson
.673	Firpo Marberry
.663	General Crowder
.627	Sad Sam Jones
.569	Dutch Leonard

Games Pitched

334	Walter Johnson
235	Firpo Mayberry
161	Sid Hudson
157	Jim Shaw
149	Chuck Stobbs

Games Started

280	Walter Johnson
130	Sid Hudson
130	Dutch Leonard
118	Early Wynn
110	Tom Zachary

Complete Games

223	Walter Johnson
72	Dutch Leonard
64	Early Wynn
59	Sid Hudson
56	Bobo Newsom

Shutouts

61	Walter Johnson
17	Dutch Leonard
14	Bob Porterfield
13	Walt Masterson
12	Jim Shaw

Saves

37	Firpo Marberry
17	Dick Hyde
15	Tom Ferrick
13	Allen Russell
12	Mickey Harris

Innings Pitched

2551⅓	Walter Johnson
1017	Dutch Leonard
1009	Sid Hudson
908⅓	Early Wynn
873	Firpo Marberry

Walks

537	Walter Johnson
386	Sid Hudson
367	Walt Masterson
363	Bobo Newsom
361	Jim Shaw

Intentional Walks

1516	Walter Johnson
522	Camilo Pascual
421	Jim Shaw
385	Bump Hadley
373	Firpo Marberry

Games Started

1516	Walter Johnson
522	Camilo Pascual
421	Jim Shaw
385	Bump Hadley
373	Firpo Marberry

Home Runs Allowed

84	Pedro Ramos
59	Chuck Stobbs
44	Camilo Pascual
42	Russ Kemmerer
39	Walter Johnson

Hit by Pitch

82	Walter Johnson
28	Bump Hadley
25	Joe Boehling
23	Doc Ayers
21	Harry Harper

Wild Pitches

46	Walter Johnson
31	Dutch Leonard
29	Harry Harper
29	Jim Shaw
20	Ken Chase

SINGLE-SEASON LEADERS AT GRIFFITH STADIUM

BATTING

Games: 81 by Eddie Foster, 1916; Clyde Milan, 1916

Plate appearances: 371 by Buddy Lewis, 1938

At-bats: 341 by Buddy Lewis, 1937

Runs: 72 by Joe Cronin, 1930

Hits: 116 by Buddy Lewis, 1937

Doubles: 31 by Joe Cronin, 1932

Triples: 14 by Goose Goslin, 1924

Home runs: 26 by Roy Sievers, 1957

RBIs: 67 by Joe Cronin, 1932

Walks: 77 by Eddie Yost, 1956

Intentional walks: 13 by Stan Spence, 1947

Strikeouts: 78 by Jim Lemon, 1956

Hit by pitch: 16 by Kid Elberfeld, 1911

Batting average: .381 by John Stone, 1936

On-base percentage: .479 by John Stone, 1936

Slugging percentage: .615 by Roy Sievers, 1957

OPS: 1.067 by John Stone, 1936

Stolen bases: 40 by Clyde Milan, 1912

PITCHING

ERA: 0.99 by Roger Wolff, 1945

Wins: 17 by Walter Johnson, 1915; Walter Johnson, 1916

Losses: 11 by Pedro Ramos, 1959

Games pitched: 31 by Dick Hyde, 1958

Games started: 20 by Bob Groom, 1912; Bobo Newsom, 1936; Dutch Leonard, 1941; Pedro Ramos, 1958; Pedro Ramos, 1960

Complete games: 19 by Walter Johnson, 1916

Shutouts: 7 by Walter Johnson, 1913

Saves: 14 by Dick Hyde, 1958

Innings pitched: 193⅓ by Walter Johnson, 1912

Walks: 80 by Jim Shaw, 1917

Intentional walks: 7 by Camilo Pascual, 1954

Strikeouts: 172 by Walter Johnson, 1912

Home runs allowed: 21 by Pedro Ramos, 1958

Hit by pitch: 12 by Walter Johnson, 1915

Wild pitches: 9 by Ken Chase, 1940

SINGLE-GAME LEADERS AT GRIFFITH STADIUM

(* = extra-inning game)

BATTING

Runs: 5 by Harry Hooper, Boston Red Sox, June 24, 1915; Ty Cobb, Detroit Tigers, July 30, 1917; Babe Ruth, New York Yankees, April 20, 1926; Ben Chapman, Cleveland Indians, September 19, 1939; Vic Wertz, Detroit Tigers, September 14, 1947 (first game of doubleheader); Hank Bauer, New York Yankees, August 12, 1953

Hits: 6 by George Sisler, St. Louis Browns, August 9, 1921*; Frank Brower, Cleveland Indians, August 7, 1923

Doubles: 3 on 38 occasions. The only player to accomplish the feat three times was Sam West (on July 14, 1928; August 2, 1931; and July 15, 1932, all with the Senators). Five players did it twice: Joe Cronin (August 6, 1931, with the Senators, and April 26, 1938, with the Boston Red Sox), Charlie Gehringer (June 7, 1929, and August 28, 1932, both with the Detroit Tigers), Goose Goslin (April 25, 1926,* and June 11, 1933, both with the Senators), Babe Ruth (May 9, 1918,* with the Boston Red Sox, and April 29, 1930, with the New York Yankees), and Mickey Vernon (July 18, 1948 [second game of doubleheader],* and May 23, 1954, both with the Senators).

Triples: 3 by Joe Judge, Senators, August 9, 1921*; Charlie Gehringer, Detroit Tigers, August 5, 1929

Home runs: 3 by Joe DiMaggio, New York Yankees, September 10, 1950; Jim Lemon, Senators, August 31, 1956; Rocky Colavito, Detroit Tigers, August 27, 1961 (second game of doubleheader)

RBIs: 7 by Doc Gessler, Senators, June 2, 1911; Frank LaPorte, St. Louis Browns, August 7, 1911 (second game of doubleheader); Rip Williams, Senators, July 3, 1914 (first game of doubleheader); Charlie Gehringer, Detroit Tigers, June 7, 1929; Buddy Myer, Senators, August 5, 1929; Tom McBride, Boston Red Sox, August 4, 1945 (second game of doubleheader); Roy Sievers, Senators, September 2, 1954; Jim Lemon, Senators, September 5, 1959

Walks: 5 by Tris Speaker, Boston Red Sox, October 1, 1912; Eddie Yost, Senators, September 10, 1955

Intentional walks: 3 by Stan Spence, Senators, July 8, 1944; Joe Kuhel, Senators, September 5, 1945 (second game of doubleheader)

Strikeouts: 6 by Carl Weilman, St. Louis Browns, July 25, 1913*

Stolen bases: 4 by Lena Blackburne, Chicago White Sox, May 13, 1914; Chick Gandil, Senators, June 23, 1915; Ty Cobb, Detroit Tigers, September 24, 1917 (first game of doubleheader)

PITCHING

Innings pitched: 19 by Dixie Davis, St. Louis Browns, August 9, 1921*

Runs allowed: 20 by Tom Sheehan, Philadelphia Athletics, September 29, 1915 (second game of doubleheader)

Hits allowed: 23 Tom Sheehan, Philadelphia Athletics, September 29, 1915 (second game of doubleheader)

Walks: 14 by Skipper Friday, Senators, June 17, 1923*

Intentional walks: 3 by Eddie Rommel, Philadelphia Athletics, April 13, 1926*; Red Ruffing, New York Yankees, June 29, 1939 (first game of doubleheader)*; Sig Jakucki, St. Louis Browns, July 8, 1944; Atley Donald, New York Yankees, August 25, 1944*; Jim Turner, New York Yankees, August 27, 1944 (second game of doubleheader); Boo Ferriss, Boston Red Sox, August 5, 1947; Saul Rogovin, Chicago White Sox, June 17, 1953

Strikeouts: 17 by Bill Monbouquette, Boston Red Sox, May 12, 1961

Home runs allowed: 4 by Russ Kemmerer, Senators, July 30, 1957; Pedro Ramos, Senators, September 28, 1958; Herb Score, Cleveland Indians, June 14, 1959 (second game of doubleheader); Jack Fisher, Baltimore Orioles, July 10, 1959

Hit by pitch: 3 on 17 occasions. The only player to accomplish the feat twice was Carl Cashion (on October 3, 1911 (first game of doubleheader), and September 6, 1913, both with the Senators).

Wild pitches: 4 by Bert Gallia, Senators, June 9, 1917

SOURCES

Society for American Baseball Research. *The SABR Baseball List and Record Book* (New York: Scribner, 2007).

Sugar, Bert Randolph, ed. *The Baseball Maniac's Almanac* (fifth edition) (New York: Sports Publishing, 2019).

Baseball-Reference.com

NationalPastime.com

Retrosheet.org/boxesetc/W/PK_WAS09.htm

CAST OF CONTRIBUTORS

Adam Berenbak lives in Washington and is an archivist at the National Archives Center for Legislative Archives. In addition to an interest in D.C. baseball (which was capped off by the Nats' 2019 World Series run!), he has written about baseball in Japan, as well as baseball and Congress, in publications such as SABR's *Baseball Research Journal* and *Prologue*, and has presented on these subjects at the Cooperstown Symposium on Baseball and American Culture. A graduate of North Carolina Central University and a former Steele Intern at the National Baseball Hall of Fame and Museum's Giamatti Library, he has curated exhibitions at the Japanese Embassy's Cultural Center in D.C. and in Durham, North Carolina.

John Bauer resides with his wife and two children in Bedford, New Hampshire, having recently relocated from Kansas City. By day, he is an attorney specializing in insurance regulatory law and corporate law. By night, he spends many spring and summer evenings cheering for the San Francisco Giants and many fall and winter evenings reading history. He is a past and ongoing contributor to other SABR projects.

Nathan Bierma is a SABR member and SABR Games Project contributor living in Grand Rapids, Michigan. His writing has appeared in the *Chicago Tribune*, *Chicago Sports Review*, and *Detroit Free Press*, and in SABR's recent books on the greatest games at Wrigley Field and Comiskey Park. He is the author of *The Eclectic Encyclopedia of English: Language at Its Most Enigmatic, Ephemeral, and Egregious*. His website is www.nathanbierma.com.

Derek Blair is currently an undergraduate student at the University of Pittsburgh. He is the founder of Dingerball.com, a baseball analytics blog, and oversees a team of writers and a podcast. He continues to write regularly for the site as well. Derek is the author of "Bullpenning: Why It Works," which dives into a deep analysis of a new pitching strategy. Derek was the recipient of the 2018 Jack Kavanagh Research Award from SABR for an essay that he wrote about the Seattle Pilots franchise.

Luis A. Blandon, a Washington native, is a producer, writer, and researcher in video and documentary film production and in archival, manuscript, historical, film, and image research. His creative storytelling has garnered numerous awards, including three regional Emmys®, regional and national Edward R. Murrow Awards, two TELLY awards and a New York Festival World Medal. He worked as a researcher and/or producer on several documentaries including *Jeremiah*; *Feast Your Ears: The Story of WHFS 102.3*; and *#GeorgeWashington*. Most recently, he was co-producer of the documentary *The Lost Battalion*. He was senior researcher and manager of the story development team for two national programs for Retirement Living Television. He has worked as a historian for two public policy research firms, Morgan Angel & Associates and MLL Consulting LLC. He recently served as the principal researcher for *The League of Wives* by Heath Hardage Lee. He has a master of arts in international affairs from the George Washington University.

Thomas J. Brown Jr. is a lifelong Mets fan who became a Durham Bulls fan after moving to North Carolina in the early 1980s. He was a national-board-certified high-school science teacher for 34 years before retiring in 2016. Tom still volunteers with the ELL students at his former high school, serving as a mentor to those students and the teachers who are now working with them. He also provides support and guidance for his former ELL students when they embark on different career paths after graduation. Tom has been a member of SABR since 1995, when he learned about the organization during a visit to Cooperstown on his honeymoon. He has become active in the organization since his retirement and has written numerous biographies and game stories, mostly about the New York Mets. Tom also enjoys traveling as much as possible with his wife and has visited major-league and minor-league ballparks across the country on his many trips. He also loves to cook and makes all the meals at his house while writing about those meals on his blog, Cooking and My Family.

A lifelong White Sox fan surrounded by Cubs fans in the northern suburbs of Chicago, **Ken Carrano** works as a chief financial officer for a large landscaping firm and as a soccer referee. A SABR member since 1992, Ken and his Brewers' fan wife, Ann, share two children, two golden retrievers, and a mutual disdain for the blue side of Chicago.

Alan Cohen has been a SABR member since 2010, and he attended his first SABR convention in 2012 in Minneapolis. He serves as vice president-treasurer of the Connecticut Smoky Joe Wood Chapter and is datacaster (MiLB First Pitch stringer) for the Hartford Yard Goats, the Double-A affiliate of the Colorado Rockies. His biographies, game stories, and essays have appeared in more than 40 SABR publications. Since his first *Baseball Research Journal* article appeared in 2013, Alan has continued to expand his research into the Homestead Grays and Josh Gibson who in 1943 had more home runs at Griffith Stadium in 38 games than the Washington Senators as a team had in 76 games. He has four children and eight grandchildren and resides in Connecticut with wife Frances, their cats, Morty, Ava, and Zoe, and their dog, Buddy.

Richard Cuicchi joined SABR in 1983 and is an active member of the Schott-Pelican Chapter. Since his retirement as an information technology executive, Richard has authored *Family Ties: A Comprehensive Collection of Facts and Trivia about Baseball's Relatives*. He has contributed to numerous SABR BioProject and Games publications. He does freelance writing and blogging about a variety of baseball topics on his website, TheTenthInning.com. Richard lives in New Orleans with his wife, Mary.

Paul E. Doutrich is professor emeritus at York College of Pennsylvania, where he taught American history for 30 years. He now lives in Brewster, Massachusetts. Among the courses he taught was a one entitled "Baseball History." He has written scholarly articles and contributed to several anthologies about the Revolutionary era, and has written a book about Jacksonian America. He has also curated several museum exhibits. His recent scholarship has focused on baseball history. He has contributed numerous manuscripts to various SABR publications and is the author of *The Cardinals and the Yankees, 1926: A Classical Season and St. Louis in Seven.*

Dan Fields has contributed to many SABR books He is senior manuscript editor at the *New England Journal of Medicine* and a longtime volunteer with the Grief Support Services program of Samaritans, Inc. He lives in Framingham, Massachusetts, and can be reached at dfields820@gmail.com.

Jeff Findley is a native of Eastern Iowa, where he did the logical thing growing up in the heart of the Cubs/Cardinals rivalry – he embraced the 1969 Baltimore Orioles and became a lifelong fan. An information-security professional for a Fortune 50 Financial Services company in Central Illinois, he also compiles a daily sports "Pages Past" column for his local newspaper.

James Forr is a recovering Pirates fan in the heart of Cardinals country. His book *Pie Traynor: A Baseball Biography*, co-authored with David Proctor, was a nominee for the 2010 CASEY Award. He is a winner of the McFarland-SABR Baseball Research Award and was a speaker at the 2019 Frederick Ivor-Campbell 19th Century Base Ball Conference.

Brian Frank is passionate about documenting the history of major- and minor-league baseball. He is the creator of the website The Herd Chronicles (herdchronicles.com), which is dedicated to preserving the history of the Buffalo Bisons. His articles can also be read on the official website of the Bisons. He was an assistant editor of the book *The Seasons of Buffalo Baseball, 1857-2020,* and he's a frequent contributor to SABR publications. Brian and his wife, Jenny, enjoy traveling around the country in their camper to major- and minor-league ballparks and taking an annual trip to Europe. Brian was a history major at Canisius College, where he earned a bachelor of arts. He also received a juris doctor from the University at Buffalo School of Law.

Gordon J. Gattie is an engineer for the US Navy. His baseball research interests include ballparks, historical trends, and statistical analysis. A SABR member since 1998, Gordon earned his Ph.D. from SUNY Buffalo, where he used baseball to investigate judgment performance in complex dynamic environments. Ever the optimist, he dreams of a Cleveland Indians-Washington Nationals World Series matchup, especially after the Nationals' 2019 World Series championship. Lisa, his wonderful wife, who roots for the Yankees, and Morrigan, their beloved yellow Labrador, enjoy traveling across the country to visit ballparks and other baseball-related sites. Gordon has contributed to several SABR publications and the Games Project.

Clark Griffith, the son of former Minnesota Twins owner Calvin Griffith and the great-nephew of former Washington Senators owner Clark C. Griffith, grew up in Washington. He worked for the Twins after graduating from Dartmouth. Griffith served as the chairman of Major League Properties when it began its marketing/licensing program and was on the Player Relations Committee that developed the player control system that is in force now. Griffith, who lives in Minneapolis, also served as commissioner of the independent Northern League.

Lou Hernandez is the author of multiple baseball histories and biographies, and two young adult novels. He resides in South Florida and loyally follows the Miami Marlins.

Paul Hofmann, a SABR member since 2002, is the associate vice president for international affairs at Sacramento State University and a frequent contributor to SABR publications. Paul is a native of Detroit and a lifelong Tigers fan. He currently resides in Folsom, California.

Mike Huber is a professor of mathematics at Muhlenberg College in Allentown, Pennsylvania. A SABR member since 1996, he chairs SABR's Games Project Committee and enjoys researching and writing about rare events in baseball, to include games in which players hit for the cycle. He has been rooting for the same American League East team for more than 50 years.

Jimmy Keenan has been a SABR member since 2001. His grandfather, Jimmy Lyston, and four other family members were all professional baseball players. A frequent contributor to SABR publications, Keenan is the author of three books: *The Lystons: A Story of One Baltimore Family & Our National Pastime*; *The Life, Times and Tragic Death of Pitcher Win Mercer*; and *The Lyston Brothers: A Journey Through 19th Century Baseball.* Keenan is a 2010 inductee into the Oldtimers Baseball Association of Maryland's Hall of Fame and a 2012 inductee into Baltimore's Boys of Summer Hall of Fame.

Timothy Kearns resides just a few blocks from the site of the former Griffith Stadium in Washington with his wife and cats. An Ohio native and a longtime fan of Cleveland's team, Timothy had to turn to the practice of law to experience the thrill of victory. He is a partner in a law firm where he practices primarily in plaintiffs' side antitrust and complex financial litigation.

Thomas E. Kern was born and raised in Southwest Pennsylvania. Listening to the mellifluous voices of Bob Prince and Jim Woods, how could one not become a lifelong Pirates fan? Tom has been a SABR member dating back to the mid-1980s. He now lives in Washington and sees the Nationals and Orioles as often as possible. With a love and appreciation for Negro League baseball, Tom wrote a SABR biography of Leon Day after having met him at a baseball card show in the early 1990s. He has since written a number of Negro League bios for the SABR BioProject. Tom's day job is in the field of transportation technology.

Ben Klein grew up in Rancho Cucamonga, California, and now resides in Rockville, Maryland, with his wife and two daughters. He has been a SABR member since 2009 and has contributed to SABR books on the 1970 Baltimore Orioles and the 1965 Minnesota Twins.

Kevin Larkin retired after 24 years as a police officer in his hometown of Great Barrington, Massachusetts. He has always been a baseball fan and has been going to minor-league and major-league baseball games since he was five years old. He has authored two books on baseball: *Baseball in the Bay State* (a history of baseball in Massachusetts) and *Gehrig: Game by Game*. He co-authored *Baseball in the Berkshires: A County's Common Bond* along with James Tom Daly, James Overmyer, and Larry Moore. The book details a history of baseball in Berkshire County, where Larkin grew up. He has authored numerous articles for SABR and also published in 2020 *Legends on Deck*, a list of the top 100 Black Baseball/Negro League baseball players. Researching and learning about this great game are what drives him, and he loves researching, reading, and writing about the game's history. He does fact-checking and hyperlinking for SABR, as well as writing biographies and game accounts, and according to him, is living the dream of writing and researching about the great sport of baseball.

Bob LeMoine grew up in Maine and has lived and died with the Red Sox for most of his life. He joined SABR in 2013 and has contributed to several SABR book projects. Having a love for both history and baseball, he usually contributes to most SABR book projects. Bob lives in Rochester, New Hampshire, and works as a high-school librarian and adjunct professor.

Len Levin is retired after a long career as a newspaper editor in New England. He is currently the grammarian and copyeditor for the Rhode Island Supreme Court. He also copyedits many of

SABR's publications, including this one. His first major-league experience involved the Senators, but it was at Fenway Park against the Red Sox, not at Griffith Stadium.

SABR member and Massachusetts native **Mike Lynch** is the founder of Seamheads.com and the author of five books, including *Harry Frazee, Ban Johnson and the Feud That Nearly Destroyed the American League*, which was named a finalist for the 2009 Larry Ritter Award and was nominated for a Seymour Medal. His most recent work includes a three-book series called *Baseball's Untold History* and several articles that have appeared in SABR books. His collaboration with others on Negro Leagues history earned him the 2019 Tweed Webb Lifetime Achievement Award given by SABR's Negro Leagues Research Committee. He lives in Roslindale, Massachusetts, with Catherine and their cats, Jiggs and Pepper.

Bill Nowlin spends most of his time writing and editing as a volunteer for SABR. Editor or co-editor of a few dozen SABR books and a few hundred BioProject and Games Project stories is either a sign of insanity or is keeping him sane in retirement. He is both a former professor of political science and a co-founder of Rounder Records, celebrating its 50th year in 2020. His only visit to Griffith Stadium is through the reading of the various stories in this book and elsewhere.

A productive and energetic member of SABR, **Chris Rainey** passed away in December 2020. He was introduced to the world of baseball research by former SABR President Eugene Murdoch around 1976. He was active in the BioProject as an author and also head of the fact-checking team. An avid Cleveland fan, he had pictures of all but 12 of the team from 1901 to 2019.

Carl Riechers retired from United Parcel Service in 2012 after 35 years of service. With more free time, he became a SABR member that same year. Born and raised in the suburbs of St. Louis, he became a big fan of the Cardinals. He and his wife, Janet, have three children and he is the proud grandpa of two.

Joel Rippel, a Minnesota native and graduate of the University of Minnesota, is the author or co-author of 10 books on Minnesota sports history and has contributed as a writer and editor to SABR publications.

Paul Rogers is president of the Ernie Banks-Bobby Bragan (Dallas-Fort Worth) SABR Chapter and the co-author of four baseball books, including *The Whiz Kids and the 1950 Pennant*, written with his boyhood hero Robin Roberts, and *Lucky Me: My 65 Years in Baseball*, authored with Eddie Robinson. He is also a co-editor of recent SABR team histories of the 1951 New York Giants and the 1950 Philadelphia Phillies as well as a frequent contributor to the SABR BioProject and Games Project. His real job is as a law professor at SMU where he was dean of the law school for nine years and has served as the university's faculty athletic representative for 33 years.

Gary A. Sarnoff has been an active SABR member since 1994. A member of SABR's Bob Davids chapter, he has contributed to SABR's BioProject and Games Project, and to the annual *National Pastime* publication. He is a member of the SABR Negro Leagues committee and is chairman of the Ron Gabriel Committee. In addition, he has authored two baseball books: *The Wrecking Crew of '33* and *The First Yankees Dynasty*. He currently resides in Alexandria, Virginia.

John Schleppi, University of Dayton professor emeritus, has worked in sports history for over 50 years. He published *Chicago's Showcase of Basketball: The World Tournament of Professional Basketball and the College All-Star Game*. He founded the Dayton Chapter of SABR and was chair for 15 years.

Steven D. Schmitt is the award-winning author of *A History of Badger Baseball – The Rise and Fall of America's Pastime at the University of Wisconsin* (UW Press, 2017). He has been a SABR member since 2010 and has written biographies and game stories for SABR books and for the SABR BioProject. He is a graduate of the University of Wisconsin-Madison, with bachelor's and master's degrees in journalism and mass communication, and is a member of the Wisconsin Alumni Association. He lives in Madison, Wisconsin, with his adult daughter Natalie.

Doug Schoppert's earliest baseball memory is attending a Yankees-Senators game at Griffith Stadium. He was raised in Virginia but now lives in another city long abandoned by the major leagues: Brooklyn. Doug has worked for the federal government for over 20 years. This is his first contribution to a SABR publication.

Tom Schott is a retired professional historian. American history Ph.D. (LSU 1978) – Geaux Tigers! Chess player, dog-, music-, books-, poetry-, and wine/beer-lover. Three kids, two grandkids, one superb wife, Susan, for 53 years.

Paul Scimonelli was born, grew up, and currently resides in Maryland with his wife, Virginia. A lifelong professional bassist, Paul retired in 2014 as the director of strings of the Landon School in Bethesda, Maryland. He is on the adjunct music faculty of the Rome School of Music, Drama, and Art at The Catholic University of America. His first book, *Roy Sievers; The Sweetest Right Handed Swing in 1950's Baseball* was published by McFarland Books in 2017. His second book, *Joe Cambria; Saint or Scoundrel? The Baseball Life of the Washington Senators Super Scout* was in production in 2020.

Doug Skipper has contributed to a number of SABR publications, presented research at national and regional conventions, and written more than a dozen player, manager, and game profiles for the SABR BioProject. A SABR member since 1982, he served as president of the Halsey Hall (Minneapolis) Chapter in 2014-2015, is a member of the Deadball Era Committee and chairs the Lawrence Ritter Award Committee. He is interested in the history of Connie Mack's Philadelphia Athletics, the Boston Red Sox, the Minnesota Twins, and old ballparks. A market research consultant residing in Apple Valley, Minnesota, Doug is also a veteran of father-daughter dancing. Doug and his wife Kathy have two daughters, MacKenzie and Shanno n.

John Sokora was born in Philadelphia in 1951. He has had an avid interest in baseball history ever since he received his first copy of *The Baseball Encyclopedia* (1958 edition). He served as an Assistant U.S. Attorney in the District of Columbia, retiring in 2011. Since that time, he has been a varsity softball coach at the National Cathedral School and, currently, at John Lewis High School in Springfield, Virginia.

Mark S. Sternman lived in Washington from 1992 to 1995. While greatly enjoying listening to Jon Miller's radio broadcasts of Baltimore Orioles games, Sternman regretted that he lived in D.C. too late to see the Washington Senators or the Homestead Grays play at Griffith Stadium.

A SABR member since 1979, **Stew Thornley** is an official scorer for Major League Baseball and a member of the MLB Official Scoring Advisory Committee.

Joseph Wancho has been a SABR member since 2005. He is the vice chair of the Baseball Index. Wancho occasionally contributes to the SABR Games Project and the SABR BioProject.

Gregory H. Wolf was born in Pittsburgh, but now resides in the Chicagoland area with his wife, Margaret, and daughter, Gabriela. A professor of German studies and holder of the Dennis and Jean Bauman Endowed Chair in the Humanities at North Central College in Naperville, Illinois, he has edited a dozen books for SABR. He is currently working on projects about Shibe Park in Philadelphia and Ebbets Field in Brooklyn. Since January 2017 he has been co-director of SABR's BioProject, which you can follow on Facebook and Twitter.

Jack Zerby joined SABR in 1994 and has been active as a writer, fact-checker, and editor in both the Biography Project (2002) and the Games Project (2014) since their respective inceptions. He and SABR colleague Mel Poplock co-founded the Harold Seymour and Dorothy Seymour Mills Chapter in southwest Florida. Jack is retired from a career as an attorney and estates/trust administrator in Pennsylvania and Florida. His fan interest over the years has been focused on the Pittsburgh Pirates, Atlanta Braves, Fort Myers Miracle, and Asheville Tourists. Jack and his wife, Diana, live in Brevard, North Carolina, in the Blue Ridge Mountains.

A SABR member since 1979, **Don Zminda** retired in 2016 after two-plus decades with STATS LLC, where he served first as director of publications and then director of research for STATS-supported sports broadcasts that included the World Series, the Super Bowl, and the NCAA Final Four. Don has also written or edited over a dozen sports books, including *The Legendary Harry Caray: Baseball's Greatest Salesman*, a CASEY Award nominee, and the SABR publication *Go-Go to Glory: The 1959 Chicago White* Sox. A Chicago native, he lives in Los Angeles with his wife, Sharon.

Friends of SABR

You can become a Friend of SABR by giving as little as $10 per month or by making a one-time gift of $1,000 or more. When you do so, you will be inducted into a community of passionate baseball fans dedicated to supporting SABR's work.

Friends of SABR receive the following benefits:

- ✓ Annual Friends of SABR Commemorative Lapel Pin
- ✓ Recognition in This Week in SABR, SABR.org, and the SABR Annual Report
- ✓ Access to the SABR Annual Convention VIP donor event
- ✓ Invitations to exclusive Friends of SABR events

SABR On-Deck Circle - $10/month, $30/month, $50/month
Get in the SABR On-Deck Circle, and help SABR become the essential community for the world of baseball. Your support will build capacity around all things SABR, including publications, website content, podcast development, and community growth.

A monthly gift is deducted from your bank account or charged to a credit card until you tell us to stop. No more email, mail, or phone reminders.

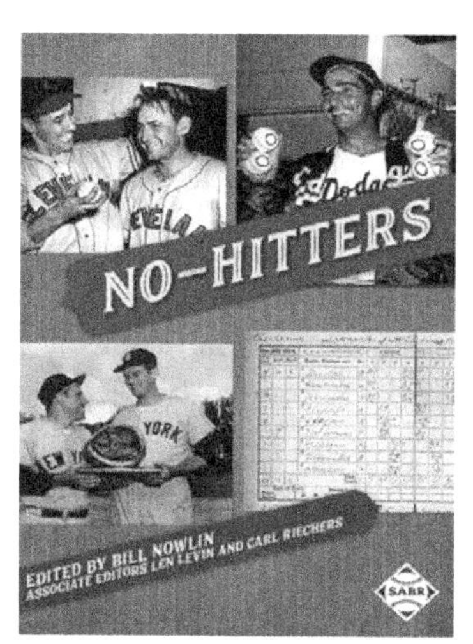

Join the SABR On-Deck Circle

Payment Info: _______Visa _______Mastercard

Name on Card: ______________________________

Card #: ______________________________

Exp. Date: ________ Security Code: ________

Signature: ______________________________

○ $10/month

○ $30/month

○ $50/month

○ Other amount ____________

Go to sabr.org/donate to make your gift online

New Books from SABR

Part of the mission of the Society for American Baseball Research has always been to disseminate member research. In addition to the *Baseball Research Journal*, SABR publishes books that include player biographies, historical game recaps, and statistical analysis. All SABR books are available in print and ebook formats. SABR members can access the entire SABR Digital Library for free and purchase print copies at significant member discounts of 40 to 50% off cover price.

JEFF BAGWELL IN CONNECTICUT:
A Consistent Lad in the Land of Steady Habits
This volume of articles, interviews, and essays by members of the Connecticut chapter of SABR chronicles the life and career of Connecticut's favorite baseball son, Hall-of-Famer Jeff Bagwell, with special attention on his high school and college years.
Edited by Karl Cicitto, Bill Nowlin, & Len Levin
$19.95 paperback (ISBN 978-1-943816-97-2)
$9.99 ebook (ISBN 978-1-943816-96-5)
7"x10", 246 pages, 45 photos

1995 CLEVELAND INDIANS:
The Sleeping Giant Awakens
After almost 40 years of sub-500 baseball, the Sleeping Giant woke in 1995, the first season in the Indians spent in their new home of Jacob's Field. The biographies of all the players, coaches, and broadcasters from that year are here, sprinkled with personal perspectives, as well as game stories from key matchups during the 1995 season, information about Jacob's Field, and other essays.
Edited by Joseph Wancho
$19.95 paperback (ISBN 978-1-943816-95-8)
$9.99 ebook (ISBN 978-1-943816-94-1)
8.5"X11", 410 pages, 76 photos

TIME FOR EXPANSION BASEBALL
The LA Angels and "new" Washington Senators ushered in MLB expansion in 1960, followed by the Houston Colt .45s and New York Mets. By 1998, 10 additional teams had launched: the Kansas City Royals, Seattle Pilots, Toronto Blue Jays, and Tampa Bay Devil Tays in the AL, and the Montreal Expos, San Diego Padres, Colorado Rockies, Florida Marlins, and Arizona Diamondbacks in the NL. *Time for Expansion Baseball* tells each team's origin and includes biographies of key players.
Edited by Maxwell Kates and Bill Nowlin
$24.95 paperback (ISBN 978-1-933599-89-7)
$9.99 ebook (ISBN 978-1-933599-88-0)
8.5"X11", 430 pages, 150 photos

Base Ball's 19th Century "Winter" Meetings
1857-1900
A look at the business meetings of base ball's earliest days (not all of which were in the winter). As John Thorn writes in his Foreword, "This monumental volume traces the development of the game from its birth as an organized institution to its very near suicide at the dawn of the next century."
Edited by Jeremy K. Hodges and Bill Nowlin
$29.95 paperback (ISBN 978-1-943816-91-0)
$9.99 ebook (ISBN978-1-943816-90-3)
8.5"x11", 390 pages, 50 photos

MET-ROSPECTIVES:
A Collection of the Greatest Games in New York Mets History
This book's 57 game stories—coinciding with the number of Mets years through 2018—are strictly for the eternal optimist. They include the team's very first victory in April 1962 at Forbes Field, Tom Seaver's "Imperfect Game" in July '69, the unforgettable Game Sixes in October '86, the "Grand Slam Single" in the 1999 NLCS, and concludes with the extra-innings heroics in September 2016 at Citi Field that helped ensure a wild-card berth.
edited by Brian Wright and Bill Nowlin
$14.95 paperback (ISBN 978-1-943816-87-3)
$9.99 ebook (ISBN 978-1-943816-86-6)
8.5"X11", 148 pages, 44 photos

CINCINNATI'S CROSLEY FIELD:
A Gem in the Queen City
This book evokes memories of Crosley Field through detailed summaries of more than 85 historic and monumental games played there, and 10 insightful feature essays about the history of the ballpark. Former Reds players Johnny Edwards and Art Shamsky share their memories of the park in introductions.
Edited by Gregory H. Wolf
$19.95 paperback (ISBN 978-1-943816-75-0)
$9.99 ebook (ISBN 978-1-943816-74-3)
8.5"X11", 320 pages, 43 photos

MOMENTS OF JOY AND HEARTBREAK:
66 Significant Episodes in the History of the Pittsburgh Pirates
In this book we relive no-hitters, World Series-winning homers, and the last tripleheader ever played in major-league baseball. Famous Pirates like Honus Wagner and Roberto Clemente—and infamous ones like Dock Ellis—make their appearances, as well as recent stars like Andrew McCutcheon.
Edited by Jorge Iber and Bill Nowlin
$19.95 paperback (ISBN 978-1-943816-73-6)
$9.99 ebook (ISBN 978-1-943816-72-9)
8.5"X11", 208 pages, 36 photos

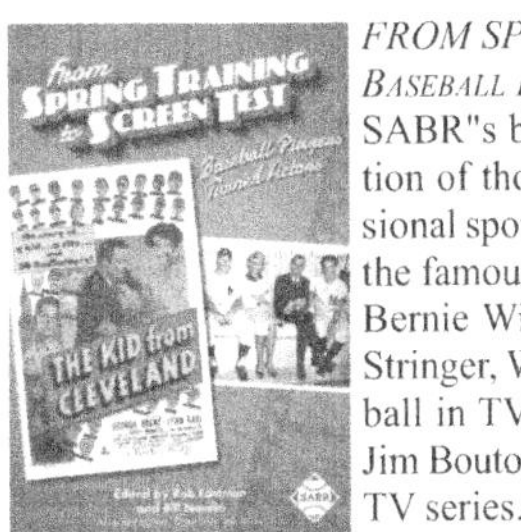

FROM SPRING TRAINING TO SCREEN TEST:
Baseball Players Turned Actors
SABR"s book of baseball's "matinee stars," a selection of those who crossed the lines between professional sports and popular entertainment. Included are the famous (Gene Autry, Joe DiMaggio, Jim Thorpe, Bernie Williams) and the forgotten (Al Gettel, Lou Stringer, Wally Hebert, Wally Hood), essays on baseball in TV shows and Coca-Cola commercials, and Jim Bouton's casting as "Jim Barton" in the *Ball Four* TV series.
Edited by Rob Edelman and Bill Nowlin
$19.95 paperback (ISBN 978-1-943816-71-2)
$9.99 ebook (ISBN 978-1-943816-70-5)
8.5"X11", 410 pages, 89 photos

To learn more about how to receive these publications for free or at member discount as a member of SABR, visit the website: sabr.org/join